INDEPENDENT
RETAILING
A Money-Making Manual

Published in cooperation
with the
National Retail Merchants Association
100 West 31st St.
New York, N.Y. 10001

INDEPENDENT RETAILING

A Money-Making Manual

HAROLD SHAFFER, B. Com.

Vice President, Retail Electronic Systems,
Staten Island, N.Y.
Formerly Director,
Sir George Williams School of Retailing
Concordia University,
Montreal, Canada

HERBERT GREENWALD

President, Herbert Greenwald Retail Consultants, Inc.
New York, N.Y.

Formerly Vice President, Amos Parrish & Co.
New York, N.Y.
and advertising executive for
Macy's, New York, and Gimbel's, New York

PRENTICE-HALL, INC., Englewood Cliffs, New Jersey

Library of Congress Cataloging in Publication Data

SHAFFER, HAROLD.
  Independent retailing.

  Bibliography: p.
  Includes index.
    1. Retail trade—Management. I. Greenwald,
Herbert, 1912-   joint author. II. Title.
HF5429.S488   658.8'7   76–9076
ISBN 0-13-456780-3

10 9 8 7 6 5 4 3 2 1

Prentice-Hall International, Inc., *London*
Prentice-Hall of Australia Pty. Limited, *Sydney*
Prentice-Hall of Canada, Ltd., *Toronto*
Prentice-Hall of India Private Limited, *New Delhi*
Prentice-Hall of Japan, Inc., *Tokyo*
Prentice-Hall of Southeast Asia Pte. Ltd., *Singapore*
Whitehall Books Limited, *Wellington, New Zealand*

DEDICATION

To the two million and more
small and medium size retailers
in the United States and Canada
who want to grow
and live the good life
of an independent merchant
under our free enterprise system.

Contents

Preface

The objective of this book is to give independent retailers a practical management manual that they will find easy to understand, identify with and apply to improve their operations and net profits. To accomplish this objective we have consciously planned the book's chapter sequence, format, text and illustrations to provide maximum guidance for all independent merchants. The result is a book that in many respects radically differs from most academic texts that cover the same fundamental retail principles and practices.

Because the book is primarily concerned with how independents can make a profit from their operations, the opening chapters plunge right into the buying, stockkeeping, pricing and inventory control functions. Most academic texts of a general nature on retailing delay discussing these topics until the student has waded well into the text.

Again, the tone of the book differs considerably from that used by most academic texts. We seek to communicate with our readers on an eye to eye, and "you and we" basis because we assume that our readers are not students but practicing retailers who want reassurance that they are operating their businesses according to the principles and practices currently used by most successful merchants, or that they are seeking solutions to problems they feel they cannot solve without expert advice.

However, we believe that students of marketing or retailing will find this text can offer them considerable insight into the reality of retailing.

Further, as we know that most busy retailers have little time or inclination to engage in searching for information, chapter headings have been developed that indicate what retail area each chapter will discuss and each one opens with a short statement outlining its contents. This technique permits the reader to select quickly the subjects that interest him at a particular time.

As we realize that the educational background of retailers is so varied, wherever possible we have eliminated academic nomenclature and phraseology. Instead, we have attempted to use commonly understood words and uncomplicated sentence structure as well as current retail jargon. We believe this approach will make it easy for retailers to understand the text whatever their educational background may be, as well as to further identify the book as one that has been written exclusively for them.

In line with our dedication to the principles of swift comprehension and immediate identification by independent retailers, all examples and illustrations have been carefully selected so that our readers can easily relate them to their own experience.

Finally, each chapter concludes with a short, cogent summary of its highlights so that the reader need only refer to a series of simple statements to recall its contents. The index, too, has been prepared for ease in subject reference.

We have included a list of some of the major publishers of books and trade journals devoted to retailing in the hope that our readers will want to increase their knowledge of the subject. These have been listed because we know that retailing books and publications often disappear from publishers' lists, and our readers will want to obtain current information by directly contacting the publishers mentioned in the list. Again, because trade associations are important to the retail industry, we have added a list of the major ones and have suggested a method of contacting others.

Although this manual has been written as a nonacademic text, nevertheless it covers all the principles of operating a retail institution that are discussed by academic texts of a general nature. Thus, in writing it, we have drawn on up-to-date information and illustrations from academic texts as well as from independent merchants, retail associations and trade papers whom we have worked with, interviewed or read about. To acknowledge all these sources would be impractical but we recognize such academic pragmatists as Drs. John W. Wingate, Elmer O. Schaller, Charles M. Edwards, Jr., Delbert J. Duncan, Charles F. Phillips, and Fred M. Jones, as well as the newer generation of authors who use a conceptual and interdisciplinarian approach to retailing like Drs. Robert D. Enterberg, David J. Rachman, and Rom J. Markin, Jr.

The many retailers who provided the authors with valued counsel as well as indispensable source material come from all over the United States and Canada. Thus we are able to present sound recommendations that reflect the policies and practices of a substantial number of independent merchants. Among these are: Louis L. Berger, Jr., L.L. Berger, Buffalo, N.Y., Seymour A. Dimond and A. John Dimond, Bergman's, Kingston, Pa., Joel Schur, The Capitol, Fayetteville, N.C., Robert M. Welham and John Blandford, Danks, Lewistown, Pa., David Merkel, Jr., Merkel's, Plattsburg, N.Y., James L. Mosteller, Mosteller's, West Chester, Pa.,

John W. Proffitt and Harwell W. Proffitt, Proffitt's, Alcoa, Tenn., James N. Hersch, Rosenbaum's, Elmira, N.Y., James N. Rothschild and John C. Nagle, Rothschild's, Ithaca, N.Y., Myrtle H. Green, Wieboldt's, Chicago, Ill., Peter G. Trier and the late Maurice G. Jackson, Worth's, Waterbury, Conn.

Canadian independents who offered valuable help include: Ed Mirvish, Honest Ed's, Toronto, Ont., Hersh Segal, Le Chateau, Montreal, Harry and Lewis Levine, Levine's Department Stores, Fredericton, N.B., the Pascal family, Montreal, Que., Clare C. Leckie, Robinson, Little and Co., Winnipeg, Man. and Doug Payne, Universal Stores, Kitimak, B.C.

Practical guidance for several sections of this work was generously provided by Carlo Ammirati, Vice President, Franklin Simon & Co., Inc., New York, Ms. M. Barbara Byam, Toronto, John L. Cohn, Vice President, Independent Retailers Syndicate, Inc., E. Lawrence Goodman, Vice President, The Newspaper Bureau of Advertising, Inc., Elias S. Gottlieb, Vice President, Research, R. H. Macy & Co., Inc., Thomas J. McGoldrick, The Television Bureau of Advertising, Inc., and Joyce Reed, Vice President, The Radio Advertising Bureau, Inc.

The extensive retailing experience of Joseph A. Rowan, Vice President, Sales Promotion Division, NRMA, was particularly helpful during the development of this text.

We also used source material from such trade associations as The National Retail Merchants Association, The National Retail Hardware Association, The Retail Council of Canada, and The Canadian Retail Hardware Association, and found invaluable material in the various trade journals of Fairchild Publications, Inc., MacLean-Hunter Publishing Co., Ltd., Weston Publishing Co., Ltd., and Southam Business Publications, Ltd.

To all these independent merchants, academics, trade associations and publications, we give our sincere thanks.

This preface would be remiss if it did not acknowledge the debt we owe to our wives who were the main victims of our preoccupation with the book, and who soon became author-widows. The syndrome for this marital condition was the harboring of a suppressed jealousy toward the creation of the book which they attempted to camouflage and control with a pretense of interest whenever it was discussed with them.

Both wives carried added burdens: that of Frances Shaffer was to type all the correspondence, text, captions and whatever else was entailed in getting the book in shape for publication, while Carrie Greenwald had to endure numerous absentee-husband days and was saddled with the herculean task of developing the index.

However, once the book was on the press and we reverted to our day-to-day preoccupations, they regained their wifely normalcy and since then we have lived happily ever after. As all husbands know, "happily ever after" is a relative phrase.

Foreword

Perhaps no type of business demands so many general management skills as retailing, and particularly of the owner-manager of an enterprise of modest size. The independent retailer to succeed must be knowledgeable and informed in marketing; in buying merchandise; in promotion, advertising and display; in finance; in personnel supervision and motivation; in maintenance of plant and fixtures and in planning and controlling.

In the highly competitive retail world of today, even the smallest retailer must arm himself with knowledge and professionalism if he is to insure a profitable and growing operation. Therefore, the National Retail Merchants Association is pleased to have cooperated with the authors and Prentice-Hall in making the publication of this book possible. Messrs. Shaffer and Greenwald have brought forth a comprehensive book to guide merchants who are operating their own stores or who are planning to do so, as well as to students of retail marketing. *Independent Retailing: A Money-Making Manual* should be a valuable, practical text for all practitioners and students.

James R. Williams
President
National Retail Merchants Assoc.

How to
Make This Book Pay Off

This book is not a novel and so it does not tell a story about a hero who, until the last paragraph of the last chapter, despairingly pursues his loved one while he desperately fights off the forces of total destruction. Nevertheless, it has a hero. He is the small and medium-sized merchant who spends his days and often his nights running after customers while he is beset with such dangers as too much inventory, not enough clientele, too many markdowns, and not enough profit.

Although the book attempts to tell this retailer how he can successfully attract customers and overcome many of his retail problems and dangers, it does not guarantee a happy ending unless merchants use its contents correctly. Success should be achieved by any merchant who studies its principles and adapts them to his particular situation.

Read it in Segments

This book, unlike a novel, is not meant to be read from beginning to end at one sitting. You should start at the chapter that interests you most and read and re-read each segment until you make its ideas your own and begin to use them in your store. Then skip along until you come to another area that interests you and conquer that.

The table of contents at the beginning of the book will help you spot the chapters that discuss the problems in which you are particularly interested. Since each chapter begins with a short statement of its contents, by reading a few opening sentences you can decide if it is worth spending more time on the rest of the chapter. The material is summarized in note form at the end of each chapter so that you may quickly refresh your memory without having to work through the material again.

Because everything you do in the store affects the entire organization, the topics discussed in one chapter may be referred to in other parts of the book. To make sure that you have covered everything the authors have to say about a subject, turn to the index at the back of the book. Beside each subject heading you will find listed all the pages on which the subject is discussed or mentioned.

If you feel that you want more information, consult the trade journals, associations, and book publishers listed at the end of the book.

This book contains what the authors consider to be the best principles and practices on each subject that they have gathered in approximately 80 years of working in small and medium-sized stores, augmented by serving as management consultants to retailers, as well as teaching retailing subjects at colleges and universities. However, they know full well that there are exceptions to every rule and that sometimes the retailer's unique personality, drive, and ambition can overcome what are considered today to be poor retail practices. But by studying what is agreed to be the right way to run a store successfully, a merchant will at least know what most authorities think should be done.

If after he studies the opinions and ideas expressed in this book, a retailer still feels that he should strike off on his own, the chances are he will become a bigger success than if he simply followed along the road that most retailers walk. Moreover, as a pioneer, he will join the illustrious company of Rowland H. Macy, Marshall Field, Timothy Eaton, Charles Digby Harrod, and others who have made their retail businesses such a success. He will also have the authors' heartiest best wishes, for retailing today needs more men like him.

Most merchants, however, will do best by following the rules and practices this book establishes because these rules should lead to a successful business that will continue to grow and earn them an ever-increasing net income after taxes.

1

Your One and Only Boss—
The Customer

WHAT THIS CHAPTER IS ABOUT

To do business, you must have customers; but just having people in your store does not necessarily mean that you are operating a successful business. Customers must buy enough merchandise at prices that are profitable for you to be able to keep your business healthy. People today are mobile. They come and go in a constant stream. Therefore, it is almost impossible to maintain a steady clientele. This chapter tells you how to attract customers and how to keep more of them coming to your store to buy merchandise.

When the Customer Was Not Considered Important

When stores were very few and far between, merchants could run their businesses to please themselves rather than their customers. It was so inconvenient for people to travel from one store to another that retailers could be ornery, carry shoddy merchandise, charge fancy prices, and still stay in business. But with increased competition, growing consumer affluence, and ease of travel, merchants were forced to change their attitudes and business methods, particularly when retailers like Marshall Field and Adam Gimbel credited a large part of their success to their ability to please their customers.

3

Today, the wise merchant realizes that although he may own his own store, he is not its boss. His boss is his customer and, to be successful, he must do everything to please the customer, not himself. This fundamental fact of retail life applies as much to the largest department stores as it does to the smallest corner grocery.

Customer and Consumer

Although at times the customer and the consumer may be the same person, retailers should understand the difference between the two terms. A *customer* is one who comes into your store for the purpose of buying merchandise. A *consumer* is one who uses the item purchased. For example, a woman buys a shirt for her husband. She is the customer and her husband is the consumer.

This may be a most profitable distinction for retailers. For example, the lingerie department in the downtown branch of a large department store noticed that many women who purchased lingerie would inquire the way to the men's socks department. Eventually, management placed a socks counter in the center aisle of the department. It proved so successful that the store not only increased the number of socks counters, it also traded up on the price of the merchandise that was sold. After this profitable lesson on the value of pleasing the customer, not the consumer, the store began to feminize its men's accessory department and this, too, proved successful.

When the company repeated these policies in its shopping center stores, however, it met a decidedly negative customer response. The company then discovered that although many women bought men's accessories in the downtown store, most men did their own shopping in the suburbs and resented the feminine atmosphere in what they considered their own special department. This firm is now aware that it must constantly think of pleasing both customers and consumers at the same time.

Choose Your Customer Segment

Not even Sears and Penney's working together could please everyone. Yet, many small retailers try to attract and satisfy everyone who passes their doors. The smart merchant knows that the smaller his capital is, the narrower must be the consumer segment to whom he can successfully cater. He seeks to please this group by studying their likes, dislikes, motivations, and shopping habits and then he tries to make his shop so attractive that they will come to him whenever they require any of the merchandise he carries.

Successful merchants have adopted this slogan: "Ours not to reason why, ours but to please or die."

This means that if you run a fashion shop, you do not question customers when they decide that they want their waistlines accentuated and you agree with them when they tell you that *now* they want less emphasis on their silhouettes. You also learn to accustom yourself to their other whims, such as thinking that one size too small is just right or that two sizes too large is form fitting. You accept as normal their passing fancy for materials that drape without shape or those that are so stiff that they stand away from the body like frozen sheets in a high wind.

It is *not* your job to say to your customer, "Now see here, how silly can you get?" It *is* your job to anticipate your customers' wants before they do and then shop the market and order the best merchandise you can get into the store and so be adequately prepared for their next fashion demands.

Stock What Your Customers Like Best

If you feel that your store is operating on too broad a merchandise base, cut it down by reviewing your sales records and then developing only the areas your customers like best. Make certain, however, that you leave yourself a sufficient market to do a profitable business and that everything you carry is related as to kind of merchandise and price. This does not mean that you should be a one-line shop. A visit to a supermarket or junior department store should make you realize that the trend today is toward item diversification. A hardware store might open a sporting goods or hobby department that will pay better than its paint section does at present, but the price and the merchandise selection of the sporting goods and the hobby items must suit the majority of customers who patronize the store.

Study Customer Trends

By studying government, trade publications and related information, you can judge whether customer trends are good or bad for your kind of business and begin to do something about it. In general, population is increasing and so is the number of family units, infants, and the older people. This means that the retail business should increase as the years go by and that wide-awake merchants are now developing techniques to cater to smaller groups of different customer segments. For example, while some retailers are planning to enlarge their infants' and children's business, other retailers are introducing shops that cater to the special needs of older people. In fact, the needs of consumers in each of these areas are so standard that a good merchant should have little trouble in developing a chain store system that would appeal to any of these specialized groups.

Study Your Area Trend

However, what is happening in the country as a whole may not be taking place in your immediate area. For example, although regional statistics may show that incomes are rising, many consumers in your area may be unemployed. Therefore, the most important trends to investigate are the age, income, length of residence, marital status, size of the family, sex, occupation, avocation, and nationality of the people in *your* area. You will have to dig for this information by using such sources as your city hall, chamber of commerce, real estate offices, the research departments of your local newspaper and other advertising media, etc. Also remember that figures for one year tell you very little. You must compare a number of years to see a *trend*. The trouble you take will pay off when you operate a store that goes along with your area trends.

More Time for Relaxation and Play

More and more people are working and living in areas adjacent to cities. Furthermore, the work week has been shortened considerably so that today there is more time for relaxation and play. Both these trends have resulted in a number of important changes for retailers. Formal occasions are now kept to an extreme minimum and emphasis is placed on even more casual living. This means that soft goods retailers, for example, should investigate whether or not it would pay to minimize the formal sections of their stores and enlarge and emphasize their sections for sportswear and casual clothes; hardware merchants should think about specializing to a greater extent in hobby, sporting goods, and do-it-yourself items; furniture stores should concentrate on merchandise that can be used for casual and outdoor living.

More Income per Family

Today, a large number of women, both married and single, are working and when their salaries are added to those of the males in the family, they represent a very substantial income. Again, in a highly technical and unionized economy, most workers seek and receive very substantial wages. Even unskilled labor is paid a fairly high hourly wage. Consequently, when people stop buying goods, it is not because they are poor; it is because retailers are not exerting themselves to make their merchandise sufficiently attractive to consumers for them to spend their disposable income, that is, what they have left after they have paid for food, rent, and taxes. Whenever this situation occurs, the whole economy falters, because if the retailer cannot sell his merchandise, he stops ordering from the manufacturer who, in turn, closes down his production. Consequently, more unemployment results. If, however, retailers become active and increase their sales, more merchandise must be produced, more people work, and the economy moves ahead once more.

Self-sufficient Customers

Customers today are not the helpless souls they were years ago. They are now conditioned to perform a large number of traditional shopping functions themselves and so are able to buy most of their needs without sales help. Still, many customers want to be waited on and guided in their buying, especially in such merchandise areas as home furnishings and appliances.

They Shop in a Hurry

Because most customers work or are otherwise occupied, they frequently shop in a hurry. If you want to make them appreciate your store, your staff should be trained to be not only courteous and helpful, but quick as well—particularly after customers have decided on their purchases.

Product Knowledge

Most of today's advertising gives consumers a great deal of product knowledge. This means that your staff must be prepared to answer accurately specific questions about the merchandise they are trying to sell. If your staff appears ignorant or foolish, customers will lose confidence in your store and will seek a store in which they will feel that they will get proper help and information.

Store Loyalty

Rapid employee turnover and customer mobility have broken down store loyalty. Today, people shop where they feel that they can obtain the best values. This means that you must not only meet competitive pricing, you must seek to build up a strong personalized relationship between your staff and your customers. Otherwise, you will not be able to enjoy even a semblance of a steady clientele. A good customer-store relationship can be easily built by the smaller merchant and it is a large plus in doing business today. Shopping has become so cold and scientific that people immediately respond to the warmth of a store that makes a policy of treating customers like human beings and showing real interest in their personal problems. Such a store is so unusual today that customers will come back again and again and will tell their friends. Such valuable word-of-mouth advertising always leads to an increasing clientele.

What Shoppers Like

In a recent survey[1] shoppers were asked to list in order of importance the factors that influence them to shop in certain stores. Following are the results:

1. Price/value relationship
2. Store specialization
3. Quality of merchandise
4. Salesclerk service (availability, competence, congeniality, etc.)
5. Store location
6. Variety and assortment
7. Guarantee, exchange, and adjustment policies
8. Customer habit or routine
9. Legitimacy of sales
10. Other convenience factors (delivery, parking, store hours, etc.)
11. Credit and billing policies
12. Store layout and atmosphere
13. Merchandise displays
14. Suitability of advertising

What Shoppers Dislike

Another survey asked shoppers to rank what they dislike about certain stores. The results of this survey are as follows:

1. Limited assortment of merchandise
2. Too much pressure to buy
3. Mistakes made by and indifference in attitude of salespeople
4. Prices out of line with what the *customer* thinks is fair value
5. Long waits for service, change, or parcels
6. False promises about delivery
7. Carelessly wrapped parcels
8. Being told that they are hard to fit or hard to please

[1]Marvin A. Jolson and Walter F. Spath, "Understanding and Fulfilling Shoppers' Requirements," *Journal of Retailing,* (Summer 1973), p. 41.

9. Overheated, underheated, and poorly ventilated stores
10. Dark or poorly lighted stores
11. Evidence of poor or careless housekeeping
12. Lack of courtesy
13. Idlers inside or outside the store

How Do You Rate?

Even though these surveys are very limited in scope, they contain enough truth in them for you to judge how your store rates and, what is more important, what you can do to make shopping in it a more pleasurable experience for your customers.

Why Customers Buy

In order to please your customers, you must know more about them than just their shopping habits and their likes and dislikes. You should try to find out *why* they buy. Of course, they purchase items as they need them, but they also buy for the following reasons:

Economy

Most people like bargains. Buying a bargain pleases their egos and also permits them to use their "savings" to purchase something else they need. This is why so many people are attracted to premiums, trading stamps, two-for-one sales, and other giveaway promotions. Except for most shoppers in the lower-income groups, however, people understand that "economy" can mean more than just price. They include in "economy" such features as better quality and style. In fact, they become suspicious of a store that continually advertises giveaways or below-cost bargains. They know that a merchant must make a reasonable profit if he is to exist (Fig. 1.1).

Status and social approval

These are two of the strongest motivations that men and women have for buying anything. Within their economic and social group, they want to be attractive to the opposite sex and make their friends and business acquaintances envious of their possessions. Your store should carry merchandise that is highly acceptable to your customer group, yet sufficiently distinctive to make them want to buy goods from you and not your competitors. This takes imagination and buying skill, and these qualities are essential to becoming a successful retailer (Fig. 1.2).

Leisure living

With the shorter work week, casual clothes, sports equipment, and aids to outdoor living are now very important consumer items. Even for action sports, men and women no longer accept apparel that is uncomfortable and unattractive or gear that is heavy or awkward to handle. Instead, they want outfits that are smartly styled, functional, warm or cool, light of weight, comfortable to wear, and easy to pack and to

FIGURE 1.1 Note how this ad dramatically headlines the drastic price reductions of "famous make" goods. Highly visible comparative pricing emphasizes the "big savings."

Courtesy, Philadelphia Sales, Binghamton, N.Y.

FIGURE 1.2 This ad is full of prestige. The emphasis of the
format is directed to the status-seeking customer by focusing
on the name of a leading designer well-known among fashion-
conscious women.

Courtesy Harridges, Toronto, Canada.

FIGURE 1.3 Here, the advertiser cleverly appeals to today's
leisure-living customer by using key selling statements like
"chill chaser," "zip-snug," "shapeholding," and "comfort."

Courtesy Feron's, New York, N.Y.

clean. They want equipment that is well-designed and compact. Merchants who are aware of these consumer desires and who have exploited
them have watched with amazement how large their sportswear and
outdoor business has become in relation to total sales (Fig. 1.3).

Health

People are very concerned with their health and they eagerly seek
items that will prevent sickness and help them live longer. This motivation has increased not only the sales of health aids but also special kinds
of foods and specially designed furniture. Retailers have performed a
good job of influencing customers to buy for health reasons and this
has been reinforced by consumer groups and protective consumer
legislation. Thus, even though many of these items cost more, if they
are properly presented, they will increase your sales and profits (Fig.
1.4).

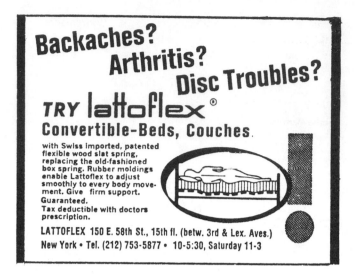

FIGURE 1.4 Backache and arthritic sufferers will be attracted to this small ad because it promises relief. Note the reassuring details in the text. Since price is not the main consideration, it is not mentioned.

Courtesy Lattoflex, New York, N.Y.

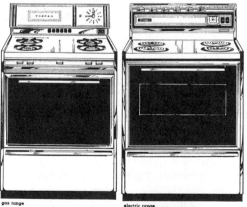
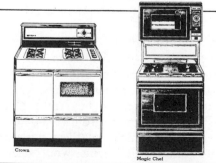

FIGURE 1.5 "Save time and work" is the headline's principal appeal to the housewife who wants to spend more of her time in leisure and recreational pursuits.

Courtesy Wieboldt's, Chicago, Ill.

Most people want to spend their leisure in relaxation and recreation. **Convenience**
Therefore, they appreciate such modern labor-saving conveniences as
automatic defrosting refrigerators, self-cleaning ovens, and easy-care
fabrics. They also like shops that are conveniently located and where
they can obtain quick service that is also helpful, interested, and courteous. If you are either losing customers or not getting your quota, it
could be that you have not developed this motivation fully. Consumers
are quick to appreciate any item or policy that demonstrates to them
that you are thinking of their comfort or convenience (Fig. 1.5).

Romance appeals to everyone from 8 to 80. Retailers can exploit an **Romance**
endless series of situations in which this motivation comes into play.
The right fashion ensemble, after-shave lotion, cosmetic, beverage, or
even a certain kind of pie can be the trigger that sets off a happy ending
for consumers as well as retailers. You would do well to study the
promotional efforts used by manufacturers and adapt them to the needs
of your store.

This is a negative approach, but occasionally it can be used with **Fear**
justification. Safer tires, nonflammable draperies, and anti-theft devices
are examples of items bought through the motivation of fear and the
consumer's desire for safety (Fig. 1.6).

FIGURE 1.6 This ad demonstrates a
wide selection of anti-theft protection
devices available to consumers who
are concerned with the need for safe-
guarding their property.

Courtesy Wieboldt's, Chicago, Ill.

Not every motive is required for every buying decision. Not every motive has the same strength or appeal in every situation. Use them only as circumstances arise. For example, if your customers are mostly economically minded, play up this aspect of your merchandise and never mind the romance angle. If, however, social approval is what your customers desire, then emphasize social approval and leave the other motivations alone. If you and your staff use these appeals properly, you should see a great improvement in your sales volume.

Consumers' Changing Spending Patterns

It is important for you to know how consumers' wants change, for you must go with the cycle. For example, during World War II all kinds of merchandise were in short supply and consumers bought everything that retailers stocked and for some time after that war they still kept buying whatever they saw. Because the majority of consumers had plenty of money and wished to spend, they bought durable merchandise like cars, major home appliances, and furniture. Sales of soft goods suffered until supply overcame demand in heavy cost merchandise. Then consumers remembered their wardrobes and began to build them up. For a while, soft goods merchants prospered, but as durables became old-fashioned or worn out, people replaced them and eased up on buying clothes. Thus, the cycle began to repeat itself.

A new consumer spending trend began to appear in the 1950s. This was the increasing amount of money spent on leisure and play merchandise. Today, informal and sports clothes of all types, materials, and sizes have become big business and so have pre-fab cottages, recreational vehicles, camping equipment, outdoor grills, and patio furniture. Because these markets have only been scratched, you should investigate how you can take advantage of their tremendous potential.

Customers' Shopping Preferences

Because customer shopping patterns change so rapidly, you should review the months, days, and times of day in which most of your customers like to shop. Then compare outside trend figures with those in your store. Any major differences between them should be carefully examined and decisions should be made on what action you should take. For example, if outside figures show that August is the best month for furniture sales, but this is not true in your store, try to find out why and then decide whether or not you should do something about it.

The best method of discovering your customers' monthly preferences is through your sales records. These should be checked back for three to five years and compared to outside figures. In this way, you can discover and exploit present and future trends before your competition does, and thus bring more customers into your store. For example, some stores today have discovered that they can sell winter vacation wear early in November. Other stores promote fall and winter coats in August. This expands their selling season and gives them an early indication of runners as well as reducing the necessity for markdowns.

Is Saturday Still the Best Day?

Your customers' best shopping day or night may have changed. It could have been Saturday or Friday night, but now some other time has replaced it. Take advantage of this trend. There is little value in running promotions on days or nights when your customers are not planning to shop. For example, if you are in a district in which there are one or two large industries, your advertising and promotional efforts should be geared to the industries' paydays and to their employees' shopping habits.

What Time of Day or Night Is Best?

The time of day or night your customers like to shop is just as important as their monthly or daily preferences. In some districts they shop in the morning; in others they like to buy in the late afternoon; in still others, they prefer noon or night. Knowing this, you can plan to have sufficient help for rush hours and be on the floor yourself. Special promotions, for example, fashion shows or visits of celebrities, should take place during these hours. Few customers will go out of their way to visit your store at a time that is inconvenient for them.

Your Customer Is Boss

In 1951 when Emily Kimbrough was gathering material for a book on the Marshall Field store in Chicago, she was told that her morning appointment with Mr. Hughston McBain, the Chairman of the Board, had to be postponed until the afternoon. Since Mr. McBain was known to be very meticulous about keeping appointments, she wondered what had caused the delay. His secretary explained that the night before an old lady had told Mr. McBain that she was disappointed in Field's because something she had ordered had not arrived. The next morning Mr. McBain traced the order and found that it was a special that had just arrived. He sent for his car and delivered the parcel himself. He was late for his appointment with Miss Kimbrough, but he had satisfied an old customer.

This example can be matched by anecdotes about merchants as

great as Macy, Eaton, or Field himself or as small as the successful owner of a 12 by 18 foot variety store who, before he opens up in the morning, delivers milk to customers who are too ill to come themselves. He does this because he feels that he has a responsibility to the people who patronize him. These merchants realize that customers do not have to please retailers but that retailers, to be successful, must study their customers and seek ways to please them. The sad truth, then, is that although customers can afford to ignore your wishes, you cannot afford to ignore theirs and still stay in business.

WHAT THIS CHAPTER TOLD YOU

1. To be a successful retailer, you must constantly think of how to please your customers, not yourself.

2. It is sometimes important to distinguish between a customer and a consumer.

3. The smaller your capital, the narrower your customer segment must be and the more careful you should be to stock your store with merchandise that your customers, not you, will like.

4. Study customer trends, particularly those in your area, and then plan how to change your business to meet changing conditions.

5. Today, most people live informally, have more income per family, and have little store loyalty. Successful retailers study these and other consumer characteristics and then change their business policies accordingly.

6. Customers often buy for reasons other than replacement or need. The main buying motivations are economy, prestige and approval, recreation, health, convenience, romance, and fear. Retailers who learn how to use these motivations increase their sales.

7. Consumer shopping habits are changing and you must investigate what month, day, and hour are most popular for those in your area. Then plan your promotions to take place during shopping peaks.

2

Good Buying
Means Profitable
Selling

WHAT THIS CHAPTER IS ABOUT

This chapter deals with what you should know about merchandise *before* you buy. This aspect of your work is important because when customers are required to serve themselves, as they so often do today, the retailer's buying mistakes become costlier.

In the next two chapters, *where* and *how* to buy will be discussed and in Chapter 5 some ideas about how to obtain more value for your purchase dollar will be suggested.

Retail Buying Used to Be Easy

Up to the early 1900s buying for a retail store was a fairly simple operation. The merchant put as much money as he could into stock. Even small clothing stores purchased men's underwear in wooden crates so large that they had to put a ladder *inside* the crates to unpack the merchandise. Merchants would also buy hundreds of dozens of men's shirts and hundreds of pairs of ladies' shoes at one time. It is true that this merchandise stayed in the store for years, but retailers were not worried. They felt that they could always sell what they had bought. They had never heard of obsolescence, turnover, interest on inventory, or any of today's merchandising techniques.

Between World Wars I and II revolutionary changes occurred in the retail field. Manufacturers not only learned how to produce merchandise in great quantities, they also developed marketing techniques to create constant consumer demands for style changes in practically every

item that a retailer could carry. Retail buying became more of a gamble and a headache. Merchants had to be more selective about the items and the quantities they bought.

It was during this period that the terms *lemons* and *dogs* were coined to describe slow-moving merchandise in a store. Although this merchandise presented a problem, it was not an insurmountable one. The retailer realized that customers could be influenced by his sales staff and so he developed the technique of offering commissions, or "P.M.s" (Premium Money) on his lemons and thus moved a certain amount of his poor buys without too great a loss.

Retail Buying Becomes Difficult

During and immediately after World War II customers in most stores no longer required or were offered sales help; they either served themselves or were waited on by sales personnel most of whom were unreliable. Under these conditions, lemons stayed on the shelves until their prices were reduced sufficiently to be attractive to bargain hunters. This meant large markdowns which, as most retailers by then had learned, were undesirable. By that time, too, some retailers had become aware of the importance of turnover and maintained markups and had forced themselves to live within strictly controlled merchandise budgets. Unexpected markdowns had a very unfavorable effect on the controls they had established.

At the same time, in carefully merchandised stores, vendor salesmen were exerting strong pressures on store buyers to purchase an increasing number of new items. Yet, if the buyers bought too much, the merchandise office closed down on them; if they underbought, the same office sent them a memo asking why their departments had so many "want slips." Worse still, if they bought too many lemons, their maintained markup fell and they were in for a very uncomfortable time with their superiors.

Owning a store did not lessen buying difficulties. Too much stock, too little stock, or too many unwanted items could lead to a series of poor seasons and eventual bankruptcy. Soon, one of the best ways to acquire ulcers was to become a store buyer.

To minimize these risks, buyers in larger stores began to study, exchange ideas, and put down in a formal way what they knew about the business of buying for retail stores. They soon developed a number of principles and techniques for effective buying that any retailer could use.

Shortages

Since the 1970s retail buyers have had to contend with a new buying problem, that of material shortages. Until then, except for periods when there was a wartime economy, supply was usually ahead of demand. Sometimes an item would become difficult to get because it was so popular that everyone wanted it at the same time. But this was a manufacturing problem, not a supply problem. The materials to make the item were available—it was putting them together that created the problem.

Today, however, even slow-selling items are held up because components such as petro-chemicals, natural or man-made fibers, or minerals are either difficult or impossible to obtain. Nevertheless, although material shortages may aggravate your buying problems, using the principles and techniques discussed below is still the best way to buy goods for your store. Material shortages only mean that you have to be more careful in selecting vendor offerings than you did before shortages became a problem.

How to Make Retail Buying Easier

The first buying principle for you to remember, whether your store is large or small, is that you are buying to please your customer, *not* yourself. This idea was introduced in Chapter 1. It is mentioned again now because the customer area in which you are operating is very important when you are deciding what to buy.

Buy to please your customer

Because your capital and store area limit the quantity of goods you can carry, you have to decide on how many different items called *breadth* and how many of each item called *depth* you should carry in stock. For example, should you go in for a wide assortment of styles and carry a few items in each range or would it be better to have fewer styles and more items in each style? In general, if you carry fashion goods, it is better to begin each season with wide assortments and then, as you spot best sellers, convert your stock from breadth to depth on these items.

Breadth and depth

Since you should never be out of staple goods, they should always be carried in depth. Sometimes, however, fashion merchandise becomes staple and the demand for staples may become smaller or even disappear. For example, once silk stockings were considered a staple. Then they were replaced by rayon stockings and then by nylon stockings. Who knows what is coming next? Even such staple items as hammers, screw drivers, lawn mowers, fishing tackle, garden hose, lawn sprinklers, etc., are subject to fairly rapid technological and material changes under today's marketing conditions.

For example, A. C. Nielsen in *Progressive Grocer* (July 1972) reported that in one year a group of 38 chain, cooperative, and wholesale warehouses dropped 5,543 items but added 7,303 new ones. Although these figures tell us that the group made 12,846 merchandise decisions, we have no idea of the great number of new items they looked at and rejected. What the figures do suggest, however, is the enormous amount

of yes and no merchandise decisions most retailers are forced to make
in any given period. Thus, if you want to be a successful merchant, you
must constantly watch your merchandise and decide which items are
moving from fashion to staple, from staple to fashion, or out of the
picture altogether. Then you can decide how to stock each item.

Judging Customer Wants From Inside Sources

One of the best ways of judging trends is to use sales records
properly. If you break them down according to style, price, or some
other category, you can actually see how each item is moving in your
store. This is one area in which using an electronic data processing
reporting system will pay dividends.

Sales records and reorders

Another way is to keep track of your reorders. They can tell you
which items are growing in demand and which are lemons.

The above methods will tell you, to a great extent, which merchandise your customers like, but it is just as important to know which
merchandise your customers do *not* like. You should know what they
want to buy from you and cannot because you do not stock it. This you
learn by carefully recording and analyzing customer returns (Figs. 2.1
and 2.2). Every return is a potential danger signal and the reason for
each one should be sought. Only neurotics take pleasure in bringing
back merchandise. Most people find it an embarrassing experience and
prefer to keep what they buy if it is at all possible.

Customer returns

The difficulty here is to make certain that the reason that the
customer gives for returning an item is the *real* reason. For example,
she might have been pressured into buying something that was beyond

What is the real reason?

```
ADJUSTMENT CLAIM
_____ 19 _____

Name & Address _____

Complaint _____

_____

How adjusted: _____

_____

In your opinion was complaint justified? _____

Was adjustment satisfactory to customer? _____

Claim adjusted by _____
           Please comment on reverse side.
```

FIGURE 2.1 This simple form
records the reasons for a customer's
return or adjustment and indicates
how this was handled.

Courtesy Proffitt's Dept. Store, Alcoa,
Tenn.

Proffitt's

DEPARTMENT STORE

ALCOA, TENNESSEE

Mrs. James Doe
5613 Palmer Ave.
Anytown, Tenn. 37846

January 25, 1940

Dear *Mrs. Doe*:

According to our records you returned *one sweater*
on *January 18* and obtained a cash refund of *10.88*.

One of our primary goals as a retail institution in this community is to offer to our customers the best service and the best selection of merchandise that is available.

Would you please take a minute of your time and tell us the reason for returning the above mentioned merchandise so that we may make some improvement that would help us to give you and our other customers better service in the future.

We hope you'll feel free to make your comments on the back of this letter and return it in the self-addressed, stamped envelope that is enclosed for your convenience.

Thank you very much.

Very truly yours,

Proffitt's, Inc.

R. M. Smith

Store Manager

/lbe

FIGURE 2.2 This letter serves three purposes: (1) it verifies that the item was actually returned, (2) it verifies the exact amount of cash refunded to the customer, (3) it encourages the customer to comment on her reasons for the return.

Courtesy Proffitt's Dept. Store, Alcoa, Tenn.

her means. By the time she gets home she is beginning to feel guilty, and so back it comes. The customer is ashamed to say that she cannot afford the item or that she was oversold; instead, she says, "It doesn't fit" or "It doesn't suit me."

Some merchandise comes back because it left the store in poor condition. Sometimes the merchandise has to be used or washed before the weakness becomes apparent. When this merchandise is brought back, you should carefully examine every similar item you have in the store to see if any more of them are imperfect. If they are, send them back immediately, have them repaired, or reduce the price and sell them as seconds or imperfects. You should realize that for every customer who returns an imperfect article, many do not return items because it is either too embarrassing or too much trouble. But they will pass by, *not into,* your store on their next shopping expedition and they will tell their friends about the imperfect merchandise you carry.

Poor condition

For example, a ladies' sports shop sold 30 bathing suits before 8 of them were returned because the zippers were not strong enough to stand strain. The proprietor was not so concerned about the 8 customers who brought the suits back as he was about the 22 who did not. He knew that a torn zipper in a swim suit could be most embarrassing and that the customers would blame the store, not the manufacturer.

Defective goods became such a problem that in January 1974 the National Retail Merchants Association (NRMA) established a vendor information program. This program is computerized to maintain up-to-date lists of their members' complaints against vendors of apparel, home furnishings, and related items who repeatedly ship them defective merchandise. The retailer's name is kept confidential by NRMA, but the supplier is notified of the complaint and is thus offered an opportunity to correct it. The file is constantly updated. Once the supplier lets NRMA know that he has corrected the fault, the reported incident becomes inactive. If, however, the supplier does nothing about it or his solution proves unsatisfactory, member retailers will soon reactivate the complaint.

NRMA Vendor Information Program

Thus, if you are a member of NRMA, you should report to them names of suppliers who repeatedly send you defective merchandise. You also have the right to ask the Association if they have anything on file on those vendors whose current returns history you wish to investigate.

Because consumerism is making customers more alert to poor quality merchandise, customers are more aggressive about returning faulty items. However, some customers are now bringing back goods that they believe are of poor value. If this happens to you, you must consider the return from their point of view and if they are right, thank them for bringing the item to your attention and go out of your way to satisfy them by an allowance, exchange, or refund. If you do not give them satisfaction, they may report the incident to a local consumer group or to a government agency and then you will have a real problem on your hands.

Consumerism increases merchandise returns

Once you have settled with the customer, treat the item in the same way that you would goods that have been shipped in poor condition.

If you are a member of NRMA and a supplier is consistently remiss in the quality of merchandise he sends you, report him to the Association and ask them to send you his current standing with other retailers. You may then make a better judgment on whether or not you want to continue dealing with him.

Because few people today have the leisure to come into a shop just to pass time, you may take it for granted that when people enter your store, they want to buy, are seeking information about the merchandise you carry, or are comparing your merchandise with that of a competitor. In every case, they are interested in your store and are potential customers. If they walk out unsold, you should know why.

In most stores it is impossible to find out why people don't buy unless there is a system that tells which merchandise customers are asking for that is not in stock. This system can be as simple as a series of printed slips with information about each unsatisfied customer's request (Fig. 2.3).

Most stores that use want slips have found that the system is only as good as the person in charge makes it. If salespeople go to considerable trouble to fill in want slips which are then ignored, the whole

Figure 2.3 Suggested customer want slip to be filled in by sales personnel. Notice that each slip must indicate the buyer's answer. The answer should then be communicated to the salesperson concerned.

Courtesy Mosteller's Inc., West Chester, Pa.

Lost ... a Sale!

Because we were out of:

Item: _____

Mfg. _____

Style No. _____

Color _____

Size _____

☐ Out of Stock   ☐ Not Carried

A sale lost is money lost in the Profit Sharing Plan.

We don't know you're out of something 'til you tell us.

Don't wait . . . tell us now before you lose another sale.

Name_____ Dept. No._____

Buyer's Answer:

system is useless. If, however, the manager or buyer personally answers each slip and tells the employee why he cannot stock the item wanted or that he will try to get it, the system can be very effective.

Remember that every request must be analyzed carefully. The demand may be created by a sudden shortage of a particular item of merchandise in your area. If you and your competitors order heavily, every store will soon carry too much stock because a few persistent customers created a false demand by going from shop to shop. On the other hand, a new "want" may be developing and if you order now, you will be ahead of your competitors.

Analyze want slips carefully

Sometimes salespeople like an item so much that they use want slips to build up a demand for it. Also, vendor's salesmen have been known to bribe sales personnel to create pressure for their particular product.

With all its faults and dangers, however, there is no method as helpful in discovering what you should be stocking as a well-run, constantly analyzed want slip system.

Your store can organize a customer panel by inviting a carefully selected group of customers to meet and discuss what they think can be done to improve your merchandise selection. These people should be paid in some way in order to make their services worthwhile both to you and to themselves. Customer panels are only valuable if store owners can stand criticism and are open to suggestions.

Customer panels

Stores frequently pre-test an item by obtaining a sample order and then watching customer response. If customers show no interest, the stock is disposed of with little loss. If it moves out rapidly, it is re-ordered in depth.

Pre-testing

The caution here is that to be valid, a pre-test requires sufficient stock assortment, display, and employee excitement. If you starve the item by insufficient breadth and depth or if you are not prepared to push it by window display, interior display, and sales personnel, do not bother with it at all. Unless you treat it fairly, the results are bound to be disappointing.

If properly encouraged, salespeople can be your best source of information about customer wants. But if your relationship with your staff is poor, they will either freeze up and give you no information at all or they will try to please by telling you what they think you want to hear, and this may be entirely opposite to your customer wants. Again, sales personnel are very prone to be subjective in their conclusions, that is, they interpret customers' remarks in terms of themselves. You must weigh what salespeople say against what you know of their personal biases. For example, if they like high-fashion merchandise, they will tend to make you think you are missing sales because you are

Reports from sales personnel

not carrying sufficiently advanced styles. If they are conservative, they will build up customer wants along these lines.

Judging Customer Wants From Outside Sources

You can learn what your customer wants not only from *inside* the store but also from various sources *outside* the store.

A fund of information, most of it reliable, is provided by vendor salesmen. They see a great number of retailers who are catering to the same customer segment as you are, and they form opinions based on a wider knowledge than you can obtain by just observing what is happening in your store.

Vendor salesmen

Your problem is how to evaluate this information. The great majority of salesmen know that the day of the drummer who misrepresented his merchandise in an attempt to obtain the biggest possible order is over. Since today's salesman wants to come back again and again, he tries to obtain the retailer's trust. Moreover, because he feels that his job is that of an agent or consultant for the vendor whom he represents, he tries to be as honest and sincere as possible.

The trouble is that salesmen generally are over-enthusiastic about the merchandise they carry. They like selling and writing orders; that is their job and their livelihood depends on it. When they tell you that a number is selling well, you may believe it, but what might be a hot item in most stores may turn out to be a first-class lemon in yours. Always remember that you are buying to please *your* customer, not your competitors'.

Again, the salesman is merely reporting the retailers' reactions to his lines and does not know what they think about competing lines. For this reason, you must take the information he gives you with some reservation.

If you are in the fashion field, you can discover customer wants by frequenting the social functions that your customers attend. You can then see what styles are coming in, have arrived, or are on their way out, and just how this should affect your buying.

Social events

Another good outside source for customer wants is your competitors' windows, advertisements, and promotions. Once you know how a retailer thinks, you can tell from the items he promotes which are his runners and which he considers dogs. You should also watch very closely a store or two above and below your customer segment. Then you can judge which merchandise your customers *will* want, what they want to buy *now,* and which merchandise is going out of style.

Watch your competitors

It is difficult to ask your competitors direct questions. However, one young man starting out in business found out when and where the more successful merchants on the street had coffee. He worked his way into their group and by asking questions received very sound advice about retailing. Today he advises others because he has become a very successful merchant indeed.

When you go out of town, visit stores similar to those of your own community. Out-of-town retailers will talk to you freely because you are not a competitor and they will answer your questions.

Every retailer should try to attend as many trade shows and market weeks as possible, not only to order merchandise but also to learn what is new and to exchange information. These events will give you the best concentrated idea of what is in your own field, as well as those above and below it, and so permit you to judge your customer wants at the

Trade shows and market weeks

moment. The danger in these events is that the excitement that they generate sometimes encourages retailers to order more than they should. Chapter 3 will discuss how to obtain the best value out of these shows.

Another good source of customer information is the resident buying office (Fig. 2.4). Its job depends on its ability to judge manufacturers' offerings and decide how they will sell in your store. But like vendor salesmen, buyers for resident buying offices cannot be as intimate with

Resident buying offices

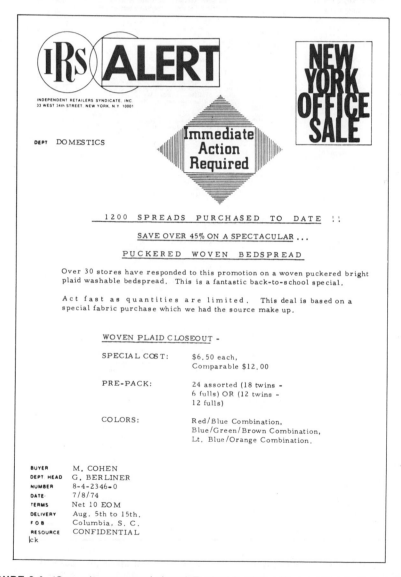

FIGURE 2.4 (Opposite page and above) Typical buying office market bulletins that inform member stores of merchandise opportunities. The one on the opposite page highlights a new item; the bulletin above alerts the client to a highly promotional offering.

Courtesy Independent Retailers Syndicate Inc., New York, N.Y.

RAM reports

MISSES SPORTSWEAR & SEPARATES
Best Selling Looks — Best Selling Style Numbers
Sold Through Ram Panel of Key Stores
Mideast Fashion Merchandising Area —
Fall / Holiday

WOVEN SHIRTS

	RESOURCE	STYLE #	PRICE	RESOURCE COMMENT
SHIRT NECKLINE LONG SLEEVE PATTERNED	LADY ARROW	5257	9.00	Stripe shirt with detachable bow, sold up.
	LADY ARROW	4020	7.50	Available for at once delivery.
	LADY ARROW	5262	9.00	Sold up. Ultressa® prints avail. for spring.
	LADY ARROW	5261	9.00	Sold up. Other Ultressa® prints avail. for spring.
	LADY ARROW	4016	7.50	Available for at once delivery.
	LADY ARROW	9381	10.00	Chiffon sheer shirt, avail. for reorders.
	VILLAGER	5020	8.50	Sold up.
	LADY ARROW	5108	7.00	Sold up.
	JUDY BOND	8418	6.38	Sold up. Now avail. as 8663 @6.00.
	CATALINA	4A758	8.00	Sold up. Similar style 5G752 avail. in knit on cruise line.

	RESOURCE	STYLE #	PRICE	RESOURCE COMMENT
SHIRT NECKLINE LONG SLEEVE SOLID COLOR	LADY ARROW	3799	7.00	Ultressa® shirt available for reorders.
	LADY ARROW	3543	6.75	Basic shirt, available for at once delivery.
	LADY ARROW	3794	8.50	Satin stripe, avail. for reorders.
	JUDY BOND	9476	6.75	Sold up.
	LADY ARROW	3059	11.00	Available for at once del. on reorders.

WOVEN BLOUSES

	RESOURCE	STYLE #	PRICE	RESOURCE COMMENT
TIE BOW LONG SLEEVE	JUDY BOND	1475	7.75	Available for reorders, 12/15 delivery.
	LADY ARROW	5252	9.00	Sold up. Ultressa® prints avail. again for spring.
	JUDY BOND	2516	7.79	Now part of 3714R @8.16. Avail. for reorders.
	JUDY BOND	2439	7.79	Now part of 3714R @8.16.
	JUDY BOND	2301	7.79	Now part of 3714R @8.16.
	JUDY BOND	2514	7.79	Now part of 3714R @ 8.16. Avail. for reorders.
	LADY ARROW	5260	9.00	Sold up. Ultressa® prints avail. for spring.
	JUDY BOND	2302	7.79	Now part of 3714R @8.16.

TUNICS & SHIRT JACKETS

	RESOURCE	STYLE #	PRICE	RESOURCE COMMENT
SHIRT NECKLINE LONG SLEEVE FULL FRONT CLOSING	TRISSI	423	9.00	Available for 2-3 week delivery on reorders.
	TRISSI	418	8.30	Available for 2-3 week delivery on reorders.
	WHITE STAG	4L241	9.40	Available for reorders, 2 week delivery.
	TRISSI	421	8.30	Available for 2-3 week delivery on reorders.
	TRISSI	419	8.30	Available for 2-3 week delivery on reorders.
	LADY ARROW	4002	12.00	Available for reorders, at once delivery.
	TRISSI	424	8.30	Available for 2-3 week delivery on reorders.

INNERWEAR JACKETS

	RESOURCE	STYLE #	PRICE	RESOURCE COMMENT
SHIRT NECKLINE LONG SLEEVE	LATCH ON LTD	6120	11.00	The well known velveteen blazer from Latch On!
	TRISSI	9119	11.20	Shirtjac 100% poly basket weave coord w/pant 9145.
	ANGUS BAILEY	1762	22.75	Basketweave poly safari shirtjac, avail. for reorders.
	ANGUS BAILEY	1825	17.75	Poly shirtjac, coordinates with pant #1826.
	BROOKVALLEY	6601	12.75	Lg/sl shirtjac, 2 patch pkts. basic & fashion colors, 2 wk del.
	VILLAGER	5814	20.00	Sold up. Similar style avail. in new colors for Dec. del.
	CENTURY	4302	26.75	3 button velveteen, fully lined, av. in 6 survival colors, 3 wk. del.
	ACT III	6125	24.75	Paisley belted jacket, Dec. delivery.
	HILTON HEAD	8444	8.50	Sold up. Avail. in new Spring colors in poly gab.
	TRISSI	9114	11.75	Avail. in Holiday colors for 2-3 week delivery.
	WHITE STAG	41225	18.75	Available for reorders. 2 week delivery.
	WHITE STAG	41022	18.75	Available for reorders. 2 week delivery.
	CATALINA	4A708	18.00	Doubleknit poly sold up. Similar style av. cruise line.
	CENTURY	4305	18.75	Velveteen shirtjac. 6 survival colors. 3 week del.
	LATCH ON LTD	5600	11.00	Blazer, now avail. in pastel corduroy as #1902, 2 wk. del.

FIGURE 2.5 An example of a trade journal service. This one emphasizes current best-selling items.

Courtesy RAM Services, Inc., and *Women's Wear Daily,* New York, N.Y.

your customer wants as you are and so what they report must be evaluated by you for your store and your store alone.

There are a number of specialized reporting services to which you can subscribe. They concentrate on a single area such as merchandise, advertising, or display and report what the leaders are doing in these fields. These services can be costly and there is a short lag between the time something happens in other stores and the time you get the report. If, however, you need stimulation or want to know what the most progressive retailers are doing, these services can be most useful and well worth the expense.

Specialized reporting services

You should subscribe to trade publications that specialize in your retail field. These are full of valuable information, but few merchants really know how to use them. They thumb through the pages quickly and then let the publications gather dust. It would be better to cut down on the number of trade publications you receive and read a few carefully. Try to get one workable idea out of each publication you study. The number of good suggestions to be found in each edition will surprise you, as will the number of times that these suggestions will pay off in terms of a more profitable store (Fig. 2.5).

Trade publications

It is a good idea to buy both a general and a specialized textbook on retailing and keep them handy in your office. As an experienced retailer, you have a better basis for understanding the contents than does a young student who does not know a retail store from a wholesaler's display room. Use the indexes in the books. They tell you where the information you want is discussed.

Textbooks

If you use the resources discussed in the above sections, you will learn a great deal about customer wants even before you go to buy. Armed with this information, you will look through vendors' offerings and buy the merchandise that will bring customers flocking to your store.

Know before you buy

WHAT THIS CHAPTER TOLD YOU

1. Because of poor sales staffs and/or self-service arrangements, lemons stay on the shelves until they are sufficiently reduced in price to attract bargain hunters. These markdowns create losses.

2. By the same token, good buys create a very satisfactory turnover and profit picture.

3. The first step in successful buying is to buy for your customer, not for yourself.

4. By concentrating on specific customer segments, you can best judge who your customers are.

5. You should make up your mind whether each item is to be carried in breadth or in depth.

6. Sales records tell you what your customers are buying.

7. Reorders tell you which items are runners.

8. Customer returns tell you which merchandise they do not like and which merchandise is imperfect.

9. To find out which merchandise you should be buying, use (a) want slips, (b) customer panels, (c) pre-tests of new merchandise, and (d) cooperation of sales personnel.

10. You can discover customer wants *outside* your store through (a) vendor salesmen, (b) frequenting social events, (c) watching competitors, (d) asking for information from noncompeting retailers, (e) trade shows and market weeks, (f) resident buying offices, (g) specialized services, (h) trade publications, and (i) retail textbooks.

3

Where to Buy

Knowing *what* to buy is only one-third of the buying operation. You must also know *where* to obtain the merchandise and *how much* to buy. This chapter will discuss the where part of the buying procedure; the next chapter will deal with how much to buy.

Buying from Manufacturers

In the old days, when staples were the main goods sold, retailers were unable to buy directly from manufacturers. They had to go to wholesalers because wholesalers were the only ones with sufficient sales volume to buy the quantities that manufacturers were prepared to sell. Eventually, retailers like John Wanamaker and F. W. Woolworth increased their business until they could buy in even larger quantities than wholesale houses. At this point, they went to the manufacturers and after some negotiations were successful in buying directly and in obtaining quantity prices. An exception to the rule was the fashion field in which manufacturers always tended to sell to stores directly because wholesalers were not set up to handle this merchandise and because quantity buying was not a major factor.

Today, most manufacturers will sell to any retailer who can buy in large enough quantities, but if it is legally permissible, manufacturers will quote different prices for wholesalers, department stores, and small stores.

31

Because manufacturers are constantly turning out goods, their merchandise is usually fresher and has more customer appeal than that bought from wholesalers, who must keep items on their shelves for some time before the items can be shipped to retailers. In hard goods, fresh-looking merchandise may not be a big factor, but in soft goods it is an important part of the appeal that is so necessary for good selling.

Merchandise may be fresher

When merchandise moves directly from manufacturer to retailer, the costs of handling by wholesalers are eliminated. Therefore, retailers who buy directly should receive some of this saving. This is truer for staple goods and other items where the longer the time the maker's machines work the less each unit costs, than in fashion or soft goods where human labor makes up the greater proportion of the cost. But even in soft goods a lower price can be obtained if you arrange to order merchandise that can be made in a slow season when the manufacturer is willing to lower his price just to keep his help and his factory going.

Merchandise may be lower in price

If you want to carry items made to your own specification, it is best to go directly to the manufacturer. A small store can seldom order large enough quantities to make it worth a manufacturer's time and effort, but some manufacturers will agree to produce special items for you, stock them, and ship them as you need them. In this way, you get the goods you ordered and pay for them as they are delivered.

Specification buying

If you order directly from the manufacturer, you may sometimes receive quicker delivery. You must remember, however, that since a manufacturer does not process orders until he has enough of them on hand to make production profitable, your order may be held up until sufficient orders are accumulated. If you order seasonal items directly, you may miss the best selling period before you receive the goods. Wholesalers, however, usually order enough merchandise at one time for immediate processing and quicker delivery.

Quicker delivery

If you give a manufacturer enough business during the season to make a good impression on him, he may offer you job lots or clearance merchandise to help you through your own clearance program. The dangers inherent in this kind of buying are discussed in Chapter 4 and should be considered very carefully.

Job lot clearances

When you buy directly from the manufacturer, you should be able to get quicker adjustments because sometimes your complaint goes through the wholesaler-manufacturer-wholesaler-retailer process. This is important in customer relations, for nothing annoys a customer more than having to wait for an adjustment for something that he or she feels is your fault in the first place. In some instances, returns

Better adjustments

create a real hardship for the customer who cannot buy another article until the adjustment is made and who still requires the item for his or her immediate comfort or convenience. The quicker returns are handled, the better it is all around.

If you represent a fairly important account to a manufacturer, he will tend to be more lenient with his adjustment policy than if you are a casual buyer. If you have a long-standing good relationship with him, you might take a calculated risk and settle the return with the customer at once, knowing that the manufacturer will stand behind your decision.

The wholesaler carries merchandise from a number of different vendors and usually shows little preference about whose products you buy. He seldom tells you why one vendor's merchandise is better than another's or seldom explains the selling points of the goods he offers you. The manufacturer, however, is very eager to have you buy *his* merchandise. He will therefore present his goods carefully and give you as much product knowledge and selling help as he can. This will aid you in making buying decisions, promoting goods, and giving sales talks to your staff.

More product knowledge

Buying from Wholesalers

Wholesalers shop a great number of vendors and then select what they think you will need for your store. This merchandise is ordered in large quantities and stocked until you are ready to handle it. In this way, the wholesaler saves you a great deal of shopping time and expense. In fact, he performs the same function for the retailer as the retailer does for his customers.

Although wholesalers buy in bulk, they sell in small quantities. It is possible to order one-twelfth of a dozen or even a few boxes of merchandise from a wholesaler and to do this as often as his supplies last. Thus, retailers who buy through wholesalers are able to keep their inventories down to a minimum because they can rebuy as quickly as they sell. This increases turnover and decreases markdowns because very little old, unsalable or counter-soiled merchandise need be carried by the retailer.

Buying in small quantities

Many large stores use wholesalers for certain departments or for items that they feel they must have for customer convenience or because the items round out their store personality but do not warrant the time and expense of a buyer. They set up basic stocks and then buy from wholesalers as the stock is sold. In this way, they pay more for the merchandise than if they bought directly, but they save money because they work with smaller inventories, increased turnover, fewer markdowns, and no buyers' salaries.

Both large and small stores use wholesalers for immediate replacement of regular merchandise. Although wholesalers would prefer to have the original orders, they are glad to accept stopgap orders because they amount in total to a large volume and enable them to buy in larger quantities and obtain better turnover.

When wholesalers were the only source of goods for retailers, they sold to merchants all over the country, but as retailers began to bypass them, wholesalers developed a number of techniques to keep alive. One of these was to specialize both in the kind of goods they carried and in the regions they wished to serve. Today, most wholesalers are local and they make a point of knowing their trading area intimately. This can be of immense help to small retailers who require knowledge about developments in the immediate area around their stores. Manufacturers' representatives usually have too large a territory to help these merchants. They can only tell them what is selling or what conditions are like in general terms.

Since wholesalers today realize that their very existence depends on the retailers' ability to dispose of merchandise, they have become very eager to help merchants run their businesses better. With their knowledge of what other stores are selling in the area, some wholesalers will suggest basic stock items not only to merchants who are just getting established but also to merchants who are already in business. They will also offer merchandise and expense control systems, advise retailers on store alterations and fixture arrangements, and provide retail counseling for the smaller merchants.

Wholesalers have always extended credit to retailers and today this forms an important part of their policy. In fact, if a retailer learns to use the wholesaler's services properly, he should be able to operate his store on a minimum inventory and a maximum credit. This means that he can make every cent of his capital work to its best advantage. Moreover, sometimes when a retailer feels that he needs extra merchandise to round out his assortments or bring in traffic, the wholesaler may give him what he requires at easier terms.

Some wholesalers have formed groups of *independent* merchants who are willing to buy most of their merchandise requirements from them. In return, the wholesaler grants price concessions to the retailers in the group and permits them to use a common store name. Eventually, the wholesaler acts very much like the central office of a large chain. He sells merchandise to his member stores at prices comparable to chains, handles the group's promotions, develops the chain's own branded items, suggests ways to establish a chain-store image, establishes merchandising controls, and so on. Yet, each member of the group maintains his independence. (See Fig. 3.1.)

Some manufacturers and retailers operate as wholesalers by operating franchise or agency stores. Franchise manufacturers place great emphasis on encouraging member stores to sell *their* products. Independents who join a retailers' franchise group are offered the mer-

FIGURE 3.1 Notice the extensive variety of services a grocery group's operation can offer its member stores.

Courtesy M. Loeb Ltd., Ottawa, Canada.

chandising knowledge and leadership of the originating merchant who runs the franchise.

Whichever way it is organized, a properly run retail–wholesale group permits each member to operate his store with all the advantages of a chain-store operation and yet retain the greatest of all retail assets—the human relationship with his customers.

Although these wholesale-independent-retail groups handle fairly staple merchandise, even fashion goods could be group merchandised. This would give independents greater buying and sales strength by permitting them to compete more successfully against the retail giants.

Resident Buyers

Because of the growing number of vendors and the rapid changes in merchandise and marketing techniques, store buyers find it increasingly difficult to keep up with what is happening in the market. To help solve this problem, specialized buying services called *merchandise brokers* and *resident buyers* are situated in important market cities and can be used by retailers who find difficulty in keeping up-to-date with many resources in their merchandise area.

Merchandise brokers receive their fees from the vendors they represent, not from the retailers who use their services. A merchant sends requests for merchandise to the broker, who fills them as best he can. Because the broker's livelihood depends on his ability to know the market and deal only with the best sources, buyers often find that they receive better merchandise from these specialists than if they shopped the market themselves. This can only happen, however, when the merchandise broker's office has capable personnel who are thoroughly familiar with the particular field and customer segment in which the retailer specializes.

Resident buyers act as agents for stores and receive retainers from them. Their main function is to shop the market and report their findings to their clients. They also perform many useful services. Resident buying offices are used by both small as well as medium and large stores.

Trade Fairs and Market Weeks

There is a growing tendency today for manufacturers and wholesalers to show their lines in the larger centers at the same time. This has a great many advantages for both vendors and retailers. Manufacturers must meet the trade show sponsor's deadline if they want to show their full line, and retailers can shop and place orders with a minimum of effort and time.

Markets, however, have dangers for both vendors and retailers. On one hand, the vendor must keep his door open to all comers and so must deal with a large number of merchants, some of whom he would ordinarily want to ignore. On the other hand, the open-door policy makes it possible for vendors to contact many new prospects who would otherwise never visit their showrooms.

These events give the retailer the advantage of being able to make direct comparisons. Because he can walk easily from one resource to another, he is better able to decide which vendor he should buy from. Otherwise, he has to base his buying on memory because salesmen visit him days and weeks apart. But the market creates a "buy now" fever and unless a merchant comes with a buying plan, uses it, and controls himself very rigidly, he will end up buying much more merchandise than he would if he saw one vendor at a time and made his buying decisions without market pressure.

Buy from All Sources

Whether the retailer does his own buying or uses a resident buying office, he can go to only two main sources—the manufacturer and the wholesaler. He should therefore learn when to deal with both of them because in some areas the manufacturer is best and in other areas the wholesaler is best. He should also realize that what is true today may not be true tomorrow and so he must be flexible enough to change vendors whenever it seems desirable or profitable.

How to Pick Individual Resources

With the constantly growing number of new products and the development of better marketing techniques, merchants are under severe and ever-increasing pressure to buy more merchandise than thcy can safely handle. One of the best ways of controlling this serious situation is to select as few suppliers as possible and give them the bulk of your business. In this way, you become a good account to the suppliers concerned and you gain whatever benefits accrue from quantity buying. Be as loyal as you can to your suppliers because continuity helps your relationship with them. This does not mean that you should stick with a vendor even when his merchandise fails to sell in your store or when his service is unsatisfactory. You should feel free to sever connections with any supplier who cannot make the grade, just as you should be forever on the alert for new vendors who will improve your merchandise selection. Your customers will show little loyalty to you if you cease to perform your function as their super shopper, but your clientele will grow whenever you move from good suppliers to better ones.

Does the vendor suit your store?

Whenever you see a vendor's line, ask yourself whether his merchandise will sell in *your* store. His merchandise may be terrific in large stores and even in the shops next to you, but this is no reason why it should sell well in your store. Remember that you don't buy merchandise because everyone else has it, but because it moves out of your store profitably.

What is the vendor's reputation?

If the vendor is new to you, judge him not only by his line, but also by whether or not his operational policies suit your kind of business. Is he a style leader or a follower? Is he known to cut prices in season? Does he stand behind his merchandise? If his pattern suggests he may give you trouble, forget him and look elsewhere for what you want. If his policies are those you like and his merchandise is acceptable, you may look forward to a happy relationship.

How does the vendor deliver?

Some lines look so good and the sales presentation is so forceful that you forget that the merchandise has to be properly delivered and has to have the same appeal in your store as it did in the showroom. Some vendors are unable to fill even placing orders as written. Because merchandise comes in with broken sizes and colors, it cannot be properly presented. Styles are cancelled and substitutions are made without your being notified. Vendors sometimes ship goods that are not the same as the sample or deliver the goods so late that you lose your selling season. Vendors who operate this way are harmful to your store for they create extra work, cause you to worry needlessly and lose business, and they harm your reputation.

Suppliers who ship placing orders on time and according to specifications still have to pass another test. How are they on repeat business? In fashion goods especially, original orders make very little profit because the retailer is probing his customers' wants. Since real profit comes from his runners, he must deal with vendors who can fill repeat orders quickly and accurately. Nothing is more frustrating in the retail business than to spot a hot number, order it, and then watch customer after customer walk out of the store because the manufacturer has not shipped it.

How does the vendor handle repeats?

The shorter the distance between you and your vendors, the better the service that you can usually obtain from them. Even today's fast communications and delivery systems cannot compete with the ability to get in touch quickly with your vendors by phone or personal visit. When this is possible, you can operate on a smaller inventory, with better turnover, more special buys, etc. You will also receive better timing in deliveries.

The larger stores protect themselves against suppliers who do not stand behind their products by maintaining special bureaus that test vendors' claims or by specifying the materials and the way they want their goods manufactured. Since the small and medium-sized merchants have no facilities for this kind of buying, they must trust the manufacturer not only to deliver the merchandise according to sample but also to stand behind his goods. This means, among other things, taking back merchandise because it was not shipped as ordered and handling returns from the store's customers with speed and understanding.

Does the vendor stand behind his merchandise?

The vendor's ethics should also be considered. Is he known as a manipulator, a high-pressure promoter, or a man who quotes low prices on a generous sample and then cheapens the merchandise he actually delivers? Is he full of promises that never become facts? Does he run down his competitors? Is he unreliable? Does he sometimes live up to his promises and at other times fail you completely?

It will also pay you to check a new supplier's financial status through your bank or your buying office. Before some vendors go into bankruptcy, they seek to save themselves by a number of very unethical practices. For example, they may offer you what appears to be a tremendous buy and make it even more interesting by granting you a large discount for cash. But by the time the merchandise is processed in the

What is the vendor's financial status?

store and its faults begin to show up, the vendor is bankrupt and you must get rid of the goods as best you can. Unsettled merchandise returns only give you creditor status, which usually means less than 100 cents on a dollar.

Since small and medium-sized retailers require all kinds of selling aids, vendors who supply these extra services become good buying sources. Some of these services are extended credit arrangements, merchandising control systems, point-of-sale display material, and such promotional aids as cooperative advertising allowances, advertising art or layout and copy suggestions. Private branding can be of immense competitive value against national brands to the small and medium-sized retailer; however, he must be careful to see whether the supplier of the private brand protects him with a good markup or squeezes the markup but still forces the store to carry his merchandise by building up consumer demand.

Does the vendor help you sell?

WHAT THIS CHAPTER TOLD YOU

1. Knowing *where* to buy is as important as knowing *what* and *how* to buy.

2. The two main sources of supply for retailers are manufacturers and wholesalers.

3. Both of these sources have advantages and disadvantages. The retailer should be flexible enough not only to buy from both but also to move from one to the other as conditions warrant.

4. In addition to going directly to the market, retailers should use the services of commission brokers and buying offices.

5. Although trade fairs and market weeks aid retailers in buying, they also present many dangers.

6. Retailers should carefully select as few vendors as possible and then be as loyal to them as they can. But they should change suppliers if the new ones will result in more profitable business.

7. In selecting a vendor, ask yourself the following questions:
   (a) Does his line suit your store?
   (b) What is his reputation?
   (c) How does he deliver?
   (d) How does he handle repeats?
   (e) Does he stand behind his merchandise?
   (f) What is his financial status?
   (g) Does he help you sell?

4

How to Buy
and Save Money

There is a lot more to buying for a store than knowing what your customers want and where you can get it. Before every season you feel that most of your suppliers have what you think your customers will want, but as soon as the season opens, only a few of them seem to stock the best sellers and they can never fill your orders quickly enough. This chapter discusses how to deal with suppliers so that you can obtain from them not only favorable prices and service but also as many other concessions as possible.

Importance of Your Relationship with Salesmen

The customers you like best are those who treat you with respect and who buy a great deal from your store. You will go beyond the call of business to please these people and retain them as customers. Casual shoppers receive minimum service and few favors, and those who keep bothering you with returns or complaints of one kind or another often receive scant treatment.

Vendor salesmen are even more sensitive about your treatment of them than you are about your relationship with your customers. During the day, many shoppers come into your store, so that if one of them leaves without buying, the results are not too serious. But a sales-man is lucky if he shows his line to six people in a day. Therefore, every potential buyer becomes very important to him and he is anxious to get an order from each one he calls on. This puts him on such an unequal basis with the store buyer that he becomes very sensitive to the buyer's conduct and reacts violently for or against the buyer. For this reason, salesmen can never be neutral; they are either a buyer's best friend or his worst enemy.

How to Get Salesmen to Help You

If you treat a salesman pleasantly and courteously, he will respond by actively helping you to buy. He may offer you a number of promotions that are on allocation or he may cut you in on items that his firm is making on a confined basis for large retail organizations and give them to you at the big retailer's price. He will talk freely about his line and point out what he thinks is best for your store. Because he has an intimate knowledge of the way his merchandise has been received, his suggestions are worth considering, although you must weigh against them his desire to get an order. Occasionally a salesman has an opportunity to dispose of an extraordinarily good but small clearance or job lot. The store to which he first offers this merchandise usually has a buyer toward whom he feels most friendly.

How Salesmen Are Antagonized

Some buyers look upon salesmen as an annoyance that they would sooner do without. Salesmen bother them because they take up time and force them to make buying decisions. They do not realize that salesmen *save* buyers a great deal of time and that they can help them make *successful* buying decisions. These buyers have many ways of insulting and humiliating salesmen. They ignore them while they gossip with their staff, deliberately forget to keep appointments, or make a habit of arriving late and disrupting the salesman's appointment schedule. If these buyers were treated this way by a shopper, they would throw the shopper out of the store. Although the salesman would swallow his pride and do what he could to get the order, he would remember rude buyers and make no attempt to help them. He would simply show them the line and write down the order. He would never go out of his way to assist these buyers with a promotion or help them by arranging early deliveries so that their store could get ahead of competition; he would not look after special orders and he would not try to make some arrangements to take back overbought or slow-moving merchandise.

Vendor Relationships

Good vendor relationships pay off almost as well as friendly associations with salesmen, although here your personal contact is not so

important nor so intimate as it is with salesmen. The vendor is most
appreciative when you pay your bills promptly, are fair about returns and complaints, and do not put too much pressure on him for bargains and promotions. In the last analysis, the vendor may countermand whatever his salesman wants to do for you and when you come to the market or reorder running numbers, he may either be liberal and fill your order quickly or tell you that he is sold out and is unable to make another item for the balance of the season.

Remember that as a buyer you may be treated like a king but your subjects are very sensitive to the way they are handled. You can make them either loyal and helpful or disgruntled and harmful. It does not take much effort or thought for a buyer to be a gentleman and it certainly pays dividends (Fig. 4.1).

See as Many Vendors as Possible

Being on good terms with vendors and their salesmen does not mean that you should buy from every salesman who comes into the store, but you should examine all offerings in your merchandise segment and then inspect as many other lines as time permits. This will tell you what is happening in the market. It is especially wise to look at the lines of a few reputable vendors who carry merchandise above and below your customer segment. Then you can judge where you fit into the total consumer picture and how your merchandise compares in style, price, value, etc. For a fashion merchant, this technique should indicate when styles are moving into and out of his customer segment so that he can then act accordingly.

Buy From as Few Vendors as Possible

Although you should be courteous to all salesmen, buy from as few vendors as possible. In this way, you become a worthwile customer to those you think will supply you with the best merchandise. For example, if during a six-month period you give $25,000 to ten suppliers, each receives an average of $2,500 and you only make a slight impression on them. If, however, you spend the $25,000 among three vendors, you become a worthwhile account for each of them. You can then ask them for the occasional favor and the vendors themselves will go out of their way to keep you satisfied.

How to Buy Staple Goods

Whenever possible, arrange to buy staples from only one or two suppliers. In return, they will give you good service, extra discounts, and other benefits. If your past records are complete and you order

BUILD GOOD VENDOR RELATIONS

1. Remember that although a saleman's livelihood depends on you, yours, to a great extent, depends on him.
2. Treat all salesmen as people from whom you expect favors.
3. If you have no intention of buying a salesman's line, tell him so. If he still wants you to see it, it is his responsibility if you don't give him an order.
4. To a salesman, time is money. Don't waste it by making him stand around waiting to arrange an appointment. Do it as quickly as possible and let him go about his business.
5. Keep all appointments that you make with salesmen and be there on time.
6. Schedule your buying in advance so that you will waste as little of the salesman's time as possible.
7. Let him show you the line in his own way. He has probably spent a lot of time working out a presentation that will highlight his best items.
8. Don't insult the salesman or his merchandise. If you must criticize, be as gentle and as constructive as possible. Remember that he is emotionally and financially involved in the firm and its merchandise and will strongly resent any attempt to undermine his livelihood.
9. Be as loyal as you can to a firm, but if you feel that you can no longer buy the line, tell the salesman why you must drop it.
10. Don't try to beat down the price of every item you want to buy. Most suppliers have set prices from which they will not vary. However, you should bargain when you are offered job lots or clearances.
11. Confirm your orders to vendors as soon as possible.
12. Don't cancel merchandise without a good reason and then only if the vendor has not put it into production or agrees to dispose of it.
13. Take all discounts offered, but do not take cash discounts after the time limit.
14. Pay invoices on their due dates.
15. Don't break up payments when they become due.
16. Don't cut prices of brand or well-established lines without the vendor's permission.
17. Do not refuse or return merchandise unless
    a. It has been shipped too far ahead of your "start-ship" date or too long after your "stop-ship" date.
    b. It is not as the sample in workmanship, style, color, size, assortment, etc. In this case, write the vendor your reasons for the return.
    c. Customers return defective merchandise and a stock check reveals that there is more merchandise in poor condition.
    d. Prices or quantities on the invoice differ from those on the store's order form.
    e. Vendor ships merchandise without an order.
    f. Vendor agrees to take the merchandise back in overbought situations.
    g. The merchandise is on consignment.

FIGURE 4.1 These rules should be studied and frequently reviewed by all buyers and merchandising executives.

conservatively but according to trends, you can sometimes give these
vendors a blanket or quantity order. A blanket order gives the vendor an idea of how much of his goods you expect to use during the season. It is not necessary to break it down into styles or units at that time. On the strength of such retail commitments, he proceeds to plan and order his requirements in large enough quantities to obtain discounts from his suppliers. He passes on some of this saving to you. When the line comes out, you place your opening requirements as usual and continue to order for the balance of the season as business warrants. To get your discount, the total of all your purchases for the period should add up to the original commitment.

Quantity orders are different. Here you must order a definite amount and as you increase your quantities, the price goes down or the discounts increase. For example, if you order one gross of a staple item, it might cost you $100. If you order two gross, the price might be reduced to $95, i.e., you will be given a discount of 5 percent. At five gross, there may be another discount, and so on.

Group Buying

If you are too small for blanket or quantity discounts, try to get together with a number of noncompeting merchants who appeal to the same customer segment as you do or, if possible, work through a buying office. As a group you can obtain whatever large discounts are available, although no one of you could do so alone.

Practice Guessing Prices

Your customers are constantly pricing food, clothing, hard goods, and in fact, everything they buy. They have become expert at judging comparative retail values in their consumer range. You, too, should practice pricing everything you see, from cars to candy, because it will help you to develop a relationship between items that your customers could buy and the merchandise you offer them. Once you become expert at this guessing game, be careful about ordering any merchandise that you have "priced" lower than its actual value. The salesman may point out valid reasons why the item must be more expensive than you judged it, but most of your customers' reactions will be the same as yours and they will not have the time or inclination to listen to your salespeople's explanations. Of course, if you are catering to an exclusive clientele to whom uniqueness, not price, is paramount, the special qualities of the merchandise become a plus factor that makes for easier selling. But in most stores these items will only become lemons that will not move until the prices are reduced.

A manufacturer's costing methods should enable you to estimate his prices. It takes just so much cloth to make a man's suit or just so much leather to make a pair of woman's shoes. To this the manufacturer adds the cost of the other materials in the item as well as a percentage that represents his overhead and desired profit, and so arrives at his wholesale price (Fig. 4.2). Most manufacturers use similar pricing systems and if a supplier differs, he will boast about the way he has outsmarted his competitors and thus is able to give you a real bargain. With some practice, you will become sufficiently competent to question any manufacturer about his prices and perhaps suggest where he could cut costs and give you a better wholesale price. This, of course, leads to better buying and more customer satisfaction. In some instances, however, your customers' ready acceptance of a manufacturer's products permits him to raise the suggested price higher than normal and this, in turn, should give you a better than normal markup.

Compare Wholesale and Retail Prices

With constant pricing practice, you not only become expert in judging retail and wholesale prices, you also become sharper in your buying judgments. By continually comparing the prices of one vendor's line with another's, you begin to see which is best for your customers and why. You learn to look for and remember the hidden as well as the obvious qualities of a line and this, of course, makes you a better judge of values.

When, Where, and How to Bargain

You can bargain for lower cost prices, except where they are affected by government regulations. You must be very careful when, where, and how you use this technique, for just as you usually dislike customers who bargain with you, so vendors dislike retailers who constantly try to beat them down. But bargaining is justifiable for special store events or for job lots. Begin by establishing a price in your own mind, but try to get the vendor to declare his price first. It may be lower than yours and you stand to gain.

If you know the market and your own secret price appears reasonable but the vendor's offer is too high, you should be able to point out to him why his quotation is out of line. Be as fair as you can when you bargain. Vendors do not want to lose a good account and will do what they can to satisfy a buyer, but they dislike being pressured too hard.

Behind the Price Tag of a $110 Summer Dress

Cotton and polyester dress: Wholesale price $59.75
Retail price $110.00

Manufacturer's Cost

Fabric
(2¹¹/₁₆ yards
at $1.60)   **$4.30**

Lining
(1 ¾ yards at .75,
plus interlining,
¾ yards at .60)   **1.54**

Belt
(Including covered
snaps, elastic)   **2.28**

Labor, wages
(Operator, finisher,
presser)   **21.03**

**Labor,
fringe benefits**
(Health and welfare,
Social Security,
vacation, pension)   **6.73**

Overhead
(Rent, insurance,
utilities, salaries,
costs of samples,
trade discounts, etc.)   **19.87**

Total cost   **$55.75**

Taxes   2.00

Profit   2.00
_____

**Wholesale cost
of dress**   **$59.75**

Retailer's Cost

$59.75 less discount for
prompt payment   **$55.00**

Markdowns
(Averaged over all
dresses in stock)   **$11.00**

**Shortages,
pilferage, etc.**   2.00

Alterations
(Cost of maintaining
department
averaged out)   2.00

Salaries
Sales staff   5.00

**Merchandising and
buying staff**
(Including expenses)   3.00

Clerical and stock room
(Receiving, marking,
deliveries, etc.;
including expenses)   3.00

**Advertising, display,
sales promotion**   4.00

Administrative
(Executives, credit and
accounting offices,
including expenses)   8.00

**Employe fringe
benefits**   2.00

Overhead
(Rent, insurance, utilities,
cleaning, security)   9.00

Miscellaneous   2.00
_____

Total   **$106.00**

Taxes   2.00

Profit   2.00

Selling price   **$110.00**
                           (plus tax)

Figure 4.2 This is an excellent example of the cost breakdowns of a manufacturer and a retailer that result in their respective selling prices. Notice that although the retailer's price is double that of the manufacturer's ($110 versus $55), both make the same $2 profit.

© 1974 by the New York Times Company. Reprinted by permission.

Learn to give and take. Everyone likes to win and if you give the vendor a small concession, he is more likely to yield a big one. If he feels that you want to beat him down on every price, he becomes uncompromising and simply raises his original price higher than usual. In this way, he ends up where he wanted to in the first place. But he resents your tactics because they make him feel unhappy and so he will not do you any real favors.

Get Other Concessions Besides Price

There are other concessions besides price that you can rightfully obtain from a regular supplier. These include cash discounts, longer dating, more advantageous shipping terms, advertising allowances, point of sale promotions, or a promise from the vendor to send one of his personnel to demonstrate a product or dress your windows and interior displays. He may also supply you with direct mail pieces, information labels, package inserts, or advertising material. Again, you might get him to offer premiums or special packaging.

Consignment Merchandise

This means that the vendor puts merchandise that he owns into your store and permits you to handle it as your own. At an agreed time, you send back what you still have in stock and pay him only for what was sold. This is sometimes a good way to give your customers a wider selection of merchandise than you could otherwise afford, or it may enable you to test a new item without risk. Consignment stock should never be accepted, however, if it competes with merchandise that you have bought and paid for, if it crowds your store, or if it does not suit your store personality.

Job Lots and Clearance Merchandise

One way to make a high markup is to purchase job lots or other clearance goods but for any store except promotional ones, this kind of buying is very dangerous because it is one of the easiest ways to build up an overlarge and unbalanced inventory. A job lot is a group of assorted merchandise that a vendor has been unable to sell at regular prices and is now offering at a lot price that is supposed to be well below the total normal value of the items in the lot.

Usually, the price of the lot is very attractive, but unless you make a specialty of this kind of buying, *examine the merchandise very carefully* and consider what effect it will have on your store before you purchase it. Stores that normally buy jobs have found that a lot is only worth buying if it can be purchased at a price so low that they can dispose of it quickly and at a profit. If you have to put the merchandise away for months or if your reductions to clear the last half or quarter of the lot are so drastic that you lose your profit, the purchase is not worthwhile.

The first thing to do with either offer is to sort it out according to your estimate of the normal retail prices of the items it contains. If it consists of 100 pieces that would ordinarily sell at $500 and the lot is being offered at $150 wholesale, it looks interesting and worth further consideration. Then put each price group into sizes, materials, colors,

How to examine a job lot or supplier's clearance

47

etc., and see how this works out. Be very realistic at this point. Jobs usually contain a *few* good styles, colors, sizes, etc., but for the most part, they generally consist of unwanted styles, colors, and end sizes. Remember that your customers will not buy certain merchandise no matter what the price. If a customer wears size 6½ gloves, she will not buy size 8 even if you offer her a pair of $10 gloves for $3.88.

The lot, as a whole, must appeal to your customer segment. If people do not expect to see the merchandise in your store, they will ignore it or be suspicious of it. It could also build ill will and make you lose prestige with your regular customers.

Does the job lot appeal to your customers?

Buying a lot too late in the season is very dangerous. Remember this rule: To be worthwhile, a job lot must sell quickly and profitably. If you have to put it away, you increase its cost because it ties up capital, lowers turnover, reduces the current and next season's open-to-buy, etc. You must also pay interest, insurance charges, storage, and rent on the extra merchandise. Your greatest loss on a lot could be caused by obsolescence. The goods could look old when they come on the floor next year and there might be such style and material changes that the lot is unsalable at any price; or retail prices could have dropped so much that new goods would sell at the price that you want to get for the job merchandise. Thus, even under current conditions of temporary shortages, if a retailer wants to gamble, he should take risks on stocks or real estate, not on merchandise for his store.

Is the job lot too late in the season?

A lot that will lower your regular prices even temporarily has to be considered very carefully. If you buy a lot of lamp shades to retail at $3.88, which you are now selling at $6.98, its effect on your store could be disastrous, not only to your present stock of lamp shades but also to related merchandise. If you can sell the entire lot in a special promotion and then bring the lamp shades back to regular prices, it might be worthwhile. But if the quantity is large and you have to carry it at reduced prices for a long time and you already have an adequate reserve of regular lamp shades, the lot will prove an unfortunate buy.

How will the job lot affect your current prices?

Will the lot fit into your current stock or will it cheapen the store? Will it make your regular merchandise look too expensive? What are you going to do with the balance of the lot after the cream has been skimmed off? Can it then be handled as regular merchandise or will you put it into boxes, store it in some obscure corner, and then forget it? What will this cost?

How will the job lot affect your stock situation?

How much of your staff's time is going to be devoted to receiving, marking, and handling the lot? How much shifting and re-shifting of regular stock is going to be required? What effect will this have on your clerks and your customers?

How much work will the job lot involve?

If the lot consists of many more units than you can possibly handle quickly and profitably, perhaps you know of a number of noncompeting retailers who would share it with you. Group participation is a worthwhile method of disposing of large lots.

Frequently, only a certain amount of the lot is worth buying. Offer the vendor a price for what you can use. If your offer is attractive enough and your relations with him are good, he may take it. Otherwise, leave it alone. Once you buy it, you have to pay for it whether you dispose of it at a profit or a loss.

Although it is well to recognize the dangers of job lot buying, the benefit of a good lot in stimulating sales and creating promotions and and customer excitement is enormous. Therefore, whenever you are offered a clearance, give it a great deal of careful consideration. If you have built up good vendor relations, manufacturers or salesmen may offer you job lots of canceled merchandise or goods taken back from a bankrupt retailer, as well as end of season clearances. These can be sold at reduced prices, and bargaining is permissible. **Vendor relations and job lots**

As the season advances, vendors begin to clear, but there is only a a short time when they offer the best bargains. You learn when this is through experience and good vendor relations. Timing and being able to arrive at quick decisions are most important in job lot buying. You are not the only retailer who knows about the vendors' offers, and the best lots move quickly. **The right time to buy lots**

Before you sign an order for job lots, special deals, goods on consignment, or, for that matter, regular goods, make sure that the merchandise fits into your buying plan and will not damage your store image. No bargain, no matter how cheaply it can be obtained, is worthwhile if you cannot sell it quickly and, at the same time, create customer goodwill. Remember that what may be a tremendous promotion for someone else can become just one big headache for you. *Caveat emptor* (let the buyer beware) is as true in trading today as it was in Roman times. **Caution**

The best way to handle job lots is to plan early enough how much you want to buy and then go out in the market and find it. **Job lot and clearance buying for profit**

Suppliers always have odd quantities of merchandise lying about that they usually cannot clear until the end of the season. They will be happy to let you take them off their hands early in the season and should give you forward dating as well as a good discount.

If you control your job lot buying properly, the bulk of your clearance stock should consist of popular merchandise in depth, which you can offer at discount prices and still make a handsome profit. In this way, you give customers what they want at prices that are real bargains. This creates customer goodwill and favorable word-of-mouth advertising.

You must be able to discipline yourself and know when to stop buying clearance merchandise. At the end of every season job lots are offered at increasingly lower prices. You unconsciously relate these prices to those you paid for the same goods in season, or even two weeks ago. The current price seems so low that you simply cannot lose.

Beware of that last buy

You are, however, thinking of the merchandise in terms of its *value,* not in terms of its *sales potential.* The last buy, then, may cause you to lose money because it ties up capital and curtails open-to-buy. Be thankful that you had a profitable season and do not tempt fortune too far. It is better to lose a few sales because your end stock is low than to lose a season's profit to make every last sale. Remember that most customers will ignore merchandise they are not in a mood to buy, no matter how much of a bargain it is.

WHAT THIS CHAPTER TOLD YOU

1. Your relationships with salesmen and vendors can enormously help or hinder your ability to buy merchandise.

2. See as many lines as you can, but buy from as few vendors as possible.

3. Practice pricing, both at retail and wholesale levels.

4. Try to order in sufficiently large amounts to take advantage of quantity and cumulative discounts. But never increase an order just for the discount.

5. Unless you are a promotional house, always look for but be careful about buying job lots.

6. By proper planning and merchandise control, you can obtain clearance merchandise that you can sell at a good profit and still create customer goodwill.

7. Know when to stop buying job lots and clearances.

5

How to Write an Order

WHAT THIS CHAPTER IS ABOUT

Too many retailers allow vendors to use their own order forms and they also go along with whatever routine and conditions the vendors insist on when writing up the order. This can only lead to the loss of control and many good opportunities for the retailer to gain cash discounts, longer dating, and many other concessions that reduce the actual price of the merchandise ordered.

This chapter discusses the value of discounts and other conditions that you should ask for in order to obtain the best possible deal. It also tells you why the use of your *own* order form is one of the best ways to protect your merchandise and control your orders.

Make Certain All Prices, Discounts, and Other Concessions Are Legal

There are many restrictions against vendors agreeing to special prices, discounts, or other concessions. Since retailers are as liable as suppliers for any illegal agreement, make certain that all arrangements between you and the vendor meet federal and state laws. Chapter 20 discusses some of these laws. If you are in doubt about any arrangement, seek advice from a trade association like the NRMA before you accept it.

One of the easiest ways for a small retailer to pay less than the quoted wholesale price for his merchandise is to ask for and take as many discounts as he can. The main discounts are called *trade, quantity,* and *cash*. You should be aware of the advantages they have for the vendor as well as for you (Fig. 5.1).

Trade discounts are usually given when suppliers sell merchandise to **Trade discounts** retailers through catalogues in which the vendor illustrates and describes the items he carries and gives them suggested retail prices called *list prices*. He encloses a separate sheet in the catalogue which tells the merchant that the goods will cost him a certain percentage off list. For example, if a watch is listed at $20 and the retailer is allowed 40 percent off list, his discount is 40/100 of $20, or $8. He therefore pays $20 minus $8, or $12. An easier way to calculate net price after discount is to subtract the discount from 100 percent and multiply the result by the list price, e.g.,

$$100\% - 40\% = 60\% \times \$20 = \$12$$

It takes months to compile and mail a catalogue. During that time the prices of all or some of the items in the catalogue may change. If the supplier had to issue a new catalogue with every price change, he would soon go out of business. To deal with price fluctuations, therefore, he simply mails additional discount notices to his clients. But a series of discounts *does not* equal their sum. For example, discounts of 40 percent + 5 percent + 10 percent equal a single discount of 48.7 percent, *not* 55 percent. To prove this, suppose that an item lists at $100, and the retailer is given discounts of 40 percent, 5 percent, and 10 percent. The first discount equals 40 percent × $100, or $40, and the cost to the retailer is $60. The second discount is 5 percent × $60, which brings the cost down to $60 − $3, or $57. The third discount is 10 percent of $57, which is $5.70, making the cost to the retailer now $51.30. If you subtract $51.30 from $100.00, you get the true single discount, $48.70.

Although a discount series of 40 percent, 5 percent, and 10 percent cannot be added, it does not matter whether you take the 5 percent first, or the 10 percent first, or the 10 percent second. No matter in which order you calculate this series, the result will still be equal to a single discount of 48.7 percent.

Because the cost of processing one large order is usually less than **Quantity** that of handling a number of small ones, the vendor sometimes offers **discounts** retailers quantity discounts. He also hopes that the extra sales volume that these discounts encourage will more than compensate for the loss of markup he incurs. Quantity discounts can be quoted in dollars or in

ORDER AHEAD — AND GET THE FOLLOWING DISCOUNTS

Early Order Discount

All orders placed before January 15, for immediate delivery, will qualify for a special early order discount of 1%.

Quantity Cash Discount

All orders placed before February 15 will qualify for the ADDITIONAL quantity cash discounts as follows, subject to unit availability.

Quantity (units)	Cash Discount if paid by:						
	Jan. 1st	Feb. 1st	Mar. 1st	Apr. 1st	Apr. 15th	May 1st	May 15th
1 - 5	2½%	2 %	1½%	1 %	net	—	—
6 - 14	4 %	3½%	3 %	2½%	2 %	1½%	net
15 - 24	5 %	4½%	4 %	3½%	3 %	2½%	net
25 - 39	6½%	6 %	5½%	5 %	4½%	4 %	net
40 - 49	7½%	7 %	6½%	6 %	5½%	5 %	net
50 and over	8½%	8 %	7½%	7 %	6½%	6 %	net

Continuing Discount

All customers placing spring dated orders for 6 or more units per above, will qualify for a special continuing discount on all further orders for dealer line units during the season ending August 31st (depending on the initial quantity ordered) as follows:

Initial Quantity	Continuing Discount
6 - 14	1%
15 - 24	2%
25 - 39	3%
40 - 49	4%
50 and over	5%

The continuing discount applies only if the customer's account is kept on a current basis. On other than spring dating orders our standard terms are 2% for payment 10 days from date of invoice, 1% for payment 10th of the month following shipment, due for payment Net the 20th of the month following shipment.

NOTE: All orders are subject to the usual credit approval.

All prices are subject to change without notice.

All prices are subject to prices in effect at time of shipment.

FIGURE 5.1 An example of the number of discounts that a wholesaler sometimes offers to retailers. In this case, if a retailer ordered 15 units and took advantage of all discounts—1 percent for early ordering, 5 percent for quantity, and 3½ percent cash discount—he would get the equivalent of a single discount of 9.24 percent. He would also be able to take a continuing discount of 2 percent, thus achieving a final discount of 11.05 percent.

units. For example, if a retailer orders either more than $1,000 worth of an item or more than 200 units, he may receive a 2 percent quantity discount. Sometimes the discounts are graduated, e.g., either over $1,000 or over 200 units, 2 percent discount; either over $5,000 or over 1,000 units, 5 percent discount; and so on.

Vendors use cumulative discounts to encourage customer loyalty. They are discounts that are figured at the end of a period and are graded according to the total amount of the purchases that the retailer has made in that period. They do not oblige the merchant to order heavily, but they tend to make him give as much business as he can to a single supplier. Cumulative discounts are figured on either dollar amounts or units of merchandise.

Cumulative discounts

Trade discounts are *given* to everyone in a certain category. Quantity discounts and cumulative discounts are *given* to everyone who buys in sufficient quantities. Cash discounts are *offered* to those who pay their bills in a shorter time than custom dictates. Vendors grant a cash discount because it saves them money, they have less collection expense and they have the use of the merchant's cash earlier than if he had taken the full time to pay. A cash discount policy gives the vendor a good selling point because, all things being equal, the smart retailer will deal with suppliers who offer the best cash discounts.

Cash discounts

A supplier who ordinarily gives a merchant 30 days to pay for his merchandise may offer him a discount of 2 percent if the account is cleared within 10 days after invoice date. Or he may offer 5 percent in 10 days, 2 percent in 30 days, 1 percent in 60 days, or the net price in 90 days. This would be written 5/10, 2/30, 1/60, n/90. Merchants may reject cash discounts, but they are very foolish if they do, for 2/10 can work out to an annual interest rate of 36.7 percent. Figure it out this way: A creditor offers you 2/10, n/30 on an invoice of $1,000. If you pay it in 10 days, you take off $20 and pay the vendor $980; if you pay 20 days later, the merchandise will cost you $1,000. By lending the vendor $980 for 20 days, you save $20. This is equal to $1 a day or $360 a year. The interest rate of $360 on a principal of $980 equals $360/980 \times 100$, or 36.7 percent. If you had to borrow the $980 at 6 percent per annum from the bank, you would still be far ahead. Also, when a retailer takes cash discounts, he not only makes a huge profit, he also enhances his credit standing because his creditors feel that he has the cash and that he is a smart businessman. Table 5.1 shows the approximate savings available from the cash discounts that are most commonly offered.

Anticipation is a method of paying vendors before due date. Because the effect of this action is the same as lending them money,

Anticipation

TABLE 5.1 Cash discount values, figured on the period between discount date and net payment date.

Approximate Cash Discount Values

½% in 10 days, net 30 days	9% a year
1% in 10 days, net 30 days	18% a year
1½% in 10 days, net 30 days	27% a year
2% in 10 days, net 30 days	36% a year
2% in 10 days, net 60 days	14% a year
2% in 30 days, net 60 days	24% a year
2% in 30 days, net 120 days	8% a year
3% in 10 days, net 120 days	10% a year
3% in 10 days, net 60 days	21% a year
3% in 30 days, net 60 days	36% a year

vendors pay you an agreed interest on the amount you lend them. Suppose that an invoice for $500 is dated September 29th, 3/10 EOM, with anticipation set at 6 percent. If the trade considers invoices dated on or after the 25th of the month as coming due the month following, and if you paid it on November 10th, you would deduct a cash discount of $15 (3 percent of $500). But if you pay it on October 10th, you are in effect lending the vendor $500 for 30 days, i.e., $\frac{1}{12}$ of a year. Therefore, you charge him $2.50 interest ($500 $\times$ .06 $\div$ 12). Thus, all you pay him is

$$\$482.50\ [\$500 - (\$15 + \$2.50)]$$

Anticipation takes many forms and not all vendors will accept it, or even cash discounts. Moreover, many small retailers do not even know that anticipation exists. But if you have the cash, ask for cash discounts and anticipation. Both reduce merchandise costs and improve your credit standing in the trade.

Sometimes a vendor offers special discounts to retailers who are willing to cooperate in reducing his costs. For example, if the retailer is willing to order his next season's requirements before the customary placing time, he is given an early placing discount; or if he is willing to accept the merchandise as it is processed, which usually means that he must store it for some time before he can sell it, he receives an early shipping discount. Merchants can also obtain bulk shipment discounts, transportation discounts, and discounts in the form of cooperative advertising.

Miscellaneous discounts

You should be aware of the fact that if you can save the vendor any expense, you should receive part of the benefit in the form of a discount. You enhance your standing if you ask for discounts because you demonstrate that you are a keen buyer. The worst reaction that you could receive would only be a "No" from the vendor.

You can reap only benefits from taking *cash* discounts or anticipation, but quantity, cumulative, and other discounts may be very harmful. Think carefully before you increase an order just to take advantage of certain discounts. For example, you may be offered a 3 percent discount, or $30, on a purchase of $1,000, but if it takes you three times as long to sell this much merchandise as it would take to sell your usual $350 worth, you will lose more than $30 through slower turnover, tied-up capital, markdowns, and all the other expenses that occur when merchandise moves slowly. If you are too small to take advantage of quantity or other discounts, see whether or not you can form a group or work through a buying office. Then no one will get stuck and all will benefit.

Take every cash discount, but think about the other discounts

Dating

When to pay

Unless you get a cash discount or can take advantage of anticipation, it is foolish to pay out money before you have to because you can use it as well as your vendors can. Therefore, always figure out the last day on which to meet a discount. Most discounts are based on the date of the invoice, *not* the date you ordered the merchandise, *not* the shipping day, and *not* the receiving day. If the invoice date is May 27th and you are offered 2/10, you should pay on June 6th. With optional discounts such as 5/10, 3/30, n/60, always take the first discount offered—in this example, 5 percent in ten days. If the invoice contains trade or quantity discounts, the cash discount is figured on the net amount, i.e., the balance *after* the other discounts are deducted. Handle anticipation in the same way.

Even when you are not offered cash discounts or anticipation, proper dating of your payment is important. Unless you pay COD (cash on delivery) or CBD (cash before delivery) for your merchandise, the more time you can obtain between the invoice date and the day you pay for the goods, the greater the chance you have to sell the merchandise and realize a profit on the supplier's money.

Ordinary dating

Customarily, "30 days" means one month from invoice date. An invoice dated June 10th, terms n/30, should be paid July 10th. If the invoice offers you a cash discount, say 2/10, you should take off 2 percent and pay it on June 20th.

EOM dating

Some suppliers accept the end of the month as the base date. Thus, an invoice dated June 10th with terms of payment 2/10, EOM, permits you to take 2 percent discount and pay the balance on July 10th. Sometimes all invoices dated on or after the 25th of the month are permitted EOM treatment, so that an invoice dated June 26th could be treated as though it were dated June 30th. Thus, an invoice dated June 26th, 2/10, n/30 becomes payable with 2 percent cash discount on July 10th, or without the discount, July 31st. Anticipation may also be figured in this way. If your suppliers accept this kind of dating, order your merchandise to be shipped on or after the 25th of the month whenever possible.

If the supplier is a long distance away from your store, he sometimes bases his payment terms on the date you receive the merchandise instead of on the invoice date.

**ROG
(receipt of goods)**

With certain merchandise for which advance promotion is an advantage even though it produces few early sales, some suppliers will ship merchandise ahead of the season but date the invoice as though the goods were shipped at the beginning of the season. Seasonal dating is important to retailers who handle big ticket items because it gives them time to spot runners and price lines, etc., even before the season starts.

Seasonal dating

Although long dating is certainly an advantage to any retailer, to ask for it may have a bad effect on your credit. The vendor may feel that you want it because your cash position is poor and, if this idea gets rumored among your suppliers, you may end up by receiving no credit at all. Nevertheless, in the case of certain merchandise such as Christmas toys being shipped in August, you should ask for dating that begins at the usual opening of the season.

**Be cautious
about dating**

Shipping Terms

You should be concerned with the carrier, the transportation costs, and who is responsible, i.e., who has *title* to the goods from the time the shipment leaves the supplier until it is received at your store. Make certain that the vendor knows not only how to ship the bulk of your order but also how to ship any balances, for small shipments dribbling in can be very expensive.

This is the usual method of shipping. The retailer pays the full transportation charges and assumes title as soon as the merchandise leaves the vendor's premises. For example, if a retailer in Buffalo buys furniture in Martinsville, Virginia, and it is shipped FOB Buffalo, he pays the freight charges to the carrier and if anything goes wrong with the goods in transit, he must negotiate a settlement with the carrier.

FOB origin

Here title or ownership passes to the retailer when the goods leave the manufacturer's warehouse. The retailer pays the freight charges to the carrier, but he deducts the charges from his net payment to the vendor.

**FOB origin—
freight allowed**

When manufacturers who are some distance from the main market want to meet competition, they sometimes pay freight charges to a market

**FOB origin—
freight equalized**

center, and the retailer pays freight from there on. If, for example, the retailer in Buffalo bought the furniture from a factory in Martinsville, Virginia, and had it shipped through Pittsburgh, under the terms "FOB origin—freight equalized," the manufacturer would pay the charges from Martinsville to Pittsburgh and the retailer would pay the charges from Pittsburgh to Buffalo. Nevertheless, title to the furniture would pass to the retailer as soon as it left the factory in Martinsville.

Here the manufacturer pays the freight charges and also assumes responsibility for the merchandise until it reaches the store.

FOB destination

In this arrangement the manufacturer maintains title to the goods until they arrive at the store and also pays transportation costs. The retailer, however, must pay back these charges to the vendor.

FOB destination— charges reversed

When merchandise is shipped so that the retailer is responsible for the goods in transit, he usually has no idea of the value of any specific shipment until it reaches his store and thus he cannot insure it properly. To help him out, some manufacturers inform the carrier of the value of each shipment and the carrier adds the insurance charges to the freight charges. Over the year these insurance charges can add up to a considerable sum and if anything goes wrong, the retailer has the trouble of filing a claim with the carrier. To reduce insurance expenses and eliminate the aggravation of time lost in settling claims, insurance companies have evolved a transit policy which is sometimes called *blanket insurance,* for which the retailer pays a premium on his estimated value of his next year's purchases. At the end of the year the actual amount is established and the retailer either pays a further premium or receives a rebate. In the event of any loss or damage to the merchandise in transit, the insurance company pays the retailer and then registers a claim against the carrier. Thus, the merchant gets his cash right away and is saved the time and bother of claiming against the transit company.

When to use "blanket" insurance

If you have a transit policy, put a notice on your order form instructing the vendor not to put a value on the shipment. Notify any vendor who disregards the directive and follow this up with another notification that tells him that you will deduct future insurance charges from his invoice. After one or two deductions, the vendor will stop putting values on your shipments.

Buyer's Order Forms

If you use the vendors' order forms, you soon collect a great many sheets of paper that differ in shape, size, color, and information. Worse still, they may contain rulings and conditions of sale that are devised for the vendors' convenience and protection, not yours. Remember that every order confirmed by the vendor and yourself becomes a legal contract and its terms can be made the subject of a lawsuit.

Importance of your own order form

IMPORTANT
1. DO NOT INSURE SHIPMENTS.
2. ALL GOODS SHIPPED AFTER THE 20th OF THE MONTH ARE TO BE BILLED AS 1st OF THE FOLLOWING MONTH.

Mosteller's
WEST CHESTER
PA.... 19380

SHIP AND BILL TO:
MOSTELLER'S, INC.
19 - 27 N. Church St.
WEST CHESTER, PA. 19380

(215) 696-0582

PURCHASE ORDER NO.
03200
MUST APPEAR ON INVOICE

THIS DEPT. NUMBER
MUST APPEAR
ON INVOICE
AND PACKAGE

DETACH

THIS

PORTION

BEFORE

SENDING

TO

VENDOR

RESOURCE_____

ADDRESS_____

CITY_____ PHONE_____

STATE_____ ZIP_____

SALESMAN_____

ORDER DATE   WHEN SHIP

AUTO. CANCELLATION DATE

TERMS_____ F.O.B._____

SHIP VIA_____

RESOURCE SHIPPING CLERK_____

DATE REC'D.	STYLE NO.	COLOR	DESCRIPTION										QUANTITY EACH DOZ.	UNIT COST	TOTAL COST		CLASS	UNIT RETAIL	TOTAL RETAIL

REMARKS

BUYER

MERCHANDISE MANAGER

AUTH.

FIGURE 5.2   A very flexible order form containing all the necessary elements for essential information.

Courtesy Mosteller's Inc., West Chester, Pa.

To regularize your order system and protect yourself, it is best to print your own order forms. Because they will be uniform in size and numbered, they may be easily filed and referred to and any missing order may be checked with the buyer concerned.

Figure 5.2 shows a very flexible order form. It is made in triplicate. The original goes to the vendor, the duplicate goes to the retailer's office for processing, and the third is kept by the department that wrote the order or the receiving room and is used to check the goods as they arrive. Each order should cover merchandise for one department only. If a buyer is ordering goods for a number of departments from the same supplier, he must use a separate order form for each department. Otherwise, office records, the

59

merchandise control system, and the receiving department's work become needlessly complicated.

Print Resource Information in Full.   Because many corporations have similar names, make sure that you write the vendor's full name in block letters. Then fill in his correct address and telephone number in order to further identify the vendor and help the office and the buyer in case they need to write or phone the supplier. It is very annoying and time-consuming to have to look up this information when you are in a hurry, and it takes only a second when the order is written.

Ship and Bill To.   Your store name, address, and telephone number should be printed on the form.

Purchase Order Number.   This is the serial number of the order and can be used for filing and reference purposes. Each buyer should be responsible for his own order book and be accountable for all missing order numbers.

Department Number.   The department number should be made part of the shipment's address. Otherwise, the order will travel around the store needlessly.

Order Date.   The order date should be the date that you phoned or mailed the order to the vendor. You may not confirm an order on the day you write it, but once it is confirmed it is important to process it as quickly as possible. Since most vendors date orders as they are received, if you delay sending the order and then argue that it has a very early date on it, the vendor will tell you when *he* received it and why you are not going to get good service from him.

When Ship.   This is a most important date because you may refuse any merchandise shipped to you before that date. It should be set to coincide with your plans to begin processing the merchandise. Of course, in season this box could read "Rush" or "As ready," but for placing, it should be used thoughtfully.

Automatic Cancellation Date.   This date is even more important than "when ship," for after the cancellation date you control the outstanding portion of the order and you may legally refuse to accept any more merchandise or may accept only part of it. The cutoff date should be a little before the end of your best selling period. However, the period between "when ship" and "automatic cancellation date" should be long enough to give your supplier time to fill the order. Experience and the supplier's capabilities should guide you in setting these two dates.

Terms.   The buyer should always ask for terms. "Usual" should not be accepted. The store that goes after terms makes a lot of extra money at a very small cost. Two percent 10 days (2/10) amounts to 36.7 percent per annum when net payment is due in 30 days, and it pays to borrow if necessary to take this discount. It also gives you a good credit rating. If you cannot get a discount, ask for longer dating if this will not hurt your credit.

FOB. This is a question not only of who pays for the shipment but also who owns it in transit. If the shipment is prepaid, the shipper has title until it is signed for by your receiver. If it is collect, you are responsible the moment the carrier signs his name at the vendor's door.

Ship via. The mode of transport must be filled in on every order, and "cheapest" will not do. Freight is sometimes cheapest, but at other times air freight will pay off in terms of profit and customer convenience. Some stores give buyers a schedule of transportation costs and explain to them how they should be used.

Do Not Insure Shipments. In Figure 5.2 this appears in the upper left-hand box under "Important—1." It is used by retailers who receive most of their shipments collect and have a blanket policy. Item 2 in that box becomes effective if the resource accepts the order.

Salesman. The name of the vendor's salesman may be important if you should need him instead of the shipping clerk.

Resource Shipping Clerk. The vendor's shipping clerk is seldomly known by his last name, but he knows more about your order than do his boss, the salesman, or anyone else on your supplier's staff. Get to know him personally and treat him well. He will pay you back many times over.

Remarks. If you have made any special arrangements or deals with the vendor's salesman, write them out in the remarks box. If they need more space, write them on the back of the order and have him sign it. Then, if the vendor accepts the order, he has to carry out the agreement.

Buyer. This is for your buyer's or your own signature.

Merchandise Manager. This is the buyer's best excuse to reconsider the order. If the buyer is certain that he wants the goods, he can confirm the order at once, but if he is not sure, he can tell the salesman that someone else, that is, the merchandise manager, must fill in this box.

Format for Actual Order. The ruled lines should be flexible enough to handle all the items the store carries.

Detach This Portion. In order to keep the retail price from the resource, the original sheet of this section should be perforated. The buyer fills out the classification and the unit retail and then tears off this portion before the order is mailed. The office extends the retail prices into the total column of the other sheets and then deducts the total dollar amount from the department's open-to-buy.

Write Legibly. Make sure that you write legibly and that the carbon copies are clear. If you do not, many mistakes may occur in the way either the vendor or your own store interprets the order.

WHAT THIS CHAPTER TOLD YOU

1. To protect your business and keep better merchandise control, have your own order forms printed and serially numbered.

2. Ask for and take all cash discounts.

3. Get as many vendor concessions as will fit into your merchandising policy. Do not take any that may prove harmful.

4. If you cannot get a cash discount, ask for longer dating if it will not hurt your credit.

5. Make sure that you use the right carrier for every shipment.

6. Write orders legibly.

6

How to Take Care
of the Merchandise
You Buy

WHAT THIS CHAPTER IS ABOUT

Merchandise costs a lot of money. Why pay more for it through careless or thoughtless handling? Good stockkeeping is more than a matter of pride; it is profitable. This chapter discusses the various steps that a small merchant can take to keep his stockkeeping costs down and his profits up.

Receiving and Marking Rooms

No matter how small the store, space should be set aside for receiving and marking shipments, and a careful receiving and marking routine should be worked out. At first glance, it seems ridiculous to take the time and trouble to develop such systems. It would seem much faster to put down parcels wherever there is a vacant space, open them, and get the merchandise on the floor as quickly as possible.

But this "easy" method leads to much duplication of effort, possible unrecoverable loss of merchandise, poor records, overlooking cash discounts, and inability to make anyone responsible for errors. Merchandise arrives in small amounts but in six months it adds up to a lot of money. Invoices tell you how much you paid for the merchandise, but you will never know how much more the goods cost because they were stolen, misplaced, mismarked, or damaged through poor handling once they reach your store.

Only certain employees should be delegated to receive merchandise. They should be told how to go about it and then should be held accountable for errors in receiving shipments. When the merchandise is brought into the receiving area, the receiving clerk should see that the package or carton has not been broken into or damaged. If he notices anything suspicious, he refuses the shipment and points out his findings to the carrier's employee. If the carrier's employee agrees to act as a witness, the receiving clerk may open the parcel and inspect the contents for loss or damage. The findings should be noted on both the carrier's and the store's slip and then signed by your receiving clerk and the delivery man.

Claims for loss or damage should be made promptly to the carrier (Fig. 6.1) or, if you have a blanket transit policy, your insurance agent should be advised.

If the shipment is intact, the receiving clerk checks the address, the number of cartons, and estimates the weight. With some experience, he will become expert at judging weights, but if errors occur too frequently, buy a scale. The weight is then checked against the cost schedule that should be conveniently posted in the area. If all is in order, the receiving clerk and the delivery man sign the appropriate slips and the parcel is now ready to be processed further.

Checking Merchandise

It is sometimes possible to have the receiving, checking, and marking room in the same area, but frequently checking and marking must be done in another part of the store. When this is so, move the parcels from the receiving room as quickly as possible because as long as they stay in the receiving room, they are in the way and cannot be processed. In a small store an employee can be designated as the receiver to open and examine shipments. This can be a clerk who is given a certain amount of time off the floor for this job. As the store grows, nonselling personnel should be hired for this. In this way you obtain employee accountability and as the employee gains experience, he or she not only works faster but also learns to spot mistakes in pricing, vendor substitutes, etc. By reporting various shipping errors, receivers can soon earn you more than their salaries.

Checking Quantity First

The checker *first checks the quantity* against the invoice or shipping memo. If an error is found, the receiver should immediately notify the buyer concerned who will then check with the vendor.

If the quantity is right, the checker proceeds to check the goods against the buyer's orders. Any difference in quantity, quality, style numbers,

Standard Form for Presentation of Loss and Damage Claims

Approved by the Interstate Commerce Commission, The Freight Claim Association, National Industrial Traffic League and the National Association of Railway Commissioners.

.... (Claimant's Number) §

....
(Name of person to whom claim is presented) (Address of claimant)

....
(Name of carrier) (Date) (Carrier's Number)

....
(Address)

This claim for $..............................is made against the carrier named above by ....
(Amount of claim) (Name of claimant)

for..............................in connection with the following described shipments:
(Loss or damage)

Description of shipment..

Name and address of consignor shipper)..

Shipped from.., To..
(City, town or station) (City, town or station)

Final Destination..Routed via..
(City, town or station)

Bill of Lading issued by..Co.; Date of Bill of Lading..

Paid Freight Bill (Pro) Number..; Original Car Number and Initial ....

Name and address of consignee (Whom shipped to)..

If shipment reconsigned enroute, state particulars:..

....

DETAILED STATEMENT SHOWING HOW AMOUNT CLAIMED IS DETERMINED.

(Number and description of articles, nature and extent of loss or damage, invoice price of articles, amount of claim, etc.)

....	
....	
....	
....	
....	
....	
....	
Total Amount Claimed	

IN ADDITION TO THE INFORMATION GIVEN ABOVE, THE FOLLOWING DOCUMENTS ARE SUBMITTED IN SUPPORT OF THIS CLAIM.*

( ) 1. Original bill of lading, if not previously surrendered to carrier.
( ) 2. Original paid freight (" expense ") bill.
( ) 3. Original invoice or certified copy.
4. Other particulars obtainable in proof of loss or damage claimed:

....

....

Remarks ....

....

....

The foregoing statement of facts is hereby certified to as correct.

By..
(Signature of claimant)

§Claimant should assign to each claim a number, inserting same in the space provided at the upper right-hand corner of this form. Reference should be made thereto in all correspondence pertaining to this claim.
*Claimant will please place check (x) before such of the documents mentioned as have been attached, and explain under "Remarks" the absence of any of the documents called for in connection with this claim. When for any reason it is impossible for claimant to produce original bill of lading, if required, or paid freight bill, claimant should indemnify carrier or carriers against duplicate claim supported by original documents.

FIGURE 6.1 In case of a claim, it is important for a retailer to immediately inform either the carrier or the insurance company if he has a "blanket" policy. If possible, the damaged package should be left as it was received until an inspector arrives.

colors, sizes, etc., should be immediately brought to the buyer's attention.
It is presumed that buyers order only what they require in order to maintain
the best assortments of merchandise for their customers. If they wanted the
vendor's substitutes, they would have ordered them in the first place.
Nevertheless, conditions might have changed since the order was given and
buyers may now be able to use all or part of the substituted merchandise, or
they may want to keep it as a favor to the vendor. However, too many
substitutions are bound to affect stock assortments and vendors who often
substitute without permission should be avoided.

Merchandise that is damaged or not ordered should be returned as
quickly as possible because the longer the unwanted goods remain in the
store, the more difficult it becomes to receive proper adjustment and the
more ill will you will build up between the supplier and yourself. You do not
like customers who keep your merchandise for weeks or months before
returning it for an adjustment. Treat the manufacturer as you yourself want
to be treated.

Returns to Vendors

Since many vendors have their own return procedures, find out what
they are before sending back any merchandise. This avoids having the
vendors refuse the return, your being forced to write a series of letters to
straighten out the return, or your having to undergo a long delay before it is
satisfactorily handled. Whatever routine the vendor uses, returns should be
made on your own serially numbered form, similar to the one illustrated in
Figure 6.2. These slips are usually made in triplicate: The original is enclosed
in the parcel, the second goes to the office, and the third goes to the buyer.

Although different items may be shipped together, every return should
have its own form. This makes it easier for both offices to process the return
properly. The vendor may send you a credit note for one return, ship
replacement merchandise for another, and dispute a third. If you put more
than one item on a single return slip, handling that slip may become very
complicated. Extra forms are much cheaper than office employees' time.
The office copy of the return slip should be attached to the invoice or shipping memo. Otherwise, the office will pay the full amount and then have
trouble collecting for the return.

Collect versus Prepaid Returns

If the vendor is doing you a favor by accepting the return, prepay it. If
it is his fault, ship it back collect and note on the return that if he wishes to
send merchandise instead of a credit note, he should prepay the substitute.
Where a vendor ships unauthorized merchandise collect, return it collect
and inform him by letter that you are deducting your transportation cost
from the balance you now owe him. Vendors who try to do business this
way will soon learn to ship you only the merchandise you order.

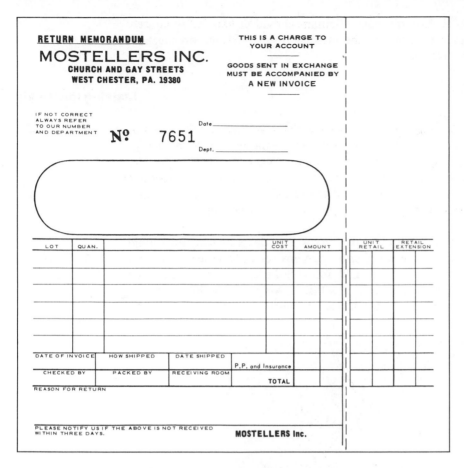

FIGURE 6.2 This return memorandum is a three-sheet form completed by the office when returning merchandise to a supplier. It is essential that goods that have been signed into the store are not returned to a supplier without a return memorandum.

Courtesy Mosteller's Inc., West Chester, Pa.

Return Slips

A lot of money can be tied up in returns. Make certain that your office has a system for keeping after the vendors who neglect to straighten out returns. The quicker these are disposed of, the sooner the money can be used for other merchandise and the smaller the risk of the vendor's going bankrupt, leaving you with a poor chance of ever receiving the full amount owed to you.

When Merchandise Is Checked O.K.

When the checker is satisfied that the merchandise is in order, he or she signs the invoice or shipping memo and sends it to the office for further processing. Invoices that offer cash discounts should be handled separately and sometimes even paid before the merchandise is received or checked. Never miss a cash discount.

Marking the Goods

Tickets and marking equipment differ with the volume and the kinds of merchandise you handle, but it is essential to have the *right* ticketing equipment for your operation. For example, double tickets and those specially designed for fragile goods or nonreturnable merchandise are more expensive than standard ones, but the savings in merchandise control, merchandise spoilage, and customer returns will make the extra outlay profitable (Fig. 6.3).

If your operation is large enough, the cost of a ticketing machine should be considered. There are any number of inexpensive ones on the market or a second-hand machine may be bought for very little. It might require an overhaul and new type fonts, but if it will save you marking time and produce a neater and more easily read ticket, it is worth purchasing.

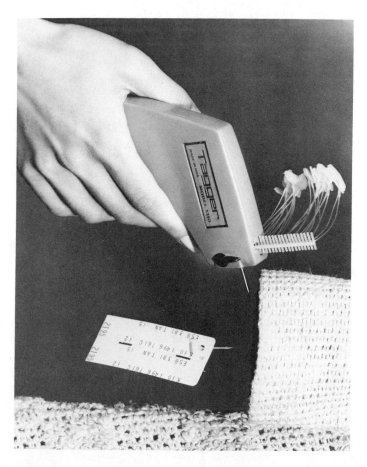

FIGURE 6.3 This machine secures the tag to the merchandise in such a way that it cannot be removed unless it is cut. This eliminates tag switching by customers and/or their using the item and then returning it with the tag attached.

Courtesy Monarch Marking Systems, Inc., a subsidiary of Pitney Bowes, Inc., Dayton, Ohio.

Using fancy tickets or a machine that has a number of useless gadgets, however, is very expensive, both in money and time lost handling a system that is too advanced for your business. Investigate a sufficient number of firms who manufacture ticketing and marking machines before deciding what you require. Then install the right system. You can afford it because it will make your marking and ticketing operations more efficient and it will pay its way in no time at all.

Ticketing

In self-service departments, good ticketing is a must and in self-selection departments an informative and easily read ticket will enable the customer to move from item to item with assurance and without sales help. Tickets that not only show the retail price but also the age of the item, vendor, style, number, etc., help the buyer to decide on markdowns and adjustments, and they may be used to organize a stock control system. Well-marked tickets also provide the quickest and most accurate method of taking stock.

Marking tickets

To be of any value, all the information on the ticket should be legible. A machine does this best and most economically. Retail prices should be clearly readable but codes may be used for other information. Mark all your merchandise as soon as it comes in, even if it is to be put away for future sale. This policy forces you to check the merchandise at once so that any necessary adjustments may be made while the goods are still fresh in everyone's memory. Also, once the merchandise is ticketed, it can go into active stock at any time.

Locking up tickets and machine

Merchandise should not be ticketed before it has been processed by the checker. If this rule is broken, the whole system of accountability breaks down. This is why it is best to keep tickets and the marking machine locked away from everyone but those responsible for their use.

Controlling the number of tickets

If you are careless with tickets and the marking machine, substitute tickets may be used in a way that can cost you a lot of money. Tickets should be allocated against specific merchandise and any unused or spoiled tickets should be accounted for by those responsible for them.

Try to standardize checking and marking procedures. It makes for better and more productive work. Review receiving, checking, and marking systems frequently and look for easier and faster ways to perform these tasks. Any streamlining that saves time saves money. More important, it gets the merchandise to the floor faster and should produce more sales and more satisfied customers.

What should go on a ticket

The information on tickets varies with their use. Some may have only the retail price, others the cost and retail, and still others may contain such detailed information as department, style, age, vendor, color, classification, and price.

There is a right ticket for every kind of merchandise, e.g., a snap type for hosiery, a string tag for furniture, a gum label for books, a security ticket for dresses, etc. In some cases the manufacturer will ticket the goods for you. This may be done when he wants to protect his suggested retail price. But remember that in every instance you are legally free to set your own retail and either put your price on his tickets or destroy them and use your own.

Using the right ticket and marking methods

For small, fast-moving items that offer close markups, for example, those handled in variety and hardware stores, individual ticketing may be too expensive. Bins should be used for this merchandise with one kind of item and one price to a bin. A card showing the retail price should be attached to the bin. Prices may be stamped on groceries. A special marking pencil or an adhesive ticket may be used on glassware.

The objective of security tickets is to discourage customers from using goods and then returning them as unused and demanding refunds or credit notes. Once a security ticket is removed from a garment, any attempt to put it back is easily noticed by the store's personnel.

Security tickets and anti-pilferage devices

Anti-pilferage devices must be desensitized by store employees or they will trigger an alarm as they pass through designated areas in the store. Thus, anti-pilferage devices attempt to apprehend shoppers who plan to take goods out of a department or store without paying for them.

Although security tickets minimize unwarranted returns and anti-pilferage devices reduce customer stealing, they increase ticketing costs. Therefore, they should only be placed on merchandise that obviously warrants the additional expense.

In this system the manufacturer marks the goods before they are shipped. He either uses preprinted tickets sent to him by the retailer or prints his own with the information the retailer gives him. However, the Robinson-Patman Act specifies that any manufacturer who offers this service to one retailer must offer it to all his customers in the same category. Source marking has two main advantages; it reduces marking expenses at the store level and also moves goods more quickly from the receiving room onto the floor. But since some manufacturers charge for this service, you should decide whether or not it is worth the cost.

Source marking

You should set a strict policy about how to show markdowns on your tickets. Some stores mark down manually right in the department on the original ticket while others send the merchandise back to the marking room for new tickets. The latter method is best because your salespeople's time can be used to better advantage than marking merchandise, the record of the markdown is double-checked, all tickets are printed so that they are easier to read, and the cashier can question any ticket bearing handwritten prices.

Showing markdowns

Receiving rooms should be as close to the receiving door as possible. This is usually at the rear of the store, but if your goods come in from the street, move the parcels out of the front area as soon as possible. The front is your best selling space and sets the store atmosphere. To have it cluttered with parcels creates a poor impression on customers and is bad business.

The marking room need not be near the receiving room, but it must be large enough to handle the merchandise properly and quickly. An overly crowded, poorly arranged marking area is very wasteful in time and money. It may be located in a dead area of the street floor or, whenever possible, in the basement or an upper floor so that it does not take up expensive space and is as large as necessary to handle your kind of merchandise. You should, of course, allow more space for receiving and marking bulky articles than for small items.

If the area is also used as a stock room, the marking section should be partitioned off so that only authorized employees are permitted into each section and so that they can be held accountable for the merchandise in their area. Wire mesh is cheap and so are two-by-fours and locks and keys.

A separate marking room saves you money because it is organized just for that operation. Spend a little time and investigate the kind of equipment you might use, as well as the best arrangement for speedy processing of the merchandise.

Stockkeeping and Housekeeping

If reserve and/or stockrooms are necessary, they should be as close to the department concerned as possible. Once they are walled off and locked, they can become the responsibility of the buyer who should know which merchandise is in the room and where it is. Some stores keep a stock room plan on which they mark the position of the goods in the room; other stores keep a unit control system so that they know whether an item is there or not. This saves time for both clerks and customers.

Stockkeeping in reserve and stock rooms

The buyer should be responsible for packing and storing between-season merchandise. These goods should be carefully inspected before they are put away. They should be segregated, reticketed if necessary, and hung up or packed so that they may be reached easily. For example, in the fall, men's short-sleeved summer shirts should be sized and packed in boxes that are clearly labeled and stored in a planned sequence. Then if there is a sudden change in weather and the demand for these shirts becomes high, they may be brought onto the selling floor quickly and without fuss.

It is best not to sell the shirts at the original price for most customers know that they are old stock and will resent such a pricing policy. Your storage price, then, should be a compromise between the original and the lowest price put on them at the end of the season. Storage selling may be done with winter garments too. For example, people look for warm clothing when they and their children go camping. Any store that is alert to their wants and makes it a point to satisfy them without making customers feel that they are imposing on the clerks or that they are being overcharged will soon build up a good off-season business because one customer will tell another. Word-of-mouth advertising spreads quickly and costs nothing.

In most small and medium-sized stores the keeping of floor stock should be the buyer's responsibility. The buyer should realize that a properly kept stock means more sales, fewer markdowns, and more stock turns with less inventory and that poorly kept stock invites stealing, loss of salespeople's time, lost sales and profits, and customer dissatisfaction. Good housekeeping brings nothing but benefits, but it requires planning and constant supervision. The department should be broken down into small areas and each day, in addition to general cleaning duties, every clerk should do a certain amount of careful and intensive stock cleaning and merchandise review.

Stockkeeping on the floor

If the buyer plans these tasks well, he or she can have the active stock reviewed every two or three weeks. Then merchandise will remain clean and fresh-looking, it will always be ticketed, and sales will not be lost because items are stored out of their size or price group. Since planned stockkeeping means more work for the buyer's staff, the staff must be supervised constantly. By setting each clerk's responsibilities, stockkeeping activities may be combined with stock taking and thus another necessary merchandise function may be accomplished simultaneously.

Before customers come into your store, they must be attracted to it by its exterior. One of your housekeeping functions, then, should be to make certain that your windows are always clean and that the metal on them is bright and shining. Window lights should be checked every day and burned out bulbs replaced with new ones, and the walls, backgrounds, and floors of the windows should always be fresh and clean. If there is any woodwork on the building, it should be repainted whenever necessary. The color need not be changed, although this sometimes makes the whole front look new and different.

Importance of an inviting exterior

What has been said about the exterior of the store also applies to the interior. Few customers like to shop or buy in a dirty store. They want to feel that the owner is as proud of his store as he is of the merchandise in it. Therefore, make certain that the interior of your store is kept clean and attractive and represents the personality you want it to have. Soap and water cost very little, paint is reasonably inexpensive, and floor wax and furniture polish are inexpensive. Used freely, they pay big dividends. Besides, since the biggest part of your day is spent in the store, why not make working there as pleasant as possible for yourself, your employees, and your customers?

Importance of an inviting interior

1. You should realize that the effort and cost of taking care of merchandise properly are the most profitable investments you can make.

2. The cost involved in running an efficient receiving room, marking room, and reserve or stock room is very small—the rewards very high.

3. Retailers should realize that to permit all their employees to receive, check, and mark merchandise and do it anywhere in the store is to invite trouble.

4. Appoint certain employees to receive merchandise and show them how to do it properly. Then they can be held accountable for mistakes.

5. Move merchandise from the receiving area to the checking and marking rooms as quickly as possible.

6. Checking and marking rooms should be enclosed and only authorized persons permitted inside.

7. Checking and marking operations should be carefully organized for quickest inflow and outflow of merchandise.

8. Proper tickets and marking machines are a must.

9. Decide what information the ticket should contain. Anything else on the ticket is useless and wasteful.

10. The checking and marking room may not be the responsibility of the buyer, but reserve and stock rooms should be.

11. Buyers should know every item in the reserve and stock rooms.

12. Merchandise should be stored so that it can be brought forward without delay.

13. Between-season stock that may have a certain amount of customer demand should be marked at prices that are compromises between the original and the end-of-season markdowns. They should then be stored according to a system that will permit the merchandise to be easily brought onto the floor.

14. Keep the exterior and interior of your store clean and attractive to your customers because your store reflects your pride and ability as a competent retailer.

7

How to
Avoid Being Overstocked

WHAT THIS CHAPTER IS ABOUT

The biggest merchandise problem facing most retailers is that of being overstocked. To keep a balanced stock, you must order according to a preconceived plan and then, as the merchandise moves in and out of the store, develop techniques that will control further purchases. In this way you will always have the right merchandise in the right place, at the right time, in the right quantities, and at the right price. Thus, you will obtain the maximum profit from your merchandise investment. This chapter discusses several ways to keep stock balanced to customer demand and so earn maximum profits.

Instinctive Buying

There are only two ways of buying merchandise: *instinctive buying* and *controlled buying.* Under the instinctive method, the merchant comes into the store, looks at a certain section of merchandise, and decides he needs to order more of it. He then guesses at the quantities, colors, sizes, etc., that he wants and sends the order to the vendor he thinks will give him the best deal. When he looks at a line, he instinctively knows whether to buy it or not. If he gives the salesman an order, he judges his quantities, etc., on what he "feels" he should have. The same buying technique is used when the sales staff tell him they are out of an item. He knows by instinct whether to reorder or forget it.

The instinctive method of buying has many advantages. It is extremely simple to operate because it requires little or no records of any kind. It is also very quick because the retailer decides to buy or not to buy almost instantly. It also gives the buyer intense personal satisfaction when a hunch pays off. But if the buyer kept a record of all the hunches that did not pay off, as well as those that did, he or she might not be so pleased with his or her buying ability.

Advantages and disadvantages of instinctive buying

Because instinctive buying usually means emotional buying, it has very serious disadvantages. For some reason, a merchant may feel that blue tones in dresses should be good this season. Therefore, he tends to overlook garments that move in other colors; he is impressed with every blue dress that is sold, for this confirms his hunch. He therefore orders heavily in blue tones and, as a result, not only loses many sales during the season but also takes heavy markdowns on blue dresses to clean up the department at the end of the season. Had he kept records, he would have found that he sold five yellow dresses to every blue dress. Because he had no records, he bought emotionally and consequently paid the price for instinctive buying by running a department that was understocked in yellows and overstocked in blues.

Again, because a certain salesman or manufacturer makes the retailer feel important, the retailer instinctively wants to carry the line. He promotes it and his hunch this time seems to be right, for he seldom carries over any of the items. However, if he had kept records, he would have discovered that the items lost money, for although he had very few of them left at the end of the season, they only began to sell when they were marked down toward the close of the season.

This buyer instinctively *knows* that he should buy a clearance because it is such a genuine bargain. What he does not realize is that his current stock is unbalanced and heavy and that the new merchandise can only complicate this already unfortunate situation.

Controlled Buying

This is the method developed by department and chain stores to help management and buyers make buying decisions based on facts, not on personal fancies. In this system the buyer refers to records of his past and current sales and then plans his merchandise requirements. Before he writes an order, he refers to his plans and records and estimates the quantities, colors, sizes, etc., he requires. He also keeps records of the way the merchandise of individual vendors moves and then reorders only from those firms whose merchandise is profitable for him.

When this buyer is offered a special promotion, he first sees if his controls permit him to buy it. Then he looks at the goods in terms of how they will affect his stock situation. In controlled buying the buyer makes decisions only after he knows the facts.

Controlled buying means that stock situations are in line with planned turnover, stock-sales ratios, profits, etc. It also tends to keep the merchandise in better balance with customer demand. The controlled buyer must still use his experience and instinct, but now he has knowledge to support these qualities.

Advantages of controlled buying

Controlled buying can become more mechanical than buying by instinct, although it need not be uninteresting. Controlled buyers are always subject to discipline, but if they are in a strong open-to-buy position, they are able to experience the thrill of playing hunches. However, even then they tend to play safe and thus the store may lose sales to buyers of other stores who are more adventurous and use the instinctive technique.

Disadvantages of controlled buying

Six-month Plans Basic to Merchandise Controls

If you feel that controlled buying is best for your store, begin by dividing your fiscal year into two six-month periods, e.g., spring and summer (from February 1st to July 31st) and fall and winter (from August 1st to January 31st). Any other six-month periods will do if they make your planning easier. Then draw up a merchandise plan form similar to the one in Figure 7.1. This form may vary according to the amount of forward planning and controls you desire. That is, if you consider promotion expense or alteration costs to be sufficiently important, you could include it in your plan. The items shown in Figure 7.1 are, however, essential.

Your merchandise plans should be drawn up about three months before the six-month period that they cover.

Enter the department by name and number, then the season involved, and then the year. Strike out the six months that are not concerned in the plan. Now, on the ''Actual'' lines, enter last year's monthly sales, beginning-of-the-month inventories, purchases, and markdowns. Use round figures as much as possible because they are easier to work with and your calculations are necessarily broad. Remember that all figures must be either at retail or at cost. You cannot use sales at retail and purchases at cost; one or the other must be converted.

How to use the merchandise plan form

By using your past records, knowledge of customer trends, economic conditions, and other sources, estimate your planned monthly sales. Try to be as realistic as possible because these estimates form the basis of your merchandise plans and controls. If you are too optimistic, you will buy too much merchandise and run into trouble. If you are too pessimistic, you will not have enough goods in the store for your peaks and will lose sales and disappoint customers. Remember to allow for Christmas, Easter, and other holidays that might affect any month's sales volume.

When this is done, estimate the amounts of your planned opening and closing inventories. These two figures must also be realistic or else your plan

YOUR STORE MERCHANDISE PLAN

Dept. No. X Season *Spring* 197?

		Feb. / Aug.	March / Sept.	April / Oct.	May / Nov.	June / Dec.	July / Jan.	Total	Avg. Stock
SALES	Actual Last Yr.	9,000	11,700	12,200	10,000	8,800	8,300	60,000	
	Plan This Yr.	9,900	12,870	13,420	11,000	9,680	9,130	66,000	+10%
	Actual This Yr.	9,500	12,000	12,600					
	Inc. or Dec.	-400	-870	-820					
Beginning of Month STOCKS	Actual Last Yr.	30,000	33,050	33,850	32,400	29,300	24,700	27,000*	30,043
	Plan This Yr.	32,000	36,700	39,430	37,210	32,510	26,430	28,500*	33,254
	Actual This Yr.	32,000	36,850	40,400	37,600				
	Inc. or Dec.	—	+150	+970	+390				
PURCHASES	Actual Last Yr.	12,500	12,700	11,000	7,200	4,600	11,000	59,000	
	Plan This Yr.	14,900	15,800	11,400	6,500	3,900	11,500	64,000	
	Actual This Yr.	14,700	15,800	10,000					
	Inc. or Dec.	-200	—	-1,400					
MARKDOWNS	Actual Last Yr.	450	200	250	300	400	400	2,000	
	Plan This Yr.	300	200	200	200	300	300	1,500	
	Actual This Yr.	350	250	200					
	Inc. or Dec.	+50	+50	—					
SALES	Revised Plan				10,300	9,050	8,550	62,000	
	Actual This Yr.								
	Inc. or Dec.								
Beginning of Month STOCKS	Revised Plan					33,050	26,750	28,000*	33,521
	Actual This Yr.								
	Inc. or Dec.								
PURCHASES	Revised Plan				6,000	3,050	10,000	59,550	
	Actual This Yr.								
	Inc. or Dec.								
MARK-DOWNS	Revised Plan				250	300	200	1,550	
	Actual This Yr.								
	Inc. or Dec.								

ALL FIGURES SHOWN ARE AT RETAIL *End of period inventory

Turnover

	Actual Last Yr.	Plan This Yr.	Revised This Yr.	M.O.R. Last Yr.
Spring	1.997	1.986	1.85	2.3
Fall				

J. Smith
Department Manager

Approved by *E.C.*

FIGURE 7.1 This six-month merchandising plan form is usually preferred by smaller stores because it contains all essential planning and control information.

will become useless. With experience, you will learn to arrive at sound estimates if you check back on previous figures and use your intelligence to avoid repeating your mistakes.

The following shows you how to find out how much you should buy for the six months in order to handle the planned sales and end up with the planned inventory:

Arriving at total purchases

Planned sales	$66,000
+ Planned closing inventory	28,500
+ Planned markdowns	1,500
Planned total of goods to be handled	96,000
Less opening inventory	32,000
Open-to-buy	$64,000

This statement says that you will require $66,000 worth of merchandise for selling purposes plus $28,500 to have in the store on July 31st. You must also provide for $1,500 worth of goods that you are going to mark down. Altogether, then, you will need $96,000 worth of merchandise during the period. But you expect to have $32,000 on hand at the beginning of the season. Therefore, your open-to-buy is $64,000.

The next problem is to spread the $64,000 open-to-buy over the six months. The plan tells you when last year's goods actually arrived, but this is usually a poor guide for placing purposes. If you have made previous merchandise plans and noted suggestions and criticisms on them, refer to them now. If you haven't, you must estimate how much merchandise you will need for a representative showing in the earlier part of the season. Unless you deal in goods that require heavy placing, for example, quality suede articles or imports, it is best to divide purchases into two sections of three months each. The heaviest ordering should be done in the first three months, with the other three months used as a sort of reserve for reordering runners, ordering fill-ins, and buying promotions and clearances. The division into two three-month periods becomes especially useful if your planned sales are too optimistic because you will be able to see your mistakes early enough to cut down your purchases during the last three months.

Arriving at monthly purchases

This is the reasoning behind the figures for planned purchases in the merchandise plan in Figure 7.1. The buyer was permitted to order 66 percent of his estimated requirements in the first three months and more than one-half of his planned purchases for the fourth, fifth, and sixth months was held back to July. This cushion should take care of any contingency.

The planned opening inventory at the beginning of each month (BOM stock) may be worked out by using the following calculation:

Planning monthly opening inventory

	February	March
Planned BOM Stock	$32,000	$36,700
+ Planned Purchases	14,900	15,800
Planned Total Merchandise Handled	$46,900	$52,500
− Planned Sales	9,900	12,870
	$37,000	$39,630
− Planned Markdowns	300	200
Planned End of Month (EOM) Stock (This is the same as BOM stock, following month)	$36,700	$39,430

You will note that the plan ends with a planned inventory of $28,500 for the end of July. This figure becomes the planned inventory for August 1st, which begins the fall and winter season.

Planning markdowns

Planning markdowns is done in the same way as you plan sales and inventories; that is, you review the actual markdowns of a sufficient number of previous years to establish a trend and then adjust this to the plan. You can proceed either by estimating each month's markdowns and then getting a total or by taking a percentage of sales as your total markdown figure and then breaking it up into months.

Checking plan for turnover

Once the plan is drawn up, check it to see if it will give you sufficient turnover. This can be found by first dividing the sum of the six beginning-of-the-month inventories plus the one end-of-the-period inventory by seven; thus:

$$\frac{\$232,780}{7} = \$33,254 \text{ (average inventory)}$$

Then divide this figure into the total planned sales to obtain the planned turnover.

$$\frac{\$66,000}{\$33,254} = 1.984 \text{ (see Chapter 22 on turnover)}$$

Checking department plans against store plans

It is advisable to make a merchandise plan for the entire store without referring to the department plans. Then take the department plans and consolidate them. Next check the store plan against the consolidated plan. If there are too many discrepancies, review the department plans and the overall store plan and make sufficient revisions to bring them closer together.

Operating plans in season

Once the season opens, enter on the merchandise plan what actually takes place. If your planned figures are not too far out, let them stand. They are only guides and need not be too exact. By the middle of the third month, you should know how your season is shaping up. If it is going according to plan, you may begin to shop the market for clearances of proven runners and order these according to your best sizes, colors, etc. They will cost you less than if you wait for the manufacturer's end-of-the-season odds and ends and you will get much more profit and better customer goodwill from them. By controlling your buying, you should be able to keep your markdowns and clearances of regular merchandise to a minimum and you should have very good markups on the merchandise you had time to purchase at bargain prices. Controlled buying and planned clearances then lead to excellent profit-taking at clearance time, and your customers receive wonderful values and the best of assortments of wanted merchandise. Competitive pricing in this case is negligible.

If your merchandise plan is too optimistic and gets very far out of line, it should be revised. Figure 7.1 shows you how this is done for the months of May, June, and July. Notice how a more realistic sales projection for the balance of the season affects all the areas, especially the planned purchase picture. If you must revise your plans in this way, you should undertake a review of your current stock situation before you go to the market to buy clearance merchandise. Maybe you will have to clear so much regular stock that you cannot buy anything else.

If plans do not work

A too pessimistic plan should also be revised as early as possible; otherwise, you will run short of wanted merchandise, lose sales, and create ill will during the best part of the selling season. If you attempt to build up stocks during the heart of the season, you must take what you can get, not what you want. Since this kind of buying leaves you with goods that can only be cleared with heavy markdowns, try to determine your needs and place your orders as early in the season as you possibly can.

A realistically projected and revised six-month plan is a must for any retailer who wants to control his buyers. Such a plan leads to disciplined buying because it makes buyers become very sensitive to their open-to-buy position. They constantly review unshipped portions of their orders and cancel whatever they think they cannot use. This gives them a better active stock situation and increases their OTB for wanted merchandise. The plan also helps them to realize that successful buyers are those who keep their opening and closing inventories as low as possible but build high stocks during the peak selling periods.

Six-month plan control buyers

The plan also informs buyers how much they are allowed to spend at any particular time. This knowledge is very important not only when they place their opening orders but also during the season when suppliers offer them new merchandise or special promotions.

The six-month plan is sometimes called a *dollar merchandise plan* because it tells the buyer how much *money* he or she is allowed to spend. However, it does not tell the buyer on which goods it is to be spent. In the

Dollar control leads to unit control

sample merchandise plan in Figure 7.1 the buyer is permitted to buy up to $14,900 in February and $42,100 in the first three months, but the plan does not tell the buyer to buy more of one item than another, and it does not tell the buyer which vendors, sizes, colors, styles, etc., are best for a merchandise category. The dollar control, then, must be supplemented by a system that informs the buyer *how* the dollars should be used to give the best merchandise assortment for his or her department.

Most buyers spend their merchandise dollars in two ways—placing and reordering—and stores have developed separate systems for handling each process. Under a *placing* control system, the buyer knows in great detail the number of units he will order and how many items he plans to place with a particular vendor before he looks at next season's merchandise. It then becomes a matter of changing his plans as actual lines are inspected. Once the season starts, however, he reverts to an *active* unit control system that tells him how each item is moving in his department. He may then spot his runners, price lines, colors and materials, as well as his sleepers, and recognize merchandise gaps early enough to have his stock in the best possible shape for customer selection. Both control systems require time, thought, and energy, but they pay off with cleaner, easier to handle, and more profitable stock than if goods are bought instinctively.

**Placing control
and active
unit control**

Model Stock Planning

Model stock planning is a method that buyers use to plan the best possible merchandise assortments for their customers with the dollars they have at their disposal. It may be developed in one of two ways. You may either begin with the money you plan to spend and then find out how many items this will buy or you may start with the number of units you plan to place and see what they add up to. Either way, the dollar and the units must be close enough to make the plan workable. If they are too far apart, you must go back and revise the plan until they approximate each other. Once this is done, you are able to plan how you want the units broken down into styles, colors, sizes, materials, etc., so that when the goods arrive in the store, your customers will see the best possible assortment of merchandise for the money you spend on that category of goods.

Suppose that your spring and summer sales last year were $90,000 and you planned this year's volume to be $100,000. Last year's turnover was 3½, but you feel that this year you can get a 4 turn. Your planned average inventory, then, would be $100,000/4, or $25,000.

**Planning a model
stock from
dollars to units**

You know that in order to give your customers a good assortment of merchandise at the beginning of the season, you will need to show them more than $25,000 worth of merchandise. In fact, you figure that $40,000 would be about right. You also feel that you will start the season with $15,000 worth of salable old stock and that you should keep back a lump sum of $5,000 for early season promotions. This means that you are open to place $20,000 as follows:

Planned Opening Inventory Beginning of Season	$40,000
Less Old Stock	15,000
TOTAL	$25,000
Less Promotions	5,000
Open to Place	$20,000

The problem now is to divide the $20,000 into the various kinds of items you want to open the season with. This should be done from the customers' point of view, not yours. Will you have enough of each item in size, color, etc., to give your customers sufficient choice? It is their selection patterns rather than your planned sales that should guide your stock proportions. For example, if you are buying three sizes (small, medium, and large) and have found from past records that your customers buy 20 percent small, 50 percent medium, and 30 percent large, you might be wise to plan your placing as follows:

Size	Sales Distribution	Stock Distribution
S	20	25
M	50	40
L	30	35

With this distribution, you would carry the largest stock where the sales are highest and the smallest stock where the sales are lowest, but your inventory would not be distributed in exact ratio to sales. In the above example, if 50 percent of the stock were ordered for medium sizes, you would be carrying far more of this size than you would require at any given time, while if only 20 percent of your opening stock were ordered in small sizes, your customers would not have much to choose from and you would lose sales or find selling difficult. By ordering less stock of mediums and more smalls and larges, you are able to give these customers a better selection and make more sales without sacrificing any of your medium sizes. This technique will also turn over your merchandise faster and give you more profit on your investment. Figure 7.2 shows a model stock plan. Notice how the percentages of planned stock differ from those of planned sales. This is done to allow you to begin the season with sufficient merchandise assortments in your fastest moving styles and still create the maximum of sales in the slower ones. If the plan works as expected, your highest turnover will be in styles XYZ and ABC because, without losing any sales, you will move these styles in and out of your store more times than if you carry them according to your planned sales figures. Although the turnover

STYLES	DESCRIPTION	% OF PLANNED SALES	INITIAL % PLANNED STOCK	ADJUSTED % PLANNED STOCK	ADJUSTED STOCK IN $
XYZ		38	35	30	6,000
ABC		32	30	25	5,000
DEF		13	13	26	5,200
GHI		5	6	3	600
KLM		7	8	8	1,600
NOP		3	5	5	1,000
RST		2	3	3	600
TOTAL		100	100	100	20,000

FIGURE 7.2 Model stock plan.

in styles NOP and RST will be low, their sales will be higher than if their opening inventories were held at 3 percent and 2 percent of sales.

The next step is to find out how many *units* you can place with the amount of money you have allocated to each style. Suppose that the average price of style XYZ is $10. Then the number of units would be $7,000/$10, or 700. If this seems too few or too many, you must revise your dollar figures to match the units. Notice that although you may have to order an item in dozens, gross, or other bulk quantities, the planning should be done in units. Seventy-two dozen sweaters may not seem very many, but when you convert this figure into 864 single ones, you may feel that you will have difficulty stocking that many in your store and begin to doubt if you will be able to make 864 sales.

Once the units approximate their dollar allocations, you are able to plan how they should be distributed in prices, sizes, colors, materials, etc. Figure 7.4 (vendor history), Figure 7.5 (vendor activity), and Figure 7.7 (vendor placing) are examples of how this can be done. The final step is to decide which units you plan to give each vendor.

Once this plan is finished, you can put it aside until you begin to examine the actual merchandise. Then the plan should be changed according to the way you see how the actual market shapes up. For example, you now feel that styles XYZ and ABC will be fair instead of good sellers and that style DEF will be the season's best number. And then you decide to go light on style GHI. Your adjusted buying plan then might look like Figure 7.3.

Another change you had not anticipated when you made your original plan was a rise in prices. For example, the average price of XYZ is now $11. Thus, the units you would place under the adjusted plan would be $6,000/$11, or 545 units. If these are boxed in threes, it would work out to 182 boxes. Now, if this amount of units is too high or too low, you have to revise your dollar figures.

STYLES	DESCRIPTION	% OF PLANNED SALES	% OF PLANNED STOCK	PLANNED STOCK IN DOLLARS
XYZ		38	35	7,000
ABC		32	30	6,000
DEF		13	13	2,600
GHI		5	6	1,200
KLM		7	8	1,600
NOP		3	5	1,000
RST		2	3	600
TOTAL		100	100	$20,000

FIGURE 7.3 Adjusted buying plan.

Suppose that a retailer plans to buy as simple and staple an item as boys' swim shorts in the size range of 8 to 14 and that he has only one year's experience to draw on. He begins by entering his last year's history of this item, as shown in Table 7.1. This table tells him that last year he began his season with 20 swim shorts, received 144, and returned 15. This means that he actually handled 149 swim shorts throughout the season.

Planning a model stock from units to dollars

TABLE 7.1   Unit sales history

On Hand			20
Received	144		
Returned		15	129
Units Handled			149
Left			23
Sold			126
Next Year's Target.....................			170
This Year's Placing			114

At summer's end, he had 23 swim shorts on hand. By subtracting 23 from 149, he knows that he sold 126 in this size range. Now if he had carried these for some years and this number was an increase over what he sold the year before and it in turn was an increase over the previous year, he would know that he was working on an uptrend and that he should be able to increase the store's swim shorts sales in the year to come. He would weigh this conclusion against the fact that last year the summer began early and developed into a hot and long season. Finally, he would have to decide whether or not business conditions next year will be as good as they were last year.

After considering all these points, he concludes that next year he should increase his sales of 126 units to 170.

If he is to sell 170 swim shorts and he has 23 on hand, how many should he place? He knows that he has to buy swim shorts in dozen and half-dozen lots and that repeats are very difficult (see Fig. 7.9, remarks 1 and 6). Therefore, he plans for 114 units, or 9½ dozen swim shorts. This will start his season with 134 swim shorts or 11 more than he sold during the entire season last year. Although this seems too many, it will permit him to order three dozen additional swim shorts if the season works out as he anticipates; if the season proves disappointing, he should still be able to sell the old stock and most of the swim shorts he will place.

With the amount of swim shorts settled, he has to decide where to order them. Figure 7.4 shows last year's vendor history, and Figure 7.5 tells him about their activity last year.

VENDOR	RECEIVED	RETURNED	HANDLED	REDUCE	LEFT	SOLD
X	48	8	40	15	10	30
Y	60	5	55	15	8	47
T	36	2	34	7	5	29
TOTALS	144	15	129	37	23	106

FIGURE 7.4 Vendor history.

VENDOR	PLACING	PLACING PRICES AND QUANTITIES					REORDERS	NUMBER ORDERED
		$2.98	$3.98	$5.50	$6.98	TOTAL		
X	36	24	12			36	12	48
Y	48		36	12		48	12	60
T	24		24			24	12	36
TOTALS	108	24	72	12		108	36	144

FIGURE 7.5 Vendor activity.

Figure 7.4 tells him that he bought swim shorts from three vendors and that X was the least satisfactory of the three vendors. X shipped 48 swim shorts, but the store returned 8, reduced 15, and 10 were still unsold. Figure 7.5 tells him that X is the most inexpensive vendor and that only one dozen was ordered from him during the season. At this point, the retailer might look up his invoices or stock records to see exactly what numbers and price groups X did ship. But it would seem that he should look around for another vendor who sells inexpensive swim shorts.

He now consults Figure 7.6, which gives him the price breakdowns for

PRICE	NUMBER HANDLED	NUMBER REDUCED	NUMBER LEFT	SOLD
$2.98	24	6 to $1.88		24
$3.98	55	12 to $1.88	6	49
$4.50	20	10 to $2.88	8	12
$5.50	18	9 to $2.88	5	13
$6.95	12	8 to $3.88	4	8
TOTALS	129	45	23	106

FIGURE 7.6 Price breakdown.

last year when he had five price groups. This seems too many for the number of swim shorts sold. If he could cut out one price group, he could carry a better selection and more depth in each of the remaining groups. This table also tells the merchant that the $4.50 group was the most unproductive. This is substantiated by Figure 7.9, remark 3. He also notes that $3.98 was the best price and that $6.95 sold very poorly.

The retailer is now ready to develop the store's placing breakdown of vendors, i.e., the *right-hand side* of Figure 7.7. This totals $456, and if this approximates his dollar allocation for boys' swim shorts, he can put it away until suppliers begin to show him their lines.

Note that this breakdown is done *before the merchant sees a vendor.* In fact, the sooner that the breakdown is completed after the season closes, the better it will be, for then the experience of the season just finished is still fresh in the retailer's mind. In addition, once it is completed, he is ready to look at vendors' lines as they contact him.

How the plan changes

The planned vendor's placing can and should be changed as the merchant inspects sample merchandise, but as he changes his planned prices, quantities, etc., he does so under control and discipline. The *left-hand side* of Figure 7.7 shows what the retailer actually placed. He found a new vendor, A, who he felt made better swim shorts at $2.98 than X did and so gave him a trial order of two dozen. He still kept X because he did not know if A would live up to expectations. However, he knows that four vendors are too many and hopes to eliminate one of them by next year.

Because Y's line proved disappointing, he ordered only one dozen $3.98 swim shorts from him. T had the best line and from him he ordered three dozen $3.98, one dozen $5.50, and a half-dozen $6.95, which he bought for prestige and window dressing. Although his original plan has been changed, the units and dollar amounts remain the same. Therefore, he need not readjust his department's planned dollar allocations.

The left side of Figure 7.7, plus the old stock, represents the swim shorts this buyer thinks would give his customers the best possible selection at the beginning of the season. Of course, this ideal selection can never

	ACTUAL				VENDOR	PLANNED				
TOTAL	$2.98	$3.98	$5.50	$6.95		$2.98	$3.98	$5.50	$6.95	TOTAL
24	12	12			X	36	12			48
12		12			Y		12	12	6	30
54		36	12	6	T		36			36
24	24				A					
114	36	60	12	6	UNIT TOTALS	36	60	12	6	114
456.	108.	240.	66	42	$ TOTALS	$108	$240	$66	$42	$456

FIGURE 7.7 Vendor's placing.

materialize, for by the time all of it has arrived, some swim shorts will have been sold and the stock will have begun to shift from an ideal to a basic one.

Once the buyer decides to order an item, he must break it down into sizes, colors, materials, etc. This should be done by the way his customer wants to buy it. For example, in boys' swim shorts, size is of prime importance; for no matter how many swim shorts you may have in your store, if you are out of size 10 and that is the size the customer wants, the sale stops right there. If, however, she comes in to buy a size 10 swim short in red, but if you do not stock that color in 10's, she may be coaxed into taking a green. Some customers make price, material, or style their second most important factor and are not too stubborn about the item's other characteristics. Buyers, then, must be aware of their customers' rigidity factors to any item, that is, the *characteristics* they must have to make a sale possible.

Order according to the rigidity factors

Because size is the prime rigidity factor in swim shorts, the buyer will use Figure 7.8 as a guide for placing orders. For example, the buyer may decide to begin the next season by reducing the five $4.50 size 8's to $3.98 (they were being sold at $3.88 at the end of last year's season). The buyer would then place very few size 8's at $3.98 but would also make sure that enough 8's are ordered at each price point to cover expected sales. If colors

SIZE	$2.98	$3.98	$4.50	$5.50	$6.98	TOTAL
8	0	0	5	1	2	8
10	0	1	2	2	1	6
12	0	2	1	1	1	5
14	0	3	0	1	0	4
TOTALS	0	6	8	5	4	23

FIGURE 7.8 Size breakdown of old stock.

and materials were important rigidity factors to the customers, the buyer would treat these characteristics in the same way that sizes are treated.

Complete tables early

The stock plan tables should be completed as soon as possible after the season ends. Then they may be forgotten until vendors begin to show their next year's lines. At that time, by simply looking at the tables, the retailer has a set of controls that enables him to place his requirements with ease and discipline. He no longer *thinks* he knows what he is doing—he *knows* and this helps to change him from a good buyer to a better one.

1) Place heavier.
2) Shouldn't have bought $6.95 after season opened.
3) $4.50 no good. Hard to sell. Customers & clerks can't tell difference between them and $3.98.
4) Try for more navy blues.
5) Boxer shorts still best.
6) Reorders hard to get in season.

FIGURE 7.9 These remarks were recorded by the retailer during the previous season to guide him in his placing.

The above routine may seem a lot of work in order to buy so simple an item as swim shorts, but if the forms are duplicated and if proper records are kept as the merchandise moves in and out of the store, it would take a retailer less time to plan next year's buying of swim shorts sizes 8 to 14, or any other item, than it would to read this section.

Model stocks never materialize

Of course, model stocks never happen in real life. New merchandise seldom comes in at one time or as it is ordered. Also, the old stock begins to move out and so the plan is changed. Nevertheless, by using this technique, you will always order under control. This should not only cut down buying mistakes, it would also maintain an open-to-buy position.

1. Both instinctive and controlled buying have advantages and disadvantages, but controlled buying, backed up by instinct and experience, is best.

2. The six-month merchandise plan is the basis for controlled buying because it tells you how many dollars you can spend in any given period.

3. Model stock planning gives customers the best possible merchandise assortments for the dollars you plan to spend on inventory.

4. A model stock may be planned in units and then translated into dollars or it may be planned in dollars and then translated into units.

5. You should plan your model stock *placing* as soon as possible after a season ends.

6. Remember that model stocks are only *guides* to buying and should be revised when you see the actual merchandise.

7. Merchandise should be ordered according to your customers' rigidity factors.

8. Although model stocks never materialize, they are important because they permit you to control your buying, reduce buying errors, and maintain an effective open-to-buy position.

8

How to Control
Stocks in Season

WHAT THIS CHAPTER IS ABOUT

Some merchants do very well with placing their orders but become hopelessly lost once the season opens and the goods begin to move in and out of their stores. They can only guess at when to order, what to order, and even how much to order. The usual results of this method of buying are poor assortments, lost sales, customer dissatisfaction, large markdowns, and small profits. This chapter discusses three ways to help you control your buying *in season* so that you may get the most profit out of every item you carry.

How to Switch from Placing to Active Model Stocks

If you place your orders correctly, you should have the best possible merchandise assortments your money can buy *before* the season opens. Once the goods begin to move, however, this model situation breaks down and you are faced with the problem of maintaining assortments that are best under actual selling conditions. To do this, you must switch from the placing model to an active one; that is, you must cut down your breadth and develop runners in depth. Usually, the placing model contains broader merchandise assortments than the active model because when you begin a season you must order a certain amount of fringe sizes, prices, colors, and styles as well as special promotional stock. As the season develops, you

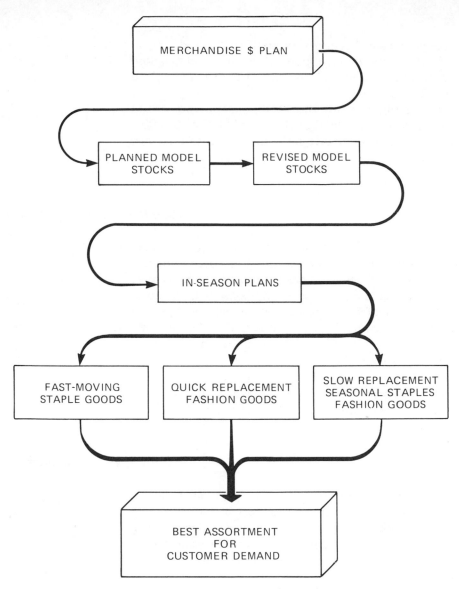

FIGURE 8.1 This diagram shows how the merchandise dollar plan flows through various planning and actual buying stages so that the buyer achieves the best assortments for his dollar allotment.

work the merchandise down from its placing stock to an active one by simply eliminating the lemons and carrying only runners. This is done by developing active unit control systems (Fig. 8.1).

Active Unit Control Systems

The purpose of these systems is to keep inventory low and turnover high. This permits you to do a maximum of business with a minimum of capital and thus make your capital return very gratifying indeed. If you have an average of $50,000 invested in stock on which you could maintain a gross profit of 50 percent on cost and you turned it over twice, you would make $25,000 × 2, or $50,000.

If you can increase the turnover just once more, that is, from two to three times, your gross profit would be three times $25,000, or $75,000. Now, since three turnovers usually involve little more expense than two turnovers, you would have an extra $25,000 to divide between yourself and the income tax departments.

How to Increase Turnover

You increase turnover by first recognizing that in most stores a small percentage of merchandise does most of the volume. It has been estimated that in some stores 10 percent of the items stocked produce 80 percent of the sales. For example, an area survey of Minneapolis grocery stores showed that they carried a total of 77 different brands of tea, yet 65 percent of all the sales were made in one brand, 13 percent in a second brand, and 3 percent in a third brand. Therefore, 81 percent of all the tea sales in the stores surveyed were made with only three brands of tea.

If a grocer carried these three brands and perhaps two or three more to appeal to neighborhood minority tastes, he would satisfy almost every customer who walked into the store. Why, then, should he carry 77 brands—or even 12 brands?

Runners Versus Sleepers

The same conditions prevail in most stores. What most retailers do not realize is the importance of both runners and sleepers in their turnover picture. Runners should be spotted early enough to be kept in depth during the selling season, but sleepers should be discovered just as early and should be quickly moved out of the store. Money realized from the sale of slow-moving merchandise can then be used for purchasing runners.

As you learn to control your merchandise, you obtain better and better turnover.

Variety in Unit Control Systems

There is a great variety of unit control systems because each one depends on what you want the control to tell you and the kind of merchandise involved. Nevertheless, everything in your store should fall into the following three large control groups:

1. Merchandise that is staple, sells fairly regularly, and on which you can get good vendor delivery, e.g., hosiery, groceries, drug items, most items carried by wholesalers.

2. Fashion goods which sell quickly in season and which the vendor can replace within a reasonable time or for which you can find a substitute in a week or two, e.g., jewelry, sportswear, etc.

3. Seasonable staples and fashion goods that are replaced slowly. This merchandise is difficult to reorder and receive in season because it either takes too long for manufacturers to fill the orders or the season is too short for reordering to be of any value. Therefore, placing must be heavy. Some examples are novelty shoes, leather coats, portable electric fans, etc.

In classifying your merchandise under these three headings, give careful thought to the right category for each item. Staples are constantly changing into fashion goods and fashion goods into staples. For example, wool sweaters were once considered a staple; now in most stores they have been replaced by man-made fiber sweaters. Again, many manufacturers today keep reserves in some items that would ordinarily be in the third category. If you deal with such vendors, treat such items as belonging to either the first or second classification.

Review Constantly

Under today's dynamic retail conditions, some items change categories quickly. You should constantly review your merchandise to see that it is properly classified. Once you have the items categorized, you are ready to work out a system that will tell you what to order, when to order, and how much to order.

What Information Do You Want to Know?

The first step is to decide what information you want a control to tell you. Do not try to ask too much from it, particularly in the beginning. Be satisfied if it tells you about the movement of the items involved.

If the system fails after a preliminary trial, determine if it has collapsed because of your inability to understand it, because of your unwillingness to do what it tells you, or because you are working it improperly. When you discover the trouble, you can then decide either to throw it out or to learn to understand it and do what it tells you.

Example of Staple Unit Control System

Once your merchandise is placed into the three general categories, you may proceed to build up a different system for each one. Category 1 might contain, for example, long-sleeved, textured shirts at $9.95 and you can control this item by using the form illustrated in Figure 8.2. This shows the movement of style 850. The symbols are translated as follows: col. = color, min. stk. = minimum stock (this is the smallest number of units you want in the store at a particular time), OH = on hand (this is the number of

L.S. Shirt $9.95
#850
Textured
Convertible Collar

SIZE 14	COL.	MIN. STK.	2/2 OH	OO	SOLD	16/2 OH	OO	SOLD	2/3 OH	OO	SOLD	16/3 OH	OO	SOLD	OH	OO	SOLD	SUMMARY Feb. 2 to July 27 OPENING INVENTORY	RECEIVED	CLOSING INVENTORY	SOLD
	B	3	2		0	2		2	0	3	2	1	3	1	3			2	9	2	9
	P	6	4	3	2	2	3	1	4		3	1	6	0	7			4	60	5	59
	W	6 9⁄6	8		4	4	6③	3	4	3	5	5	6	4	7			8	108	9	107
	R	6	3	3	2	4	2*	0	6		3	3	3	1	5			3	36	4	35
	Y	3	3		0	3		2	1	3	0	4	1	1	3			3	6	1	8

FIGURE 8.2 Staple unit control system (category 1).

items you have in the store on the date they were counted), and OO = on order. The number of shirts sold between the counting dates is found by adding the OH at the beginning to the OO column and subtracting the quantity OH at the next count. For example, look at size 14, col. R. On February 2nd there were three on hand and three on order which came in before February 16th. Six, therefore, were handled in the two weeks, February 2nd to 16th. When the item was counted on February 16th, there were four left. Therefore, two must have been sold. The next time this item was counted, it was found that two came back (2*). On March 2nd, therefore, there were six on hand.

If you look at 14's, col. W, min. stk., you will see that the buyer set the min. stk. at 6, then increased it to 9, then to 10, and then, as the season waned, dropped it back to 6. The form also shows that on February 16th, she ordered one-half dozen 14 W. Only three came in by the time the count came around again on March 2nd, but she ordered three more anyway. These three, plus those ordered on February 16th came in before the March 16th count.

You will notice how rapidly you can pick out runners and sleepers even from this slow-moving sample. Obviously, 14, col. W, is the best of the lot and perhaps col. B and col. Y. should be discontinued and money used for other purposes. This is further confirmed in the summary in which only 9 B and 8 Y were sold during the six months. Remember that you are not in business to please everyone who comes into the store. Your job is to satisfy as many customers as you can with your space and capital.

Counts Must Be Regular

Although the counts in the sample form were spaced two weeks apart, they could be done every week during the busy season and then cut back to two-, three-, or four-week counts in off-seasons. Whatever the period, the counts must be done on the dates set. If you plan so that only a certain number of items are counted each day and you insist on taking the count, your staff will find sufficient time to do the job as part of their day's work.

EDP Eliminates Manual Counts

A properly installed electronic data processing system (EDP) not only eliminates manual counts, it also gives you quicker and more accurate information on how each item you want to control is selling. Thus, EDP permits your staff to spend more time on their housekeeping and selling functions. Again, because it should be more accurate and faster than manual counts, you should be able to reduce your stock and increase your sales and turnover. The drawbacks of EDP are the cost of installing and maintaining the system and your ability to interpret properly the information it gives you (see Chapter 24) for a more detailed discussion of the advantages and disadvantages of EDP for a smaller store).

Control in the second category must be flexible because it deals with such fast-moving, high style items as dresses which, during the season, should be examined and reordered at least once a week. This gives you the opportunity to keep runners in stock by having your vendors fill your reorders in time or, if this proves impossible, to find other vendors who will give you suitable substitute styles.

The item you want to control should first be broken down into as many classifications as you desire. These could be by price line ($25.95 and $29.95), or by price zone ($22.50 to $29.95 or $35.00 to $45.00), or by styles, materials, colors, etc. If desired, synthetics could be broken down into their own categories, such as rayon, nylon, and cotton blends. Further breakdowns could be made by vendor.

If you have proper classification control, you should be able to plan and order each category without difficulty. For example, on March 10th you review your $29.95 cotton dresses (Fig. 8.3). Since it takes three weeks for an order to come on the floor, you must plan the assortment of dresses you want to have on the racks on March 30th. By looking at this year's sales in this range and by comparing them with last year's, you estimate you should sell 28 dresses from March 10th to the 30th. You also want to have 40 dresses on hand on March 30th. Your salesclerks count 32 dresses on hand and 15 on order as of March 10th.

ITEM: *Cotton Dresses $29.95*		
DATE: *Mar. 10*		
PLANNED SALES TO *Mar. 30*		28
PLANNED STOCK ON HAND *Mar. 30*		40
PLANNED UNITS REQUIRED		68
LESS: ON HAND *Mar. 10*	32	
ON ORDER	15	47
TO ORDER *Mar. 10*		21

FIGURE 8.3 Unit buying plan by price line (category 2).

With this information, you can draw up a form similar to Fig. 8.3. It shows that you should order 21 dresses today. The problem now becomes what sizes and colors should these dresses be? This problem is solved by filling in forms similar to those shown in Figs. 8.4 and 8.5.

SIZE	IDEAL PROP.	ACT. *Mar. 10*	ON ORDER *Mar. 10*	TO ORDER *Mar. 10*	TOTAL
12	3	2	2	5	9
14	6	11	6	0	17
16	6	8	2	7	17
18	5	7	3	4	14
20	4	4	2	5	11
TOTAL	24	32	15	21	68

FIGURE 8.4 Unit buying plan by size (category 2).

COLOR	IDEAL PROP.	ACT. *Mar. 10*	ON ORDER *Mar. 10*	TO ORDER *Mar. 10*	TOTAL
Y	8	5	2	4	11
Z	4	3	—	3	6
TOTAL	12	8	2	7	17

FIGURE 8.5 Unit buying plan by color (category 2).

How to Fill in Sizes, Colors, etc.

The first two columns of Fig. 8.4 are the ideal proportions of each size for every 24 dresses. Of course, this model will vary according to your kind of customer. If you have a young adolescent trade, you will require more smaller sizes than are shown and these could be 5, 7, 9, etc. If the majority of your customers are bigger women, you will want to carry more larger sizes and even oversizes. Remember that the sizes of your model, like everything else in this system, require review and revision at frequent intervals.

Having decided on the proportions, fill in the sizes you have on hand and on order March 10th. Then, to the 32 you have on hand and the 15 on order, add the 21 you are going to order. This gives you a total of 68 dresses, which is what you want to have on your floor on March 30th. Since 68 is almost three times 24, you should make the units in the total column as nearly three times the model of 24 as possible. You are now able to fill in the "To Order" column by placing enough dresses in each size to make up the size total. For example, size 12 needs 5 dresses (2 in stock plus 2 on order plus 5 to order, equals 9).

Colors are ordered the same way (Fig. 8.5) for size 16. In fact, any other classification that you desire may be broken down and ordered in this way.

It should be noticed here that individual unit control systems main-

tained manually or by computer would help you to decide on the best
running styles and that vendor history cards (Fig. 7.4), would tell you the
best sources for repeats. You may review, reduce, or rearrange your plans,
and reorder as often as you like—every week in season or once a month as
the season slows down. But every time you write an order, you know what
you are doing. You are in control of your merchandise and you may eliminate lemons in sizes, colors, materials, etc., by reducing them and using
the cash to build up your stock of runners.

EDP Helps to Control Inventory

Although proper EDP systems may give you much faster information
than manual ones on how customers are reacting to fashion goods, cost
considerations must be considered. Therefore, before you decide to install
any computerized system to control your fashion merchandise, make sure
that it will pay off by reducing inventory and increasing sales, turnover,
and profits.

Example of Slow Replacement Merchandise

This last category is the most difficult to order because so much depends
on your original placing. For example, novelty shoes are almost impossible
to reorder in season. Remember, however, that novelties are distinct from
staple shoes, which the manufacturer will wholesale for you.

One way to plan the buying of novelties is shown in Fig. 8.6.

PROBABLE SPRING SALES BY PRICE LINES FOR NOVELTY SHOES

1	2	3	4	5	6	
RETAIL PRICE	LYF F & W SALES	TY PL SALES	STK + OR − AT END	QTY TO BUY	% ORDER NOW	UNITS TO ORDER NOW
39.95	40	45	—	45	100	45
35.95	125	150	+20	170	3/4	128
22.95	175	200	−40	160	2/3	107
19.95	70	75	+15	90	1/2	45
TOTAL	410	470		465		325

FIGURE 8.6 Buying plan for fancy goods (category 3).

Retail Price (column 1). This is a list of what you expect retail prices
will be next year.

LYF and W Sales (column 2). These are last year's fall and winter
sales. These figures are obtained from past records.

TY PL Sales (column 3). This shows this year's planned sales.

STK + or — at End (column 4). Because you always need a certain number of shoes to carry on from one season to another, this column records the amount of stock you would like to have at the end of the season. At $39.95, you want to have the same number of units that you now have, but at $35.95, you would like 20 more pairs than you now have, etc.

Qty to Buy (column 5). The quantity to buy for the entire season is arrived at by adding or subtracting columns 3 and 4.

% Order Now (column 6). At $39.95, you may want to order 100 percent of the shoes you need, but as you move down the price scale, you should order less than 100 percent because you know that you will need to reduce some of the shoes in the more expensive lines and you also want to leave yourself open for a job lot or a promotion. These will be in the lower priced lines.

Use of Forms

All these controls look easy on paper and will be even easier in practice once you decide it is worthwhile to create your own systems and use them. In fact, the more you work with controls, the less time they take and the more useful each one becomes. Notice that most of the forms can be written on any piece of paper, but it is better to have them mimeographed on standard size sheets so that they may be filed for future reference. Of course, computerized systems require forms that are supplied by the firms who operate the service.

Go Easy with Both Manual and Electronic Controls

Do not put your whole store under merchandise controls at once. If you try to accomplish too much at one time, you will only get bogged down with details, revisions, and confusion. Also, since a complete system is difficult to understand unless you have experience, if you attempt to tackle the whole job at one time, you could become so discouraged that you would give up the whole idea.

Therefore, take it easy. In fact, take it *very* easy. Select only one item in each category and manipulate the forms until you can make them give you the information you want when you want it. Then take on another set of items, then another, and gradually extend the system to the whole store. In this way, you will control your merchandise and not have it control you.

This slow but sure learning process is particularly important *before* you decide to install computers, because unless you know what you want the machines to tell you and unless you can interpret the data properly, they will be very expensive and will not give you the service you expect of them.

1. There are three main systems for active unit control:
   (a) For fast-moving staple goods that manufacturers can replace quickly.
   (b) For fashion goods that sell quickly in season and can be replaced or substituted in a week or two.
   (c) For slow replacement of seasonable staples or fashion goods when reorders have little value.

2. All items and systems must be constantly reviewed and revised or they go out of date so that controls become a hindrance, not a help, to the buyer.

3. The combination of dollar and unit controls should give high profit returns with a minimum of capital investment in merchandise.

4. Develop controls slowly. Take one item only and make sure that you understand it before you go on to another. If you move too fast, the systems will become so complicated that you will get discouraged and give up controls entirely.

5. EDP systems should only be installed when they are more profitable than manual systems.

6. EDP systems should only be installed when you are certain you know what information you want from them and that you can interpret their data properly.

9

How to Price for Profit

WHAT THIS CHAPTER IS ABOUT

Pricing the merchandise you buy is both a science and an art. If you price too low, you may do a lot of business but make little or no profit; if you price too high, you will make a big markup on everything you sell, but most of your customers will buy from your competitors and eventually you will have to reduce your goods to a point where you will make little or no profit. This chapter tells you something about the science of pricing and suggests how to apply it. The way you use these pricing techniques will help to make you a business success—or a failure.

History of Pricing

Caveat emptor

Until the time of great retail pioneers like R. H. Macy, Adam Gimbel, and Timothy Eaton, every sale was a battle between the retailer and the customer. Prices were arrived at by haggling, but the retailer had the advantage. He knew what the merchandise cost him, usually had greater merchandise knowledge, and also had a good idea of what his competitors paid for the same goods. He therefore had a price below which he would not go. Customers had the short end. They could shop other stores if there were any in the neighborhood and compare materials and prices, but their main weapon was usually a weak one: to bully the shopkeeper by threatening to give their business to another merchant.

In those days, customers were seldom aware that all goods contained hidden values and that the cheapest price could mean the most unsatisfactory merchandise. Yet, the retailer permitted neither returns nor refunds. *Caveat emptor* (let the buyer beware) was the retailer's motto.

John Wanamaker and others like him developed a new philosophy of pricing. They believed that if customers had confidence in a merchant, they would be loyal to him. This would result in repeat business and a growing clientèle, for word-of-mouth advertising plus store promotions on this theme would be bound to bring in more and more customers.

One price and merchandise return policies

These retailers marked their retail prices on every item and permitted no haggling. Moreover, if customers were dissatisfied with purchases, they could bring them back and obtain adjustments or refunds. These policies proved to be so successful that more and more retailers adopted them and today they are accepted practices with most merchants.

The original one-price merchants marked their goods up by trial and error. They knew that there must be sufficient difference between cost and selling price to pay for all their expenses and still leave them a profit. But how much should this marked-up price be? They soon learned that markups should vary according to the kind of item to be priced. For example, a fashion item required a higher markup than a staple one, and a fast-turning piece of merchandise could be sold at less markup than a slow selling one. Customer services also entered into the markup picture, for the more of these the merchant offered his clientele, the higher his prices had to be.

Early markup policy

As their businesses grew larger, merchants were unable to mark the price of each item themselves, so they began to develop markup percentages to help them in their markup procedures. In time, these standard markups were maintained by most merchants, big and small, as though they were God-given laws. For example, if a department or chain store buyer paid $21.25 a dozen, or a small store buyer $22.50, for an item, they *automatically* retailed it for $2.98. When manufacturers discovered the buyers' pricing methods, they began to build their lines on accepted retail markup standards. This pricing structure was further helped by various resale price maintenance and fair trade laws.

After World War II a few merchants began to question established markup patterns, especially in the appliance fields, and they came to the conclusion that if they eliminated a lot of "normal" services like personal selling, delivery, credit, returns, etc., they could reduce markups enormously and still make a profit. Moreover, if they refused to spend money on expensive windows, fixtures, and other items that create an attractive store atmosphere, they could mark their goods even lower. Finally, if they could build up sufficient volume to obtain quantity prices, they could pass on some of these savings as well.

Discount houses revolutionize markups

These aggressive men were as brave and adventurous as Macy, Gimbel, and Eaton, for they pioneered and developed new retail concepts that revolutionized merchandising in every distributive field. Discounters gambled by basing their operations on sales volume that could be obtained by offering consumers presold merchandise at lower than traditional markups. They stocked only well-advertised and branded goods so that customers knew the amount of every discount, but the onus for post-sale satisfaction was placed directly on the manufacturer.

Once discount houses become sufficiently competitive, traditional stores were forced to review their markup policies and decide whether to base them on competitive factors or on tradition. They were familiar with different kinds of markups because they used them for planning and controlling the merchandise in their stores. For example, they knew that they could look at any markup in three ways: if an item cost $1 and was priced at $1.50, the *dollar* markup was 50¢, but the markup could also be described as 50 percent of cost, or as 33⅓ percent of retail.

Traditional merchants revise markup policies

The difference between markup on cost and markup on retail is very important. Many a small retailer has gone bankrupt because he thought a markup on cost was the same as a markup on retail. When he bought something for $1, he added 50 percent and made the retail price $1.50. When clearance time came and he wanted to get back his cost, he took off the 50 percent he had originally put on the item. However, although he thought he was selling the merchandise at cost, he only received 75¢ for an item that had cost him $1.

Markup on cost versus markup on retail

Most small retailers think in terms of markup on cost. The larger stores, particularly those on the retail inventory method, think of markups as a percentage of retail. To make it easier to use markups at either cost or retail, a buyer may use a markup chart similar to the one in Fig. 9.1. Notice how quickly the percentages spread. For example, 25 percent of retail equals 33⅓ percent of cost; 33⅓ percent of retail equals 50 percent of cost; 50 percent of retail equals 100 percent of cost. So when a salesman claims that you make 50 percent on an item, ask him if he is talking about markup on cost or on retail. He usually means cost because cost is the larger percent and the easier one to work out mathematically. But 50 percent on cost is only 33⅓ percent of the retail.

Each item receives its own markup, and individual markups in any classification or in the store as a whole differ considerably. Yet to operate properly, buyers must know the *average* markup for their whole department and management must know the *average* markup for the whole store. They therefore accumulate markups into desired groups called *cumulative markup percentages*. This procedure permits markup planning. For example, a buyer knows that on October 1st his inventory cost him $25,000 and that it retails for $35,000. During the month of October he plans to buy merchandise at $29,000 cost and retail it for $55,000. This means that during October he will deal with $25,000 + $29,000, or $54,000 worth of merchandise at

Cumulative markups

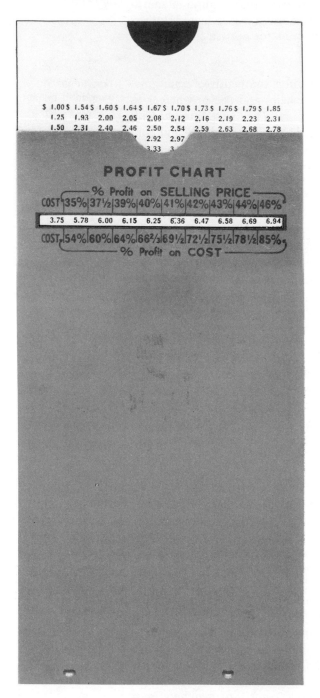

$ 1.00	$ 1.54	$ 1.60	$ 1.64	$ 1.67	$ 1.70	$ 1.73	$ 1.76	$ 1.79	$ 1.85
1.25	1.93	2.00	2.05	2.08	2.12	2.16	2.19	2.23	2.31
1.50	2.31	2.40	2.46	2.50	2.54	2.59	2.63	2.68	2.78
				2.92	2.97				
				3.33	3				

PROFIT CHART

— % Profit on **SELLING PRICE** —

COST	35%	37½	39%	40%	41%	42%	43%	44%	46%
	3.75	5.78	6.00	6.15	6.25	6.36	6.47	6.58	6.69	6.94
COST	54%	60%	64%	66⅔	69½	72½	75½	78½	85%

— % Profit on **COST** —

FIGURE 9.1 Markup chart. To use this chart, slide the inner card until you can see the unit price the vendor is quoting you. If your markup is based on *cost*, look along the *bottom* edge of the slot to check on the markup percentages (%) on cost; if your markup is based on *retail*, look along the *top* portion above the slot. If you use these markup guides, you should be able to decide how the price the supplier is quoting you will fit into your pricing structure.

Courtesy Parisian Novelty Co., Chicago, Ill.

cost. This is $90,000 worth of merchandise at retail ($35,000 + $55,000). The dollar markup, then, is $90,000 − $54,000, or $36,000.

The cumulative markup percent of retail is $36,000/$90,000 × 100, which is 40 percent. Using this percentage figure, the buyer may either go ahead or revise his plans.

Retailers know that when an item is first put on the floor, it may or may not sell at the price asked. If it does not move at the original price, it must be marked down or, occasionally, marked up. For planning and control purposes, then, there are two markups. The initial markup is the one the retailer *initially places* on each item, while the maintained markup is the one the retailer is able to *maintain* when the item is finally sold.

Initial markups versus maintained markups

Markups in dollars are very important because, taken together, they must be sufficient to cover the cost of the entire operation of the store and still give the merchant an adequate profit. But management and buyers use *percentages* instead of actual dollar figures to plan and control merchandise operations. In this way, an entire department or groups of similar merchandise may be given fixed percentages. Buyers then price individual items with both initial and maintained markups in mind. They become very conscious of the fact that if they price certain items below these percentages, they must compensate for it by pricing other goods above them.

Importance of markup percentages

The initial markup (IMU) must be high enough to cover the following:

What goes into the initial markup

All store expenses:

This figure includes the cost of alterations to goods, but *not* the transportation of goods to your store.

Deduct vendor cash discounts.

PROFIT

The total of these two items is called:

MAINTAINED MARKUP (MMU)

INITIAL MARKUP (IMU)

Markdowns.
Discounts to employees and customers.
Shortages

The total of these three items is called:

REDUCTIONS (RED.)

To make the IMU figure into a useful tool for planning, it must be translated into a percentage of your planned initial retail price. To get this figure, add the planned dollars you expect to take in (net sales) to your planned reductions (markdowns, discounts to employees and customers,

How to find IMU percent

and shortages). You then obtain a figure that would result if you sold all your goods at the prices that you originally wanted to get for them. To calculate your IMU percent, use the following equation:

$$IMU\% = \frac{MMU\% + Red.\%}{Net\ Sales\% + Red.\%}$$

Example: You plan your next year's operations as follows:

	Dollars	Percent
Net Sales	100,000	1.00
Expenses	31,000	0.31
Profit	3,000	0.03
Reductions	10,000	0.10

Therefore,

$$MMU = \$31,000 + \$3,000 = \$34,000$$
$$MMU\% = .31 + .03 = .34$$

Substituting your planned percentages into the equation, you get

$$IMU\% = \frac{.34 + .10}{1. + .10} = \frac{.44}{1.10} = .40,\ or\ 40\%$$

Now express this percentage of net sales as a dollar figure, that is, 40 percent of $100,000, or $40,000.

The IMU% is a very useful planning tool. It tells you what margin you must try to make *initially* on your goods in each merchandise classification, in each department, and in the store as a whole. Planned initial markups, however, are useful only if they are computed realistically and if, when they are applied to individual items, the prices appeal to your customer segment. If you feel that your first attempt at a planned IMU% will be rejected by your customers, then the elements in the equation must be revised until a better IMU% is obtained. You do this by very carefully reviewing the elements that go into the IMU% figure. See where you can reduce expenses, shortages, and markdowns and, at the same time, attempt to increase vendor cash discounts and increase your sales volume.

How to use the IMU% equation in planning

You go to the market to buy $10,000 worth of goods at retail. Your planned IMU% is set at 40 percent. At the end of the second day your

How to use the IMU% in practice

purchases total $4,400 at cost and $8,000 at retail. You know that you are now in a position to look for promotions, but you want to know just what IMU% you require on the balance of your open-to-buy. To find out, make the following calculations:

$$\text{OTB at retail} = \$10,000 = 100\%$$

If the IMU% equals 40 percent, then cost must equal 60 percent.

	Cost	Retail	IMU%
You set out to buy goods at	$6,000	$10,000	40%
You have already purchased goods at	4,400	8,000	45%
Therefore, you can now buy goods at	$1,600	$2,000	20%

As the season progresses, the prices you set initially, based on your IMU%, become less and less attractive to your customers. The original prices must be reduced. In order to find out how much you may reduce the goods and still end up with your planned profit on operations, use the MMU% equation, which is

How to find MMU%

$$\text{MMU}\% = \text{IMU}\% - \text{Red.}\% \ (\text{Net Sales}\% - \text{IMU}\%)$$

Example: You plan as follows:

	Dollars	Percent
Net Sales	100,000	1.00
IMU	40,000	0.40
Reductions	10,000	0.10

Substitute actual percentages into the equation, as follows:

$$
\begin{aligned}
\text{MMU}\% &= .40 - .10(1. - .40) \\
&= .40 - .10 \times .60 \\
&= .40 - .06 \\
&= .34 \text{ or } 34\%
\end{aligned}
$$

In dollars, this percentage of net sales is .34 × $100,000, or $34,000.

When you are satisfied with your planned IMU% and MMU%, you may use them to solve pricing problems. For example, you have bought 100 pairs of slacks at $7 a pair. If your IMU% is 33⅓ percent of retail, you make them $10.50 a pair. After you have sold 80 pairs at this price, you want to reduce the balance. You look up your planned MMU% and find that it is 30 percent. This information enables you to figure out what the reduced price should be. The following shows you how it is done:

How to move from IMU% to MMU%

MMU% required is 30 percent of retail. Therefore, cost of goods is 70 percent of retail.

Actual dollar cost of goods is 100 pairs @ $7 = $700.
If 70 percent of retail is $700, the original retail of the whole lot is

$$\frac{100 \times \$700}{70} \qquad \$1,000.00$$

Sales to date: 80 pairs @ $10.50   840.00

Sales still needed $ 160.00

You may therefore retail each of the 20 remaining pairs at one-twentieth of $160, which is $8 a pair. In practice, if you sell the 20 pairs at $7.97, or $7.99 a pair, you will have made your MMU% on the lot.

Sometimes you want to find what percent you can allow on a lot of goods that needs to be reduced and still end up with your planned MMU%. To do this, use the following equation:

How to find reduction percent

$$\text{Red. \%} = \frac{\text{IMU\%} - \text{MMU\%}}{\text{Net Sales\%} - \text{IMU\%}}$$

Example: Your planned figures are as follows:

	Dollars	Percent
Net Sales	100,000	1.00
IMU	40,000	0.40
MMU	34,000	0.34

Substitute actual percentages into the equation:

$$\text{Red. \%} = \frac{.40 - .34}{1. - .40}$$

$$= \frac{.06}{.60}$$

$$= .10, \text{ or } 10\%$$

In dollars, this percentage of net sales is .10 × $100,000, or $10,000.

Your planned IMU% has been set at 40 percent, planned expenses at 33 percent, and planned profit at 1 percent. What reductions would these figures allow you to make?

Using the reduction equation in a practical way

Solution:

$$\text{MMU\%} = .33 + .01 = .34$$

Using the reduction percent equation, we get

$$\text{Red.}\% = \frac{.40 - .34}{1. - .40} = \frac{.06}{.60} \times 100 = 10\%$$

If shortages are planned at 1 percent (1.0) and discounts to employees and customers at ½ percent (.005) of net sales, your markdowns will be .10 − .015 or 8½%. On planned sales of $100,000, then, your markdowns can total $8,500.

Although it is best to work the equations out by percentages, always translate the answer into dollars. Sometimes you might be making a high markup percent, but the cash equivalent is so small that it hardly pays to carry the item. For example, you may want to carry a slow-selling item that costs 5¢ and sells for 10¢. Your profit would be 100 percent on cost, or 50 percent on retail. But is the 5¢ profit enough to carry the item? Would it be better to use the space for a fast-selling item that costs you 50¢ and sells for 75¢? The markup percent is not as big as it is on the first item, but the dollar amount is and the quicker turnover makes for higher profits.

Always translate percentages into their dollar figures

The scientific method of setting IMU%, MMU%, and Red.% is only as good as you make it. If you use accurate figures from past seasons and sound estimates for next season's business and you stick to your plans, then the three equations will be useful to you. But you must keep checking your percentages from time to time to see that your actual figures do not wander too far from your planned figures. If they do, review your plans and, when necessary, revise them to fit the facts.

Planned percentages must be realistic

In order to understand the interaction between the elements that can make your store either a success or a failure, it is important to play "if" not only with the IMU%, MMU%, and Red.% but also with the other factors that go into profit planning.

Play "If" with all the elements

For example, "if" we raise the planned net sales in the example on page 106 by 10 percent, i.e., from $100,000 to $110,000, the expenses are bound to go up. These may increase $1,000, i.e., from $31,000 to $32,000. However, "if" we could maintain our planned IMU% of 40 percent, MMU% of 34 percent, and Red. % of 10 percent of net sales, what would happen to the net profit?

Solution: Because we are not considering vendor cash discounts or work room costs, the MMU is the same as the gross margin.

MMU = expenses + profit
MMU = 34% of $110,000 = $37,400
Expenses   = $32,000

Profit, therefore   = $ 5,400

According to this "if," you stand to make a profit of $5,400, or 4.9 percent of net sales, instead of $3,000, or 3 percent that you would have made on sales of only $100,000.

Since every item has to be marked up separately, group IMU%'s and MMU%'s can only be used as *guides*. If you want to know what is the most profitable price for a single item, estimate the number of units that you can sell at given prices. For example, if an item costs $5, you could draw up the following schedule:

Unit Selling Price	Estimate of Units Sold	Cost per Unit	Gross Profit
$8.00	300	$5.00	$ 900
7.50	400	5.00	1,000
7.00	600	5.00	1,200
6.50	900	5.00	1,350
6.00	1,100	5.00	1,100
5.50	1,300	5.00	650

In this instance, $6.50 is the most profitable price, but a change in either the cost or the demand for the article would cause the most profitable selling price to move up or down. For example, in inflationary periods the same item could cost $6. Then your table would read as follows:

Unit Selling Price	Estimate of Units Sold	Cost per Unit	Gross Profit
$9.50	200	$6.00	$ 700
9.00	300	6.00	900
8.50	400	6.00	1,000
8.00	700	6.00	1,400
7.50	900	6.00	1,350
7.00	1,200	6.00	1,200

According to this table, $8 would be the most profitable price, but it, too, would change if incomes and the general price level continued to rise. In any event, because a retailer can never really estimate exactly how many units could be sold at each price level, planning for maximum profits is, at the most, experienced guess work.

WHAT THIS CHAPTER TOLD YOU

1. Markup is the difference between the cost of an item and its retail price.
2. Markups may be figured either at cost or at retail.
3. Most successful retailers think in terms of markup at retail.

4. To mark up merchandise profitably, the retailer should understand the science of pricing and how to apply it.

5. There are two kinds of markups: (a) initial markup is the amount you put on the goods originally, i.e., what you would *like* to make by selling the merchandise; (b) maintained markup is what you *actually* make when the goods are sold.

6. The initial markup percentage equation is

$$IMU\% = \frac{MMU\% + Red.\%}{Net\ Sales\% + Red.\%}$$

7. The maintained markup percentage equation is

$$MMU\% = IMU\% - Red.\% (Net\ Sales\% - IMU\%)$$

8. The reductions percentage equation is

$$Red.\% = \frac{IMU\% - MMU\%}{Net\ Sales\% - IMU\%}$$

9. Make sure that you understand the relationships among the three equations before you use them to control your price structure.

10. Markup planning is useful only if it is based on realistic figures.

11. Prices are affected by such a great number of influences that you may not be able to price all items at their maximum profit.

10

Right Pricing
Means Profitable Selling

WHAT THIS CHAPTER IS ABOUT

The subjects covered in Chapter 9—knowing what goes into a markup and making plans to control prices in general—are the easiest steps in arriving at a retail price. The most difficult decision in pricing is the actual setting of a selling price for each item you handle; for in practice, a few cents one way may move goods quickly, whereas a few cents the other way may keep them in the store and lead to drastic price reductions. There is a lot to know about practical pricing and a lot to gain by carefully thinking through what your pricing policy should be. This chapter tells you about most of the methods a merchant can use to price each item in his store for maximum sales and profits.

Methods of Pricing

Single unit

Retailers should know as many different ways of pricing merchandise as possible and when to use them. The most commonly used method is to set an initial retail price on each article and watch its movement. If you have presented it properly, but without success, it should be marked down. Some stores mark the new price on the original tickets to show customers that the merchandise has been reduced, while others make new tickets. Sometimes the price of the item should be *increased*. This happens when the article is priced so low that customers become suspicious of the bargain. In this case, new tickets should be made for your marked-up price.

You can try to increase your volume or obtain quicker turnover by encouraging customers to buy more than one item at a time. You could, for example, charge $8 for a shirt, but sell two for $14.50. Some stores quote *only* multiple prices and the customers lose the difference if they buy less than the units offered; that is, if they want only one of an item priced at two for 69¢, they must pay 35¢.

Multiple units

You should remember that multiple pricing reduces markup (Fig. 10.1) and this fact should be considered when setting the original price. Multiple

Multiple pricing reduces markup

FIGURE 10.1 The effect of markdowns on maintained markup. Find the initial mark-up (percent of markup on inventory and purchases) achieved in the first column and the reductions achieved in the first line across the form. From the reduction figure, read down on the form to the line on which the markup appears at the left. The lower figure in this square is the resultant maintained markup. The black figure immediately above it is the reduction percent times the complement to the markup percent. For example, if the initial markup is 42 percent and the reductions 3 percent, the maintained markup is 40.26 percent.

From John W. Wingate and Elmer O. Schaller, *Techniques of Retail Merchandising,* 2nd ed., © 1956, p. 136. By permission of Prentice–Hall, Inc., Englewood Cliffs, N.J.

MARKUP AND RETAIL PRICE

% Mark-up on Inventory and Purchases	% OF REDUCTIONS TO SALES												
	3	4	5	6	7	8	9	10	12	14	16	18	20
	1.74	2.32	2.90	3.48	4.06	4.64	5.22	5.80	6.96	8.12	9.28	10.44	11.60
42	40.26	39.68	39.10	38.52	37.91	37.36	36.78	36.20	35.04	33.88	32.72	31.56	30.40
	1.77	2.36	2.95	3.54	4.13	4.72	5.31	5.90	7.08	8.26	9.44	10.62	11.80
41	39.23	38.64	38.05	37.45	36.87	36.28	35.69	35.10	33.92	32.74	31.56	30.38	29.20
	1.80	2.40	3.00	3.60	4.20	4.80	5.40	6.00	7.20	8.40	9.60	10.80	12.00
40	38.20	37.60	37.00	36.40	35.80	35.20	34.60	34.00	32.80	31.60	30.40	29.20	28.00
	1.83	2.44	3.05	3.66	4.27	4.88	5.49	6.10	7.32	8.54	9.76	10.98	12.20
39	37.17	36.56	35.95	35.34	34.73	34.12	33.51	32.90	31.68	30.46	29.24	28.02	26.80
	1.86	2.48	3.10	3.72	4.34	4.96	5.58	6.20	7.44	8.68	9.92	11.16	12.40
38	36.14	35.52	34.90	34.28	33.66	33.04	32.42	31.80	30.56	29.32	28.08	26.84	25.60
	1.89	2.52	3.15	3.78	4.41	5.04	5.67	6.30	7.56	8.82	10.08	11.34	12.60
37	35.11	34.48	33.85	33.22	32.59	31.96	31.33	30.70	29.44	28.18	26.92	25.66	24.40
	1.92	2.56	3.20	3.84	4.48	5.12	5.76	6.40	7.68	8.96	10.24	11.52	12.80
36	34.08	33.44	32.80	32.16	31.52	30.88	30.24	29.60	28.32	27.04	25.76	24.48	23.20
	1.95	2.60	3.25	3.90	4.55	5.20	5.85	6.50	7.80	9.10	10.40	11.70	13.00
35	33.05	32.40	31.75	31.10	30.45	29.80	29.15	28.50	27.20	25.90	24.60	23.30	22.00
	1.98	2.64	3.30	3.96	4.62	5.28	5.94	6.60	7.92	9.24	10.56	11.88	13.20
34	32.02	31.36	30.70	30.04	29.38	28.72	28.06	27.40	26.08	24.76	23.44	22.12	20.80
	2.01	2.68	3.35	4.02	4.69	5.36	6.03	6.70	8.04	9.38	10.72	12.06	13.40
33	30.99	30.32	29.65	28.98	28.31	27.64	26.97	26.30	24.96	23.62	22.28	20.94	19.60

pricing may be used if more volume is expected or if the merchandise is to be cleared quickly regardless of markup. Sometimes a multiple price is offered either to create excitement or to reduce an overstocked situation. In these cases, the offer is limited by time or quantity. Mass merchandisers use multiple pricing as a regular policy, but other stores should use this technique very carefully. Figure 10.2 clearly shows how many more sales are required to make a normal gross margin if prices are reduced.

IF YOU CUT THE PRICE →			5%	10%	15%	20%	25%	30%	35%	40%	45%	50%
ON	25% →	THE	25.0%	66.7%	150.0%	400.0%						
	30% →	ADDITIONAL	20.0%	50.0%	100.0%	200.0%	500.0%					
MER-	35% →	UNIT	16.6%	40.0%	75.0%	133.0%	250.0%	600.0%				
CHANDISE	40% →	VOLUME OF	14.3%	33.3%	60.0%	100.0%	166.6%	300.0%	700.0%			
THAT	45% →	BUSINESS	12.5%	28.6%	50.0%	80.0%	125.0%	200.0%	350.0%	800.0%		
HAS	50% →	REQUIRED TO MAKE UP	11.1%	25.0%	42.8%	66.6%	100.0%	150.0%	233.0%	400.0%	900.0%	
BEEN	55% →	THE SAME	10.0%	22.2%	37.5%	57.1%	83.3%	120.0%	175.0%	266.0%	450.0%	1000%
NORMALLY	60% →	DOLLARS	9.0%	20.0%	33.3%	50.0%	70.2%	100.0%	140.0%	200.0%	300.0%	500%
MARKED	65% →	AND CENTS	8.3%	·18.2%	30.0%	44.4%	62.5%	85.7%	116.7%	160.0%	225.0%	333%
	70% →	MARGIN	7.7%	16.6%	27.3%	40.0%	55.5%	75.0%	100.0%	133.3%	180.0%	250%
UP	75% →	WILL BE	7.1%	15.3%	25.0%	36.3%	50.0%	66.7%	87.5%	114.3%	150.0%	200%

COURTESY NOTION AND NOVELTY REVIEW

FIGURE 10.2 Increases in transactions needed to offset price cuts.

From John W. Wingate and Elmer O. Schaller, *Techniques of Retail Merchandising,* 2nd ed., © 1956, p. 145. By permission of Prentice–Hall, Inc., Englewood Cliffs, N.J.

Free gifts

Some stores offer ''free'' gifts which may be based on a percentage of what the customer buys, may supplement a regular purchase, or may be offered to a limited number of people. Although the gift may be free to the customer, it costs the retailer money and so it should be considered as reducing the markup percent of the department concerned. If you give a free gift worth $6 retail to a woman who is buying a $60 layette, you are reducing your profit. If the markup on the $60 sale is $20 and the ''free'' gift costs you $4, you net only $16. Free gifts, then, should be used only for reasons similar to those for multiple pricing.

Seasonal pricing

A retailer of fashion goods usually obtains a higher than normal markup at the beginning of the season. Certain consumers like to own a "first," whether it be soft goods, an appliance, or an automobile and they are willing to pay for that privilege. Buying a fashion "first" also gives them a longer time to use the item, so it is less expensive than it appears to be. Again, the high price establishes a prestige factor which, to some customers, is very important.

As the season advances, runners become apparent, not only to you but also to your competitors and vendors. Someone is bound to reduce prices because he wants to increase sales during the heart of the season. He is justified in doing so because there is less risk in handling the merchandise now that its popularity is established. Also, from the customer's point of view, the goods are not worth as much as they were at the beginning of the season because they offer less prestige and have less use value. Therefore, after the start of the season, you should know when to begin to lower prices to levels that will appeal to most of your customers.

As the season reaches its end, prices should be further reduced to clearance levels. Every effort should now be made to avoid carrying over fashion merchandise into the next season. Little profit can be made by clearance merchandise like this, but, as explained in Chapter 9, if the retailer plans and controls his buying, he can offer his customers "clearance" priced merchandise and still retain his normal or better-than-normal overall markup.

Odd price endings

There is much controversy over prices that end in odd amounts, such as 98¢, 99¢, etc. These endings may have originated from translating English pounds into American dollars or because early retailers realized that making change would help to prevent their personnel from stealing. Whatever the origin of odd price endings, they had definite customer appeal. Selling an item at 98¢ meant that the customers got not only their purchases but also some change out of their dollars. To the more observant retailer, it was soon apparent that for some unknown reason, endings such as 95¢, 98¢, or 99¢ attracted more customers than those ending in 94¢ or 96¢. Today, promotional stores use odd price endings much more than medium or better stores do, but it is an almost universal retail practice.

It is best for each retailer to set his own price-ending policy. For example, he might use 98¢ as the ending for all prices up to $5. Then he could shift to a 95¢ ending up to $100. Even endings could be quoted on prices above $100. Such a policy helps to create the store's personality and makes the buyer's pricing job easier. (Customers no longer wonder why similar items vary by a few cents.) Goodwill and better selling usually result from an overall price-ending policy.

Use even price endings whenever possible

Some stores, particularly those that cater to high-income clientele, have successfully eliminated odd price endings, and you should experiment with this too because it will increase your markup percent and dollar profits. For example, changing the price of an item that costs you 60¢ from 95¢ to $1 increases your IMU from 36.8 percent to 40 percent and gives you an extra

5¢ on every item sold. If, however, you find that your customers reject even price endings, go back to odd price endings as quickly as possible.

Price Points and Price Lining

Merchants who follow planned initial markup percentages too strictly soon offer their customers a great number of retail prices with very small dollar-and-cents differences between each price. For example, they may carry raincoats at $33.50, $34.50, $35.50, $36.95, etc. These slight variations in price points might be of value to promotional stores where price is a major consideration or to exclusive shops where price is a minor buying motivation, but the fewer prices a middle-income store has, the better. In these stores, prices should be set wide enough apart to make the difference in the comparative value of the merchandise easy for customers to see. Few people can tell why one raincoat shoud sell at $33.50 and another at $35.50. Coats between $33.50 and $36.95, then, should be grouped together and sold at a single price, say $35. Price lining is particularly important in self-service and self-selection stores, but even in salon selling it is useful because both the salesperson and the customer can understand the differences in merchandise values without too much difficulty.

Figure 10.3 lists the unit sales of women's white and colored blouses and sweaters by price points. You can see from the percentage figures which of the various price points could be eliminated, unless there is a specific reason for keeping them. For example, white blouses at $14.95, colored blouses between $17.95 and $21.95, and sweaters at $15.50 to $15.95 are the

How to set price points and price lines

FIGURE 10.3 Accessory unit sales by price points.

Prices $	White blouses %	Colored blouses %	Sweaters %
4.49	3.5	20.3	...
5.95	...	8.7	...
7.95			2.6
	14.9	29.3	
7.99			
9.95	56.5	11.9	
			3.2
11.95	16.5	13.7	
14.95	0.7	8.5	14.6
15.50			
	5.9	4.0	1.5
15.95			
17.95	...		75.5
19.95	2.0		2.6
		0.3	
21.50	. . .		. . .
21.95	. . .		. . .
25.95	. . .	3.3	. . .
	100.0	100.0	100.0

poorest sellers. Perhaps these price lines should be maintained, but only after a very careful re-examination. On the surface, it would appear that money involved in stocking these price lines should be spent on better selling price points such as the white blouse at $9.95, which have 56.5 percent of the sales volume.

Advantages of Price Lining

If customers have little trouble in seeing why prices differ, they come to quicker buying decisions. Also, by building up a series of price lines, merchants soon discover which price points please most of their customers, e.g., the white blouses at $9.95 in Fig. 10.3.

**Customers buy
more easily**

To price line properly, the retailer must first set his low and high prices and then estimate his points in between. This makes his buying easier for he does not have to look at merchandise that would be too high or too low for his store or that would be at in-between prices. For example, if a retailer decided to carry blouses from $7.95 to $29.95, he need only look at a few $5.95 and $35 lines in order to satisfy himself that the blouses he is carrying compare favorably with blouses outside his price range. And if he has established $5.95, $7.95, $9.95, etc., as his price points, he should pass up merchandise at $6.95, $8.95, etc. Since he is able to spend most of his time examining blouses in his best price lines, he soon becomes an expert in buying the best selling price points in these lines.

**Buying is made
easier**

Price lining gives you more depth and breadth with less stock because it forces you to concentrate your merchandise into definite price categories. For example, if you had 100 units divided among four prices, you would have little breadth or depth at any one price. If, however, you carried these 100 units at only two prices, you would have approximately 50 units in each price and this would give you double the amount of depth or breadth.

Price lining saves you a lot of time in sales training. Since salespeople do not have to remember as many prices, it is easy for them to distinguish between merchandise at one price and at another, and therefore their sales presentations can be developed quickly.

**Get more depth
and breadth**

Handling merchandise becomes easier when price lining is used. Stock checkers and price markers soon learn to spot off-price merchandise as well as items that do not seem good value at the prices you have set. Marking is simplified and time is saved because instead of having to make two dozen tickets at $2.98, two dozen at $2.99, and two dozen at $3, the marker simply makes six dozen tickets at $2.98.

**Stockkeeping
easier**

Markdowns are reduced because prices are usually set at the going and accepted price, that is, $2.98 instead of $2.96. Also, because you have more depth and breadth at your single price, you give your customers better selection and this sells merchandise faster.

**Markdowns
reduced**

When you establish price lines, remember to allocate prices between regular lines for sales purposes. For example, if you have a regular $1.98 price, the sale price could be 88¢; on the $2.98 line, the sale price could be $1.88, etc. By using this technique, you can give your customers greater satisfaction in each sale group because you have more depth and breadth of merchandise at each price. One hundred dresses clearing at a variety of prices, say $22.79, $24.99, $26.79, and $28.99 will make a very poor promotion because there is insufficient merchandise at any one price. But if there are only two prices, say $23.79 and $27.99, the promotion offers more advertising and selling possibilities and it enables you to compete more successfully with larger retailers.

Sales promotion is more effective

If you price point properly, you should stock only the best values in each price line. Customers will soon appreciate your expert shopping ability and will tell their friends. This is the best advertisement that any store, and particularly a small store, can get. Yet, you spend fewer instead of more dollars to obtain this valuable advantage, for price lining results in smaller and cleaner inventory. Too many price points force you to carry a minimum of materials, styles, sizes, and colors at each price point, even though they may be only a few cents apart. For example, a minimum of 100 units may be necessary for a price line between $8.50 and $9.95, with price points at $8.50, $9.50, and $9.95. A single price point of $8.95 could give customers more variety and depth with perhaps only 60 units. This, of course, means better turnover, easier merchandise control, and less money tied up in merchandise.

Customer goodwill is increased

Although price points and price lines for most stores have many advantages, it can be dangerous. If your prices do not appeal to your customers, they will not buy. Therefore, you must set your lower and upper limits with the customer in mind. There is no use carrying stereo players under $59.95 if your clientele is not interested in any price lower than this.

How to establish price points and price lines

Try to establish the same price lines as those of typical stores in your field. If you are not sure of a price, survey your competitors and see not only where they are strong but also where they are weak. Sometimes you can make their weak price lines your strong ones; or if a price line seems to be missing, find out why and then see if you can do something about it.

Vendor salesmen in your area know which price lines are popular. Ask them to suggest the lines that should be best for your store. Want slips, too, can tell you which prices are selling, which are not selling, and which are missing. Your salespeople can be trained to report any price difficulties they may have with customers.

One way to tell whether to trade up or down and just how to go about it is to analyze the sales in each department or classification by price lines. If you have three prices in any item, the middle one should be your best seller. If this is not so, there is something wrong with your price lining.

Price lines tell when to trade up or down

Sometimes you may discover that a low price line produces 30 percent of the sales volume but is responsible for only 10 percent of the gross margin of a department or line of merchandise. A higher price line may produce only 10 percent of the sales but is responsible for 30 percent of the gross margin. This does *not* mean that you should discontinue the lower price line because it might be a customer traffic builder. It *does* mean that you should try to increase your sales in the higher price line. Remember that it is not necessary to carry full stocks in all price lines; only the best selling lines should be carried in both depth and breadth. The other ranges should be bought in a staggered fashion.

Prices may vary from season to season, but this should not worry you if everyone else is changing his prices at the same time you are.

However, once a price line is established, it should not be changed during the season unless it is absolutely necessary. Yet, it is difficult to maintain the same price for the same quality in times of rising prices. This is when your knowledge of your customers is most important. If they buy mainly for price, you must lower your quality, but if they buy mainly for quality, then you can raise your price safely. In times of recession or extensive unemployment customers shop more carefully than they do when everyone is working, and price becomes most important. Your only concern then is to meet competition.

Whenever you want to add a new price line, think it through carefully. Will the extra volume of the new line compensate for the space and the capital that you have to invest? Will it interfere with the sale of an item that you now have? In the last analysis, customers come to your store to buy an item, not a price, so price line according to the way you feel that your customers are thinking.

WHAT THIS CHAPTER TOLD YOU

1. Different ways of pricing are single unit, multiple units, and free gifts. Each method has its advantages and disadvantages and must be carefully used.

2. Prices for fashion goods vary according to the season. High prices may be obtained at the beginning of any season, but as the season advances, prices should be lowered to appeal to the majority of your customers. As the season ends, merchandise should be cleared at any price.

3. Develop a price-ending policy. It helps to maintain your store personality and makes for better price lining.

4. Price pointing and price lining are techniques that have many advantages for most stores.

5. Price lining should tell you when to trade up or down.

6. In times of rapidly increasing prices you should decide whether price or quality is more important to your customers and act accordingly.

7. In times of recession or extensive unemployment your prices should be competitive.

11

Why Take Inventory?

Because the stock in your store is the body of your business, you should understand how it functions. To do this, you must develop a sensitive merchandise control system and learn how to interpret it. Then you will be able to correct whatever seems to be going wrong with your merchandise soon enough to keep your store in a continually healthy state. You begin to understand your business only when you know the true condition and value of the merchandise in your store. This chapter tells you how to gain this knowledge and how to use it.

Taking Inventory Need Not Be Disturbing

Most retailers dislike taking inventory because they find the whole process disturbing from beginning to end. Your staff starts bothering you months ahead and as "I-Day" approaches, they seem to dream up all sorts of queer problems that must be solved at once. Customers become more of a nuisance than ever; seeing salesman, planning advertisements, and other day-to-day details are pushed aside until the stock is actually counted and the sheets are collected and turned over to the office for extending.

This is definitely the wrong approach to taking inventory. If you plan ahead and know what you are doing and what you want to get out of your inventory figures, the job may be accomplished without straining anybody's nerves and you will obtain very important information about how your store is doing.

Inventory may be taken in different ways. You can take it carelessly and then work it to a predetermined figure that will make your income tax "comfortable" and still permit your accountant to accept it as a basis of his annual statements without too many qualms of conscience. But such an inventory is of little use because you never know how much merchandise you really have in your store. Therefore, you cannot determine your merchandise shortage, turnover, age, or even compare your operation with that of other stores. In fact, inaccurate inventory figures are positively dangerous because most retailers tend to insure their goods at their book value, which after some years can become as little as one-half of their true value. In case of fire or other merchandise damage, a retailer can lose much more than the few thousands he "saved" by lowering his inventory for tax purposes. Such losses have put some retailers out of business or into bankruptcy.

Of course, just looking at your entire stock once a year does *some* good. It will turn up merchandise you had forgotten or misplaced and it might even make you think that you have too much stock. On the whole, however, inventories that are taken because they are an important element in your P & L statements have little value.

The Value of Taking a True Inventory

A *true* inventory is very valuable if you take a good hard look at your stock situation at least twice a year and try to understand what it means by using some method of comparison. Otherwise, you never really know what is happening to your business. This lack of information can lead to very serious consequences. By taking a proper inventory, you know where you are going and you are also conscious of how much your merchandise is worth at a definite time. You can then decide whether to reduce or to build up the capital you have invested in stock.

Aging Your Stock

A properly taken inventory *ages* the merchandise so that you know whether or not you have too much old stock. Merchandise in your store is not at all like money in the bank. It earns nothing until it is sold at a profit. Since every minute that stock lies on your shelves costs you money, holding on to old stock becomes a very expensive business.

When you take a properly planned inventory, both your staff and you will discover merchandise that for some reason was pushed into drawers, packed away in the stock room, or simply put in the wrong place and forgotten. When these items are brought to your attention, you can do something about them before they become older and cost you even more money. Sometimes they have only to be cleaned up before they can be put out for sale. Sometimes just moving them around helps sell them.

A properly taken inventory tells you what you want to know about the stock in each merchandise classification and department. Even the smallest shop should divide its merchandise into a number of separate classifications; a men's store, for example, could break down its stock into shirts, ties, socks, etc.; the store itself could be divided into clothing department, furnishings department, etc. An inventory that is properly taken and properly interpreted gives you the facts and lets you know whether you are running a paying operation with good turnover and clean stock or whether you are permitting your store to slip into a dangerous situation that requires immediate action.

How to Value Inventory

If you use the retail inventory method, simply value the merchandise at the retail price on your price tickets. Then convert it to cost by the method discussed in Chapter 22.

If you use the cost method, make certain that you value each item at the lower of its cost or market value. For example, although you paid $20 for a suit two years ago, you may know that today it is worth only $8 wholesale. Therefore, $8 is the inventory price of this suit. But if its value today is $25, take it at $20 for inventory purposes, i.e., lower of cost or market value.

How to Take Inventory

Before you begin, decide what information you want from your inventory in addition to its value at a certain date. For example, as long as you have to list each item of merchandise, why not divide it up according to classification and age? Then you will know how much old stock you have and where it is.

How to Use Inventory Sheets

An inventory sheet that is widely used is discussed in detail below with an example of a sheet and a summary sheet from an independent men's furnishing store (Figs. 11.1 and 11.2).

Headings on the Inventory Sheet

Since the sheets must be carefully accounted for, they must be numbered consecutively.

Sheet numbers

Because the sheets are in looseleaf form, they are sometimes misplaced or torn out of their binding. If each sheet is dated as well as numbered, it can be returned to its proper place.

Date inventory taken

MEN'S WEAR INC.   Sheet Number 3

Dept: 70   Classification: *Men's Dress Shirts*   Date Invt. Taken: *Jan. 31, 1978*

Location: *East Wall*   Fixture: 5   Counted by: *H. W.*   Extended by: *L. A.*

Listed by: *D. B.*   Totalled by: *E. R.*

Checked by: *B. H.*   Checked by: *O. H.*

NOTICE TO INVENTORY TAKERS:

1. Only ONE classification of merchandise may appear on this sheet.
2. EVERY sheet, whether used, unused, or cancelled must be RETURNED.
3. Do NOT write in columns 6, 7, 8, 9 or 10.

PERIOD RECEIVED	DESCRIPTION	QUANTITY NO. of UNITS	KIND of UNIT	PRICE PER UNIT DOLLARS CENTS	1 to 6 mos.	7 to 12 mos.	13 to 18 mos.	19 mos. and older	TOTAL
1	2	3	4	5	6	7	8	9	10
7	white broad shirts	8	ea.	2 00		16 00			16 00
6		14		4 00	56 00				56 00
7	///	3		5 00		15 00			15 00
9	THL THL	10		2 50				25 00	25 00
TOTAL	DO NOT WRITE IN THIS AREA				56 00	31 00		25 00	112 00

SIGNATURE DEPT. MANAGER *J.C.*

FIGURE 11.1 An inventory ruling that is very flexible and also allows for the aging of merchandise.

MEN'S WEAR INC.   Sheet Number *Summary*

Dept: 70   Classification: *Furnishings – Summary*   Date Invt. Taken: *Jan. 31, 1978*

Location: Fixture: Counted by: Extended by: *L. A.*

Listed by: Totalled by: *E. R.*

Checked by: Checked by: *O. H.*

NOTICE TO INVENTORY TAKERS:

1. Only ONE classification of merchandise may appear on this sheet.
2. EVERY sheet, whether used, unused, or cancelled must be RETURNED.
3. Do NOT write in columns 6, 7, 8, 9 or 10.

PERIOD RECEIVED	DESCRIPTION	QUANTITY NO. of UNITS	KIND of UNIT	PRICE PER UNIT DOLLARS CENTS	1 to 6 mos.	7 to 12 mos.	13 to 18 mos.	19 mos. and older	TOTAL
1	2	3	4	5	6	7	8	9	10
Jan. 31, 1961	*Total*				2,977 –	1,852 –	678 –	1,450 –	6,957 –
	% of Total				42. 8	26. 6	9. 8	20. 8	
Jan. 31, 1960	*Total*				3,645 –	1,782 –	1,211 –	2,312 –	8,950 –
	% of Total				40. 7	19. 9	13. 5	25. 9	
	Difference				–668 –	70 –	–533 –	–862 –	–1,993 –
	% Inc. or Dec.				–18. 3	3. 9	–44. 0	–37. 3	–22. 3
TOTAL	DO NOT WRITE IN THIS AREA								

SIGNATURE DEPT. MANAGER *J.C.*

FIGURE 11.2 Inventory summary sheet. This sheet should be very carefully examined by management and the buyer. It is one of the most useful tools a merchandiser can obtain.

If numbers or letters are used to designate departments, insert them here; in this example, 70 represents the men's furnishings department. This heading allows easier sheet identification.

Department

Write in after this heading the name of the merchandise that is to be taken on this particular sheet. It is important to remember that *every* sheet is to have *only one* classification on it; for example, if a fixture contains both shirts and ties, use two sheets, one for shirts, the other for ties.

Classification

"East wall, Fixture #5." It is best to prepare a master plan of your store and to place the sheets in a definite pattern. Then if a sheet is lost, it may be traced on the master plan and a new one used to replace it. Every shelf, drawer, table top, etc., should have its own inventory sheet or sheets if it contains merchandise of more than one classification.

Location and fixture number

It is best for the *counter* to be familiar with the stock. The *lister* need not have any merchandise knowledge; his only job is to carefully write down the information as it is called to him.

When the merchant or department manager gathers up the sheets, he should quickly look at the actual merchandise that is listed on them. If it seems to agree with the information on the sheets, he initials the sheets beside the words "checked by." If, however, he is suspicious about what he finds on a sheet, he should immediately and carefully check the merchandise against the sheet. In any event, he should spot-check the odd sheet to convince himself that the units, prices, and aging are correct.

Counted by, listed by, and checked by

These headings are for office use and are self-explanatory.

Extended by, totaled by, and checked by

1. Only *one* classification of merchandise may appear on a sheet. This has been explained under the heading "Location and Fixture Number."

Notice to inventory takers

2. *Every* sheet, whether used, unused, or canceled, must be *returned*. Because it has been given a definite place in the master plan of locations and fixtures, it must be accounted for. Carelessness here leads to stock not being counted, or if counted, not being included in the inventory. Sheets discovered after the inventory has been tabulated can lead to a great deal of annoyance and extra office work.

3. Do *not* write in columns, 6, 7, 8, 9, or 10. The office uses these columns for aging and totaling. See below how this should be done.

(Column 1). This refers to the *age* of the items. The counter must say if the item goes into column 6, 7, 8, or 9. For example, if the inventory is being taken in January, column 6 would refer to items that came in since August, that is, this year's fall and winter merchandise. Even if it was

Period received

received in July but was meant for fall and winter selling, it should be identified as fall and winter stock.

Column 7 refers to merchandise that is 7 to 12 months old, that is, items that were left over from last spring and summer seasons. Column 8 contains last year's fall and winter merchandise, Column 9 is for stock that is at least one and a half years old, whether fall and winter or spring and summer merchandise.

A Special Note. If you want to include spring and summer merchandise that has arrived in January, you must segregate it and enter it *separately* in column 6. Otherwise, this merchandise will affect this year's fall and winter inventory total.

(Column 2).

Description

This column permits you to make use of as narrow or as broad a classification as you wish, for example, men's shirts, men's broadcloth shirts, or men's white broadcloth shirts, etc.

(Column 3 and 4).

Quantity: number of units, kind of unit

These columns must be considered together. Column 4 tells the office whether you have counted the merchandise in single units or in dozens, gross, etc.

(Column 5).

Price per unit

This is the price you set on the merchandise you have counted. In the retail inventory method the retail price on the ticket is used; in the cost method, the counter must evaluate each item at the lower of its cost or market value. Usually, the cost code is on the ticket and the counter judges any price variations from this value.

These columns were explained above and are used for aging. After the office calculates the price of each item by using columns 3, 4, and 5, the results are entered in the column designated in column 1. For example, if column 1 shows a "7," if column 2 shows "white broadcloth shirts," if column 3 shows an "8," if column 4 shows "ea." (each), and column 5 shows "$2," the office would multiply 8 by $2 and get $16 which it would then place in column 7.

Columns 6, 7, 8, and 9

(Column 10).

The *total* column

It is used to balance each page (i.e., the totals of columns 6, 7, 8, and 9 must equal that of column 10) to give those interested in the inventory a quick summary of each page and to compile classification, department, and total figures.

This places the responsibility for columns 1 through 5 on the department manager.

Signature department manager

Is There a Satisfactory Method of Preparing the Inventory?

Yes, by planning ahead and leaving yourself plenty of time to carry out the plan. Count your reserve and slow-moving merchandise before inventory day, but remember to mark off merchandise that is sold between the time it was counted and I-Day. Some stores have developed elaborate mark-off systems, but in a small store the owner need only impress his staff with the value of accuracy.

Before inventory day arrives, try to segregate as much active merchandise as possible; separate this year's $7.98 shirts from last year's $7.98 shirts, etc. Then on inventory day all these items can be counted and aged much more easily and quickly.

By going over all your stock before counting it, you will discover unticketed merchandise and so save yourself annoyance and wasted time on inventory day. Another advantage in preparing your merchandise beforehand is that you can examine and mark down items to their proper value before they are entered on the inventory sheets.

The best way to take inventory

Plan ahead and do as much counting and entering as possible before inventory day. Then a single evening or morning is all that should be needed to complete the inventory.

It is faster and more accurate to have your staff take inventory in teams of two: a counter who should know the merchandise and a lister who need only be careful how he writes the information on the sheets.

As an added check, some stores have the counter and the lister change places when the merchandise is put back in stock. This is very time-consuming and is unnecessary if everyone realizes the value of proper inventory.

It is important to train your staff to list the inventory directly on the sheets. It is ridiculous to take it on little bits of paper or odd pieces of cardboard, consolidate the data, and then list the information on the inventory sheets. This is not only time-consuming, it also leads to many errors and reduces the value of inventory planning. Remember that each sheet should represent the merchandise in a definite physical location so that if you want to see any item, the sheets will tell you where to find it.

Some stores eliminate counters and listers by having only one employee record the inventory on a tape recorder. Since the information must be entered on inventory sheets before it can be tabulated, the cost and percentage of error of this technique should be carefully weighed against more traditional methods.

Special areas to check before completing inventory

Be sure to clear up returns, credit notes, and other items that exist between you and your vendors.

Be sure to list the merchandise in your window and interior displays.

Be sure that all customer returns have been reticketed and returned to stock.

126

Be sure to account for all goods that are not sold but are either out of the store for cleaning or alterations or on consignment or approval and not charged directly to a customer.

If the next season's merchandise has arrived and you do not want to take it into stock, be sure to mark it *and* the invoice "NOT TAKEN."

Make Certain that All Inventory Has Been Accounted For

Once the inventory sheets have been gathered and the information on them has been confirmed and initialed, they should be sorted into numerical order and checked off against the master plan. Spoiled or unused sheets should also be checked and accounted for.

The Office Takes Over

The sheets should be turned over to the office as soon as possible for extending, totaling, and comparing figures. While you are waiting, begin to examine the questionable merchandise that has come to your attention while the inventory was being taken and decide what to do with it. Some stores that use the Retail Inventory Method take inventory during the *first* week of January and the *first* week of July. They have found that they can run their clearance sales much more intelligently if they review their merchandise as early as possible in these clearance months. If they delayed inventory taking until the end of January and the end of July, the best period for clearance sales would pass before the final inventory figures could be used as a basis for reductions. This clearance sales technique is extremely difficult under the cost method of taking inventory.

How to Read the Office Figures

Compare the current *value* of the stock against that of other years. Then compare the *age* of the stock itself and that of other years. For example, examine the summary sheet of the furnishings department as of January 31st. (Fig. 11.2). Column 10 tells you that this year this department had almost $2000 less stock on January 31st than it had at the same time the previous year. Whether this is good or bad depends on a number of factors. Taken by itself, this figure could mean that either the department still has too much fat or that its stock has been cut so much that sales are being lost.

Column 9 informs the merchant that, compared with last year, he has done a fairly good job of cleaning out the really old stock but that he still has a long way to go. Having 20.8 percent of the inventory in the store for more than a year and a half is not good at all. By turning to the individual sheets and checking each one carefully, he can look at the actual merchandise and then make up his mind about the best way to dispose of each item. One thing is certain: This stock is very expensive and is costing him a great deal of money every minute it lies on the shelves.

Column 8 shows that $678 worth of last year's fall and winter stock is still on hand on January 31st. This is a considerable improvement over the stock situation last year; in fact, it is 44 percent better, but it still represents almost 10 percent of the current stock. Therefore, a very earnest attempt should be made to dispose of this merchandise while customers may still want it. Remember that stock that is put away represents nonproducing capital.

Column 7 shows that a $70 increase has taken place in the spring and summer stock. This looks like an insignificant sum until you see that the total amount of column 7 spring and summer merchandise represents 26.6 percent of the total stock, which is not good. The retailer should examine the merchandise and immediately plan how quickly he can turn this stock, plus the spring and summer merchandise in column 9, into cash as soon as the new season opens.

When he looks at column 6, the merchant might be pleased because it shows a reduction of 18.3 percent in dollar value compared with last year. Better still, it represents 42.8 percent of this year's stock against 40.7 percent last year. However, $3000 in current stock may be too low to meet the department's day-to-day requirements; therefore, the retailer should examine the inventory sheets to see if he is running short on basic items. If he is, orders should be put through for them immediately.

Compare Your Inventory Against the Average

More can be done with the inventory figures than just observing the store trend. The percentages should be compared with outside averages which can be obtained by subscribing to such organizations as NRMA, your trade association, or government agencies. In the case of our example, it might be found that the average stock in men's furnishings under six months would be higher than our merchant is showing. This would mean that, compared to averages, his store still has a long way to go in cleaning up its old stock.

Other Uses of the Inventory Sheets

It is a good idea to compile separate lists of merchandise that should be watched and checked every week. This is a valuable aid in moving unwanted merchandise because if your salespeople know that you have your eye on these items, they will make an effort to get rid of them.

Your accountant should use the inventory figures to arrive at the store's gross margin. They can also be used for controlling stock shortages, arriving at a series of important turnover trends, and comparing with outside sources.

There are many other things that you can do with inventory figures, but no matter how you use them, when you have taken inventory properly the figures are exact and represent real values. They are all down in black and white, and neither you nor your department heads can argue them away, forget them, or neglect to do something about the merchandise *at once*.

"Experts" say that everyone who wants to remain healthy and prevent serious illness should see his doctor once a year and follow his advice. Similarly, if you want your store to be healthy and your business to prosper, take a proper inventory twice a year. Read the results. Then do what the figures tell you—even if it hurts.

WHAT THIS CHAPTER TOLD YOU

1. Knowing the value and age of your merchandise is the first step in keeping your store healthy.

2. Taking inventory is not difficult if you know what you want it to tell you and if you plan ahead.

3. If you use the retail method, take the price on the tickets. Then its cost complement will give you its market value.

4. If you use the cost system, value each item at the lower of cost or market value.

5. Inventory should be listed on inventory sheets.

6. Compare the inventory results with (a) other years to see your store trend and (b) outside sources to see where you stand against other operations.

7. Know where your old stock is and what to do about it.

8. Know where you have too much or too little merchandise.

9. Use inventory figures as a basis for controlling stock shortages and arriving at your gross margin, turnover, and other necessary ratios.

12

How to Get More Customers
into Your Store

WHAT THIS CHAPTER IS ABOUT

The more people who are attracted to your store and who are willing and able to buy your goods, the better chance you have of running a successful business. To bring them to your store, you must first make potential customers notice it and then you must induce them to come to and enter it. Then you must be able to attract them to *the point of sale.* The various methods of accomplishing this are called *sales promotion.*

This chapter will tell you *how to plan* your store's sales promotion activities and the next chapter will discuss how to use the most important tools of sales promotion.

What Is Sales Promotion?

Any effort you make or any devices you employ to attract customers to the point of sale are considered sales promotion. These can be advertising in newspapers, on radio or television, circulars mailed to prospective customers, or giveaway handbills inside or in the vicinity of the store. Attractive windows and informative interior displays are especially effective sales promotion activities. Fashion shows, product demonstrations, even clowns in front of the store can sometimes be considered worthwhile tools of sales promotion. Favorable news stories about your store, usually called *publicity,* are also included as an important function of your sales promotion activity.

No matter what size store you operate or how limited or extensive your sales promotion budget is, you will succeed in getting a meaningful return on your promotional investment if you use the following four objectives as guides for your planning: (1) Build a clearly defined store personality. (2) Generate traffic. (3) Reflect accurately your store's merchandising strengths. (4) Increase your gross margin.

Your sales promotion methods should tell people exactly what kind of store you operate and the kind of goods you sell. By impressing a clear-cut personality of your store on your potential customers, you should be able to have them think of you first when they want to buy the goods you carry.

Objective 1. Build a clearly defined store personality

There are three major store personalities: (a) institutional stores, (b) aggressive-promotional stores, (c) semi-promotional stores.

Institutional Stores. These stores concentrate on presenting distinctive merchandise of quality and good taste. Customer services are extensive and varied to meet the expectations of their clientele. These stores should be extremely careful in their sales promotion activities. They must direct their promotional energies and money toward creating an image that reflects the store's distinctive personality. Rarely do institutional stores blatantly emphasize price except during clearance periods. Their main promotional style is directed to focusing on the newness or the quality and good taste of their merchandise as well as on the prestige of the store among its customers. Frequently, some institutional stores will use tasteful sales promotion to highlight their reputation for good service or any special customer services they offer.

Advertising in newspapers or for mailings is developed in a highly individual manner that uses good taste to enhance the store's special character. Patrons are expected to react to these ads as if they were personal invitations from the store (Fig. 12.1).

Windows and interior displays are particularly important for institutional stores because much of their individuality will depend on the imaginative, creative, and tasteful presentation of the merchandise. Avant-garde mannequins, distinctive showcases, merchandise tables and stands, and other display fixtures can be of considerable help in projecting a particular store character.

Institutional stores often use in-store promotional activities such as product demonstrations or fashion shows to accent the new in merchandise. Because these activities must be consistent with the store's image, the store should try to avoid in-store promotions that attract great crowds, for these promotions will not increase business and they may even alienate loyal clientele.

FIGURE 12.1 A highly individual ad that enhances this store's very special personality. Notice that the handwritten style suggests a personal invitation.

Courtesy Jermies, Inc., Richmond, Va.

Aggressive-Promotional Stores. These stores operate and live by continually promoting price-appeal goods. They have many storewide sales and departmental events as well as item promotions that vigorously stress prices. Their newspaper ads are usually jam-packed with items and the ads use highly visible emphasis on prices and savings; their radio or TV advertising style follows this pattern as well (Fig. 12.2).

These stores offer few customer services and much of their goods is sold on a cash-and-carry basis. However, most of these retailers offer some form of credit, either through their own or through external charge plans.

Aggressive-promotional stores use low-cost, well-designed merchandise fixtures that present as much goods as possible. Although these stores use a minimal amount of window and interior displays, they are skillfully designed to attract the shopper's attention to the values and prices of their merchandise. Consequently, signs are a most valuable part of their display with emphasis on prices and savings.

Aggressive-promotional stores can use many crowd-attracting in-store promotion ideas. For example, various legal lucky number "drawings" can attract a large number of customers to the store and strolling clowns or musicians can draw traffic all over the store. Using famous personalities is another good way that an aggressive-promotion store can create excitement not only for the total store but also for drawing attention to a particular department. For instance, a well-known athlete appearing in a sporting goods store or department can attract considerable prospective customers, even for the short time that he appears. Such in-store promotion adds further to the store's image as an up-to-the-minute promotional store and an exciting place to shop.

FIGURE 12.2 This quality retailer's advertising consistently retains its basic format whether it is used to present new fashions or emphasize extensive assortments in a special shop or promote an off-price event. Note how the format is effective for single item units as well as in multiple item advertising. Courtesy L. L. Berger, Buffalo, N.Y.

Semi-Promotional Stores. These stores are not as loud or as continuous in shouting their wares as are the aggressive-promotion stores. Their sales promotion character is divided between the approach of the institutional stores and the high-powered methods of the aggressive retailers. Because of this division, the semi-promotional store must use an easily recognized interrelationship in all of its promotion activity. Whether the store is having a strong price promotion or is introducing a new product, there should be a personality resemblance in its promotion character, especially in its advertising (Fig. 12.2).

Stores in this category rarely use windows or interior displays for aggressive promotion that focuses on price appeal. Instead, store signs, posters, or counter cards are planned to highlight a storewide sale or specially priced merchandise. Since good taste and distinction in display adds so much to the image of the semi-promotional store, these qualities should not be sacrificed for short-term price promotions, no matter how imperative they may be considered at the moment.

The semi-promotional store should not get involved with big crowd-attracting in-store promotions of the highly promotional store. Instead, it should concentrate on the more unusual and ideaful promotions of special interest to the customers who prefer this kind of store. It should plan in-store activities that focus on the current life-styles of their clientele. Promotion ideas based on import (or foreign country) weeks, gourmet cookery demonstrations, home decorating workshops, or do-it-yourself presentations can draw their share of interested customers without crowding the store so that sales volume is interrupted.

Decide on the Kind of Store You Are Operating. Once you make a decision on what promotional image is best for your store, concentrate on the proper sales promotion techniques that will emphasize this personality. Furthermore, make sure that every sales promotion action you take will add more luster to your store's personality. Keep your sales promotion activity consistent and continuous so that your identity is constantly presented to the public.

Objective 2. Generate traffic

No matter what kind of store you are operating, concentrate your sales promotion efforts on the goods that *most* of your customers want. By doing this consistently, rather than spending promotion energy on the odd item that appeals to the few, you can be certain of attracting much more traffic to your store.

Customers' wants vary from season to season, month to month, week to week, and even day to day. Therefore, to be sure of always getting traffic, your sales promotion planning must be flexible enough to accommodate these variations. Since at the beginning of a season more people are interested in the new in merchandise, plan your sales promotion to concentrate on answering your customers when they ask, "What's new?" For example, in the spring, women are most interested in the new fashions; therefore if you run a fashion store, promote these. At this time of the year many men are interested in their gardens, their houses, or lawns. If you operate a hardware store, this is the best time to concentrate your promotion activity on gardening tools and supplies as well as on house paints, brushes, ladders, etc. Do not waste money on less important goods that will not draw maximum traffic.

At the end of a season customers want values and savings more than they want the new in merchandise. This is the time to promote special purchases or important markdowns.

Again, there are times when customers are thinking about gifts, for example, Mother's Day, Father's Day, or Christmas. This is when you should direct your promotion efforts to emphasize your gift merchandise.

Since strengths have developed from "customer preference items," capitalize on them by concentrating your sales promotion on those items your customers tell you they prefer the most. By focusing promotion efforts on your strengths, you will attract more shoppers to your store and they will buy other items that possess good potential, but which are not yet worthy of promotion expense.

Again, allotting an important part of your budget to customer preference merchandise will avoid wasting promotion money on goods that have not earned sufficient customer acceptance to have promotion dollars spent on them.

Objective 3. Reflect accurately your store's merchandising strengths

To produce more gross margin you should concentrate your sales promotion on the most profitable departments and classifications. These profit-making areas can more easily support promotion expense than your less profitable ones and they will also generate even more traffic for less profitable departments.

The tendency of most retailers is to try to increase their gross margin by increasing their sales peaks, using an *excess of promotion dollars* to accomplish this. But adding more money to promote sales peaks may not produce an equivalent increase in volume and profit. Moreover, doing this may weaken the budget of those periods when sales are in the "valleys." If this money were properly applied to stimulate more business during slower periods, the increase in sales would speed up turnover and add to your store's gross margin. Also, you would avoid the promotion feast and famine cycle which can limit the development of your store's personality through sales promotion.

Objective 4. Increase your gross margin

Define Your Sales Promotion Objectives

No matter what kind of store you operate and what its personality represents, unless you understand what your sales promotion objectives should be, you can easily waste your money. Each promotion, then, should be directed toward a specific target. Many successful retailers use the simple

A-B-C formula as an easily controllable method of defining their various sales promotion objectives.

Promotion Objective "A"—for Action. Sales promotion in this category is directed toward getting *immediate customer response* and *maximum customer traffic.* "A" promotion includes storewide sales, department or item price-appeal events, clearances, and manufacturer closeouts. The prime purpose in action promotion is to make your merchandise so attractive to price-conscious customers that they will stop what they are doing and rush to your store (Fig. 12.3). Although "A" promotion is the lifeblood of mass-merchandising stores, it can also be used successfully in other kinds of stores.

FIGURE 12.3 This "A" ad is planned for immediate customer action by extra emphasis on price and stressing the limited period of the promotion. Visual impact is created by the strong use of type, carefully planned to white space, and an eye-catching border.

Courtesy of V. I. P. Yarn & Creative Craft, Buffalo, N.Y.

BLACK VELVET

You...in the lush plush touch of this velvety panné evening suit. You...in this long length of skirt with classic blazer. You... out on the town in elegance exquisitely understated. A never-fail fashion when you team it with a bow-tied blouse, ascot, sweater or whatever. Also smashing in emerald or ruby for sizes 10 to 18. Grant Avenue Dresses, fifth floor. The suit 36.

RANSOHOFFS
GEARY AT GRANT

FIGURE 12.4 This "B" ad builds a favorable impression of this store's merchandise leadership in quality fashions at an attractive price.

Courtesy Ransohoff's, San Francisco, Calif.

Promotion Objective "B"—for Building. This is used to *build favorable impressions* of your store's leadership in merchandise assortments, quality goods, attractive price points, brand development (famous names or your own private brand), etc. "B" promotion also involves introducing new products and emphasizing exclusive lines. Although its primary purpose is to create an important long-range reputation for your business, it frequently produces the same immediate sales results as an "A" effort (Fig. 12.4). "B" promotion is a significant part of promotion planning of institutional stores and semi-promotional stores.

Promotion Objective "C"—for Creating Store Character. This objective is concerned with creating *goodwill* for your store by focusing on the store's special character and distinctions that are not directly related to your merchandise. "C" promotion is used to emphasize the quality of your service, the convenience of your location, special store hours, or your

FIGURE 12.5 The objective of this "C" advertising is to create customer goodwill by announcing the opening of a new floor. It also emphasizes increased ease of shopping and more selection of merchandise.

Courtesy McLean's, Binghampton, N. Y.

store's activities for the good of the community. Promotion to reactivate or increase charge accounts falls into the "C" group. In fact, any event that will highlight your store as an "institution" belongs in the "C" promotion category (Fig. 12.5). Although "C" promotion is used to considerable advantage by institutional and semi-promotional stores, aggressive-promotional stores primarily use it to announce new store openings or to introduce new departments.

Aggressive-Promotional Stores.   By definition, the aggressive-promotional store is committed to a continual program of action-getting promotion, for it depends on heavy daily traffic to maintain or increase its sales. This requires a large "A" promotion expense to produce the immediate response it needs and to continually reflect the bargain filled store image it wants to create.

Thus, when these stores are under pressure to produce extra traffic, they sometimes use promotional exaggerations that give customers reason either to mistrust the promotion or be disappointed in its values. Also, a considerable waste of promotion expense occurs if the aggressive-promotional store is not in a prime traffic location and is incapable of attracting a great number of passing shoppers.

Institutional Stores.   These stores must consider carefully the planning of "A" promotion. Too much emphasis can quickly dilute the store's prestigious character. In addition, the retail prices must *justify* an action-getting promotion. Disappointing merchandise or a weak price point can build customer ill will that can affect the store's fine reputation for quality and value. "A" promotion events can also bring serious complaints from patrons who paid the regular price a few days before the "A" promotion took place.

In addition, too many of these promotions place a heavy burden on the store's ability to serve its customers. Even though it generates extra traffic, salespeople may be so overworked that they may make mistakes or irritate loyal clientele because service has suffered. Again, insufficiently trained extra help can fail to make the expected sales and may further annoy regular patrons.

Another danger in overemphasizing "A" promotion for the institutional store is that many customers will postpone some of their regular purchases and wait for these events. They are willing to take a chance on finding the goods they want at lower prices during "A" promotion periods. The result of this overemphasis is that regular clientele will soon find that there is little or no reason to trade at regular prices.

Again, valuable buying time and energy of the staff can be wasted in looking for "A" promotion goods. This reduces the buying efficiency required for getting the right merchandise on which the store's reputation rests.

Finally, many "A" promotions not only increase promotion expense, their success also depends on lower markups. Thus, the added sales they create may not produce a desirable profit. When this disappointment is considered along with the possible loss in prestige, deterioration in service, and alienation of loyal patrons, the dangers of too many "A" promotions can be quickly realized.

Semi-Promotional Stores.   The semi-promotional store must also carefully weigh its decisions to use "A" promotion to attract immediate response. Overemphasis in this area can quickly distort the store's image.

Because the semi-promotional store must present a much more rounded, better balanced personality, considerable thought should be given to the proper mix of "A," "B," and "C" promotion activities. Variations of this mix should change from season to season and even month to month.

However, drastic changes in the economy or intensive competition may provoke the store into overemphasis of its "A" promotion planning. If this is accomplished by draining the promotion budget allocation for "building," the store's reputation, the store's prestige, and promotion personality can suffer.

Therefore, semi-promotional stores should make sure that their "B" promotion program is not interrupted despite the urgent need for *immediate response* promotion. Thoughtful shifting of money from "B" and "C" plans should help the store to meet its increased "A" objectives. But pushing the panic button and assigning too much of the planning to "hurry-in-now . . . get-the-big-buys" promotion can rapidly change the semi-promotional store into a weak aggressive-promotional one.

Which Departments to Promote

A store exists on profits. As a general rule, the most profitable department should get the biggest share of the budget, but every department should be considered separately. There is a point beyond which money spent for promotion of certain departments cannot bring in returns commensurate with the amount of money spent. Department sales are affected by poor locations, the wrong kind of merchandise, inadequate salespeople, or by improper lighting. Remember that even unlimited promotion dollars cannot cure a sick operation. Therefore, spend money to cure poorly performing departments or classifications before you budget one cent for their sales promotion.

Many departments thrive on store traffic generated by the effective promotions of other departments. Since these merchandise areas require very little of your promotion budget, concentrate your promotion expense and energies on those departments or classifications that have proved that they can be extra productive because of good sales promotion. They have the greatest customer acceptance and can also draw enough extra traffic to support weaker departments.

When it comes to sharing promotion money, the principle should be "the rich get richer." For example, if department X is successful because of its superior location and the excellence of its merchandising techniques, overpromotion will not be justified. A careful study of department Y shows that it is successful mainly because it gets good response from sales promotion. In these cases, it is better to limit the promotion dollars of department X and increase the budget for department Y.

Underpromoting a growing department or classification that demonstrates promise is just as wasteful as pouring promotion money into a weak department. Therefore, set aside a small, but not insignificant part of your promotion budget to subsidize departments that have growth potential; then study sales trends by departments and ask yourself which ones might perform better if they had more promotion attention than they are currently getting and divide your subsidy money between them.

The Sales Promotion Cycle

The amount and the character of promotion varies from season to season, month to month, and often day to day. Fall, obviously, is good for footballs, sweaters, and dinnerware. Christmas is right for toys, jewelry, and lingerie. And, in any season, the day before payday in a factory community is the best time to plan for "A" promotions that will bring you a lot of immediate-response traffic.

It has been found that, notwithstanding powerful pressures, customers will not buy when they are not in a buying mood. Therefore, consideration of your customers' buying moods is the only way to plan your sales promotion cycle. Usually, this cycle is divided into three broad time periods: *early-season, in-season,* and *post-season.*

Early season sales promotion

This should focus on the introduction of the news in merchandise that is appropriate to the season. This is an ideal time for institutional and semi-institutional stores to concentrate on "B" promotions because it provides an important opportunity for them to build up their stores' reputations. Therefore, a large percentage of their "B" budget should be allocated for advertising, displays, and signs to inform customers of important style news and new product information and to reinforce their reputations for quality merchandise.

The proper use of advertising, display, and in-store presentations could launch new products and styles in the goods you stock. This is the time to profitably promote your merchandise at regular prices because your customers expect to find complete selections and an abundance of new merchandise ideas.

Early season promotion should enable you to discover customer preference items and which of these items possess the potential of becoming profitable runners. Without this promotion exposure, most of these items might never be noticed by shoppers and you could lose many opportunities to increase sales and profits while at the same time, build up runner inventory for the in-season selling period.

In-season sales promotion

This capitalizes to a great degree on the information you gained during the previous period. Plan to promote the runners you carried over from the prior period. You may increase their promotion attraction by taking limited markdowns on these runners. The in-season period can also be used for promoting early markdowns on slow-selling goods. Many of your regular resources will start taking their own markdowns at this time. Consequently, you should get special offerings to be able to develop a storewide or departmental price-promotion event.

A good deal of your "A" promotion budget should be used during the in-season period because you should make your price promotions more important. Even though your customers are shopping for your special values at this time, you should plan part of your promotion program for new, regularly priced merchandise to be able to *continue building* the store's personality.

Here, the main objective is to help you clear your stocks and reduce your inventory at a time when customers are looking for bargains and savings. During this period the customer is ready to accept odds and ends, broken sizes, etc., as long as you promote worthwhile savings. Allocate most of your "A" promotion budget to post-season sales and clearances to be sure that you *quickly convert your investment from merchandise to cash.*

The Six-Month Promotion Plan

Most stores can fairly accurately plan their sales goals for at least six months by combining seasonal periods such as spring-summer or fall-winter. In a similar manner they can plan their six months' sales promotion expense by relating it to the goals of their sales plan.

Therefore, the first important stage of promotion planning is the *six-month promotion plan* (Fig. 12.6).

Essentially, this is the dollar breakdown of what you intend to spend on promotion for each month in this period. You establish how much you will spend by first determining *what percentage of your six-month sales you can afford* for sales promotion. This percentage varies by size of store, by kinds of merchandise, and by certain conditions determined by location, competition, or past experience. Some stores can afford only 2 percent of sales for promotion expense, but others find it necessary to spend 3.6 percent or more in order to maintain or increase their sales. The important consideration is how much can you *afford,* not what is the average expense of other stores like yours.

Then break down this total into monthly dollar allocations, relating each one to its promotional needs rather than to a fixed percentage to sales. These variations can be determined by competitive situations, growth opportunities, etc. Your monthly allocations at this stage should include budgeting for your traditional promotion events (anniversary sales, end-of-season clearance, pre-holiday events, etc.).

At this stage of planning, it is not necessary to assign promotion funds to particular departments. It is a good time, however, to set aside a reserve for emergencies or sudden opportunities that might arise.

The six-month plan is not necessarily a fully committed plan. Various market factors, economic conditions, or competitive situations may cause

1974 ANNUAL LONG RANGE SALES — PROMOTION PLANNING CHART

FEBRUARY
February 1973 produced 5.5% of average total store sales for the year

	ACTUAL 1973	PLANNED 1974
Sales	$16,800	$18,800
Total Advertising	$ 2.14	$ 282.
Total Adv. Percentage	1.85	1.60
% of year's sales in Feb	4.88	4.81
% of year's adv. in Feb	2.55	2.35

Lincoln's + Washington's Birthdays Promotion "A" money $240.

Note: Transfer $52 to March.

MARCH
March 1973 produced 7.5% of average total store sales for the year

	ACTUAL 1973	PLANNED 1974
Sales	$18,300	$19,800
Total Advertising	$ 288.	$ 396.
Total Adv. Percentage	1.80	2.00
% of year's sales in March	6.29	5.24
% of year's adv. in March	3.03	3.86

Pre-Easter Event "A" money $252.
2 item ads on spring goods "B" money $126.
Post-Easter Clearance "A" money $63.
total $441.

APRIL
April 1973 produced 7.8% of average total store sales for the year

	ACTUAL 1973	PLANNED 1974
Sales	$12,000	$12,200
Total Advertising	$ 360.	$ 462.
Total Adv. Percentage	1.80	2.10
% of year's sales in April	5.88	5.74
% of year's adv. in April	2.78	4.50

Annual Event "A" money $378.
2 item ads on new goods—Brands "B" money $126.
total $504.
NOTE: Pick up extra money from May + July.

MAY
May 1973 produced 8.0% of average total store sales for the year

	ACTUAL 1973	PLANNED 1974
Sales	$22,800	$24,240
Total Advertising	$ 608.	$ 649.
Total Adv. Percentage	2.60	2.79
% of year's sales in May	6.28	6.77
% of year's adv. in May	6.34	6.52

Mother's Day Gifts "B" money $252.
2 Summer items "B" money $126.
Pre-Holiday Event "A" money $240.
total $618.

Mother's Day—May 4
Memorial Day in Monday 5/26

JUNE
June 1973 produced 8.1% of average total store sales for the year

	ACTUAL 1973	PLANNED 1974
Sales	$24,000	$26,840
Total Advertising	$ 612.	$ 750.
Total Adv. Percentage	2.50	2.79
% of year's sales in June	7.18	7.06
% of year's adv. in June	6.41	7.31

Father's Day Gifts "B" money $320.
Graduation Gifts "B" money $189.
Vacation Item Prom. "A" money $189.
"A" money $240.
total $708.

Note: Father's Day—June 15

JULY
July 1973 produced 7.5% of average total store sales for the year

	ACTUAL 1973	PLANNED 1974
Sales	$17,000	$17,340
Total Advertising	$ 317.	$ 393.
Total Adv. Percentage	1.80	2.01
% of year's sales in July	5.18	5.09
% of year's adv. in July	3.33	3.39

Summer Clearances (start after July 4) "A" money $120.
Sidewalk Sales "A" money $150.
total $270.

AUGUST
August 1973 produced 8.2% of average total store sales for the year

	ACTUAL 1973	PLANNED 1974
Sales	$	$
Total Advertising	$	$
Total Adv. Percentage	%	%
% of year's sales in August	%	%
% of year's adv. in August	%	%

SEPTEMBER
September 1973 produced 8.7% of average total store sales for the year

	ACTUAL 1973	PLANNED 1974
Sales	$	$
Total Advertising	$	$
Total Adv. Percentage	%	%
% of year's sales in Sept	%	%
% of year's adv. in Sept	%	%

OCTOBER
October 1973 produced 7.8% of average total store sales for the year

	ACTUAL 1973	PLANNED 1974
Sales	$	$
Total Advertising	$	$
Total Adv. Percentage	%	%
% of year's sales in Oct	%	%
% of year's adv. in Oct	%	%

NOVEMBER
November 1973 produced 10.7% of average total store sales for the year

	ACTUAL 1973	PLANNED 1974
Sales	$	$
Total Advertising	$	$
Total Adv. Percentage	%	%
% of year's sales in Nov	%	%
% of year's adv. in Nov	%	%

DECEMBER
December 1973 produced 14.7% of average total store sales for the year

	ACTUAL 1973	PLANNED 1974
Sales	$	$
Total Advertising	$	$
Total Adv. Percentage	%	%
% of year's sales in Dec	%	%
% of year's adv. in Dec	%	%

JANUARY
January 1974 produced 6.5% of average total store sales for the year

	ACTUAL 1973	PLANNED 1974
Sales	$	$
Total Advertising	$	$
Total Adv. Percentage	%	%
% of year's sales in Jan	%	%
% of year's adv. in Jan	%	%

FIGURE 12.6 This store's actual sales last year were $340,000 and its promotion expense was $9,520, or 2.8 percent of sales. The planned sales for the coming year are $380,000 with a planned promotion expense of $10,260, or 2.7 percent of sales. Notice that the planned sales are increased while the planned promotion expense is decreased as a percentage of sales even though the dollar amount has been increased. This promotion plan, for the first six months, demonstrates how each monthly allocation of promotion dollars is related to the store's promotional needs rather than to a fixed percentage to sales. Study how the money allocations are shifted from certain months that can use less than a fixed percentage to those months that require more of the planned money to achieve effective promotion.

Many retailers also use this phase of planning to establish the timing of traditional or special events as well as indicating other important promotion information. Note that a small reserve of money has been deliberately set aside for any unforeseen promotion needs or possible emergency.

Calendar courtesy National Retail Merchants Association [NRMA], New York you to revise your planned sales. This, in turn, means an equivalent revision in your six-month promotion plan.

The Three-Month Promotion Plan

Every three months you should review your six-month plan so that you can act on any changes in the sales forecast. At the same time you should allocate the actual sales promotion expense for the three months you are planning. This is a most important stage in the promotion planning process. Not only do you realistically decide on the promotion expense for this period, you also plan what you will actually advertise or display. This is the time when you determine which departments and items will get "A" or "B" promotion money and how much they will get. "C" expense is also considered. You also use the three-month plan to determine exactly on which days your promotions take place. Thus, every promotion activity is decided on and budgeted for in the three-month promotion plan (Fig. 12.7).

Many retailers use their three-month planning calendar to determine all advertising media, including newspapers, direct mail, radio, and television. A separate calendar form should be used for scheduling displays.

The NRMA publishes a very useful sales promotion calendar. If, however, you concentrate your sales promotion in the newspapers, you will find the plan book of the Newspaper Advertising Bureau Inc. helpful. Again, your trade association or trade paper may publish equally worthwhile planning calendars.

During this particular planning stage you should clearly see the picture of your store's entire sales promotion activities for three months. This can be your opportunity to increase price-promotion emphasis if your sales trend indicates that this is necessary; or you can increase your "B" or "C" budgets to improve the image of your store.

After the three-month promotion plan is completed down to the last details possible, you should inform all those who will be involved with it of the decisions that have been made. You can make copies of each of the three calendar pages and distribute them to those who will be responsible for the various activities in the plan. It's up to you to make sure that the plan is followed and that all promotion efforts are well coordinated.

The Monthly Promotion Plan

This is the final planning phase before the various elements go into actual production. Because of this, you must complete the monthly plan with every detail accounted for. You should make the specific decisions on what goods you want to feature in newspaper advertising, display, or on the air. Since you are closer to the delivery of the items to be promoted or have possession of the goods by this time, you can decide on the prices you will use and even select the merchandise to be illustrated in ads or used in dis-

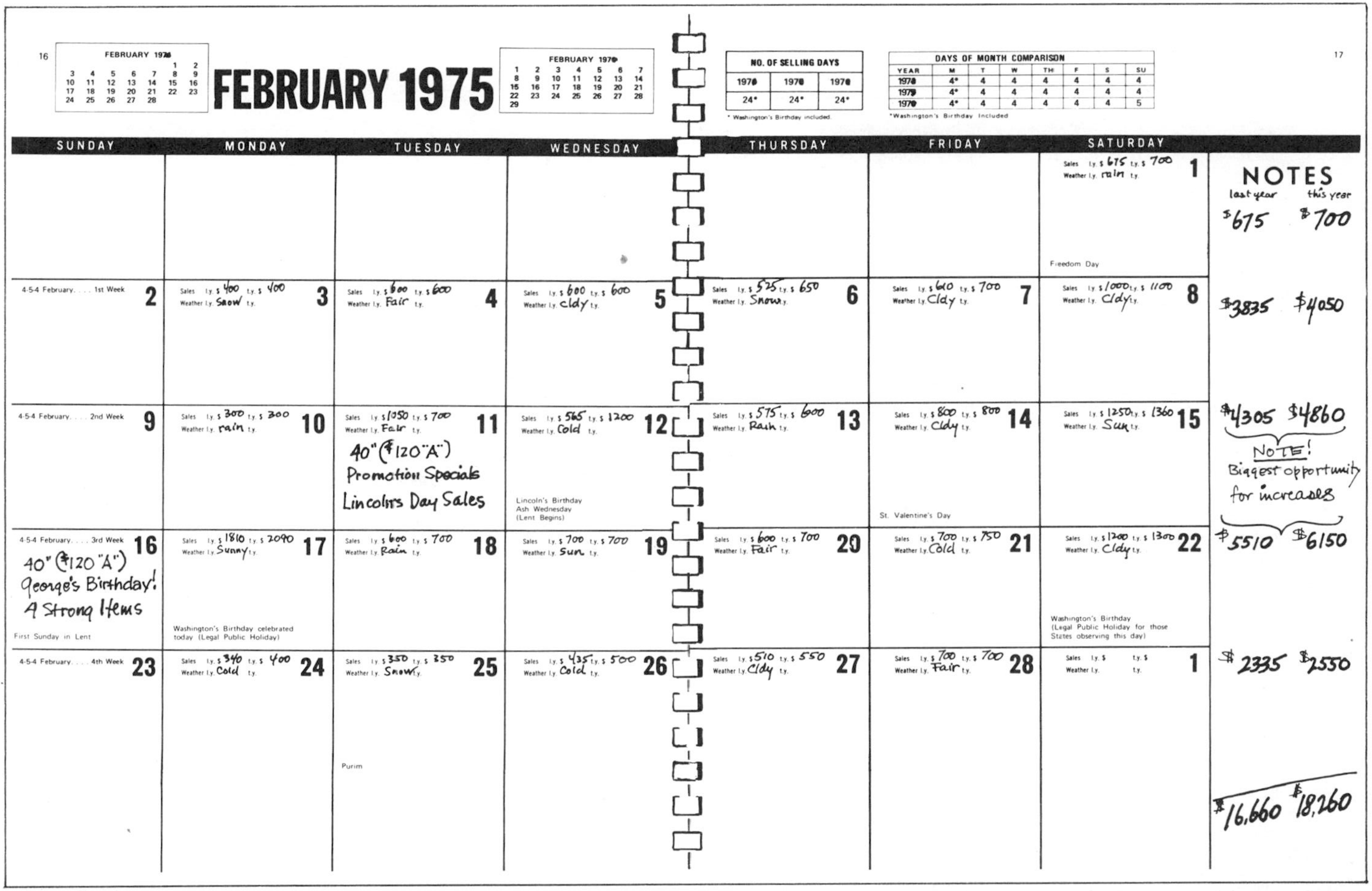

FIGURE 12.7 In the three-month plan the promotion dollars are converted to inches of newspaper space scheduled for specific advertising days. In this planning stage the "A," "B," or "C" promotion objectives are established for each ad. For planning purposes, this store uses an average ad space cost of $3 per inch. Calendar courtesy of National Retail Merchants Association [NRMA], N. Y.

MARCH 1975

MARCH 1974 — 3 4 5 6 7 1 2 / 10 11 12 13 14 8 9 / 17 18 19 20 21 15 16 / 24 25 26 27 28 22 23 / 31 29 30

MARCH 1976 — 1 2 3 4 5 6 / 7 8 9 10 11 12 13 / 14 15 16 17 18 19 20 / 21 22 23 24 25 26 27 / 28 29 30 31

NO. OF SELLING DAYS		
1974	1975	1976
26	26	27

DAYS OF MONTH COMPARISON

YEAR	M	T	W	T	F	S	SU
1974	4	4	4	4	5	5	5
1975	5	4	4	4	4	5	5
1976	5	5	5	4	4	4	4

SUNDAY	MONDAY	TUESDAY	WEDNESDAY	THURSDAY	FRIDAY	SATURDAY	NOTES
						1 Sales ly $1100 ty $1200 · Weather ty Fair	last year this year $1100 $1200
2 4-5-4 March....1st Week — 21"($63 "B") New Spring Brand Item	**3** Sales ly $400 ty $500 · Weather ty Cldy	**4** Sales ly $400 ty $500 · Weather ty Cldy	**5** Sales ly $500 ty $500 · Weather ty Rain	**6** Sales ly $400 ty $450 · Weather ty Cldy	**7** Sales ly $510 ty $550 · Weather ty Fair	**8** Sales ly $1150 ty $1200 · Weather ty Fair	$3360 $3600
9 4-5-4 March....2nd Week · Sales ly $500 ty $550 · Weather ty Cold	**10** Sales ly $500 ty $550 · Weather ty Cold	**11** Sales ly $520 ty $650 · Weather ty Cldy	**12** Sales ly $500 ty $535 · Weather ty Fair	**13** Sales ly $525 ty $600 · Weather ty Fair — 21"($63 "B") Spring Item Feature style	**14** Sales ly $600 ty $675 · Weather ty Cldy · Purim	**15** Sales ly $1200 ty $1300 · Weather ty Fair	$3845 $7210
16 4-5-4 March....3rd Week · Sales ly $560 ty $550 · Weather ty Rain	**17** Sales ly $560 ty $550 · Weather ty Rain · St. Patrick's Day	**18** Sales ly $600 ty $650 · Weather ty Cldy	**19** Sales ly $1000 ty $600 · Weather ty Rain — 42"($126 "A") Pre-Easter Sale 2 or 3 Values	**20** Sales ly $625 ty $750 · Weather ty Cldy — 21"($63 "B")	**21** Sales ly $710 ty $820 · Weather ty Fair · Spring Begins	**22** Sales ly $1250 ty $1400 · Weather ty Sun · Lent Ends	$4305 $4770 Pre-Easter
23 4-5-4 March....4th Week · Sales ly $1650 ty $1725 · Weather ty Sun	**24** Sales ly $1650 ty $1725 · Weather ty Sun	**25** Sales ly $710 ty $800 · Weather ty Fair	**26** Sales ly $650 ty $700 · Weather ty Fair — 42"($126 "A") Easter Promotion 2 Features	**27** Sales ly $750 ty $825 · Weather ty Cldy · Passover (First Day)	**28** Sales ly $830 ty $900 · Weather ty Cldy · Good Friday	**29** Sales ly $1200 ty $1330 · Weather ty Cldy	$4990 $5270 Pre-Easter
30 4-5-4 March....5th Week · Sales ly $600 ty $750 · Weather ty Sun — 21"($63 "A") CLEARANCE! Palm Sunday (Passion Sunday) Easter Sunday	**31** Sales ly $600 ty $750 · Weather ty Sun	**1** Sales ly $ ty · Weather ty	**2** Sales ly $ ty · Weather ty	**3** Sales ly $ ty · Weather ty	**4** Sales ly $ ty · Weather ty	**5** Sales ly $ ty · Weather ty	$690 $750 $18,000 $19,800

FIGURE 12.7 (continued)

APRIL 1975

APRIL 1975						
	1	2	3	4	5	6
7	8	9	10	11	12	13
14	15	16	17	18	19	20
21	22	23	24	25	26	27
28	29	30				

APRIL 1975						
			1	2	3	4
5	6	7	8	9	10	11
12	13	14	15	16	17	18
19	20	21	22	23	24	25
26	27	28	29	30		

NO. OF SELLING DAYS

	1974	1975	1976
	26	26	26

DAYS OF MONTH COMPARISON

YEAR	M	T	W	TH	F	S	SU
1974	5	5	4	4	4	4	4
1975	4	4	5	5	4	4	4
1976	4	4	4	4	5	4	4

Calendar Grid

SUNDAY | MONDAY | TUESDAY | WEDNESDAY | THURSDAY | FRIDAY | SATURDAY

Week of 1st
- MONDAY: (blank)
- TUESDAY **1** — April Fool's Day
- WEDNESDAY **2** — Sales ty $740 ty $550; Weather ty Cldy
- THURSDAY **3** — Sales ty $650 ty $650; Weather ty Fair
- FRIDAY **4** — Sales ty $700 ty $900; Weather ty Fair
- SATURDAY **5** — Sales ty $650 ty $1400; Weather ty Sun
- NOTES: last year this year $4900 $5100 — Pre-Palm Sunday last year

4-5-4 April....1st Week
- SUNDAY **6**
- MONDAY **7** — Sales ty $700 ty $550; Weather ty Fair
- TUESDAY **8** — Sales ty $600 ty $500; Weather ty Cldy
- WEDNESDAY **9** — Sales ty $700 ty $550; Weather ty Fair — 21" ($63 "B") Brand Item for Spring-into-Summer
- THURSDAY **10** — Sales ty $650 ty $700; Weather ty Cldy — Passover (Last Day)
- FRIDAY **11** — Sales ty $650 ty $750; Weather ty Fair
- SATURDAY **12** — Sales ty $1800 ty $1500; Weather ty Fair
- NOTES: $5600 $4500 Pre-Easter last year

4-5-4 April....2nd Week
- SUNDAY **13**
- MONDAY **14** — Sales ty $650 ty $750; Weather ty Fair
- TUESDAY **15** — Sales ty $500 ty $625; Weather ty Cldy
- WEDNESDAY **16** — Sales ty $550 ty $750; Weather ty Cldy — 21" ($63 "B") Runner Item on Spring goods
- THURSDAY **17** — Sales ty $640 ty $825; Weather ty Fair
- FRIDAY **18** — Sales ty $600 ty $850; Weather ty Fair
- SATURDAY **19** — Sales ty $1200 ty $1550; Weather ty Sun
- NOTES: $4000 $5350

4-5-4 April....3rd Week
- SUNDAY **20** — 84" ($252 "A") Spring-into-Summer SALES 6 items
- MONDAY **21** — Sales ty $550 ty $1250; Weather ty Fair
- TUESDAY **22** — Sales ty $500 ty $800; Weather ty Fair
- WEDNESDAY **23** — Sales ty $550 ty $700; Weather ty Cldy — 42" ($126 "A") LAST 3 DAYS of SALE
- THURSDAY **24** — Sales ty $600 ty $800; Weather ty Sun
- FRIDAY **25** — Sales ty $600 ty $900; Weather ty Warm
- SATURDAY **26** — Sales ty $1200 ty $1800; Weather ty Warm
- NOTES: $4000 $6350

4-5-4 April....4th Week
- SUNDAY **27** — No N.P. advertising. Use "interior advertising for E.O.M. Bargain Tables!
- MONDAY **28** — Sales ty $525 ty $650; Weather ty Fair
- TUESDAY **29** — Sales ty $550 ty $600; Weather ty Cldy
- WEDNESDAY **30** — Sales ty $575 ty $550; Weather ty Cldy
- THURSDAY **1** — Sales ty $ ty $; Weather ty
- FRIDAY **2** — Sales ty $ ty $; Weather ty
- SATURDAY **3** — Sales ty $ ty $; Weather ty
- NOTES: $1600 $1800; $20,000 22,000

FIGURE 12.7 (continued)

plays. The signs that you plan to use are started at this stage of the plan. The monthly promotion plan actually "locks in" the sales promotion planning that started months back. Finally, this is your last opportunity to make necessary changes, additions, or eliminations in your promotion plan (Fig. 12.8).

Plan Far Enough in Advance

As stated earlier, allow enough advance time for each of the three stages in the planning sequence. All your planning should begin *no later than one month* before the specific planning period involved. To delay your planning timing can easily leave you frantically scheduling promotion at the last moment.

Generally, most retailers find that planning their sales promotion in these three stages is the most efficient method and coordinates effectively with the store's other planning procedures. When most of the sales promotion is carefully planned well enough in advance, there is still sufficient flexibility to handle the few promotion emergencies that may occur.

Some stores add the weekly plan to their planning sequence. These are mostly highly promotional merchants who feel it is necessary to plan as close to the selling period as possible. This demands a quick-moving, fast-decision-making management backed up by an equally fast merchandising and sales promotion staff.

The Importance of Pre-planning Promotion Expense

Plan a sales promotion program you can afford and then stick to it. Use the principles defined in the section on the three stages of promotion planning as guides for pre-planning your promotion expenditures. If you don't, you may find that you have overspent your allocation before you have completed a season. Or you may discover that you have under promoted your business which has retarded your growth.

Promotion budgets should also be based on past experience, today's needs, and future trends. Once you know how much you are going to spend on promotion, you can more accurately plan the various promotional activities and think about the merchandise you will feature in them. However, both your budget and your promotion plans should be flexible enough so that they can take advantage of any sudden opportunity that might arise.

Need for Coordination

Using the three-month plan and the monthly plan as a guide, you can schedule the merchandise involved to be in the store in time for the promotion. You should also be ready with sufficient, properly trained staff to handle the promotion whether it is a storewide event or the introduction of

MONTH __APRIL__ __YEAR 19XX__

SUNDAY	MONDAY	TUESDAY	WEDNESDAY	THURSDAY	FRIDAY	SATURDAY
		1 *Special note* after-Easter Clearance continues! Use Bargain Tables with *eye-catching signs*	2	3	4	5
6	7	8	9 Dept.24 21" Ⓑ Daily Journal Make Famous Tennis Shirts 2 illustrations	10 NOTE! Start production of signs, etc. for Spring-into Summer SALES	11	12
13	14	15	16 Dept.18 21" Ⓑ Daily Journal New Mood in Co-ordinates 1 illustration	17 "Violette" TRUNK Fashion Show 11 am to 2:30 pm in Dept 14	18	19 note for Display at end of day... Sale Signs go on all displays
20 Dept's 12,18,29 32, 37, 41 84" Ⓐ Sunday Express "Spring-into-Summer SALES	21 Radio time for Sale $100 WRHG-WCWL 30 seconds Run of Program	22	23 all depts. 42" Ⓐ Daily Journal LAST 3 DAYS OF SALE good listings!	24	25 Radio Last 3 Days $85 WRHG-WCWL 30 seconds A.M.&P.M. Drive time	26 WINDOW SIGNS LAST DAY OF SALE
27	28 *Special note:* No N.P. Ads for E.O.M Clearance. Plenty of Bargain Tables with appropriate signs!	29	30			

FIGURE 12.8 In this detailed monthly plan the retailer has scheduled those departments that will have advertising as well as which specific merchandise will be advertised. The timing of promotion is confirmed and media selection is determined along with the promotion objective of each ad. In this final planning stage, special attention is given to interior advertising, such as signs, bargain tables, and an in-store presentation of new merchandise. The reserve money set aside in the three-month plan is to be used for radio commercials to add power to the store's annual promotion event.

new products. Your window and interior displays should be timed to coordinate with your advertising and possible free publicity. You should also build enthusiasm among your staff for every major promotion so that it reaches its highest peak when the promotion is launched. If you do not use this carefully prepared plan to coordinate the entire store's energies, you will waste not only a great deal of the store's potential sales and profits but also the money you invested in the promotion.

Promote Through Display

Your store itself is your best promotion asset. It is your biggest advertising medium because it can deliver more significant customer circulation than any other advertising activity, especially when most of your customers work or live nearby or if it is located in a high-traffic shopping area. Consequently, it will pay to concentrate an important part of your promotion money and effort on window and interior display.

Window Display

Windows are the expression of your particular personality and often they are your store's *first contact* with the public. Good windows draw attention to your merchandise, and when the contents are most attractive, will invite customers into your store to the point of sale. If your store is in an enclosed shopping center where there are no store windows in the traditional manner, the entire store from the entrance should appear like a typical window. Therefore, it, too, must be attractive and inviting enough to bring shoppers into the store (Fig. 12.9).

Basic principles of window display

To be effective, your windows should attract the customers' attention enough to draw them into your store. This can best be accomplished by emphasizing one creative merchandise theme (and variations on the theme) in such a manner that it persuades customers to want to own the goods. The presentation of this theme should be simple and tasteful and should make a lasting impression of your store's personality (Fig. 12.10).

The importance of one theme

Because your windows must actually stop and hold the attention of a passerby almost in a split second, you must have a display that gets one merchandise idea across in the shortest possible time. To do this, the merchandise on display should tell just one story. For example, if you want to feature vacation fashion goods, concentrate on presenting items like swimwear, colorful tops, and shorts along with a picnic basket on a beach towel. Then make the theme meaningful by using a short, catchy phrase on an appropriate sign, for example, "Color your vacation bright!" The card should be easy to read and big enough to be visible amidst the colorful merchandise. If you were to add dressy apparel or raincoats just to show

FIGURE 12.9 How a retailer in an enclosed mall effectively uses his entrance to attractively present the entire store.

Courtesy Barnstable's, Crown Center, Kansas City, Mo. and Retail Reporting Bureau, New York.

FIGURE 12.10 In a simple, attractive presentation this pre-season window highlights a theme that heralds the new Spring fashions. The lattice effect in the background serves as a screen to reduce the visibility of the interior of the store.

Courtesy The Capitol, Fayetteville, N. C.

that you have these items in stock, you would only confuse the viewers and quickly lose their attention.

The institutional store uses its windows to express the variations in the sales promotion cycle. During the pre-season phase its windows should feature new, prestigious items in simple, imaginative arrangements that are not crowded. Theme signs emphasizing the newness of the merchandise are important and price tickets can be used if they are discreet and do not distract from the character of the display.

Dress windows for the season

As runners develop during the in-season cycle, they should get window emphasis. Theme signs should tell customers about what most shoppers want at prices they want to pay. Since price cards should get more attention at this time, they should not be too small nor hidden in the arrangement.

End-of-season windows are clearance windows. They can show more merchandise than during the previous periods, but they should not be crowded with too much goods, for this may reduce the amount of stock that can be sold in the store. Moreover, removing an item from a display to satisfy a customer is usually troublesome.

Many institutional stores create effective end-of-season displays without using any merchandise. They place large, tastefully executed signs in the windows. These signs focus on savings and price. Accompanying the signs are simple but imaginative display ideas that dramatize the savings or values at clearance time.

During the pre-season and in-season cycles the semi-promotional store employs display very much in the style of the institutional store. During the end-of-season promotion period this store also uses dramatic but tasteful signs in its windows and creates attractive groupings of clearance goods combined with highly visible price cards. It avoids the crowded appearance characteristic of the highly promotional store.

No matter what the season, the windows of the aggressive-promotional store always say, "You'll find lots of merchandise at low prices and you will get great savings as well!" To communicate this message, it packs its window with merchandise and large, colorful signs that dramatize the selling theme. Price cards feature large size prices and emphasize the savings customers can obtain if they purchase the items on display.

Make sure that your windows look balanced. Many retailers who dress their own windows are unaware that a poorly balanced arrangement looks untidy, complicated, and unattractive. To correct this, go out and look at the window from the street and then adjust the arrangement until it has correct balance.

View your windows from the street

The two kinds of balance that you can use to create your window arrangements are (a) *formal balance* which is achieved by placing articles of equal size at equal distances from the center and (b) *informal balance* which is based on placing unequally sized articles at unequal distances from the center (Fig. 12.11).

FIGURE 12.11 This window's formal balance arrangement is accomplished by placing merchandise and decorative "props" equidistant from the center unit, the suit form. The architectural shape of the background further emphasizes the formal balance.

Courtesy Bloomingdales, New York and Merchandise Display News, Westbury, N. Y.

Informal balance is achieved by placing a dominant grouping of merchandise, including a mannequin, at the left side of the window, while a smaller arrangement of merchandise and a sign are at the right side of the presentation.

Courtesy Arnold Constable, New York and Merchandise Display News, Westbury, N. Y.

FIGURE 12.12 This imaginative display employs carefully positioned spotlights to attract the viewer's attention and to highlight the details of the merchandise.

Courtesy Bergdorf Goodman, New York and Retail Reporting Bureau, New York.

Use harmonious colors

Most people are sensitive to colors. Therefore, choose those that are appropriate to a season in order to create a pleasant feeling in people who stop to look at your windows. Pale blues, yellows, grassy greens, or pinks, for example, communicate a spirit of spring; browns or tans with orange tones create a definite fall impression.

Importance of window lighting

Since most people are attracted to light, focus attention on the merchandise in your window by using light. For example, a specially placed spotlight will emphasize important details of an article (Fig. 12.12). Colored lighting effects will increase the color impressions that add to the window's attraction. However, interesting lighting treatments are of little value during the day, particularly if the sunlight is so overpowering that it seems to fill the entire window. Then your windows must depend even more on the arrangement along with the colors you choose for decorative purposes.

Keep your displays clean

A good part of your store's personality depends on the cleanliness of your windows and interior displays. Your display is like a bright stage where every speck of dirt or finger mark, every bad fold, crease, or dent is magnified to the shopper who looks at your display.

Use a good household glass cleaning preparation to clean the glass shelves in the display areas and then wipe them with a clean cloth. Wipe wood or plastic display units with clean dust cloths. Do not use oil-treated rags. Keep your window and showcase glass clean on the *inside* as well as on the outside. Check for burned out lights and replace them as soon as possible.

The more often a window is changed, the better, for windows are like newspapers—they get old fast. Dressing a window can be a chore, but every window should be changed or rearranged at least once every two weeks. After two weeks it becomes less and less attractive and just eats up money.

When to change windows

A window is easier to dress and is more attractive when you use proper fixtures. Buy inexpensive fixtures that fit your current needs but that can be discarded when more up-to-date units become available. When you buy fixtures, try to get those that serve several display purposes, and whenever possible, select the ones that can function on the selling floor as well as in the windows (Fig. 12.13).

Importance of good display fixtures

FIGURE 12.13 The versatile fixtures that display the merchandise in this window can be easily used on the selling floor or in "interior advertising."

Courtesy Arnold Constable, New York and Merchandise Display News, Westbury, N.Y.

Some windows have backgrounds that completely block out the store, others have no background at all, and still others have partial backgrounds that separate the window from the store's interior but permit shoppers to see past them into the store. Each has its advantages and disadvantages, but no matter which background you use, there are certain things you can do to obtain the most value from it.

Permanently positioned backgrounds that block off the store should be used to their fullest extent. They should not be left naked; instead, use them to hold signs, posters, decorative material, or display props. Merchandise or "props" can be suspended from them in an attractive manner or special shelving can be placed against the background for presenting smaller articles (Fig. 12.14).

FIGURE 12.14 An enlarged photoprint of an 1880 newspaper page has been attached to the permanently positioned background of this window to easily create an attractive setting for accessories.

Courtesy I. Miller, New York and Merchandise Display News, Westbury, N. Y.

If your windows have no background or just partial ones, create displays that use the store itself as a background. There are display fixtures that contain partial backgrounds attached to a unit that gives the effect of a backdrop. Or you can use "see-through" fixtures with shelves that permit the store to be part of the total effect.

Every time a window is changed, people passing by should stop to look at it. It should create sufficient interest for some of them to come in and buy. After you dress a window, check it by standing outside and observing how many people stop, what they look at, what they say, and how many walk into the store. In this way you can learn whether or not the window is drawing sufficient attention. Another method of checking a window is to count the number of people who come into the store and ask for something displayed in the window. Always shop your competitors' windows for ideas and themes, and note the good ones in your calendar for next year.

**Check your
window displays**

Interior Display

Since you spend a lot of money and energy to get shoppers into your store, once they are there, you must excite them further and intensify their interest through dramatic interior displays. Instead of using the term

FIGURE 12.15 This chart demonstrates (on the left) how retailers use fixtures, tables, ledges, and wall areas for more effective interior advertising that concentrates on one theme and uses signs correctly for a persuasive selling message. The sketches (on the right) point out display usage that should be avoided.

"interior display," think of the term "interior advertising." This means
that each interior display should attract the customers' attention to a
merchandise idea instead of being used as a decorative unit or a space filler.
Remember that prospective customers are now in your store with money to
spend and they are ready to make one or more purchase decisions. How
many of these decisions they make may well depend on your interior
advertising.

Most of the principles and techniques used to create good window
displays apply to interior advertising. For example, each display of merchandise aided by a selling message whether it is on a ledge, highlighted on
the floor, or placed on a counter or inside a showcase should tell one story
(Fig. 12.15). Interior displays should be changed more often than displays
in your windows. When you have many display areas, it is a good idea to
change one-half of them one week and the other half the following week. In
this way, you can give the appearance of having fresh new interior advertising all the time.

Because many impulse and related sales are the result of good interior
advertising, the use of open display fixtures (Fig. 12.16) is one of your most
valuable visual selling techniques. The merchandise for sale is also the
display. It frequently can be handled and examined by shoppers without

**Advantages and
disadvantages of
open interior
displays**

FIGURE 12.16 Shopper involvement is the important feature of this open interior
display. This form of interior advertising permits the customer to examine the merchandise without the help of sales people. The mannequin adds an eye-catching
benefit to this presentation.

Courtesy Belk's, Asheville, N. C.

help from salespeople. In most cases, it eliminates the barriers between your goods and your customers. Impulse buying is increased because the customer gets closely involved with the merchandise.

However, open displays have several disadvantages. If they are not skillfully arranged, they may cheapen the image of the store. They increase pilferage, and they also can create soiled or damaged merchandise.

To increase the advantages and overcome the disadvantages of certain interior displays, use your wall areas that are high enough to be seen from a distance. The tops of counters also provide highly visible display areas.

Floor units placed on platforms with a simple railing effect made of posts, chains, or decorator's cord may be used to keep customers from disarranging the display. Whenever a interior display has been disturbed, insist that the salespeople rearrange the unit immediately.

Signs

You wouldn't buy costly newspaper space and leave it blank. You wouldn't spend money on radio time and remain silent. You must not permit your interior advertising to be *mute!* Even though your attractive

FIGURE 12.17 This sign machine is useful for small stores because it can be easily operated to produce attractive signs quickly. A tasteful variety of type styles is available.

Courtesy Showcard Machine Co., Chicago, Ill.

Pure Cashmere

strikingly beautiful

$39.85

General Electric

TOASTERS

Deep chrome
finish

15.98

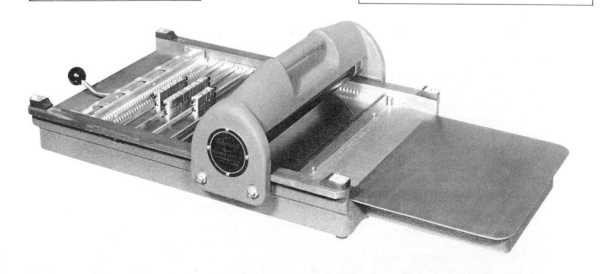

display stops the customers in the store and holds their attention, you must communicate a selling idea to them. Displays that catch the eye are doing half the job. It is the printed word that persuades the shopper to take buying action. That is why every interior and window display must have a sign. A simple, clever message is best, but even a straightforward statement is acceptable as long as the shopper is motivated to purchase the articles on display. Where possible, small price cards should be used.

Hastily or amateurishly scribbled signs will not sell goods and will not express your store's image properly. There are several sign making machines available for small stores that can be used by any employee after a short instruction session (Fig. 12.17).

Signs must be hand-lettered, expertly drawn or machine printed

Aisle Tables

Aisle tables are an excellent way of selling directly from a certain kind of interior display. These tables attract shopper attention in the same way that a well-planned display does. Moreover, when they are placed in areas where traffic is slow, you can increase shopping action if the goods are right. Some stores often create imaginative versions of aisle tables by using decorated pushcarts painted in bright colors. Display dealers often sell unusual flower carts made of bent wire that can be used as distinctive aisle tables.

Although aisle tables can be arranged to direct store traffic, if they are improperly located, they hinder or block store traffic, create congestion, and draw customers away from regular merchandise. Tables are best used for bargain items, but they can be useful in presenting new or unusual merchandise. But whether used singly or arranged in a group, tables require signs with a selling message.

WHAT THIS CHAPTER TOLD YOU

1. Everything you do to get people into the store and sell them merchandise is called sales promotion.

2. The aims of sales promotion are to (a) build a clearly defined store personality, (b) generate traffic, (c) reflect merchandise strengths, and (d) increase gross margin.

3. Decide whether you are an institutional, semi-promotional, or an aggressive-promotional store, and then promote within that framework.

4. Define your sales promotion objectives by using the A-B-C formula.

5. Concentrate promotion activity on your most profitable departments and classifications.

6. Plan your sales promotion cycle with customer buying needs in mind.

7. Plan ahead by using the six-month, three-month, and monthly promotion planning methods.

8. For most small stores, windows and interior displays are the best form of sales promotion.

13

How to Make
Your Advertising
Pay Off

WHAT THIS CHAPTER IS ABOUT

Advertising is one of the essential sales promotion tools that retailers use to bring customers to their stores. Although the majority of merchants concentrate on newspaper advertising, some find radio and TV best for their stores and others prefer direct mail. Many retailers combine all or some of the media to make their promotions successful. Since advertising costs money, this chapter discusses how you can get maximum return for your advertising dollar.

What Makes an Ad Pay Off?

Customers today are so assaulted by all forms of advertising that they turn off, tune out, or ignore advertising that instantly fails to relate to their current wants. To be effective, therefore, your advertising must *immediately turn their attention to your message.* Just as your windows must stop people passing by, so your advertising must stop newspaper readers and radio or TV audiences and have them react to your message strongly enough to take positive action.

Your advertising must *inform customers of the good quality* of your merchandise or your store. It should emphasize the details that relate to the customers' needs and dramatize them. For example, when you advertise mattresses, think about what the customer wants from a mattress. If it is sleeping comfort, your ad should dramatize how the mattress is constructed to support the user's back. If you believe that your customers are looking for values in mattresses, then your ad should focus on prices and emphasize the savings they will get.

Your advertising must *ask for the customer to take action.* The ads should contain an invitation to "come in and see how comfortable these mattresses are" or to "shop now for the best values and selection." Coupons in newspaper ads and in direct-mail advertising are good ways to ask for customer action.

Advertising Should Be Continuous

Not every one in your market needs your goods at the same time, nor do they all see or hear your advertising all the time. However, every day, every week, some of them want your kind of merchandise. Therefore, you must continually communicate with your loyal patrons as well as your prospective customers.

To reach all of your customers all the time, it is better to plan to reach them more frequently through a series of attractive smaller ads instead of using a few very big ads that can exhaust your advertising budget. Because people quickly forget advertising, it is necessary for you to remind them that you have the goods they want when they are in the market for such merchandise.

Spend Advertising Money Carefully

To maintain a continuous program of advertising requires great care in budgeting. Don't waste money by scattering precious dollars in all the media available. Plan to concentrate your media budget to achieve maximum frequency of advertising. Competition for customer interest is so intense that when your advertising appears infrequently, you become less important to customers. They will be attracted to other stores who have become important because they have adopted a policy of advertising concentration and frequency in carefully selected media. Therefore, direct your expenditures so that you become important enough in the medium that gives you the best results.

A Good Advertising Style Is Important

Successful retailers have learned that a good advertising style pays off. Therefore, to compete with the best retail advertising, your style must be equally good, or better. Whether you use newspapers, direct mail, radio, or TV, it is important that your advertising style achieves the following objectives:

FIGURE 13.1 Note the high recognition value of this group of ads. Even though they appeared over an extended period and involved varied groups of merchandise and promotion objectives, they clearly identified this store's unique character.

Courtesy B. Altman & Co. Inc., New York.

1. *Select the correct audience.* Your advertising should be directed to that segment of the total public with which you have already established a valuable relationship. Don't throw away advertising money trying to sell groups of shoppers, however large, who won't appreciate your goods or feel at home in your store.

2. *Identify the store.* Develop an advertising style that identifies the store quickly, definitely, favorably, and can be used for a long time. High recognition value is a prime requirement of good advertising (Fig. 13.1).

FIGURE 13.2 This is "A" advertising for an institutional store and an aggressive-promotional mass merchandiser. Notice how both ads emphasize price appeal to express each store's distinctive personality.

Courtesy Garfinkle's, Washington, D. C. and Neisner's Department Stores, Rochester, N. Y.

3. *Express the store's personality.* Your advertising style should clearly express the characteristics that add up to your store's particular image. If you are operating a price-promotional store, your advertising treatment should quickly transmit this impression to the customer. If you want to build a quality fashion reputation, your ad style should clearly indicate this to the customer (Fig. 13.2).

Avoid the Trial-and-Error Method

In order to establish a good advertising style suitable for your store, avoid the trial-and-error method. Rarely has this haphazard approach produced a really worthwhile advertising personality. Instead, work with a retail advertising specialist or a creative advertising agency with retail experience. Money spent for this kind of service will quickly prevent misdirecting your advertising dollars into the wrong style for your business.

What Is a Good Advertising Style?

A good advertising style is the *total impression* of the various elements that make up your advertising. All these units must work together to express the store's personality. In this way they reinforce each other to build the best advertising style for your store. These units are (1) your store signature, (2) your selling message (headlines and copy), (3) your layout, and (4) your illustrations.

Store signature

The name of your store is the most important item that you have to sell! Therefore, your store signature should be distinctive and should clearly reflect its personality. The way it looks must represent your particular store. For example, if you operate a hardware store, your advertising signature should give the impression of strength and durability. Therefore, its design should reflect a masculine personality instead of a delicate femininity (Fig. 13.3). Furthermore, your store signature should not resemble that of any other retailers in your community, no matter what kind of goods they sell.

FIGURE 13.3 The first store signature design sketch is more suitable for a hardware store because it clearly reflects the strength and durability associated with hardware goods. The other design is appropriate for a fine jewelry shop or a quality china-glassware store.

When your signature appears in print advertising (newspapers, mailings, and handbills) or on television, it should, because of its distinctive design style, quickly suggest to the customer that you are either a quality institutional store or an aggressive-promotional store. Your radio signature should also transmit to your customers the kind of store you are. Skillful use of voice, music, and sound effects can easily produce a "personality signature" that represents your store accurately.

Selling message

This should tell a specific story about the advertised merchandise or service. It should not deal in generalities, for you should assume that the customer is a very self-interested person who wants the answer to these questions: *WHAT is it? WHY is it GOOD? WHAT will it do for ME* (the customer)? *HOW MUCH is it?* (Fig. 13.4).

Your selling message does not necessarily have to appear in the order described above because this depends on what your ad should stress first. However, make sure that you direct your headlines and copy to the self-

FIGURE 13.4 This small space ad is effectively directed to the self-interest of the customer. Note how the selling message clearly answers the questions: What does it do for me? What is it? Why is it good? How much is it?

Courtesy Jacobson's, Jackson, Mich.

interest of customers who do not care about your reasons for selling the advertised goods; what they want to know is why they should own the goods.

Know the customer segment you are talking to and write for them in such a way that they can understand your message. Use every day "people talk" that expresses enthusiasm about the merchandise and the store. The message should cover the important answers to the customers' questions discussed above, but no more. Complicated phrases, tricky double meanings, and word affectations only block the delivery of the selling message.

Good copy is based on good product information; therefore, the more the person who writes the headlines and copy knows about the goods, the better the ad. You should keep the message believable by avoiding exaggerations. Words like stupendous, spectacular, fabulous, amazing, incredible, even if true, are rarely believed by the readers because they have been continually exposed to all kinds of high-pressure advertising that uses these overworked words.

Don't try to get all the merchandise features into one ad. It is better to focus on a few significant answers to the readers' questions than to lose their attention because of excess detail. Use short, easy-to-grasp sentences to hold their interest.

Layout

Essentially, this is a blueprint for building your ad. Without a layout, there is no way to tell artists, copywriters, typesetters, or printers exactly how the advertising should look. Furthermore, the layout gives you the opportunity to see what your ad will look like in the early preparation stages. You can then correct, change, or adjust the various elements of the ad before it is too late, for last-minute changes usually cost money (Fig. 13.5).

In radio advertising the layout is the script that arranges the message, music, and sound effects in the manner in which they will be broadcast. In television advertising the layout is called the *story board*. It is a series of sequence sketches of how the advertising action will appear. The story board is also a guide for the production phases of TV advertising and can be changed or amended prior to final preparation (Fig. 13.6).

Illustrations

In print or television advertising the picture is the most important element because it is the featured attention getter. When properly done, illustrations that attract the reader's eye build interest and confidence in the product and the customer goes on to read or listen to the selling message. As far as possible, the illustration should faithfully represent the merchandise.

Institutional and semi-promotional stores should use illustrations that express the special character of the store. Many such stores can create further advertising identity by using a distinctive style of illustration. Illustrations for aggressive-promotional store ads should stress the details of the merchandise (Fig. 13.7).

We let the alligators loose

but they're easy to manage, nevertheless, in our knits to put together as you please. From our David Crystal sportswear collection — an easy jacket in navy or red, 40.00 Classic white long sleeved shirt, 18.00 Both with alligator insignia. Navy pull-on pants, 22.00 All, polyester knit, sizes 8 to 18. Spectator Dress Shop, Second Floor, Lord & Taylor — call Wisconsin 7-3300 And at Manhasset, Garden City, Ridgewood-Paramus, Millburn, Westchester and Stamford

FIGURE 13.5 This is a layout for a small ad along with the actual ad as it appeared in the newspaper. This particular ad features a dominant illustration as a focal point. Note how the advertiser can easily visualize how his advertising will look before he gets involved with the expense of preparing the ad. The layout also serves as a blueprint for guiding the artist and for establishing the exact areas for the headline and copy message.

Courtesy Lord & Taylor, New York.

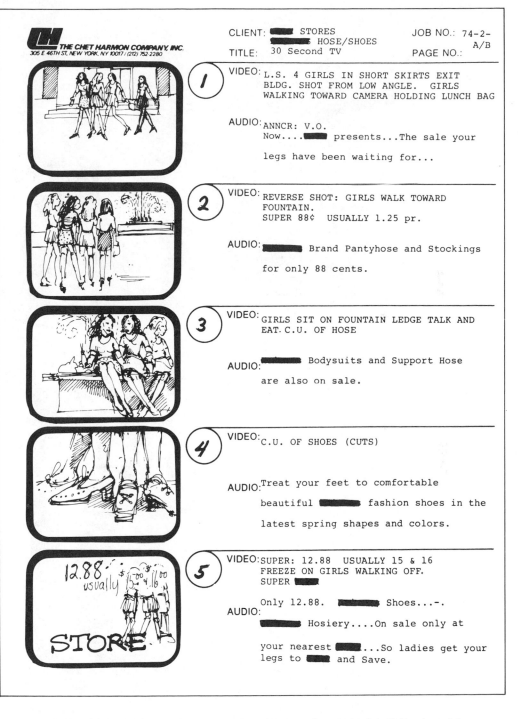

CLIENT: ████ STORES

████████ HOSE/SHOES

TITLE: 30 Second TV

JOB NO.: 74-2-A/B

PAGE NO.:

THE CHET HARMON COMPANY, INC.
305 E 46TH ST, NEW YORK, NY 10017 / (212) 752-2280

1

VIDEO: L.S. 4 GIRLS IN SHORT SKIRTS EXIT BLDG. SHOT FROM LOW ANGLE. GIRLS WALKING TOWARD CAMERA HOLDING LUNCH BAG

AUDIO: ANNCR: V.O.
Now....████ presents...The sale your legs have been waiting for...

2

VIDEO: REVERSE SHOT: GIRLS WALK TOWARD FOUNTAIN.
SUPER 88¢ USUALLY 1.25 pr.

AUDIO: ████ Brand Pantyhose and Stockings for only 88 cents.

3

VIDEO: GIRLS SIT ON FOUNTAIN LEDGE TALK AND EAT. C.U. OF HOSE

AUDIO: ████ Bodysuits and Support Hose are also on sale.

4

VIDEO: C.U. OF SHOES (CUTS)

AUDIO: Treat your feet to comfortable beautiful ████ fashion shoes in the latest spring shapes and colors.

5

VIDEO: SUPER: 12.88 USUALLY 15 & 16
FREEZE ON GIRLS WALKING OFF.
SUPER ████

AUDIO: Only 12.88. ████ Shoes...-.
████ Hosiery....On sale only at your nearest ████...So ladies get your legs to ████ and Save.

FIGURE 13.6 A television story board for a 30-second commercial. Notice how this method of planning carefully coordinates the T.V. pictures and their verbal messages.

Courtesy The Chet Harmon Co., New York.

LORD & TAYLOR'S MAJER MAN LOOKS LIKE A MILLION—
His sumptuously soft jacket is camel hair, 150.00 Slacks are a light wool,
in plaids or solids, even waist sizes, 45.00 to 55.00 Understated. Easy.
And impressively tailored. The kind of riches you'll find all through our
Majer collection in The Man's Shop, Tenth Floor, Lord & Taylor, Fifth Avenue at
39th Street, WI 7-3300—and at all Lord & Taylor stores.

Lord & Taylor · Fifth Avenue · Manhasset · Garden City · Webtchester · Millburn · Ridgewood Paramus · Stamford · West Hartford · Boston · Bala-Cynwyd · Jenkintown · Washington-Chevy Chase · Falls Church · Atlanta · Oak Brook · Woodfield · Dallas · Houston

5402 MAR'75
M.P. 39

FIGURE 13.7 The illustration at the left expresses the special character of an institutional store. The illustration on the right is ideally suited for an aggressive-promotional store.

Courtesy Lord & Taylor, New York and Metro Associated Services, Inc., New York.

Not all store advertising requires an illustration in order to be effective. Often, institutional or semi-promotional stores will employ an unusual headline in a dramatic style as an attention-getter instead of an illustration. This can be extremely productive for a special event or a price promotion (Fig. 13.8).

FIGURE 13.8 This institutional store uses only typography to dramatically attract the reader's attention. Notice how the price is the main focal point.

Courtesy Bolton's, New York.

Effective Newspaper Advertising

Because they wish to reach the largest number of potential customers, retailers, as a group, use newspapers more than any other advertising medium. Nearly everyone reads a daily paper and readers are accustomed to shop newspaper advertising to get information on the merchandise they want.

**Advantages of
newspaper
advertising**

Using newspapers for your advertising allows you to set definite times for your ads because you can choose the days that are best for you. You may prefer to advertise new items early in the week and immediate-response promotions at the end of the week. Newspaper ads also permit you to be flexible with your space; you can run a quarter-page or less one day and use a much larger unit another day.

Another advantage is that you can usually have your ad placed on the same page on those days you advertise. Readers will then become conditioned to looking for your ad when they turn to this page. Most newspapers will cooperate with you in arranging for a definite page on the days you run your ads. The more frequently you schedule your ads, the more you will find the paper willing to insure your page position. The best position can be determined only by experimentation or from the sound advice of the paper's advertising department. For example, men's wear or hardware is best placed in the sports section, while children's or ladies' fashions are good for the women's or society pages.

Because many newspapers publish special sections such as bride's supplements, home furnishing guides, or do-it-yourself sections, they help you reach very special customer groups.

Among the disadvantages of newspaper advertising are intense competition for reader attention, the short life of your ad, poor reproduction of your illustrations, and, most important, the limited time people have for newspaper reading because of distractions such as television, increased participation in community activities, and more time devoted to sports activities either as participants or spectators.

Disadvantages of newspaper advertising

Another disadvantage is that it takes more time to prepare effective ads for newspapers. Not long ago, retailers had three to four days to get their advertising prepared by the paper. Now it can take a week in many newspapers. Moreover, since many papers no longer provide proofs, in order to avoid errors the advertiser may have to go to the paper to check his ad before it appears.

A major disadvantage is *wasted* circulation. How many newspapers are bought by your market segment? You may be advertising to a very small part of the paper's total circulation. Or you may be missing potential customers because the paper's distribution, especially in suburban or rural areas, doesn't reach enough of your market.

When there is more than one paper in your area, the first point to consider is the quality of circulation. You can get circulation figures from the newspapers, but it is not how large the circulation is that counts; it is how many potential customers are within the circulation area of the papers. Also, when you examine these figures, determine if you are duplicating circulation in your particular customer segment if you advertise in more than one paper. Duplication can be wasteful.

More than one paper

Next, determine which paper has the biggest circulation among your potential customers. Remember that it is the quality of the circulation that is important, not the amount. If you play the circulation numbers game, you may not reach the biggest group of your kind of shoppers.

Another consideration is the advertising rate per inch. If two papers have the same inch rate, but paper A reaches twice as many of your potential customers as paper B, all other things being equal, B is twice as expensive as A.

People usually react to newspaper advertising in one of three ways: (1) They really don't see it, even though they may glance at it. (2) They do not like it and reject it. (3) They like what they see and are attracted to the message. According to the Newspaper Advertising Bureau Inc., "the most important single factor determining how many people will read any newspaper ad is *the skill and technique used in preparing the ad.*" If you wish to be sure that your advertising produces the results that make your expenditures worthwhile, do not ignore the importance of employing the best technical skills and advertising experience you can get.

How people react to newspaper advertising

To be effective, your layouts should contain four basic qualities. They should (1) be simple in arrangement and easy to read, (2) contain visual elements that catch the reader's eye, (3) reflect the store's personality, and (4) maintain continuity of impression. Regardless of size, ads that lack these qualities usually fail to get sufficient reader attention.

Four principles of effective newspaper ad layouts

The Layout Should Be Simple in Arrangement and Easy to Read. This requires an orderly layout of the various elements (the signature, the type areas, the illustration) so that the main idea or message is easily understood. Ads that are easily read are easy to buy from. Complicated layouts usually repel the reader.

The Layout Should Contain Elements that Catch the Reader's Eye. Your ad should arrest the reader's attention and direct the eyes to that part of the layout that conveys the dominant message. It is at this focal point that the ad takes its first step in telling your story. This focal point can be an attractive illustration or an exciting headline. Even one word or a price dramatically displayed can do this (Fig. 13.8).

The Layout Should Reflect the Store's Personality. Ads with simple layouts and eye-catching treatment are doing only half the job. The layout must also represent the character of the store. A highly promotional store should use layout to reflect its price-appeal character in a bold, aggressive style. A quality fashion or housewares store must impart its special flavor in its layout or it will lose readership. The best advertising tools for projecting your store personality properly are your signature, the type faces and borders you select, and the character of your illustrations. How your layout assembles these units into an arrangement that best suits your store's personality will determine how well your ad is identified with your store.

The Layout Should Maintain Continuity of Impression. Your layout format must be versatile enough to maintain the continuity of your distinctive ad style no matter what task it has to perform. It should be able to introduce new products or styles as well as clear old stock without sacrificing its basic character and identity or becoming boring after frequent exposure (see Fig. 13.1).

To develop advertising that best represents your kind of store, use the following creative steps as a guide.

Place Your Signature at the Top of the Ad. As stated earlier, your signature is your best ''item'' for it represents your biggest investment—your name. Shouldn't this valuable property be proudly positioned at (or near) the top of the ad instead of at the bottom buried under type or illustrations? If the signature is placed at the top, it will quickly identify the store and help establish the personality of the rest of the ad because the reader's eye has been trained to start reading from top to bottom.

Select Type Faces that Best Express the Character of Your Store. Type faces come in all sizes and weights, from very light to very heavy in appearance. Some of them stand upright (Roman) while others slant or tilt at an angle (italic). By carefully selecting type by size and weight, you can easily give readers the correct impression of your advertising personality.

LARGE
HEAVY TYPE

like this imparts to the reader that your store emphasizes aggressive price promotion.

Small light type

like this is better for a prestige store that is known for quality and style. You can select type faces that suggest delicacy and

Femininity

or you can select type faces that suggest ruggedness and

MASCULINITY

Whatever type face you choose, select one or two that will definitely establish your distinctive personality.

Use Variety in Type Faces. This technique can add further distinction and more eye-catching qualities to your advertising style. There are many interesting combinations to use that define your advertising personality.

a small light type
COMBINED WITH A
HEAVY TYPE IN
A LARGE SIZE

can create a more exciting headline style for an aggressive-promotional retailer's ads.

Reversing this format,

A tasteful
large light type
**combined with a
small heavy type**

can be suitable for a quality fashion store.

Combinations like the above provide eye attraction as well as establish your advertising personality. However, don't get reckless and use too many different type faces. Two suitable type faces are enough. Here, too, it is important to maintain simplicity when you are using type.

Place the Illustration to Stand Out Clearly. Since the art work should not interfere with the readability of the message, avoid having the illustration break the flow of the copy or separate headlines from the prices and the text. Headlines, price, and copy should be grouped into one easy-to-read arrangement by placing the illustration over or alongside the type section (Fig. 13.9). Multiple units of illustrations should be massed together as if they were one single illustration. This will keep your ad from having a scattered, complicated look that distracts the reader.

Use Type Rules, Borders, or Boxes to Tie Various Elements Together. Boxes, borders, and rules are very versatile. They can frame your ad, particularly if it is small, and thus keep neighboring ads from crowding your space (see Fig. 12.5). Rules and boxes can also keep miscellaneous elements within your ad from wandering all over the space. Boxes are especially helpful in providing the simple arrangement which is a leading quality of good ad layout.

Borders, boxes, and rules are also used to frame illustrations so that they will be more eye-catching. Headlines often will gain more attention if they are placed within an interesting box shape.

Newspapers, printers, and creative services can provide you with a

Come in, write or phone 362-3060

Livingston's

Five piece traveler: your Fall wardrober complete with cardigan, skirt, vest, pants and dicky—coordinated florals and solids in wine or green. All are machine or handwashable knits of polyester and acrylic; 12 to 20. Francisco Shop **Five pieces 50.00**

GRANT AVE. • CHESTNUT ST. • STONESTOWN • PALO ALTO • HILLSDALE • SAN JOSE • MARIN

FIGURE 13.9 This ad uses attention-getting artwork without interfering with the readability of the message. Notice how the two fashion figures are grouped together to create a massed illustration effect.

Courtesy Livingston's, San Francisco, Calif.

varied selection of decorative boxes, rules, or borders, many of which have been designed by talented artists.

Other Advertising Media

Although the newspaper is the backbone of most retail sales promotion planning, you should consider other media that many retailers, large and small, have used successfully. These include direct advertising, broadcast advertising, magazines, billboards, and special local publications. Only the biggest budgets can productively use all the media listed above. However, you should be aware of the advantages and disadvantages of all available media so that you can plan what is best for your store.

Direct advertising is divided into two segments. The first, direct mail, concerns advertising that uses the post office to reach the customer; the second concerns material that is distributed in the neighborhood or inside the store. Both forms of direct advertising have been successfully employed by retailers, often at a lower cost than other ad media.

Direct advertising

When you advertise in the newspapers or on broadcast media, you are never sure that enough customers see or hear your advertising. They may have skipped past your newspaper ad or their radios or TV sets were not turned on when your advertising was on the air. Also, there is a lot of waste circulation in reaching people who are not interested in what you are selling. Not everyone in the total market can be your customer.

Advantages of direct mail

By using direct mail advertising, you can more accurately select those people who may be your customers; and you can directly deliver your advertising message to this special segment.

Direct mail advertising can be sent to your most loyal clientele as well as to selected lists of prospects who would appreciate your store and the goods you sell. Thus, you can control your advertising circulation with a minimum of waste. In addition, you have much less advertising competition than in the mass media and your prospect can give more attention to your advertising if it is interesting and attractive.

To make your message more effective, direct mail allows you more variety of creative techniques. Instead of being limited to the one dimension of the newspaper page, the radio, or TV, you can vary your mailings from personal sales letters and post cards to colorful bill enclosures, brochures, and booklets.

With postage rates on the increase, mailing costs for each customer unit are high and may seem extravagant when compared with newspaper costs. However, constant supervision of your mail lists can not only reduce postage costs but also make certain that your advertising is reaching only the best prospects.

Disadvantages of direct mail

Another disadvantage of direct mail is the expense of preparing the mailing piece. Printing costs money and the more elaborate the mailing, the more your budget is affected. However, to get the customers' attention and to convince them that your merchandise will suit their wants, this promotion technique may be the best method of insuring a successful result.

An important disadvantage of direct mail is the length of time it takes to prepare the mailing and deliver it to the recipient. A simple piece of direct mail can take five to ten days, but a more elaborate one may require three weeks or more before delivery.

Institutional and semi-promotional stores with charge accounts are principal users of direct mail because they have built-in basic lists. These

Who should use direct mail?

stores may also purchase additional mailing lists from companies that specialize in compiling mailing lists.

Because the aggressive-promotional store depends more on external charge plans, it usually does not have a sufficient list of names developed from its own accounts receivable to make direct mail worthwhile. Also, experience has taught these stores that they get their best customer response from newspaper advertising, radio, and/or TV. However, many aggressive-promotional retailers use newspaper-style circulars that are delivered by the post office to all homes. These mailings, addressed to "Householder," are often successful as a supplement to a strong newspaper program.

The Sales Letter. The sales letter is the most personal of direct mail techniques and is the easiest to prepare. When it is well written in an interesting, friendly style, it can be very effective.

Kinds of direct mail

The Postcard. The postcard is just as effective as the sales letter when done with taste and imagination. Some retailers, using a dramatic merchandising idea in a creative manner, have made the ordinary postcard a successful advertising tool (Fig. 13.10).

Account Statement Stuffers. These are less expensive if each stuffer's weight does not increase the original postage expense because they can be

FIGURE 13.10 This demonstrates how an innovative and dramatic merchandising idea uses an ordinary postcard to generate more sales.

Courtesy Worth's, Waterbury, Conn.

FIGURE 13.11 An attractive account statement stuffer provided by a manufacturer. This is printed in color on both sides of a single sheet and can easily be inserted into any statement envelope.

Courtesy The Capitol, Fayetteville, N. C. and Rosanna Knitted Sportswear, New York.

included in the regular postage costs of the customer's statement mailing. Many resources and buying offices supply you with such stuffers and include the store signature at little or no cost (Fig. 13.11).

Broadsides. These are printed cheaply on large sheets of paper folded to fit a mail box and are used to promote bargains. They are rarely addressed to any person but are delivered by the postman or by private distributors within a definitely set time.

Booklets and Catalogues. These are usually elaborate and colorful. They are especially important for gift periods such as Christmas, Mother's Day, or Father's Day. Buying offices and manufacturers sometimes provide gift season booklets and catalogues, and manufacturers in the home furnishings and housewares field usually offer colorful booklets for special promotions.

Handbills are a separate area of direct advertising material delivered by private firms or individuals other than the mailman. There are several advantages in using this kind of sales promotion; you can concentrate

Handbills and package stuffers

your advertising on a special market without much waste of circulation; you can reach customers in the immediate vicinity of your store when you are located in a heavily populated region. Since your only costs are printing and distribution, you eliminate or reduce the higher costs of mass-media advertising and you can prepare and print a handbill in less time than it takes to prepare a newspaper ad. Furthermore, the handbill can also be given to all customers who enter your store.

Package stuffers are useful because after customers have opened their parcels, they are reminded that you have more values for them. You can prepare special stuffers or use the account statement enclosures mentioned above.

Most aggressive-promotional and semi-promotional stores have found handbills and stuffers to be very successful. They have the advantage of being less costly than many other forms of sales promotion and they produce a satisfactory increase in sales.

For many years most retailers used radio and television as a comparatively minor supplement to newspaper and direct-mail advertising. Now, many more of them have found broadcast media to be extremely effective for selling goods and building a store's character as well. Many successful small retailers use broadcast advertising exclusively, not only to sell more merchandise but also to create a very distinctive personality for their business through excellent showmanship techniques.

The value of broadcast advertising

The human voice can be most persuasive when it is properly used—even more persuasive than the best newspaper advertising. Another important advantage of radio is its wide listening audience which makes it possible to talk to more people than you can through newspapers or mailings.

The advantages of radio

Since radio has no physical delivery problems, it can reach special segments of your total market that are usually beyond the capability of newspapers or direct mail.

You also have considerable flexibility in choosing the time when it is best for your advertising. Not only can you broadcast your message any day or days of the week you wish, you can also select the time period of each day that is right for your advertising. Furthermore, you can direct your message to special audience segments and offer specific goods to these groups. For example, you can advertise to men at certain times, to women at other periods, and to young people after school. This time selection flexibility is one of the leading reasons why so many retailers use radio.

Another important advantage of using radio is its ability to help you make fast changes in the timing and selection of goods for advertising. For example, if a sudden blizzard is on its way, you can quickly switch from a radio spot advertising a hardware item to one advertising tire chains.

Flexibility can be increased by using various advertising styles to catch the listener's atttention. For example, you can develop a catchy musical jingle to accompany a persuasive voice to sell merchandise to women, or you can use newsy, chatty talk to appeal to young people.

Radio time costs are comparatively inexpensive, especially when you consider the above advantages. In addition, there is a fairly wide range of rates for each time of the radio day you select (Fig. 13.12). The highest cost unit is usually called *class AA time* and the lowest cost unit time is *class D time*. Time cost rating schedules vary according to local radio station practices.

You can also choose various time units to tell your story. Most stations offer 30-second and 60-second units. Many stations will supplement these basic time units with 15-second "spot" announcements. Decide which of these time units are best for your advertising messages to be sure that you get as much frequency on the air as your budget permits. Many successful radio users schedule a mix of these units to add variety and frequency to their radio advertising.

Time	Time Slot	Audience	Cost
6 a.m.-10 a.m.*	AM DRIVE	Men, women, teens.	Most expensive. Prime time on most stations.
10 a.m.-3 p.m.	HOUSEWIFE	Housewives, mostly, but plenty of men available.	Third most expensive.
3 p.m.-7 p.m.	PM DRIVE	Men, women, teens.	Second most expensive on most stations, prime time on young audience stations.
7 p.m.-Midnight	EVENING	Teens, tv dropouts, hobbyists, people in cars or working.	Fourth most expensive on most stations, prime for young audiences.
Midnight-6 a.m.	NIGHTTIME	Night-shift workers, insomniacs, people retiring.	Least expensive.

*Some stations' AM DRIVE runs from 5 or 5:30 to 10.

FIGURE 13.12 A schedule of a typical broadcast day. Using this schedule, a retailer can decide what time of the day is best for him to reach special audience segments.

Courtesy The Radio Advertising Bureau, Inc., New York.

The disadvantages of radio

Radio cannot picture your merchandise as print or TV advertising can. Since the message must be brief and to the point, you cannot tell a long story or broadcast a lot of items over the air. Furthermore, its short life makes your message highly perishable. It is gone before potential customers are aware of it, and they cannot refer to it as they can in print advertising. This can be overcome by scheduling radio time to achieve frequency of impression.

Buy enough radio time to make your store important by buying time in quantity units to get quantity discounts. Make sure that your message sounds exciting, enthusiastic, interesting, and distinctive. The success of your radio advertising will not only depend on the goods you are promoting but also on the way the message sounds.

Important rules for radio advertisers

Your local station(s) can help you create a distinctive radio personality for a small fee; or you can get expert help from specialists in this field. Consult the Radio Advertising Bureau in New York for guidance in time buying as well as for techniques you can use to create a special radio format for your store.

Television is ideally suited for retailers because its ability to show a picture of merchandise in action along with a persuasive selling voice combines the advantages of print advertising and radio. Its effect is almost like having your salesperson in every viewer's home at the same time.

The advantages of television

The TV audience is large, and in that audience are many kinds of prospective customers, some of whom rarely get past the front pages of a newspaper, let alone read its advertising. Since each TV station's audience extends far beyond the newspaper's circulation, you can reach new customers more easily. You can also select the exact time that you wish to reach the most important segments of your market. For example, most surveys show that afternoon and early evening programming reach women between the ages of 18 and 49, while evening programs reach the entire family. Television is similar to radio in providing quick-change flexibility that allows you to quickly switch your ad, for example, to suit a sudden change in weather.

In addition to TV time charges, there are usually production expenses of from 15 percent to 20 percent more for the ad message, because it should employ top caliber production style and creative imagination. This is necessary if the store wishes to have effective advertising that can compete with TV spots used by its biggest competitors.

Disadvantages of television

When time and production costs are totaled, you may have to spend a large portion, if not all, of your promotion budget to maintain a continual but modest impression on TV. If you want to compete more vigorously with major retail advertisers and make the strongest impression, you would have to concentrate the store's TV ad schedule to a few weeks each season, but then you would lose the important assets of continuity of advertising impression.

Furthermore, it is difficult to measure the size of your TV audience, especially at the time the advertising appeared. Unlike newspaper advertising or direct mail whose circulation figures can be pinpointed with accuracy, broadcast media are not able to establish the exact number of people who heard or saw your advertising when it actually appeared. Audience measurement figures are available through your local TV stations, but the figures are based on research methods that record the viewing habits of selected audience segments. Although analysis of these data do give clues to approximately how many people were in the audience at the time your advertising appeared, only your sales results can really answer whether or not your TV message was seen by enough people.

Finally, as in radio, your TV advertising has a short life, 30 seconds at the most each time, and it is just as perishable. If viewers miss your ad, they cannot retrieve it as they can in newspaper or direct advertising. to a limited degree this can be overcome if you can afford to repeat your TV ads frequently.

Billboards. Newspapers, direct mail, and broadcast media can be supplemented by billboards if their cost does not weaken the budget for your basic media program. Billboards are costly and must be used with discretion. They should be located on well-traveled roads that lead to your store, whether in the city, suburbs, or rural areas. They should also be placed where there are not too many other billboards because there should not be too much visual competition. Furthermore, their location must give the viewers sufficient time to absorb the message and make a decision about it.

The message should be brief and the total design should be colorful with an attractive pictorial idea. If you use billboards, they must look fresh and clean, even if this means that you have to change them frequently.

Shopping Bags. The familiar shopping bag is an effective form of advertising media, especially for small retailers. When the shopping bag is cleverly designed using distinctive graphics and attractive colors, it becomes a walking billboard. These bags quickly identify the store and project the store's image to a large audience since they are used over and over. There are many successful small stores whose total advertising effort depends on an unusually attractive, well-constructed shopping bag.

Miscellaneous Media. School publications or various social journals are in the nature of charity or gestures of good will rather than advertising. If you can support this kind of promotion, fine, but remember that the more of these ads you accept, the more you will be called upon for support by other organizations. If, however, you are in a town that has a large daily college paper circulation, carefully consider using the paper as a regular advertising medium. Many an ad series that cleverly stresses selected items for their special readership has paid off for shops that cater to college students.

1. Advertising is one of the most essential tools of sales promotion.

2. To be effective, your ad must attract attention, inform, and ask for action.

3. To get maximum return from your advertising dollar, your advertising should be continuous.

4. A good advertising style selects the correct audience, identifies the store, and expresses its personality.

5. Before you advertise, carefully weigh the advantages and disadvantages of all advertising media.

14

How to Sell
More Merchandise

While bringing people into the store and to the point of sale is the objective of sales promotion, the main objective is to sell them goods at sufficient speed and profit to make your promotion efforts worthwhile. Retail selling today is vastly different from what it was before the 1950s. Therefore, every merchant should realize that selling methods change and should be ready to meet any changes. This chapter discusses current selling techniques and tells you how to use the right ones.

Recent Selling Changes

F. W. Woolworth was one of the first retailers to realize that if prices were low enough, people would serve themselves. In the early 1900s Clarence Saunders, an independent grocer, experimented with cash-and-carry techniques and shortly after World War I he developed the Piggly-Wiggly chain which became the forerunner of today's self-service stores. But up to World War II most customers expected to be waited on and retailers went out of their way to oblige them. However, the manpower shortage created by the war affected store personnel to the extent that management was forced to streamline many operations.

One of the new techniques was to use fewer salespeople. Because customers would buy whatever was put on the counters, retailers required employees only to take care of the merchandise, give out information, and complete sales transactions. Manufacturers helped this trend by packaging bulk goods into units which customers could buy conveniently. This was most noticeable in food stores where sales help became almost nonexistent, but even screws, nails, and other hardware items came prepackaged as did such soft goods as men's shirts and ladies' blouses, sweaters, and brassieres.

When, after the war, conditions changed from a seller's to a consumers' market and retailers again began to think of personal selling, they found it difficult to obtain competent personnel because working in a store lacked prestige, required Saturday and some evening employment, and paid rather poorly. Yet, most merchants decided against attracting more competent employees with offers of increased salaries to compensate for undesirable working conditions. Instead, they preferred to spend money on repairing and updating their premises that had been neglected during the war. They also felt that by this time most customers, except the upper-income group, had become used to the nonpersonal selling techniques that had been developed and refined during the war and preferred to do their own shopping rather than go through a series of annoying experiences with incompetent and unqualified salespeople.

Selling Today

Today, a retailer can still practice salon selling techniques which rely entirely on the ability of the salesperson, or he can develop sample and pre-selection selling in which customers require a minimum of store help for advice and direction, or he can sell merchandise by self-selection and self-service in which customers do all their own shopping and only need someone to wrap the goods and take their money.

Different Personnel for Each Method

Retailers must realize that each selling method requires entirely different personnel and that a salesperson who is an expert in salon selling does very poorly when placed in a self-selection department, and vice versa.

Selling Means Helping the Customer

Selling is the act of helping customers to buy correctly. It consists of influencing people, not forcing or shaming them, into making a series of buying decisions that are beneficial to both the purchaser and the store. Ideal salespeople have the ability to put themselves in their customers' shoes and, with their training and product knowledge, sell customers the items that will best satisfy their wants. Just to "sell" customers something because they ask for it is not good selling. The items may be all wrong and so will not satisfy them at all.

For example, a customer may *want* to buy a shag nylon rug in orange for her family room because she likes its soft feel and it has a bright, comfortable look. However, when the salesman learns that the room is the main play area for her three boys, aged 12 to 18, and their dog, he knows that if the customer buys this rug, she will soon be unhappy with her purchase because the color shows dirt and the shag look will soon get flat. Therefore, he tries to persuade her to buy what he knows she *needs*. This could be a level loop, nylon rug with a blended design in browns, golds, and greens. He knows that this rug will always look the same because it has a sturdy, firm carpet finish, resists compression, and the print will mask the soiling that the activities of the children and their dog will inevitably cause. In this situation, if the salesman allowed his customer to buy what she asked for she would not be properly sold and she would be dissatisfied with the store.

What Makes a Good Salesperson?

Most salespeople are not born, they are made. Whether they are doing salon selling or performing a selling function in a self-service area, they must have the proper attitude toward their job, as well as a number of personal qualifications. Effective salespeople must like people and enjoy helping them solve their buying problems. To do this, they must be able to size up customers properly. They should have a pleasant appearance, dress to fit the store's personality, and have a sincere, not a forced, smile. Their voices, like their smiles, must be warm and pleasant and their manner friendly and courteous. They should have a good memory for names and faces, be able to talk easily to people, and in other ways show that they are genuinely interested in their customers and their needs. They must also be strong enough to handle the merchandise they sell and be able to stand on their feet most of the day without becoming so tired that it affects their outlook. Although good salespeople are competitive and aggressive, they should be able to get along easily with other employees. They must like working with things rather than ideas, must be able to express themselves easily and properly, and must have sufficient clerical skill to complete whatever sales routines the store has installed.

These characteristics must be combined with a thorough knowledge of the merchandise they sell. They must know their stock intimately and be able to judge its usefulness and satisfaction under various conditions and in various situations. Then salespeople can help their customers make proper buying decisions. But to do this they must also realize that sales can only be made in the customers' minds and that they must, when necessary, *persuade* their customers to buy not what they ask for, but what they really require. To do this, salespeople must have some grasp of psychology and the techniques of proper selling.

Although every salesperson should possess these qualities, each one will vary according to the salesperson's interests and personality. This is why a successful retailer places his sales help where they can do the best job. For example, if a salesperson personally likes informal clothes, is rather impatient, and wants to be doing something all the time, she might do well in the sportswear department. Another saleslady who has the same potential but who prefers dressier apparel, moves and thinks more slowly, and has a great deal of patience but gets flustered in a very busy convenience department like notions, might be very competent in a shopping goods department such as better coats.

Importance of Sales Training

Every effective salesperson should be trained in proper selling techniques and should learn how to use selling strategy correctly. It is not true that the longer a salesperson takes to make a sale, the better he or she is. A good salesperson works quickly and uses a minimum of time and energy. This comes from practice and the proper application of selling techniques, but it also requires making decisions about the best ways to develop selling transactions as they take place. Properly trained salespeople are seldom surprised by anything a customer may ask for, say, or do. They have not only studied most situations before they happen, they have also preplanned a method of turning them to their advantage.

Continual Sales Training Increases Sales

Continual sales training increases sales because with new items constantly flowing into the market, the selling staff's product knowledge must be constantly updated. Again, with today's turnover of sales personnel, constant sales training becomes a necessity because new help must be trained in your selling methods and techniques. Again, any change in selling systems and procedures requires thoughtful re-education programs or your staff will resist the change and it will be difficult to make it work properly. Lastly, unless you retrain yourself as changes occur, your sales staff will reject whatever new selling system you have decided to adopt.

The Five Major Selling Techniques

There are five major selling techniques: (1) salon, (2) sample, (3) pre-selection, (4) self-selection, and (5) self-service. Although it is possible to use all of these procedures in the same store, you must be very careful about where each one is practiced. Otherwise, salespeople's efforts will be largely wasted and customers will not get the service they require. For example, to use salon selling in a self-service area not only defeats the concept of both selling techniques but reduces the salesperson's efficiency, embarrasses the customers, and decreases their potential purchases. The unfortunate results of the grocery store owner who mixed up these selling methods (page 253) illustrate the importance of using the right technique in the right place.

This is the oldest and most rewarding form of selling because it presumes that the customer comes into the store with a want that she is helpless to fulfill by herself. However, because the customer must rely entirely on the salesperson, this selling technique can be very dangerous. For example, if the saleslady happens to be tired, forgetful, or irritable or if she lacks merchandise knowledge, the sale might be lost. Again, if you have not schooled her properly in the seven phases of salon selling, she will have difficulty making the sale and may even lose it entirely.

Because every salon sale is completely in the saleslady's hands, she should learn to distinguish how to use each of the following phases of salon selling:

1. *Approach*
2. *Finding out what the customer really wants*
3. *Presentation*
4. *Meeting objections*
5. *Closing the sale*
6. *Suggestion and related selling*
7. *Departure*

If any phase is missed or improperly handled, the sale may become unsuccessful. Yet, since every sale develops differently, salon selling is not only interesting and exhilarating, it also demands a professional attitude on the part of the salesperson for she must be able to recognize the beginning and end of each phase and use the proper combination of techniques that will guide the sale to a successful conclusion.

Approach

The salesperson should think of the store as if it were her home. Then every customer who walks in becomes her guest. Visitors at home are met at the door with a smile and a warm greeting. In the same way, every customer should be welcomed and greeted "Good Morning" or still better, "Good morning, Mrs. Brown." When this approach is used, the customer usually responds with "Good morning" and then asks for the item she came in to buy.

Neglecting a customer, even for a short time, will make the sale very difficult to conclude. In salon selling, customers *expect* service and they should get it. Although it is important to approach a customer as soon as possible, it is not necessary for the salesperson to drop everything she is doing and rush to the customer. If she is really busy, she should acknowledge the customer's presence with a smile and "Good morning," finish what she is doing as quickly as she can, and then attend to her. If, by this time, the customer is examining an item, the saleslady should say something that puts her into the sale immediately, for example, "Isn't that an exciting style?" or "Did you notice how crease resistant this dress is?"

189

When the Store Has the Item. When a customer asks for a specific item and the store has it, the salesperson should show it right away. She may think that the customer *needs* something else, but at this stage she really does not know. Besides, once the customer sees the item she has asked for, she can be more easily shown merchandise better suited to her needs.

Not only is the first minute with the customer more important than any time spent with her later, the first sentence after the customer has made known her wants can also make or break the sale. This is why preplanned selling sentences are so important. For example, the approach might have been perfect but if the customer says, "I would like to see something in a beige suit," and the salesperson frowns and says haltingly, "Let me see, I think we have a few left somewhere—I wonder where they are?" the sale is ruined then and there. If, however, the salesperson says, with a smile, "Yes, Mrs. Brown" and guides the customer to the proper suit rack, shows her a beige outfit, and says, "This goes so well with your coloring and is very versatile because each piece will coordinate marvelously with your wardrobe," the sale is well on its way.

During this phase the salesperson should give the customer all the attention. She should listen carefully to what the customer is saying and she should use her eyes, ears, and brain more than her voice. The customer will be flattered by this and quickly warm up, and the sale can be concluded easily. Of course, the salesperson should talk, but most of what she says should be in the form of questions. This will help her judge the kind of customer she is dealing with and whether or not the customer really *wants* what she says she does or *needs* something else.

In particular, the salesperson should avoid asking questions such as, "What price, color, or fabric are you thinking of?" These questions will force the customer to make a decision. If the store is out of the particular item or if the item is not what the shopper needs, then the salesperson will have a great deal of trouble changing the customer's mind. General questions should be asked but, better still, merchandise should be *shown* that will give the salesperson clues about the color, price, fabric, etc., that the customer prefers.

For example, a salesperson can discover what price the customer wishes to pay by simply showing a medium-priced article first. Then she is able to move up or down according to the customer's reaction. However, the salesperson should avoid confusing the customer by showing too much merchandise and leaving it visible. She should set aside all items in which there is little interest. This technique focuses attention on the items the salesperson wants to sell, protects the other merchandise from being soiled or stolen, and releases the merchandise to other salespeople and their customers.

When the Store Does Not Have the Item. If the store does not have the item asked for but stocks a reasonable substitute, the salesperson should never say, "No, we have had so few calls, we dropped it." Instead, she should say, "Yes, Mrs. Brown" and take the customer to the substitute item and point out *at once* its similarities and the best reasons why she should buy what the store has. If the customer makes no objection to the substitute, the salesperson can go ahead with the sale; if the customer remains unconvinced, the salesperson should be helpful and, if possible, tell the customer where she might find the item asked for. The customer will be surprised and pleased with this assistance and will also begin to doubt the importance of her original want. Then, if the selling presentation in the other store is poor, the customer will remember your salesperson's presentation and thoughtfulness and return to your store.

Presentation begins as soon as the salesperson moves to where the merchandise is stocked and introduces it with a preplanned selling sentence. By this time, the salesperson should have evaluated the customer and decided on the best way to conduct the sale. Figure 14.1 lists most of the ways customers act and the best ways to respond to them. The salesperson must remember that customers change from day to day and even from situation to situation. For example, Mrs. Brown might have been classified as "nervous" when she first shopped in the store, but she might have been classifed "quiet and attentive" when she came back the second time. A professional salesperson will react differently on each occasion.

By this time, too, the salesperson should know *why* the customer wants the item and should begin to build up her sales presentation around this motivation. Most goods are bought for more reasons than immediate need. People buy merchandise because they think it is a bargain or because they expect it to give them prestige. It may have conveniences they like or they feel that it will make them healthy or more attractive. Whatever the motivation, the salesperson should concentrate on it. She should introduce and use other desires, but if she feels that a customer wants a self-cleaning stove because it eliminates a disagreeable task, she should point out again and again the self-cleaning features of the model she thinks the customer should buy.

The best salesperson is the one who is able to put herself in the customer's shoes, knows what she wants, why she wants it, and then be able to present and dramatize the merchandise in a way the customer will understand and accept. It always helps a sale when the salesperson points out the obvious features of the merchandise, for example, wool is warm. Customers seldom realize that years of conditioning have gone into building up an image that wool *is* warm and that is really why she wants that particular fabric. Then the salesperson should move from the obvious characteristics of wool to its less obvious qualities, for example, wool is crease-resistant. Here, the salesperson's merchandise knowledge becomes effective and if she uses it properly, she will soon gain the respect and confidence of the customer.

The more the salesperson builds up the value of the item, the less expensive the price seems to the customer. Thus, an item at $30 might be considered a real bargain, but one at $3 might be thought too expensive.

The salesperson should make the customer sell herself by inducing her

Type of Customer	Characteristics	How Should This Customer Be Sold?	Should Few or Many Items Be Shown?	Should Full or Short Sales Talk Be Used?	Should Few or Many Questions Be Asked?	What to Avoid
Just looking	Says, "I'm just looking." Either is undecided, or fears sales pressure. Starts to leave when approached; can't be rushed. Remember—looking indicates interest.	Invite customer to look. Give facts about merchandise. Ask questions that can be answered with yes.	Many	Short	Few	Don't distract attention from merchandise by questions as to customer's needs. Don't seem overanxious to sell.
Disagreeable	Wants to argue. Makes unreasonable demands. Refuses to be pleased; is apt to talk loudly and be abrupt, sarcastic, or antagonistic.	Let customer do most of the talking; you listen. Be calm and good-natured. Offer to adjust previous difficulties.	Many	Short	Few	Don't argue. Don't let sarcastic remarks disturb you. Don't take criticisms as personal.
Inattentive	Has "far-away" expression, or has attention distracted by child or companion, by outside noise or displays of other merchandise. Doesn't listen to your sales talk.	Concentrate on few main selling points. Be alert and peppy. Arouse interest and curiosity by demonstrations.	Few	Short	Many	Don't allow your own attention to be distracted. Don't leave customer alone. Don't stop selling.
Silent	Won't answer questions or respond to usual "leads." Face is unexpressive. Apparently doesn't hear your sales talk. Is either timid, suspicious, or has language difficulty.	Be friendly and interested. Ask questions that can be answered with "Yes." Repeat selling talk in different words. Demonstrate.	Many	Full	Many	Don't repeat questions in louder tones. Don't stop talking and allow awkward pauses.
Talkative	Continues to talk. If not properly "directed" may leave without buying. Discusses personal affairs instead of concentrating on merchandise or your sales talk.	Listen sympathetically, but switch conversation back to merchandise as soon as possible. Be courteous but businesslike.	Few	Short	Few	Do not be led into discussion of your personal affairs. Do not act impatient, but do not let interest in sale be sidetracked.
Indecisive	Can't make up her mind. Wavers between one article and another. Constantly asks questions of companion or salesperson, seeking to have self-confidence bolstered up.	Be liberal with merchandise information. Give plenty of help and advice. Watch for signs of interest, and follow these leads.	Few	Full	Many	Don't allow conversation to lag. Don't act as if customer's indecision were unusual. Don't leave customer alone if you can avoid it.

Positive	Tries to display own knowledge of merchandise. Contradicts or questions salesperson's statements. May be overbearing or argumentative in manner. May know more about merchandise than salesperson does.	Welcome and use this customer's opinions and ideas. Be patient, calm, and attentive. Remember there is flattery in listening.	Few	Short	Few	Don't argue or disagree. Don't get excited or appear intimidated. Offer to call department manager for information or opinion.
Hurried	Appears impatient, nervous, fidgety. Is brisk in manner, glancing often at watch, perhaps has appointment to meet.	Listen carefully to customer's requests. Show few, well-chosen items; be brisk in your motions and talk.	Few	Short	Few	Don't allow interruptions to interfere with the sale. Don't be ''wordy,'' condense your sales talk.
Deliberate	Wants time to look and ''think it over.'' Is slow and leisurely in motion and speech. Appears to have unlimited time to listen.	Take time—repeat sales talk in different words. Give full demonstration of merchandise.	Many	Full	Many	Avoid the appearance of rushing a decision. Don't use pressure. Do not appear hurried or impatient and don't lose interest.
Confused	Is buying merchandise that is unfamiliar, or may be a stranger to your store or your town. May be old person, child, or foreigner with language difficulty.	Supply plenty of merchandise facts in simple words. Put customer at ease. Be friendly, conversational, and self-confident.	Few	Full	Few	Refrain from asking too many questions. This may add to the customer's confusion. Don't hover about if customer prefers to be alone for a while.

FIGURE 14.1 The most difficult customers—how to recognize and deal with each one.

Reproduced from Richert, *Retailing Principles and Practices*, 3rd ed., © 1954, with the permission of the Gregg Publishing Division, McGraw-Hill Book Company, Inc.

to participate in the sale. She should have her try on the garment, work the
dials on the stove, turn on the light fixture, lift the aluminum chair, etc. As the customer actively enters into the sale, the salesperson should keep her saying "Yes" by asking such questions as "Isn't this a useful time-saver?" or "Wouldn't this look just right in your living room?"

The phrases, sentences, and questions that the salesperson uses should be carefully selected beforehand and combined with the activities involved in her presentation. General phrases like "Its a mighty good buy" or negative ones like "You can't go wrong with this item" should never be used. Instead, you should train the salesperson to sell positively. For example, she should use such phrases as "You will always look attractive in this suit because . . ." or "This self-cleaning stove will permit you to spend much more time doing the things you really want to do." Again, the salesperson should never talk over the customer's head. The customer will only be confused, not impressed, with the salesperson's knowledge. If she must explain something technical, she should be sure that the customer understands the *meaning* of the term and, if possible, should show why she has used that particular expression.

The salesperson should be trained how to keep only those items in which interest is shown before the customer, and then how to narrow the choice down in order that a decision can be reached more easily. Sometimes it is wise to let the customer compare an item that she obviously will reject against one the salesperson wants her to buy. The merchandise should always be handled with care and pride; the salesperson should feel that everything presented to the customer is the best obtainable. This raises its value in the customer's eyes and makes it much more desirable for her to own.

It should be remembered that the customer is interested only in herself and what the goods will do for her, not what it did for the salesperson. She should never contradict the customer; she may win the argument but will most likely lose the sale and create ill will. She should always be ready to close. If the customer has indicated a willingness to buy, but the salesperson continues with her presentation, she can easily talk herself right out of the sale.

During the course of the presentation the customer may raise an **Meeting** objection. This is a good sign because it tells the salesperson how the sale is **objections** going and what the customer is really thinking. Customers raise objections because they do not understand what is being said, or haven't sufficient information to grasp the selling point, or need more reasons to make them buy. The salesperson should listen to objections carefully and then stop to consider why they were made and the best way to answer them. They may be *excuses* not to buy rather than *objections*. If so, the excuses must be overlooked and attempts should be made to find the real reason for them. If objections are honestly made, they should be answered as soon as practical and the answers should be geared to the customer's buying motivations as well as to the particular phase that the sale has reached.

A good way to answer an objection is to agree with it and then go on to disprove it. For example, the salesperson could say, "You are quite right, however, ..." or "There's a lot of truth in what you say, but . . . ." Another way is to keep questioning until the customer overcomes the objection herself. For example, if the customer says, "I'd like this watch but I cannot see myself paying that price," the salesclerk could answer, "How often do you buy a watch?" and then demonstrate that when the extra value of the higher priced watch is considered, the difference between it and the less expensive one is really very small in the long run.

Some Do's and Don'ts in dealing with the youth market

DO give your young customer a friendly hello. Walk toward her, not away from her.

DO leave the dressing room before she trys on a garment. Let her know you're available *just outside* when she wants you.

DO answer the questions courteously and fully. She is eager for information and grateful for your attention.

DON'T patronize her. She is a customer in her own right.

DON'T avoid her in favor of an older customer. And when she's in the dressing room, please don't disappear for what seems hours.

DON'T high pressure her or suggest that she bring her mother if she's not certain.

DON'T be disinterested if the sale is small. If she is pleased, she will always return.

FIGURE 14.2 An easy guide for serving and selling the youth market.

Adapted from *Style,* published by Maclean-Hunter Limited, Toronto, Canada.

Techniques of Closing the Sale. There is no psychological moment to close, because every sale has many opportunities for completion. One of the best ways to tell a good salesperson from a poor one is to watch her close a sale. An effective salesperson closes early and naturally; a poor one wastes much more time and then closes clumsily. She can improve her ability to close if she watches the customer carefully, because when a buying decision has been made, the customer usually shows this by relaxing her eyes, hands, and mouth. Sometimes she pauses over an item and nods her head or her voice changes. Finally, when she asks the price or information about credit or delivery, alterations, etc., or raises such objections as, "That is really what I want, but . . ." the salesperson will know that the customer is ready to make the purchase and all that is required is a reassuring answer.

The salesperson can try closing at any time during the presentation. If the customer is not ready to buy, she will simply raise an objection which the salesperson can answer. Then the salesperson continues with the presentation. Like everything else about selling, closing techniques are very varied and should be preplanned, but some methods seem to work better than others. For example, if the salesperson can get the customer to say "Yes" often enough, she will have difficulty changing her reply to "No." Again, if the salesperson can make the customer decide on a minor point like "Do you want the print or striped blouse?" she can take for granted that the customer wants a blouse.

Another way to close is to narrow the choice to two items. Sometimes it is wise to interject an obviously unwanted item for comparison. A risky close but one that sometimes works well is to take for granted that the sale is made and ask, "Shall I have it sent or will you take it with you?" Whatever the method, the salesperson should know what she is doing and compare the effect of different closing techniques on different customers and situations. In this way, she becomes very expert and can make more and more sales in less time.

Remain Friendly—Win or Lose. Remember that selling is a continuous relationship between the store and your clientele. That is why, once the sale is completed, the salesperson should continue to act friendly toward the customer. Otherwise, the customer will be offended and think that the salesclerk's interest in her was obviously not genuine and simply a technique to take her money. The salesperson should remember that the customer will soon need something else and if she prepares her *now,* future sales will be easier to make. Also, this is the time to continue selling because the customer is in a buying mood and may be receptive to any number of suggestions.

Your customers have friends who may become customers if your store is recommended to them highly enough. Therefore, after the sale is completed, the salesperson should try to spend a few minutes with the customer, reassuring her that she has bought the right merchandise and giving her a feeling of well being and confidence in her buying decisions. The salesperson can ask the customer to come back again and let her know how her friends admired the blouse and she can remind her that it is machine-washable and dryable. If the salesperson must turn to another shopper, she should excuse herself, thank the customer, and tell her how happy she will be with her purchase and how nice she was to serve.

If the salesperson loses the sale, she should be *extra pleasant.* She should thank the customer for thinking of your store and hope the next time she wants something, she will come in again. By doing this, the store loses only the sale, not the customer.

Usually, customers are not sufficiently aware that the item they purchased requires related items. For example, paint requires a roller, brushes, turpentine, sandpaper, etc. Since most customers are thankful if they are reminded of these items because it saves them extra trips to the store, this is a good way to build up good will and increase sales. Suggestion and related selling is *not* high-pressure selling; it is an important service that the sales

Suggestion and related selling

staff renders your customers by helping them buy properly. In addition to related items, the sales staff should tell customers about newly arrived or specially advertised goods. Since customers may not be aware that this merchandise is in the store, they will appreciate the information, and again you will increase good will and sales volume.

Suggestion and related selling should flow as naturally as the other five phases of the sale and it too should be preplanned and introduced from the *customer's point of view.* However, it should only be attempted *after* the main sale has been closed and *before* the parcel is wrapped. The salesperson should be specific and positive about the suggested items. For example, she should place a sweater inside the jacket the customer has just bought and say, "Look how the color of this sweater shows off your new tweed jacket." General phrases such as "Anything else?" or negative ones like "You don't want a sweater, do you?" are useless because they do not stimulate customers to think or they do not interest them in making a further purchase. By showing and demonstrating the item, the salesperson is actually going into the presentation phase of the next sale. It may work or it may stimulate customers to think of something else which they may not buy now but will later.

In salon selling the sale is finished only when the customer is walking away from your door. Therefore, if the salesperson has time, she should accompany the customer to the store entrance. On the way, the customer may decide to buy a related item that the salesperson suggested earlier, or she may see something else that interests her and for which a sale can be made. Sometimes an item in the window can prompt a sale, or, as the salesperson accompanies the customer to the door, she can build up interest toward some future purchase.

Departure

In her own home the salesperson sees her guests to the door, wishes them goodbye, and asks them to come again. She should do the same with your customers.

An Example of Salon Selling

When Mr. and Mrs. Rogers enter the lighting fixture store, the salesperson, who had been writing in a book, puts down his pen, approaches them with a friendly smile, and says, "Good morning."

Approach

Mrs. Rogers asks if he has bathroom light fixtures to hang on each side of a medicine chest. He answers, "Yes," leads the couple to a fixture display, and dramatizes it by pressing a bank of switches to light them up. He watches them move among the lighted fixtures until they stop before a single fluorescent unit and then he says, "Did you notice how quickly the fluorescent fixtures light up these days? They have developed new starters" (Merchandise knowledge).

**Finding out what
the customer
really wants**

Mrs. Rogers: I wasn't thinking of fluorescent. I had thought of long frosted bulbs.

Salesman: (Going over to a fixture and pointing to it) Is this what you mean?

Mrs. Rogers: Well, I don't know. I just heard that frosted bulb fixtures are quite new.

Salesman: (Yes—but) Yes, they are, but we found that most of our customers are changing to fluorescent. (Begins personal questions.) When was your house built?

Mrs. Rogers: About 30 years ago.

Salesman: Houses were very well constructed at that time and the rooms were large.

Mrs. Rogers: Yes, they were.

These phases in the sale demonstrate the difference between the customers' wishes and their needs.

Salesman: (pointing to a frosted bulb fixture) Notice how dull this light is compared to the fluorescent? Yet, it uses twice as much wattage. Besides, the fixture costs more, so does your electricity, and so do the bulbs. They are also much clumsier to replace. (As he talks, the salesman removes the bulbs from both the frosted light and the fluorescent fixture and hands them, not to Mrs. Rogers, but to her husband.) (Good demonstration and excellent customer psychology.)

Mr. Rogers is very impressed with this man. He feels that the salesman is not only thinking intelligently about their problem but that he is, in fact, saving them money now and in the future.

Now the salesman answers a nasty objection courteously and turns it into a selling point.

Mrs. Rogers: If the frosted light fixtures are selling so poorly, why not reduce them?

Salesman: (Smiles) Well, there is no reason to do that. We still have a sufficient demand. It is only that *in your case* I think the fluorescent fixture would be better. (He then turns on both lights.) (Dramatizes his point.)

There is no question—the fluorescent is very much brighter and Mr. Rogers likes the savings.

Mrs. Rogers: I really don't know why I thought of frosted bulbs. I just heard so much about them. But you're right, the fluorescent *is* much better.

The salesman sells only what the customer requires.

Salesman: Are you redecorating your bathroom?

Mrs. Rogers: Yes, we are.

Salesman: Well, have you thought of using only *one* fixture?

Mrs. Rogers: Yes, but I thought two would be better.

Salesman: That's true, but as long as you are repainting, it wouldn't cost much for the electrician to make a single outlet over the medicine chest. Single fixtures are neater and more modern.

Mrs. Rogers: Yes, I had thought of that, but I didn't know how expensive it might be.

The salesman builds up the sale.

Salesman: Besides, you would only have to buy one fixture, so you could buy a more interesting one than those you had planned on.

He takes the Rogers to a section that contains more expensive fixtures. By this time, Mr. Rogers has complete confidence in the salesman. He feels that he is trying to sell them the fixture which is best for their particular situation, not just trying to make the biggest sale.

Salesman: Two frosted bulb fixtures would cost $26.50. Two plain fluorescent fixtures would cost $24.50. Now, this one, for example, (pointing to a particular one) is $22.50. It saves you $4 over a pair of frosted bulbs and another $2 over a pair of plain fluorescents. Therefore, you save $6 by buying a single fluorescent fixture and it is much richer and more appropriate for your bathroom. Don't you think so?

Mrs. Rogers: It certainly looks better.

He actually begins the sale over again in the area he desires.

The salesman leaves the Rogers alone for a few minutes to look over the rest of the fixtures. Then Mrs. Rogers begins to ask questions about those that interest her. The salesman in turn asks her what color the bathroom is, how large, etc. By this time, Mr. Rogers is willing to take anything that the salesman suggests.

The salesman narrows the choice and dramatizes the one he wants to sell.

The Rogers finally arrive at a choice between two fixtures. The difference is that the more expensive one has a more elaborate shade. Since this is the one the salesman wants to sell, he begins demonstrating it. He unscrews the shade and says, "You see how the light is dispersed up and down? Now, watch." He puts the shade back and, of course, this throws the light down.

Salesman: You see how the best part of the light will be right on your mirror. Is your bathroom dark?

Mrs. Rogers: Well, yes. We always keep the blind drawn.

Salesman: You need good lighting them. (He goes on moving the shade up and down.) You see, this is easily adjustable so that you can get the best light on your mirror. Isn't that what you want?

Mrs. Rogers: Yes.

The salesman is now ready to close, which he proceeds to do by saying, **Closing the sale** "Do you want the 18- or 24-inch fixture?"

Mrs. Rogers: The 18-inch.

And that is the end of the sale.

As the salesman places the fixture into its container and *before* he makes the bill, he asks, "By the way, where is your house?" Mrs. Rogers tells him. "Oh yes, I know that area very well. There are some lovely homes there."

>   *Mrs. Rogers:* Yes, we like ours very much.
>   *Salesman:* I've just received some living-room lamps this morning that might very well fit into your home.

The Rogers go with him to look at the lamps in another section. Mr. Rogers is more than willing to be led anywhere by this man because he feels that he would not sell them anything that would make them unhappy.

The Rogers buy an expensive living-room lamp. So by saving them a few dollars on a bathroom fixture, this store made more money on an added sale. Moreover, the Rogers are happy to pay for this sale, even though the article is expensive.

As the salesman walks the Rogers to the door, another couple he had greeted while he was waiting on the Rogers move toward him. He smiles at them and says, "I'll be with you in a minute," and he continues to accompany the Rogers to the door, where he quickly reassures tham that they will be happy with their purchases, thanks them for shopping at the store, hopes that they will come again, and then says goodbye. As they walk to their car, both Mr. and Mrs. Rogers feel that they have not only bought fixtures that are well worth the price, they also feel that the interchange between the salesman and themselves has also been a highly pleasant social experience. Thus, it is very possible that both Mr. and Mrs. Rogers will recommend this store and salesman to their friends.

Salon Selling Can Increase Your Sales and Profits

Salon selling is the easiest and best way to increase your sales and profits. Expenses remain the same because it usually costs as much to sell an item at $19.95 as one at $29.95. If you make 4,000 sales with an average of $20 per sale, your volume will be $80,000. Suppose that your gross margin is 40 percent of retail and your total expenses are $24,000.

Sales (4,000 × $20)		$80,000
Cost of sales (.60 × $80,000)	$48,000	
Total expenses	24,000	72,000
Net profit		$8,000

If you could increase the average sale by only $1, your net profit would move up to $9,600.

Sales (4,000 × $21)		$84,000
Cost of sales (.60 × $84,000)	$50,400	
Total expenses	24,000	74,400
Net profit		$9,600

Watch the Cost per Sale

However, if you stress increasing the average sale too much, your sales-people may neglect casual customers or small purchasers. If this happens, your cost per sale will go up. For example, in one week you might sell 300 customers $600 worth of goods. The average sale would then be $2. The next week you might increase your average sale to $2.50, but you might sell only 200 customers, for a sales total of $500. This means that while you have increased your average sale by 50¢, you have reduced your sales volume by $100 and may have increased your cost per sale by 50 percent. So increasing the average sale is not enough. To be effective, it should be accompanied by more sales per period, resulting in a lower cost per sale.

Advantages of Salon Selling

When sales personnel are properly trained and are given sufficient time to practice salon selling, there is no better method of increasing sales and profits and creating a highly satisfying experience, socially, economically, and psychologically, between the customer and the salesperson. Thus, the store benefits from increased sales and profits, reduced employee turnover, and the building up of a growing loyal clientele.

Disadvantages of Salon Selling

The disadvantages of salon selling are many and they are growing all the time. It is very difficult to obtain the right personnel because so many other jobs offer more prestige, more money, and better working conditions. In addition, store owners often do not realize that one customer well-served is worth three who are poorly attended. They tend to keep only enough staff for minimum customer traffic, and since most people shop at the same time, any salesperson who could use salon selling techniques to advantage is unable to do so. When salespeople know that customers are waiting impatiently to be served, they sell under pressure which limits their professional selling style.

This situation is further aggravated in a salon type store because the people who are not being served have very little to interest them while they wait for a salesperson. They can look at untouchable displays, but they can't get involved with the merchandise because it is in drawers, behind glass, under counters, or in showcases. Again, counter arrangements do not always lead to the most advantageous selling conditions, for they require that the salesperson stand behind the showcase and the customer remain in front. This creates a barrier in the selling relationship and sometimes loses sales. Finally, the customer is always at the mercy of the salesperson who may be tired, uninterested, or distracted, and thus many sales are lost.

Sample and Preselection Selling Techniques

The seven phases of salon selling may also be used by sample and pre-selection personnel, but they require different techniques. In sample selling, only a sample of each item the store or department carries is displayed within the customer's reach. She selects the merchandise in which she is interested and then goes to a saleslady who gives her the exact size and color required. A shoe department is a good example of this selling technique.

Preselection requires that all the merchandise be displayed. The customer chooses what she wants, but needs some instruction or other help from a salesperson to complete the sale. For example, in a dress department arranged for preselection, the customer would have access to all the garments but once she made her choice she would have to be shown to the fitting room to try on the dress and perhaps be fitted for alterations.

In both sample and preselection arrangements the customer is expected to do the initial shopping. Therefore, displays, fixtures, tickets, and signs must do the preliminary selling. The salesperson should not approach the customer but simply acknowledge her presence with a smile and pleasant greeting and continue her stockkeeping and housekeeping duties until she sees that the shopper is having difficulty or requires help. Only then does she approach and enter into the sale.

At this point, the clerk may develop the sale through salon techniques or she may simply give the customer information or other help and then go back to her duties. For example, if a customer wants to try on a skirt, the salesperson may either show her the fitting room and leave her alone or she may become active and use salon selling methods.

If a customer decides on her purchases herself, she takes them to a salesperson who completes the sale. Sales personnel in these departments therefore, should be highly trained in suggestion and related selling, for it is at this point that they can make many extra sales. The departure, too, should be as in salon selling, except that the salesperson does not move out of her department.

Advantages of Sample and Preselection Selling

Sales personnel can handle many more customers than in salon selling and also have time for other duties. Because all the merchandise is in full view and within easy reach of the customer, she is not handicapped by a salesperson who does not feel like selling. Since the customer can take as much time as she wants to browse, try on merchandise, read labels, compare goods and prices, she is not forced to make the quick series of decisions that salon selling entails. Sales help is always available with a minimum of delay and since there is no counter barrier, the customer–salesperson relationship can be very pleasant and informal. Maximum merchandise presentation also encourages impulse buying and this, too, increases sales. There is little pressure on sales personnel. Customers who wish to be waited on but find all the salespeople busy can occupy themselves by examining merchandise until someone is free to look after them.

Disadvantages of Sample and Preselection Selling

Forcing the customer to wait on herself is ineffective in such areas as expensive or highly technical merchandise. Here, customers demand and require more help and information than any fixture or sign can give. They want the personal touch and the assurance that their purchases are the correct ones. Moreover, in sample and preselection selling customers usually buy what they think they need, not what they should have. This can lead to exchanges and customer dissatisfaction. It also loses sales because many customers feel that they should not bother the sales personnel and so walk out without buying merchandise which is in the store but which, for some reason, they did not see.

Self-selection and Self-service Techniques

Here, personal selling is almost entirely eliminated. Store employees are hired to do stockkeeping and housekeeping and to handle customer inquiries only as incidentals. Both of these selling methods require that all the merchandise be displayed and that customers do their own shopping. Self-selection differs from self-service in that self-selection requires the customer to take purchases to a salesperson in the particular department that handles the item in order to complete the sale. In self-service customers shop throughout the store and then pay for all their purchases at one time. For example, under a self-selection arrangement, a customer cannot choose a dress, a table lamp, and a pair of shoes and pay for them as she leaves the store. She must complete these purchases in three separate departments. In a self-service arrangement, however, only one transaction at the checkout counter is necessary.

In both methods of selling, customers should obtain the necessary merchandise knowledge from labels or signs and use the services of store personnel only when they pay for their purchases. Consequently, employees cannot use salon selling techniques except to be friendly and answer questions courteously. Large grocery chains foster this kind of service (Fig. 14.3). In small stores in which the owner or cashier knows the customers, a certain amount of suggestion and related selling can be accomplished. For

Friendly Courtesy is our attitude toward every customer,
rich or poor, young or old. It is our way of demonstrating that we appreciate
their patronage and that we want every customer to come back again and again.

The job of each person in our organization is dependent on
Customer Goodwill. Without customers, there would be no pay in our envelopes
at the end of each week. Thus, it is essential that everyone, from the part-
time student right on up to the President, displays friendliness each time the
opportunity arises.

Not only is Friendly Courtesy good for business, it is also a
way of life that is contagious, adding to job enrichment as well as job efficiency.
One of the best ways to show customers this feeling of friendliness is to greet
each and every one of them with a smile and a friendly "hello".

So smile at your customers and fellow employees...they may
even smile back!

"Smile and the whole world smiles with you
Frown and you frown alone".

Always use "please and "thank you", and answer questions
with a polite "yes" or "no". When you have finished serving a customer end the
conversation with "Have a nice day" or "Have a nice week-end".

TRY IT   IT WORKS

Friendly Courtesy is measured, not only in terms of words or
smiles, but also by our actions. Put yourself in the customers shoes!

Do you see the buggies scattered all over the store and
containing bits of paper, lettuce leaves, and other garbage? Or are they
where they belong, clean and in good running order?

Is the person behind the meat counter, the snack bar, attending
the scale in the Produce aisle, waiting on customers in turn? Is he or she using
the number tags where they exist?

FIGURE 14.3 A large chain store stresses to its employees its policy of "friendly courtesy."

Courtesy Dominion Stores Ltd., Toronto, Canada.

example, the grocer or clerk at the cash register could suggest to Mrs. Smith the large economy size for her big family or could mention specials.

Advantages of Self-selection and Self-service

When done properly, as in supermarkets and discount houses, self-selection and self-service are highly satisfactory. Customers seem to enjoy the freedom of moving about without being "watched" and "imposed upon" by sales personnel, and customers who want to shop quickly find it satisfactory, for they soon learn the location of the items they want. Customers who like to shop leisurely look upon the open displays as an adventure. They enjoy moving from one section to another and examining the merchandise for unexpected prices or products. Impulse buying is exceedingly high because a tremendous amount of motivational research has gone into displays, packaging, merchandise location, etc. The cost per sale is very low because these methods require very little staff and customer returns are discouraged.

Disadvantages of Self-selection and Self-service

Self-selection and self-service are best for customers who are willing to forego service for price. Since the retailer can offer little more than price, he must shout as loud as or louder than his competitors. This kind of promotion is very expensive. The retailer must also buy very shrewdly and be constantly aware that small markups and fast turnover are his life blood. Also, these stores invite pilferage which can become a major drain on profits.

Make the Most of Your Selling Method

Change your thinking to fit your selling operation. In most small stores all methods of selling can be used but the owner must be aware that if he changes his selling patterns without changing his thinking processes, he will then have as unhappy results as those of the grocer described in Chapter 17.

Sales Meetings

If you employ more than one salesperson, arrange to have a short sales meeting every week. This could be either 15 or 30 minutes before the store opens or on a slow morning. Use the meeting to review one selling phase, demonstrate new merchandise, or explain the selling points of the weekend advertisement. Once these meetings become part of the store routine, they will be one of the most valuable techniques you have for increasing sales volume and moving merchandise.

HOW MUCH A SALESPERSON SHOULD SELL

WEEKLY SALARIES ➤	$75.00	$80.00	$85.00	$90.00	$95.00	$100.00	$110.00	$120.00	$130.00	$140.00	$150.00	$160.00	$170.00	$180.00
SALARY COST PERCENTAGES														

AMOUNT OF WEEKLY SALES	$75.00	$80.00	$85.00	$90.00	$95.00	$100.00	$110.00	$120.00	$130.00	$140.00	$150.00	$160.00	$170.00	$180.00
$ 300	25.0	26.7	28.3	30.0	31.7	33.4	36.7	40.0	43.3	46.7	50.0	53.3	56.7	60.0
325	23.1	24.6	26.2	27.7	29.2	30.8	33.8	36.9	40.0	43.1	46.2	49.2	52.3	55.4
350	21.4	22.9	24.3	25.7	27.1	28.6	31.4	34.3	37.1	40.0	42.9	45.7	48.6	51.4
375	20.0	21.3	22.7	24.0	25.3	26.7	29.3	32.0	34.7	37.3	40.0	42.7	45.3	48.0
400	18.8	20.0	21.3	22.5	23.8	25.0	27.5	30.0	32.5	35.0	37.5	40.0	43.0	45.0
425	17.6	18.8	20.0	21.2	22.4	23.5	25.9	28.2	30.6	32.9	35.3	37.6	40.0	42.4
450	16.7	17.8	18.9	20.0	21.1	22.2	24.4	26.7	28.9	31.1	33.3	35.6	37.8	40.0
475	15.8	16.8	17.9	18.9	20.0	21.1	23.2	25.3	27.4	29.5	31.6	33.7	35.8	37.9
500	15.0	16.0	17.0	18.0	19.0	20.0	22.0	24.0	26.0	28.0	30.0	32.0	34.0	36.0
525	14.3	15.2	16.2	17.1	18.1	19.0	21.0	22.9	24.8	26.7	28.6	30.5	32.4	34.3
550	13.6	14.5	15.5	16.4	17.3	18.2	20.0	21.8	23.6	25.5	27.3	29.1	30.9	32.7
575	13.0	13.9	14.8	15.7	16.5	17.4	19.1	20.9	22.6	24.3	26.1	27.8	29.0	31.3
600	12.5	13.3	14.2	15.0	15.8	16.7	18.3	20.0	21.7	23.3	25.0	26.7	28.3	30.0
625	12.0	12.8	13.6	14.4	15.2	16.0	17.6	19.2	20.8	22.4	24.0	25.6	27.2	28.8
650	11.5	12.3	13.1	13.8	14.6	15.4	16.9	18.5	20.0	21.5	23.1	24.6	26.2	27.7
675	11.1	11.8	12.6	13.3	14.1	14.8	16.3	17.8	19.3	20.7	22.2	23.7	25.2	26.7
700	10.7	11.4	12.1	12.9	13.6	14.3	15.7	17.1	18.6	20.0	21.4	22.9	24.3	25.7
725	10.3	11.0	11.7	12.4	13.1	13.8	15.2	16.6	17.9	19.3	20.7	22.1	23.4	24.8
750	10.0	10.7	11.3	12.0	12.7	13.3	14.7	16.0	17.3	18.7	20.0	21.3	22.7	24.0
775	9.7	10.3	11.0	11.6	12.3	12.9	14.2	15.5	16.8	18.1	19.4	20.6	21.9	23.2
800	9.4	10.0	10.6	11.3	11.9	12.5	13.8	15.0	16.3	17.5	18.8	20.0	21.3	22.5
825	9.1	9.7	10.3	10.9	11.5	12.1	13.3	14.5	15.8	17.0	18.2	19.4	20.6	21.8
850	8.8	9.4	10.0	10.6	11.2	11.8	12.9	14.1	15.3	16.5	17.6	18.8	20.0	21.2
875	8.6	9.1	9.7	10.3	10.9	11.4	12.6	13.7	14.9	16.0	17.1	18.3	19.4	20.6
900	8.3	8.9	9.4	10.0	10.6	11.1	12.2	13.3	14.4	15.6	16.7	17.8	18.9	20.0
925	8.1	8.6	9.2	9.7	10.3	10.8	11.9	13.0	14.1	15.1	16.2	17.3	18.4	19.5
950	7.9	8.4	8.9	9.5	10.0	10.5	11.6	12.6	13.7	14.7	15.8	16.8	17.9	18.9
975	7.7	8.2	8.7	9.2	9.7	10.3	11.3	12.3	13.3	14.4	15.4	16.4	17.4	18.5
1000	7.5	8.0	8.5	9.0	9.5	10.0	11.0	12.0	13.0	14.0	15.0	16.0	17.0	18.0
1025	7.3	7.8	8.3	8.8	9.3	9.8	10.7	11.7	12.7	13.7	14.6	15.6	16.6	17.6
1050	7.1	7.6	8.1	8.6	9.1	9.5	10.5	11.4	12.4	13.3	14.3	15.2	16.2	17.1
1075	7.0	7.4	7.9	8.4	8.8	9.3	10.2	11.2	12.1	13.0	14.0	14.9	15.8	16.7
1100	6.8	7.3	7.7	8.2	8.6	9.1	10.0	10.9	11.8	12.7	13.6	14.6	15.5	16.4
1125	6.7	7.1	7.6	8.0	8.4	8.9	9.8	10.7	11.6	12.4	13.3	14.2	15.1	16.0
1150	6.5	7.0	7.4	7.8	8.3	8.7	9.6	10.4	11.3	12.2	13.0	13.9	14.8	15.7
1175	6.4	6.8	7.2	7.7	8.1	8.5	9.4	10.2	11.1	11.9	12.8	13.6	14.5	15.3
1200	6.3	6.7	7.1	7.5	7.9	8.3	9.2	10.0	10.8	11.7	12.5	13.3	14.2	15.0
1225	6.1	6.5	6.9	7.4	7.8	8.2	9.0	9.8	10.6	11.4	12.2	13.1	13.9	14.7
1250	6.0	6.4	6.8	7.2	7.6	8.0	8.8	9.6	10.4	11.2	12.0	12.8	13.6	14.4
1275	5.9	6.3	6.7	7.1	7.5	7.8	8.6	9.4	10.2	11.0	11.8	12.6	13.3	14.1
1300	5.8	6.2	6.5	6.9	7.3	7.7	8.5	9.2	10.0	10.8	11.5	12.3	13.1	13.9
1325	5.7	6.0	6.4	6.8	7.2	7.6	8.3	9.1	9.8	10.6	11.3	12.1	12.8	13.6
1350	5.6	5.9	6.3	6.7	7.0	7.4	8.2	8.9	9.6	10.4	11.1	11.9	12.6	13.3

The figures in the top line of the table represent weekly salaries. Those in the extreme left are the weekly sales required to justify the salaries according to salary cost percentages.

To determine how much a salesperson should sell, select the column headed with the weekly salary of the salesperson. Follow this column down to the salary cost percentage nearest that of your store. The dollar figures on the same line in the AMOUNT OF WEEKLY SALES column (extreme left) show what the salesperson should sell each week to earn his salary.

Example: A salesperson receives $110.00 per week in the men's wear store. The salary cost percentage for stores in this classification is 9.29. Under the column marked $110.00, locate the salary percentage or the one closest to it. The amount in the AMOUNT OF WEEKLY SALES column opposite 9.2 is $1200.00. This is the average amount of merchandise the salesperson should sell each week to earn his salary of $110.00.

If you know the average weekly sales of your salespeople, you can determine which ones deserve salary increases with this table. Find the salesperson's amount of weekly sales and follow that row across to your salary cost percentage. The weekly salary at the top of that column is what your salesperson is actually earning. If you're paying him less than the table indicates he should be paid, he may be entitled to a raise. But if you're paying him more, the difference is coming directly out of your profit.

FIGURE 14.4 How much a salesperson should sell

Courtesy NCR Corporation, Dayton, Ohio.

At a definite time each month you could have a meeting at which, if you think it desirable, you may review the month's store and individual sales records. The meeting should end with a general discussion. At first you will have to coax your staff to talk, but if you try to be informal and not act like a boss, they will soon respond. If they remain silent, the fault is yours, because salespeople like to talk and everyone has grievances. In fact, the first few meetings will be full of complaints, but as time goes on, the meetings will become more constructive.

Be careful how you answer a complaint. Be honest and, above all, be fair. Ask the staff for solutions, better methods of operating, etc. They sometimes have excellent ideas, but during business hours you and they are too busy to talk about them. All decisions, however, must come from you. What might be best for the sales staff could be harmful to the store or for you.

How to Pay Sales Personnel

The wages of sales personnel depend largely on the kind of selling they do. A salesperson employed for salon selling should receive much higher compensation than one working in a self-selection department. Sales personnel today increase their pay in many ways other than straight salary. Some of these are discussed in Chapter 19 under employee compensation.

What should salespeople cost?

If you establish a well-publicized policy of paying more than the going rate and if you are a demanding but fair employer, you should, in time, be able to command the elite of the sales personnel in your locality. It is difficult for a small retailer to accept this principle, but whenever he does, the results are very satisfying.

To the customer, the salesperson *is* the store. Happy, comparatively intelligent and efficient personnel bring customers back again and again, and your profit increases accordingly.

By keeping the wages of your sales personnel separate from other expenses and by converting the total into a percentage of sales, you can compare your current percentage with your own past records and with other sources, to learn trends. By dividing wages into the number of sales transactions, you can obtain the salesperson's cost per transaction. Figure 14.4 is a table of weekly wages and the cost percentages that can be used as a guide to setting basic wages and other compensations. Since salespeople's wages, like everything else in retailing, change, they should be reviewed and revised periodically, and appropriate action should be taken.

WHAT THIS CHAPTER TOLD YOU

1. Continual sales training pays big dividends.
2. Since the 1950s, selling techniques have undergone many significant

changes. Today they range from salon selling where the customer is presumed helpless to self-service where sales personnel are virtually nonexistent.

3. Most stores can use all selling techniques to advantage.

4. Retailers should select different people for each selling method.

5. Salon selling requires constant training in the seven phases of making a sale, as well as in the preplanning of sales talks.

6. The other selling methods can use certain of the seven steps with some changes in technique.

7. The retailer must be able to re-educate himself as well as his staff and his customers when he changes a section of his store from one type of selling to another.

8. It is advantageous to establish a reputation for paying your sales personnel more than the going rate.

15

How Much Service
Should A Customer Get?

WHAT THIS CHAPTER IS ABOUT

You can promote sales by displaying merchandise so temptingly in your windows and inside the store that shoppers are motivated to make a purchase, and you can let them know about your store and its merchandise through advertising media. Some shops stress personal selling as a method of promoting sales, and most stores try to make shopping convenient, easy, and enjoyable by offering customers such services as free parking, free delivery, credit, alterations, liberal return policies, etc. Since these services cost money, the retailer must evaluate each one in terms of whether or not it brings in at least sufficient profit to offset the expense it entails. This chapter will discuss some of the usual services offered to customers and will point out how to tell whether or not they are worthwhile for your operation.

How Services Started

Up to the middle 1800s, retailers did not offer customers any services at all. It was pioneers like Marshall Field who discovered that catering to customer needs paid off in increased sales volume and who developed many of the standard as well as fringe services that most large stores still offer today. As long as only one store gave these services, the rewards were worthwhile, but as soon as they were introduced and improved upon by other stores, the benefits for each store diminished. Nevertheless, until

World War II, competition forced larger retailers to develop more and more customer services.

Services Since World War II

After World War II, discount houses put the spotlight on customer services. Why, they reasoned, should customers who buy for cash and take their purchases home and keep them pay the same retail price as customers who phone in their orders, charge them, have them delivered, make a complaint, have the store send out employees to attempt adjustments, then have the parcels picked up and the refunds credited to their accounts? Why should customers who go into a store, select what they want themselves, pay cash for the goods, and take the items with them have to pay the same prices as customers who park their cars free, take up a lot of highly paid salespeople's time, and have the parcels gift wrapped, charged, and sent home?

Promotional stores, catalogue stores, and warehouse stores have eliminated almost all customer services for they have discovered that there are enough people who are pleased to exchange services for low prices.

Also, since World War II the expense of maintaining such traditional services as free alterations and free delivery has so skyrocketed that attempts have been made to make customers pay for, or share, their cost. Today, every small retailer must review his service policies and decide whether or not he can afford to offer them to his customers.

Returns and Adjustments

Customer returns and adjustments are as inevitable in retailing as insects and blight are in farming. Every merchant must decide on a return and adjustment policy, remembering that it will help to create and keep alive his store image. Many promotional stores discourage returns, but almost all institutional stores handle them with a smile. Sears actively promotes returns through its slogan "Satisfaction guaranteed or your money back."

Most small stores try to adjust reasonable complaints and will refund the purchase price in cash or with a credit slip because they feel that goodwill and word-of-mouth advertising are worth the cost and effort of satisfying the customer. Their policy does not assume that customers are always right, but rather that they should be given the benefit of any doubt. There are, however, certain people who get a peculiar satisfaction out of buying merchandise and bringing it back. Some return it in salable condition, but others being it back after the selling season is over in such poor condition that it can only be sold at a loss. The small retailer should be able to recognize these people quickly and discourage them from returning merchandise. When they purchase the goods, the owner might personally make the bill "no return permitted" and sign his name. Then, unless the merchandise is actually faulty, he should refuse to accept the return in spite of threats of unfavorable publicity. The store can do without these customers.

How to Handle Complaints

Before customers return merchandise to a small store, they usually go through a struggle with themselves. They not only must make a special effort to bring back the items, they also expect an argument and so they are very sensitive to the way they are treated by the store. Because of this fact store owners should avoid handling returns themselves, for they take most complaints as a personal slight on their ability to run their stores properly. It is better to let returns be handled by employees who are particularly courteous and attentive to customers and have been taught how to handle returns pleasantly. It has been found that if a store immediately shows sympathy and willingness to be fair, customers are so relieved that they will accept any reasonable adjustment.

In some cases, this involves a long wait; for example, if merchandise has to be returned to the vendor for adjustment. The customer may need the item right away and may be upset by the delay. Good vendor relationships minimize such situations, but if it is not possible to make an immediate adjustment and if the customer is going to suffer because of the delay, the retailer is wise to offer some compensation or substitution. This usually involves a small cost, but it creates enormous goodwill and customer loyalty.

Returns Are Expensive

Most merchants do not realize how very expensive a return can be. Every sale costs money. There is the time the salesperson spends in selling the merchandise, recording, wrapping, and perhaps having it delivered. If it is a telephone order, there will be handling and recording costs involved. When a customer returns merchandise, another whole series of expenses must be added to the selling costs: more of the salesperson's time, more recording, and perhaps transportation from the customer's home to the store. If the return is made over the phone, there is still further expense.

The depreciation of the returned merchandise must also be considered. Sometimes this necessitates repairs or cleaning, and even then the merchandise may have been so badly handled by the customer that it has to be reduced. At other times, the return is made so late in the season that the item has to be marked down to clearance prices. Of course, to all these expenses the retailer must add customer annoyance and the ever-present danger of creating ill will.

If the items are large (furniture, rugs, or electrical appliances), the return cost may be covered in the markup. But returns of less expensive items may easily result in the loss of more money than the goods were worth originally.

A survey of 11 department stores in the Boston area for one year showed that returns amounted to 12½ percent of total sales and that over 63 percent of the returned items were priced at $5 or less.

Price of Goods Returned			Percentage of Total Returns	
$ 0.01 to $ 0.50	3.4%			
0.51 to 1.00	7.8		34.8%	
1.01 to 2.00	23.6		not over $2	63.2%
2.01 to 5.00	28.4			not over $5
5.01 to 10.00	17.4			
10.01 to 20.00	11.6			
20.01 to 50.00	3.5			
50.01 to 100.00	1.2			
100.01 and up	3.1			
	100.0%			

It is obvious that some of these items were hardly worth the expense of picking them up and putting them back in stock.

The survey also listed the return frequency of certain kinds of goods:

	Percentage of Total Returns
Dresses	25.4
Women's and misses' wear	10.9
Shoes	10.5
Men's furnishings	6.7
Gloves	5.9
Hosiery	5.7
Furniture	3.3
Notions	3.0
Millinery	2.6
Groceries	2.4

You will note that the largest percentage of returns in this table was in clothing and that dresses were the heaviest item returned.

The survey then went on to list the reasons for returns. These were:

Reasons for Returns	Percentage of Total Returns
Wrong size	37.2
Unsatisfactory merchandise	16.5
Goods that did not match	15.6
Change of mind	15.0
Faulty merchandise	13.0
Misrepresentation by the store	1.2
Disapproval of the person for whom the merchandise was purchased	1.2
Unsatisfactory delivery service	.3
	100.0

How to Reduce Returns

Almost every one of the reasons given above can be corrected if a store attacks the return problem intelligently and consistently. For example, "wrong size" in most cases is a result of faulty sales training. Salespeople should be aware of and make allowances for differences in each manufacturer's cut and sizing methods. If the item is either sent or cannot be tried on by the customer, it should always be checked to see that the size put on by the supplier is correct.

If the order is received over the telephone, the salesperson should be trained to ask questions that will permit her to arrive at the correct size. For example, if she can obtain the customer's approximate weight and height, she should be able to judge the clothing size correctly. If the customer is in the store, the salesperson should encourage her to try on the item before deciding on the purchase. It is better to lose a sale in the first place than to go through the expense of making it and then lose it anyway.

"Unsatisfactory merchandise" and "change of mind," which accounted for 31.5 percent of the returns, can be corrected by judicious handling at the store. Frequently, these returns are not caused by faulty merchandise, but by the customers' deciding, for some reason or other, that they did not want it once they brought it home. In most cases this means that customers were sold merchandise that was either too high or too low in price. This happened because the salespeople were either too lazy or too untrained to sell properly.

"Goods that do not match" and "faulty merchandise" are usually a result of carelessness on the part of the salesperson. "Misrepresentation" can be the result of poorly made policies or poor staff training.

"Unsatisfactory delivery service," although only .3 percent of total returns, can also be corrected by using a proper delivery system. Even the 1.2 percent of the returns that are classified as "disapproval by the person for whom the merchandise was purchased" can be lowered if the salespeople are trained to ask the right questions and then sell the customers not what they think they want but what they really need.

Of course, if some of your business is done by or through the mail, returns are likely to be higher than if you do in-store selling. Also, when part of your selling technique is to permit the customer to take home items on approval, returns can be larger than normal. But no matter what business methods you use, if you realize the tangible costs of each return, you will attempt to cut them down considerably without creating inconvenience or ill will. In fact, if you eliminate as far as possible the causes of returns, customer satisfaction with your operation will increase.

Alterations and Repairs

Alterations and repairs are becoming increasingly expensive, but whenever a store that traditionally absorbed these costs attempted to charge for alterations, customer reaction was sharply negative and, in most cases, the store returned to absorbing these expenses and added them to the retail price. Yet, promotional stores never offered these services and caused no ill will. Most customers today will pay for some of their own alterations and repairs if they feel that this will give them a price advantage. Yet, sometimes free alterations can be successfully used for certain promotions if the extra volume will pay for its costs. For example, fabric shops will occasionally make "free" draperies from materials purchased in their stores. Institutional stores, of course, absorb these expenses in order to maintain their image of service.

In the meantime, ways of cutting costs should be explored. Is it better to recommend a tailor, or is it cheaper to send out work than to pay for staff, buy the necessary equipment, and stock the findings that alterations on the premises entail? Do you need two full-time employees to do this work, or can it be done with part-time help and by working overtime? Can two or more retailers get together and set up a cooperative system?

Store Credit and Credit Cards

A small retailer is always being pressured into giving credit by competition, credit card companies, and some of his customers. Even some supermarkets and most promotional stores offer some kind of credit. In most cases, credit will increase sales volume, but because it also increases operational costs, you must decide whether you should sell for cash only or use some credit combination.

Credit makes it easier for the customer to buy more goods and buy them at higher prices. Because little or no cash is involved at the time of the purchase, customers tend to think that they have more income than they actually have. Why should they not take more and better merchandise? Credit also permits them to make many purchases at different times and pay for all of them when it is most convenient for them, usually on paydays. Again, since the whole family can use one charge account, everyone tends to

Why credit increases sales

buy more goods at higher prices than they would if they paid cash on the spot. A charge customer can shop over the phone or by mail and not be bothered with CODs. Another reason for offering your own credit in a small store is the habit that a certain number of charge customers form of coming into the shop to make a payment and then buying something else.

Most retailers do not realize that when they give a customer credit, they are actually lending that customer a certain amount of money for the period agreed upon by the particular contract. For example, if the amount loaned is $100 for 60 days, the merchant in effect lends the customer $100 for a period of 2 months. Thus, it is only fair that credit customers pay the store sufficient interest on the money loaned to cover at least the finance charges the store has to pay whether it uses its own capital or borrows from a lending institution. Because of competition and the lack of understanding about credit costs, most stores charge customers only the going interest rate. Thus, they lose money because this rate does not cover such factors as risk involved or office costs. So no matter whether you give customers credit through an in-store or external arrangement, you should realize that this service costs money.

Why customers should pay for credit

The kind of merchandise handled is the main factor to consider when you think of credit as a customer service. Stores selling such quick-moving, small profit items as cigarettes and soft drinks should not offer credit, although many owners of such businesses do permit a limited number of charge customers. The best stores for active credit promotion are those carrying big-ticket items with good markups, such as clothing, furniture, or major electrical appliances.

Who should offer credit?

Originally, credit involved customers' opening charge accounts and paying what they owed whenever statements were sent them, usually once a month. But this system proved unsatisfactory for big-ticket items like furniture or furs and a new method of charging had to be developed. This was called *installment buying*. The customer was asked to make a down payment and was then permitted to pay the balance in a series of monthly or weekly installments. Interest was charged on the balance owing at the beginning of each month.

In-store credit arrangements

From these two main methods a number of variations have evolved. For example, *revolving* credit, a combination of the two, permits customers to charge up to an amount that equals a certain number of times their monthly payments. Under this scheme, if customers agree to pay $10 a month, they may be able to buy up to $60 ($10 × 6), or $100 ($10 × 10), depending on the store's revolving credit policy. As with installment accounts, customers pay a small interest charge on the balance owing at the beginning of each month. A further refinement is the *flexible revolving* account. In this case the payments vary according to the balance in the account, and customers are told how much they are required to pay when their monthly statements are mailed to them.

Truth in Lending Acts. In 1968 the federal government passed Consumer Credit Protection legislation which became known as the Truth-in-Lending Act. This was soon followed by the Federal Reserve System's Regulation Z. The major provisions of the Act and Regulation Z make it mandatory for retailers to provide their customers with a written statement that sets out exactly how much time a customer is allowed before the store can add a finance charge, how this charge is to be applied, and how it is calculated. It must also include whatever additional charges or penalties the store wishes to impose and the customer's minimum payment, if any.

When a Customer Disputes Your Bill. The Truth-in-Lending Act is very specific about what to do when customers dispute the amount of a bill you sent. According to the Act, they have sixty days from the date you mail the bill to notify you that they believe it to be in error. You must then acknowledge the letter within thirty days of receiving it, but you have ninety days to either correct the error or explain to the customer why you believe your amount is correct.

During this period neither you, a lawyer, nor a collection agency may send collection letters nor take any other action to collect the amount in dispute. You are also forbidden to threaten the customers with damage to their credit rating, sue them for the disputed amount or report the amount as delinquent to a credit bureau or to other creditors. However, you are permitted to keep sending statements, apply the disputed amount against the customers' balance and perform whatever acts are necessary to collect the undisputed amount.

If it is decided that you made the mistake in the bill, the customer does not have to pay any finance charges on the disputed amount and must be allowed the normal time to pay up the undisputed amount. However, if you have not made an error, you can add your nominal finance charges to the disputed amount, and the customer may make up any missed payments on this amount.

Other clauses state that unless customers agree that the bill is correct, you must send them a written notification of what they owe and give them ten days *after* they receive this letter to notify you that they are still not satisfied and refuse to pay the disputed amount. You are then free to report them to credit bureaus or other creditors and take your normal action to collect what they owe you. However, you must tell the customers where you have sent your notifications and that in every case you reported their side of the dispute. If, later on, the dispute is settled, you must notify those to whom you reported the customer as being delinquent of this settlement.

If you do not follow these procedures, you will not be allowed to collect the first $50 of the disputed amount plus finance charges *even though* your bill turns out to be correct.

Remember, the above paragraphs are only a brief outline of the more significant regulations of the federal Truth-in-Lending Acts. Because these acts contain many other requirements and because the state or states where you operate may have their own laws and regulations, you should obtain and study all federal and state legislation involved with customer credit.

The owner of a small store who does not actively promote credit usually knows the customer who asks him for a charge account, and thus he has a good idea of the customer's ability to pay. But if credit is being actively promoted, a system of handling applicants must be created which will separate good risks from bad ones. In such a system the initial interview is most important. It should take place in a quiet part of the store and be as private as possible. The interviewer then has an opportunity to sell the store, build goodwill, and also make certain that the customer is aware of his or her responsibilities. The interviewer attempts to obtain sufficient pertinent information from the applicant to determine whether to open a charge account or to offer another purchase plan. The form shown in Fig. 15.1 indicates some of the questions that should be asked of every applicant.

How to open charge accounts

Dishonest charge customers have developed many techniques for fooling stores. Therefore, you can never be too careful. That is why some stores have a policy of checking every applicant with the local credit bureau. These stores ask for a file report, or when necessary, obtain more detailed information. A sample credit report is shown in Fig. 15.2.

Checking charge applicants

Of course, if you refuse an applicant you must follow the regulations set out in the Fair Credit Reporting Act. This obliges you to give the customer the name and address of the reporting bureau so that he or she can examine the file for themselves. However, the law *does not* oblige you to tell the customer the specific reason(s) that made you reject him or her.

Always try to deliver the first charge because it gives you time to make a thorough check and also provides an opportunity to find out if the applicant actually lives where he says he does, what his surroundings are like, and so on.

There are many kinds of systems for handling charge accounts. Look around before installing yours, talk to firms that specialize in credit control, the NRMA Credit Division, and your trade association, as well as to retailers who already have credit account systems in operation. Find out what they like about their systems and how they would improve on them. Remember that a system is good only if it does a proper job for you at your stage of development, and remember that a wrong system can be very expensive in employee wages and customer ill will.

Credit accounting systems

Some stores have found that the best time to mail a statement is a few days before payment is due. If possible, customers should be reminded of their obligations just before they receive their wages. It is also important to set up a good system to handle customers who fail to pay on time (see Fig. 15.3). For this purpose, a series of notices and telephone calls that start off as reminders, but get tougher as the time goes on, should be used. Some-

Collecting on charge accounts

217

	DATE	LIMIT	CC	ACCOUNT NUMBER	TYPE	RT.

PLEASE PRINT ALL INFORMATION PLAINLY   FOR OFFICE USE ONLY

FIRST NAME (INCLUDE INITIAL) MR. ☐ MRS. ☐ MISS ☐ MS. ☐	LAST NAME (INCLUDING SUFFIX)
STREET ADDRESS	CARE OF OR APT. NO.
CITY OR TOWN STATE	ZIP CODE HOW LONG PHONE NUMBER

SPOUSE'S FIRST NAME

PREVIOUS ADDRESS   PLEASE CHECK   MARRIED ☐   SINGLE ☐   WIDOW(ER) ☐   DIVORCED ☐   SEPARATED ☐   OWN HOME ☐   RENT ☐   ROOMING ☐   LIVING WITH PARENTS ☐

	ADDRESS	POSITION	HOW LONG
EMPLOYER - SELF			
PREVIOUS EMPLOYER - SELF			
EMPLOYER (SPOUSE)			
PREVIOUS EMPLOYER (SPOUSE)			

CHARGE ACCOUNTS IN OTHER STORES	CITY	BANK ACCOUNT	CITY	CHECKING ☐ SAVINGS ☐
		BANK ACCOUNT	CITY	CHECKING ☐ SAVINGS ☐
		CREDIT CARDS		

PLEASE SIGN ON REVERSE SIDE OF ORIGINAL AND DUPLICATE COPY OF THIS APPLICATION

TAKEN BY	APPROVED BY	STORE #	DATE

CHARGE ACCOUNT AGREEMENT

Worth's SMILING SERVICE

P.O. Box 1430
Waterbury, CT. 06720
Tel: 754-5101

I request a Worth's charge account and agree that merchandise and services purchased by me and my immediate family will be paid for in accordance with the following terms.

1) To use this account as a **30**-day charge account without finance charges by paying the total indebtedness within **30** days after billing date, or to pay at least 1/10 of the new balance each month, or $5.00 whichever is greater. If I extend my payments beyond 30 days, I understand that there is a **finance charge** computed at a **periodic rate of 1% per month**, which is an **annual percentage rate of 12%.** I agree to pay this finance charge which will be computed **upon the average daily balance** of my account in each monthly billing period. The **average daily balance** is determined by dividing the sum of the balances outstanding for each day of the monthly billing period by the number of days in the monthly billing period.

The **balance outstanding** for each day of the monthly billing period is determined by subtracting payments and credits from the previous day's balance excluding any purchases added to the account during the monthly billing period.

2) If I fail to make payments when due, you may declare the entire unpaid balance of my account immediately due and payable, together with reasonable fees incurred, if my account is referred to an outside agency or attorney for collection.

3) If more than one person signs this agreement, the obligation hereunder shall be joint and several.

4) I authorize Worth's to investigate my credit record and report to proper persons, and bureaus my performance of this agreement.

5) I have read this agreement before signing, and I acknowledge receipt of a copy thereof.

. . . .
Date

. . . .
Signature

Date Copy Mailed:_____by_____

FIGURE 15.1   It is good procedure to keep a customer's history and credit activity on one card.
Courtesy Worth's, Waterbury, Conn.

NAME AND ADDRESS OF CREDIT BUREAU MAKING REPORT

CITY CREDIT BUREAU
ANYTOWN, USA

- [ ] SINGLE REFERENCE
- [ ] IN FILE REPORT
- [ ] TRADE REPORT
- [x] FULL REPORT
- [ ] EMPLOY & TRADE REPORT
- [ ] PREVIOUS RESIDENCE REPORT

CONFIDENTIAL *Factbilt*® REPORT

FOR

CREDIT GRANTER
100 MAIN ST
ANYTOWN, U S A   10000

Date Received
10/28/74
Date Mailed
10/28/74
In File Since
6/68

This information is furnished in response to an inquiry for the purpose of evaluating credit risks. It has been obtained from sources deemed reliable, the accuracy of which this organization does not guarantee. The inquirer has agreed to indemnify the reporting bureau for any damage arising from misuse of this information, and this report is furnished in reliance upon that indemnity. It must be held in strict confidence, and must not be revealed to the subject reported on, except by reporting agency in accordance with the Fair Credit Reporting Act.

REPORT ON (SURNAME): MR., MRS., MISS. MS.		GIVEN NAME:	SOCIAL SECURITY NUMBER:	SPOUSE'S NAME:
CONSUMER MR	JOHN Q.		99-8888-77	MARY

ADDRESS:	CITY:	STATE:	ZIP CODE:	SINCE:
3456 AVE A, ANYTOWN,	ANYSTATE		10000	

COMPLETE TO HERE FOR TRADE REPORT AND SKIP TO CREDIT HISTORY

PRESENT EMPLOYER	POSITION HELD:	SINCE:	DATE EMPLOY VERIFIED	EST. MONTHLY INCOME
ACME AUTO COMPANY	service manager	6/68	1968	$ not div.

COMPLETE TO HERE FOR EMPLOYMENT AND TRADE REPORT AND SKIP TO CREDIT HISTORY

DATE OF BIRTH	NUMBER OF DEPENDENTS INCLUDING SELF:			OTHER: (EXPLAIN)
6/1/35		[ ] OWNS OR BUYING HOME	[ ] RENTS HOME	[ ]

FORMER ADDRESS:	CITY:	STATE:	FROM:	TO:

FORMER EMPLOYER:	POSITION HELD:	FROM:	TO:	EST. MONTHLY INCOME $

SPOUSE'S EMPLOYER	POSITION HELD:	SINCE:	DATE EMPLOY VERIFIED	EST. MONTHLY INCOME $

CREDIT HISTORY *(Complete this section for all reports)*

KIND OF BUSINESS	DATE REPORTED	DATE ACCOUNT OPENED	DATE OF LAST SALE	HIGHEST CREDIT	AMOUNT OWING	AMOUNT PAST DUE	TERMS OF SALE AND USUAL MANNER OF PAYMENT
D	10/28/74	10/68	12/69	$375.00	–		R-$40-1
F	" "	4/69		$3155.00	–		I-$125-1
J	" "	5/69	9/74	$408.00		$205.00	I-$50-1
D	" "	9/68	2/71	$170.00			I-1

MEMBER

Associated Credit Bureaus, Inc.

FORM 100

1-74

FIGURE 15.2   An example of a credit bureau report. Notice the poor credit record of this applicant.

Courtesy Credit Bureau of Waterbury, Inc., Conn.

OVER 50 YEARS OF SMILING SERVICE

Worth's

WATCH WORTH'S . . . FOR OVER 50 YEARS NEARLY EVERYONE HAS

P.O. BOX 1430 • WATERBURY, CONNECTICUT • 06720

TELEPHONE (203) 754-5101 EXT. 29

We are writing to remind you that your account is presently past due in the amount of $

Very likely this has been overlooked. May we ask that you send us this amount by return mail.

If your payment has recently been made, please disregard this letter and accept our thanks for your attention.

Very truly yours,

Worth's
Credit Department

Worth's

OVER 50 YEARS OF SMILING SERVICE

P.O. BOX 1430 - WATERBURY, CONNECTICUT - 06720

TELEPHONE (203) 754-5101 EXT. 291

We have not had a response to our recent letter in which we called your attention to your account which is past due in the amount of $

In order to avoid further correspondence, please send us your check or money order by return mail.

Your prompt attention to this request will be appreciated.

Very truly yours,

Worth's
Credit Department

wn waterbury / naugatuck valley mall / waterbury plaza / torrington center / danbury mall
ɔwntown manchester / manchester parkade / meriden square mall / west farms mall

---

Worth's

OVER 50 YEARS OF SMILING SERVICE

P.O. BOX 1430 - WATERBURY, CONNECTICUT - 06720

TELEPHONE (203) 754-5101 EXT. 291

Would you please be kind enough to call or come in to see us at your earliest convenience in order that we may discuss the matter of your account to our mutual satisfaction.

This opportunity is taken to assure you of our desire to be of service to you at all times.

Very truly yours,

Worth's
Credit Department

downtown waterbury / naugatuck valley mall / waterbury plaza / torrington center /
downtown manchester / manchester parkade / meriden square mall / west farr

---

Worth's

OVER 50 YEARS OF SMILING SERVICE

P.O. BOX 1430 - WATERBURY, CONNECTICUT - 06720

TELEPHONE (203) 754-5101-EXT. 251

It has been brought to my attention that your account remains unpaid. Naturally, we are concerned.

I feel sure that if we could talk it over, we would both have a better understanding.... and very likely find a solution to the problem.

Will you please come in - or call me - within the next FIVE days.

Very truly yours,

R. M. Guerrera
Credit Manager

downtown waterbury / naugatuck valley mall / waterbury plaza / torrington center / danbury mall
downtown manchester / manchester parkade / meriden square mall / west farms mall

FIGURE 15.3 This collection sequence starts with a series of gentle reminder letters that becomes more severe in requests for payment and ends with notices that demand immediate action from the debtor.

Courtesy Worth's, Waterbury, Conn.

We cannot continue to carry your account in
its present past due condition.

Your account will be placed with our attorney
unless you pay it in full, or make satisfactory arrangements, within the next FIVE
days.

Please be fair to yourself... your immediate
action will save you the added expense of
collection fees.

Very truly you

R. M. Guerre
Credit Manag

Final Notice
BEFORE SUIT

....

....
Creditor

....
Debtor

TO THE ABOVE NAMED DEBTOR:

FIRST: *Take notice that the above named creditor claims that you are indebted to
him in the sum of $.......................*

SECOND: *Although duly demanded, the same has not been paid.*

THIRD: *Now therefore, unless you remit to the above named creditor,.......................*

*on or before the..day of...A. D., 19.........for
payment of said claim, or make provision for adjustment thereof, suit may be
brought for the total amount with interest together with the costs and disburse-
ments of the action.*

Dated this...day of..., 19........

CERTIFIED STATEMENT OF ACCOUNT

*The above creditor hereby certifies that he has examined the matter in the above
mentioned claim and has found the account to be true and correct to the best of
his knowledge and belief.*

....
Creditor

MAKE PAYMENTS DIRECT TO CREDITOR

1 sp

times customers have bad luck and you can make them loyal to you by being sympathetic and patient in arranging the payment of the balance they owe. Sometimes a bad credit risk can be a good cash or layaway customer. However, as soon as you see that a customer does not intend to pay, put pressure on him or her and, if necessary, turn the account over to a collection agency. The customer will no longer patronize your store, but you don't want his business anyway.

Have a legal contract. The form you use should be approved by a competent lawyer because there are many legal and consumer angles to installment contracts and you want yours to be as foolproof as possible.

There are three main ways to carry installment accounts: (a) conditional sales agreements, (b) chattel mortgages, and (c) lease agreements.

Conditional Sales Agreements. These are sometimes called *secured transactions* for they make the title to the goods conditional upon the buyer's meeting the payments. Sometimes the purchaser agrees to pay for other charges such as insurance, maintenance, and repairs. The merchant can repossess the item if the customer does not pay in full, and he can obtain a judgment against the purchaser for loss of value of the goods at the time of repossession and be reimbursed for costs involved in the repossession action. If the retailer wants to use the contract for finance borrowing, the customer agrees that it may be assigned to a third party. Because they are so flexible, conditional sales agreements are the most popular of installment contracts.

Chattel Mortgage. Here the title to the merchandise passes immediately to the customer when he or she signs the contract, but the customer gives the retailer a *lien* against the goods for the unpaid amount.

Lease Agreements. In this case, the merchandise is *rented* to the customer, but the store retains title. However, after a certain number of payments, the customer can obtain title if he or she pays a specified sum to the store.

Down Payment. It is very desirable for the retailer to obtain a down payment that equals at least the initial depreciation of the item. Sales resistance and competition, however, may force him to take a smaller amount or even none at all. It has been found that the smaller the down payment, the easier it is to make a sale, because most charge customers never think of the total amount of money involved. They are simply interested in the down payment, the amount of each subsequent payment, and the number of installments.

Service Charge. It is only fair to charge interest on the money that you lend customers for the goods they buy on the installment plan. The interest rate is usually set by federal and state laws, custom, and competition. It should, however, cover the cost involved in operating the installment accounts, interest on the capital invested, and a fair return for the risks incurred.

Most small stores do not really know what it costs to run a credit office. They do not attempt to separate credit expenses, and they add the installment interest they receive to their operating profit and record it as "other income." If treated this way, installment credit always *appears* to make money. It would be better for retailers to think of it as they do other services and deduct the total credit expenses from the total income they receive from installment sales. Then they would be able to see whether or not installment credit is profitable.

Credit expenses should be kept separately

Knowing your credit expenses has a number of advantages. By dividing the total credit expense by the number of credit sales you make in any period, you can find the cost of each credit transaction. This tells you at what dollar amount an account becomes profitable. Below this minimum it might be better to refuse credit and encourage the customer to use a layaway plan instead.

If you divide the total credit costs by the average number of accounts for a period, you will find out what each account costs. This figure is usually so high that it might stop you from accepting charges below a certain minimum for a one-time purchase. It will also make you understand why it pays to keep accounts active, for it costs very much less to reactivate an old account than it does to open a new one (Fig. 15.4).

When credit expenses are separated, they can be controlled and ways can be found to reduce them. Streamlined manual systems, automated machines, or EDP might mean a heavy installation outlay, but savings in salaries and increased customer goodwill could make the investment worthwhile. Before you install a system, however, make sure that it is not too expensive or complicated for your current or future credit business. Remember, too, that a new system will require re-educating yourself, your employees, and your customers. Otherwise, it will be less profitable than the old, and the change will not be justified.

Control credit expenses

When you examine credit selling expenses, you will see that it costs a lot of money to account for the collection of even good risks. With bad risks, the expense of garnisheeing, repossessing, and other means of obtaining what the customer owes you increases your costs tremendously, and even when you do get a refund of your out-of-pocket expenses, it never covers the true costs involved. Therefore, the fundamental principle of a successful credit operation should be the proper screening of risks. Most good credit customers will encourage you to consult the credit exchange or other references because they enjoy being told they are A1. Usually, it is more profitable to turn down a doubtful credit applicant and lose a sale than to make the sale and run into so many expenses that your profit is wiped out. Let the poor risk take his unprofitable business elsewhere, or if he wants the

Accept only good risks

DATE_____

"YOUR PERSONAL CREDIT CERTIFICATE WORTH $5.00"

Here is a surprise bargain for you, our Credit Certificate for $5.00-----
it has just one small string attached, one that I'm sure will please you.

We have truly enjoyed having you as a charge customer at "The Capitol" in
the past.

To show you just how much we would like you to again join the ranks as one
of our charge customers, we will deduct $5.00 on your account when you, once
again, make a CHARGE purchase in any one of our fine departments within the next
60 days.

There are three convenient locations....all chock full of smart fashions
for the entire family....all ready to give you the special service you, the
customer, deserve.

We feel that there are many advantages to you as a customer, to have an
account with The Capitol.

The following are only a few of these advantages:

1. The ability to buy what you need when you want it.
2. The money savings in taking advantage of immediate special buys.
3. The opportunity of shopping at future Special Sales for Charge
   Customers only.
4. The advance notice of future sales and merchandising events.
5. The convenience of shopping without carrying cash.
6. The prestige of saying "Charge it."

Here is how it works.....

Just present this letter within the next 60 days at one of our three
fine stores serving all of Fayetteville---Downtown, Eutaw Shopping Center,
Bordeaux Shopping Center----when you make a charge purchase on your account.

Now, isn't this a great bargain. We sure hope that you will enjoy it
and, once again, become part of our growing Capitol family.

Sincerely yours,

J. Bernard Stein
President

FIGURE 15.4 Positive customer reaction is effectively stimulated by this account reactivation letter because of the limited time for the customer to take advantage of the offer of a $5 credit certificate.

Courtesy The Capitol, Fayetteville, N. C.

goods badly enough, let him put it on a layaway until his risk is sufficiently reduced to make the charge worthwhile.

Originally, if a store was unable to carry its customers' credit or preferred not to, it would sell its accounts to a finance company at a discount which varied according to the obligations the store assumed, the kind of

External credit arrangements

merchandise, etc. In this arrangement, the store, not the finance institution, made the credit arrangements with the customer.

Then came the era of credit cards. In this system, the outside agencies, not the store, decide on the client's credit limits and also assume full collection responsibility. They may set a minimum or floor amount above which the store must obtain the credit card company's OK. The fee for this credit service usually depends on such factors as the volume the store is able to generate and the method the company uses to reimburse the store, for example, does it receive almost instant cash or does it have to wait for its money?

Cash versus credit arrangements

If you can get your customers to pay cash or hold goods on deposit and layaway without decreasing the amount they buy or the prices they pay, you should avoid all credit arrangements. However, if credit will encourage more purchases at higher prices, credit should be considered. This requires a careful study of the costs involved in installing any credit arrangement before you decide whether or not increased sales and higher prices will make credit worthwhile. After making a thorough examination, you may decide to lose money on an internal credit system because it has a potential of generating business that cash alone does not provide. For example, it will give you a mailing list of customers that would be difficult to compile if you had a cash arrangement. This list can be used for promotional material that can be inserted in monthly statements or to build customer profiles that tell you what your customers buy and do not buy in your store, as well as to find out the limits of your trading area. Internal credit arrangements may also give you a degree of customer loyalty, but external systems may improve your competitive strength. For these reasons, many stores operate internal and external credit systems.

The choice is up to you, but if you decide to give credit, you must also decide whether to move into it slowly or to promote it for all its worth. At the same time, you should recognize the difficulties you will have if you find that you have to eliminate any system.

Delivery

Delivery must be considered in relation to the kind of store you operate, its location, and the goods you sell. Supermarkets, variety, and discount stores charge for delivery, some stores that cater to the middle- and upper-income groups deliver any purchase free, and other stores set a dollar minimum before a free delivery can be made. Competition, custom, and cost should help set your delivery policy. If you must offer delivery, you can cut expenses by delivering in certain areas on set days and by encouraging customers to carry small parcels. To find out what it costs to deliver a parcel, divide the number of parcels delivered in any period into the total delivery expense. Then compare that figure with delivery figures of other stores. If it is too high, break down the expenses as completely as possible and review each element intensively.

With delivery expense ratios in mind, you can project which system is best for your operation: your own delivery trucks, a cooperative delivery, or a consolidated delivery. **Three ways to deliver**

There are many advantages in running your own delivery service. Since you have complete operational freedom, you can make delivery schedules flexible. You can also give your customers personal service because the driver represents your store. If he is trained to be pleasant and courteous, the store's goodwill is enhanced. But operating even one truck can be so expensive that it may outweigh the advantages gained by having your own delivery system.

Two or more stores can get together and run a *cooperative delivery*. This reduces delivery expenses but eliminates your identity and flexibility. It may also create disputes between the retailers who own the system because each one's wishes cannot be wholly satisfied. In a *consolidated delivery* system a private carrier charges so much per parcel, establishes a definite pickup schedule, and collects and distributes parcels for the retailer who is willing to pay his fees. In this system the merchant has little influence in the delivery operations and there is no opportunity for a personal touch.

Customer Parking

If your store has no parking facilities but most of your customers must drive to reach it, parking can become a serious service problem. If customers usually park in public or private lots, you may be able to make an arrangement with the civic authorities or private lot owners to pay for your customers' parking tickets, or you may be able to get together with other merchants to form a parking lot cooperative.

Unless customer parking is based on a time limit, some customers will take advantage of your free service and use it to shop your competitors or do other chores on your time. To eliminate this practice, in parking areas employing attendants, most stores have the lot attendant deduct from the total parking charge an amount that equals the time they feel is sufficient for the average customer to leisurely shop in their store. Of course, customers must have their parking tickets validated by the store.

What you do about customer parking depends on the store image that you wish to create and whether or not this service will increase your sales and profits sufficiently to cover parking expense. Thus, like all customer services, parking must be judged on its advantages versus its cost, and periodic reviews should be made to see if the expense can be reduced or whether or not the service can be eliminated altogether.

Store Hours

Retailers big and small must constantly review the extent to which they are prepared to keep their doors open for business. To stay open 24 hours a day, 7 days a week would offer maximum customer service, but this might be illegal and in most cases would be unnecessary. You should stay open as long as it pays. This means that whenever possible business hours should be based on when most of your customers, your staff, and you want the store to be open. Your clientele couldn't care less if your store is open when they do not want to shop in it. What they demand is that it be open when they are able to go to it. Personnel tend to seek employment in stores that are most convenient to them in terms of travel and working hours. The time you want to spend away from the store must also be considered. Of course, competition, municipal laws, and shopping center regulations may force you to keep your doors open or closed. These conditions may not satisfy your customers, your staff, and you, but if you know what times are best for you, you can sometimes arrange to keep other hours to a minimum.

However, because the life-style of your customers, staff, and yourself is subject to change, store hours must be flexible and revised to satisfy changing demands. For example, it is conceivable that while your store is now open from 9 AM to 6 PM on Tuesday, Wednesday, and Thursday, from 9 AM to 9 PM on Monday and Friday, and from 9 AM to 5 PM on Saturday, a few years from now these hours might be from 12 PM to 10 PM, seven days a week. If this situation will satisfy most of the reasons for staying open, they should be followed. Any other times would merely increase overhead without improving sales or profits.

WHAT THIS CHAPTER TOLD YOU

1. The services you offer customers are worthwhile only if they increase sales and profits. But sometimes competition and custom force you to render unprofitable services.

2. The kind of store, its location, and the items sold play a major part in any service policy.

3. Every store suffers from customer returns and you must decide how they are to be handled.

4. Most returns are made because retailers do not use enough preventive measures.

5. Alterations and repairs are services that need careful consideration.

6. Credit, whether internal, external, or both, is a very important service. It usually increases sales volume, but there is some doubt about its leading to extra profits. Only by segregating all collection expenses and deducting these from collection income can the retailer reach a valid conclusion on the value of this service.

7. If you have to deliver, examine your costs and then decide which service is best for your image.

8. For some retailers parking is a particularly vexing problem. It can be solved only by studying the costs involved in paying for customer parking against a possible loss in sales volume if customers pay for their own parking.

9. Whenever possible, store hours should be set to satisfy your clientele, employees, and yourself.

16

How to Get
the Right Location
for Your Store

WHAT THIS CHAPTER IS ABOUT

A good location gives you the best possible customer potential with a minimal effort in merchandising. Today's customers are restless and as they move into or away from a neighborhood they can alter its structure sufficiently to create a problem for the retailers in the area. This chapter discusses how to find out whether or not your community has changed and, if it has, what to do about it.

Today's Customers Are on the Move

Every year thousands of stores large and small close their doors because they no longer have sufficient reason to keep them open. Some follow their customers to other locations; others simply close their doors. For example, from 1954 to 1956 such large organizations in New York City as Ohrbach's, Hearn's, and The Hecht Company shut down their 14th Street stores which once accounted for millions of dollars worth of business annually. Ohrbach's moved to 34th Street, Hearn's went to the Bronx, and The Hecht Company closed their New York store. A major chain store policy is to close low-profit units and open new ones in areas they feel will give them a more profitable operation. The owners of these stores are aware that their customers are always on the move and that what was a 100 percent location ten years ago is not nearly as good today and they know that what is farmland now can be a flourishing shopping center in a very short time.

Have Your Customers Changed?

What about your store and its neighborhood? Was it established to cater to a high-, medium-, or low-income group? Who are its customers now? Usually, when people in higher-income brackets move to the suburbs, their former homes are occupied by middle-income families who then may sell to lower-income groups. Thus, if your store once served a higher-income community, it might now be surrounded by a low-income or ethnically different neighborhood. Of course, the change could be reversed; some low-income areas could be cleared for the construction of middle- or high-rent apartment complexes or new office buildings which would bring an influx of office workers to the area.

How to Meet the New Situation

If your area *has* changed, what can you do to meet the new situation? Of course, you can act like an ostrich and bury your head in an increasing stock of unsalable merchandise, or you can get stubborn and say, "If my old customers want to buy from me, they know where I am." Either method will solve the problem—but not in the way you want it to, for both of these solutions could be fatal.

A better approach is to look at your business as though it were up for sale and you were a stranger considering buying it. Then you would see first whether the store, as it is now operating, appeals to the people in the area, and second, whether the actual site is worthwhile now and can be improved in the future.

Is the Community Expanding or Contracting?

One of the best ways of discovering whether the community is interested in your store is to combine the techniques discussed in Chapter 1 with a personal survey of the people who live in the area. If you are surrounded by an expanding group of potential customers, you are fortunate. On the other hand, customers may be moving away so that your business is being conducted with fewer and fewer people.

How Much Money Is There Around?

Having people in your area is not enough. They must have money and be willing to spend it in your kind of store. What is the true situation? Perhaps when you started, the area consisted of workers with good, steady incomes. Now the community contains many more people, but they are workers whose salaries depend on economic conditions, union contracts, and the intentions of their employers. Or an upgrading could have occurred and people are now coming into your store who desire better merchandise than you stock. So look at your present community through eyes that see what kind of customers are there now and what they are likely to be in the future.

Have the Living Standards Changed?

Over the years the living standards of your potential customers may have changed completely. People in the higher-income levels have different wants from those in the middle- and low-income brackets. An area that once consisted of large private estates may now contain clusters of small private homes. Each group has different consumer wants, living standards, and buying habits. Are you catering to people who can buy from you today and tomorrow, or are you operating a store that, in its present location, can only be considered a museum piece?

Has Competition Changed?

Take a new look at your competition. A dime was once the highest price in the Woolworth chain, but today Woolworth carries any merchandise it thinks it can sell regardless of the retail price. Visit the mass merchandisers in your area and you will be surprised at the number of items they stock that are in your store too. Again, small stores that once concentrated on coats and dresses have added other merchandise areas such as sportswear and accessories, while hardware stores sell sporting goods and sporting goods stores stock many hardware items.

What do all these changes in merchandise mix mean to your store? If the competition is keener than you thought, and this frightens you, re-member that increased competition brings more of your kind of customers into your immediate area than you could possibly attract by your own efforts. In fact, you should really worry if you have no competition, for what is the use of a monopoly business without sufficient customers? You should welcome competition although this means that you must sharpen your merchandising techniques because more stores are trying to attract more customers away from your shop.

What about Your Actual Site?

Once you have investigated the community as it is now and have judged its future, take a new look at your actual store site. Are you in a location that was once considered 100 percent and is now no more than 50 percent? Did you once have attractive and busy stores on each side of you that are now closed or turned into buildings that bring very little traffic past your door? Has your street or shopping center grown seedy over the years and is it now showing its age? Does it require structural repairs and is the immedi-ate area also in need of renovation?

What about transportation? Were you originally on a busy, two-way street which is now one-way with parking meters in front of your door? Is it difficult to reach your store by public transportation? Are the parking facilities inconvenient? Do people find your area so inviting that they are inclined to window-shop or do they rush past it without stopping or slowing down?

What to Do about Your Present Situation

If, after the survey, you reach the conclusion that there have been considerable customer and site changes, you are faced with the following alternatives:

1. If the community has changed but the store site is still good, you can enjoy considerable prosperity if you alter your merchandising pattern to fit the new situation. Chapter 1 suggests ways of approaching and solving this problem.

2. If alternative 1 requires too radical a change in both your merchandising techniques and your own attitude, or if the site is no longer desirable, you should investigate the possibilities of moving.

Convenience versus Shopping Goods

If you decide to move, is it better to relocate in a main shopping area or will a secondary one do as well? If you carry convenience goods, that is, inexpensive, quick-turning merchandise like candy and soda pop or fast-moving health and beauty aids like toothpastes and hair sprays, you must locate in heavy pedestrian traffic areas. Most convenience items are so staple that customers will not go out of their way to purchase them.

If you carry shopping goods, that is, expensive merchandise that people buy very infrequently such as furniture, you can relocate in a quieter traffic areas. Since most people will take the time and effort to compare a number of stores' offerings before they buy these goods, being convenient is less important. However, what some customers regard as convenience goods, others treat as shopping goods. Some men will buy a suit, sport jacket, and slacks at one time while others can buy only one outfit a year and then they wait for special sales. Consider your customers' buying habits before you decide where to locate.

Downtown versus Shopping Centers

Both downtown areas and shopping centers have so many advantages and disadvantages that the ultimate choice can be very difficult indeed. In some cities and towns high concentration of large department and specialty stores offer an enormous potential in their downtown areas. They attract those who work in the district, women on a shopping spree, and visitors. But, in these cities first-class sites are not easily obtainable, rents and taxes may be very high, and the area may be losing its customer attractiveness because of its growing physical obsolescence and traffic congestion.

Shopping centers generally have the advantage of being planned, modern, convenient, and attractive. They may also offer a fairly captive customer potential, but if the center is too small, there is so little retail competition it lacks the excitement of comparative shopping that most people enjoy. Furthermore, there may be too many centers in the area, rents may be pegged too high, you may have to spend too much money modernizing your fixtures, or you may be forced by your lease to participate in group promotions that will bring in a very small return for your outlay.

Opportunities for the Future

What about the future of the community and the site? It would be extremely foolish to relocate in an area that will change in a few years and force you to move again. Moving is worthwhile only if you feel that the new site has more potential than the one you are in at present and the opportunity of growing and expanding with the community looks promising.

To help you decide what business changes are likely to take place in the area, see Chapter 1. You may feel that two shopping centers close to each other give excellent competition, but if you discover that a third one is to be built nearby in the future, you may feel that this would limit the potential of your contemplated site. Replacing slums with middle- or high-income apartments could either be very profitable for you or force you out of business before you even got started. The acquisition of the area for a government or industrial project that requires very little personnel would certainly be harmful. There may be highway plans under way that will improve or weaken the potential of your projected site.

If you decide to move, make as certain as possible that it will be a profitable venture; otherwise, stay where you are and see whether or not you can change your present store and adjust its merchandise pattern. Moving from one bad situation to a situation that may be worse is not only very expensive but also foolish.

Investigate Retail Services

If you have discovered a community with possibilities, spend a little time finding out what the area contains in the way of retail services. For example, see if there is at least one bank in the area that has a reputation for knowing how to deal with retailers. A bank manager who has had experience with retailers and is interested in them as well as in their money can give you invaluable advice and assistance when you require it. If your business demands that you operate on customer credit, find out what the credit reporting facilities are in the area. If this service is inadequate, decide whether you can afford the many losses that may incur before you have built up sufficient experience in handling customer credit to make competent credit decisions or give up your own store credit and use outside credit services instead.

What about the availability of employees for your store and what salaries and working conditions do they expect? What about the local newspapers, printers, sign writers, window dressers, and other services? Are you satisfied that they will cooperate with you and give you the attention you require? Determine the equipment of the fire and police forces and investigate the local taxes and the store opening and closing laws. You should also find out what the public transportation facilities are in the area. If possible, compare the asking rent with others in the immediate vicinity. Make sure that you know the insurance rates for your store; if it is an old building or next to a restaurant or a repair shop that uses volatile material, the insurance rates may be very high.

In other words, make a list of all your expenses both fixed and variable and try to judge what they will be before you move. Figure 16.1 suggests a checklist for this purpose.

Will You Fill a Merchandise Vacuum?

Before you make any definite plans, try to discover whether or not the community to which you would like to move really needs the kind of store you contemplate opening. If you have nothing new or better to offer the people in the area, they will have no reason to patronize you instead of the stores that are already established. However, if you feel that your shop will fill a vacuum with the merchandise you now sell and that it will be wanted by the community, you have every justification for opening your store and being confident that it will do well.

Shopping Center Considerations

Some retailers think that there is something magical about a shopping center and that if they move to, or open a store in one, they are bound to be successful. However, all the location problems discussed in this chapter apply to shopping centers as well to downtown or suburban locations. Therefore, before you sign a lease for a store in a center, make sure that enough of your kind of customers shop there to give you a living and that they will want to buy the goods you plan to offer them.

In addition to typical location problems, shopping centers have special situations that should be investigated. Is the size of the center you are considering right for your business, are there too many centers for the population of the area, and are more being contemplated? How does the center promote itself in the surrounding community, and is the drawing power of the anchor stores strong enough to attract *your* kind of customer? Does the

Worksheet for estimating

INITIAL CAPITAL REQUIREMENTS FOR AN INDEPENDENT VARIETY STORE (Limited Price)

Estimated operating ratios expressed as a percent of net sales, with examples showing
their application to various annual sales volumes (*See note 1, page 3*)

	Percent	Annual Sales Volume		
		$36,000†	$60,000†	$84,000†
Net sales................................	100.0	$36,000†	$60,000†	$84,000†
Cost of goods sold......................	66.0	23,760	39,600	55,440
Gross margin............................	34.0	12,240	20,400	28,560
Operating expenses......................	29.0	10,440	17,400	24,360
Net profit (Excluding proprietor's salary)*..	5.0	1,800	3,000	4,200
Average inventory (*See note 8, page 3*).....		7,920	13,200	18,480
Stock turn: 3 times per year				

*Total return to the proprietor or operator is the total of net profit and his salary. In the illustration below for a $60,000 store this is estimated
at a total of 11% or $6,600. (*See note 4, page 3*.)
†Estimated store sizes for these annual sales volumes are as follows:

- $36,000 = 20' by 75'
- $60,000 = 28' by 75'
- $84,000 = 34' by 75'

MONTHLY SALES AND OPERATING EXPENSES (*See note 2, page 3*)	Estimated ratios percent of sales	Dollars per month based on annual volume of $60,000	Your estimate of monthly sales and expenses based on annual volume of	INSTRUCTIONS FOR COLUMNS 3 AND 4 Enter your monthly operating expenses in column 3 based on percentages of sales in column 1, as illustrated in column 2. Enter your initial cash requirements in column 4 based on amounts shown in column 3. For several items a period of months is suggested.	Your estimate of initial cash requirements
Item	Col. 1	Col. 2	Col. 3		Col. 4
Net sales 1/12th of annual estimate	100.0	$5,000.00	$	(*See note 3, page 3*)	$
Operating expenses					
Salaries of officers, proprietors or partners	6.0	300.00		Enter 1 month or more (*Note 4, page 3*)	
All other salaries and wages	8.0	400.00		Enter 2 months or more	
Occupancy (rent for those leasing)	4.0	200.00		Enter 2 months or more (*Note 5, page 3*)	
Utilities and building service	3.0	150.00		Enter 2 months or more	
Taxes (other than income) and licenses	1.5	75.00		Consult city and state taxing authorities	
Supplies	1.0	50.00		Enter 2 months or more	
Depreciation (except buildings)	1.0	50.00		No entry in column 4 (*Note 6, page 3*)	
All other expenses				Make your own estimate for other expenses	
Telephone and telegraph				Check local rates	
Unemployment insurance				Consult your State director of unemployment insurance	

			INSTRUCTIONS FOR COLUMN 4
Other insurance			May have to pay premiums for 1 year or more (Note 7, page 3)
Donations and dues			
Advertising	4.5	225.00	Enter one-fourth annual advertising budget
Freight and shipping			Parcel post expense and freight charges
Miscellaneous			List any item not mentioned above
		$	
Total of these items should amount to 4.5% e.			
Average monthly operating expenses	29.0	$1,450.00	No entry in column 4
NONRECURRING INITIAL CAPITAL REQUIREMENTS			INSTRUCTIONS FOR COLUMN 4
Purchase of real estate	*(See note 5, second paragraph, page 3)*		
Decorating and remodeling	Enter total estimated cost		$
Fixtures and equipment	Enter total of list on page 1		
Installation of fixtures and equipment	Enter cost of installing all fixtures and equipment		
Initial inventory	Estimate and enter initial inventory from instructions in note 8, page 3		
Deposits with public utilities	Enter full amount to be deposited		
Initial advertising and promotional expense	Enter total estimated cost		
Cash	For unforeseen requirements, special purchases, etc., and for absorbing any initial losses.		
Other	List any item not mentioned above		
Total estimated initial capital requirements *(Add all items entered in column 4)*			$

FIGURE 16.1 Although this is a worksheet for estimating the initial capital requirements for a limited price variety store, it can be used for other kinds of retailing.

INITIAL CAPITAL REQUIREMENTS FOR AN
INDEPENDENT VARIETY STORE (Limited Price)

Prepared in the Office of Distribution, Business and Defense Services Administration
U.S. Department of Commerce

This worksheet is designed to assist the prospective operator of an independent variety store in estimating his total initial capital requirements. It consists of a monthly operating budget based upon operating ratios considered typical for the trade, and a list of non-recurring capital expenditures which are generally encountered when a new business is first established. Because the expenditure for furniture, fixtures, and equipment is an important consideration, a suggested list of the major items needed has also been included. The worksheet should be completed in full before any commitments are made. It is not advisable to establish any business unless available capital exceeds the initial requirements by a margin sufficient to cover personal expenses and contingencies for a number of months, since a newly established business seldom shows any appreciable profit during the first year of operation.

The capital requirements will depend to a large extent upon the merchandise and services to be offered as well as the buying arrangements made with sources of supply. These and other variables should be carefully considered when estimating the required investments in the initial inventory and the necessary expenditures for furniture, fixtures, and equipment. For advice in store layout and selection of fixtures and equipment, it is suggested that the prospective merchant consult the various equipment manufacturers and trade associations, many of which offer valuable merchant service to those in need of specialized assistance. Similarly, in estimating inventory, the merchant should consult suppliers and retail trade associations in the selection of initial inventory and the development of a stock plan.

(Explanatory notes are provided on page 3.)

SCHEDULE OF FURNITURE, FIXTURES AND EQUIPMENT

Item (Suggested list - omit or add items as required. Use separate sheets to list details under each main heading)	If cash purchase (New or used) enter full amount below and in the last column	If installment purchase (New or used) enter in the last column down payment plus at least one installment			Estimate of your initial cash requirements for furniture, fixtures and equipment
		Price	Down payment	Amount of each installment	
Display counters and fixtures					
Display shelves					
Display tables, cases, gondolos					
Garment racks					
Magazine racks					
Candy case					
Window display fixtures					
Lighting					
Mirrors					
Floor covering					
Checkout stands					
Cash register					
Safe					
Office equipment					
Air conditioning					
Outside sign					
Awnings					
Total furniture, fixtures and equipment (*Enter total on page 2 under "nonrecurring" initial capital requirements*).					

FIGURE 16.1 (continued)

image of the center appeal to your customers? Are there enough related stores in it to draw your kind of customers and so help you make more sales?

Also, find out what the center expects of you as a tenant in terms of cooperative action. Are you content with a uniform front if stipulated in your lease or do you want to identify yourself by a highly personalized exterior? Are you willing to contribute to center-wide joint ads and tie yourself into promotions with specially priced merchandise? Do you believe in cooperating with other stores on seasonal themes and are you prepared to work with them on special gimmicks such as carnivals or sidewalk sales?

Check Rental Schedules

Most centers use a graduated scale of rents which means that they set a basic rent you must pay no matter what business you do. However, when

1. The operating ratios illustrated on page 2 may be briefly defined as follows:

   NET SALES - Gross sales less all returns and allowances, and exclusive of sales tax revenue.

   COST OF GOODS SOLD - Beginning inventory, at cost, plus net purchases (gross purchases less returns and allowances, plus freight in), less ending inventory, at cost. (Percent of net sales.)

   GROSS MARGIN - Net sales less cost of goods sold. (Percent of net sales.)

   OPERATING EXPENSES - All expenses incurred in business operations - see breakdown in table on page 2. (Percent of net sales.)

   NET PROFIT - Gross margin less operating expenses. (Percent of net sales.)

   STOCK TURNS - (Number of times per year) - Cost of goods sold divided by average inventory.

   The operating ratios shown are for an independent limited price variety store and were estimated upon the basis of conditions during the past few years. It should be noted that the operations of an individual store may vary widely from the averages for the trade, these variations depending upon location, size, number and variety of lines of merchandise carried, and services offered. However, the estimated ratios shown may be used as a rough guide in determining what provision to make for initial operating expenses in relation to anticipated sales.

2. Monthly sales and operating expenses as listed on page 2 should be determined as follows:

   (1) Estimate annual sales volume (See note 3 below).

   (2) Divide by 12 to obtain estimated monthly volume.

   (3) Multiply monthly sales volume by each operating ratio to determine dollar amount for each operating expense for 1 month.

   (4) Monthly expenses for the items for which separate ratios are not shown should be individually estimated. The total of these expenses should be approximately the percent of estimated sales shown opposite the bracket around "all other expenses" (Column 1, page 2).

3. Your actual sales volume cannot be accurately determined in advance since this will depend upon the amount of business in the area, the number of competitors already sharing this business, and the amount which you may be able to obtain. However, assistance in making a careful estimate can be obtained from representatives of manufacturers and wholesalers, the trade association, your banker, the Chamber of Commerce, and other business men who may be familiar with local conditions and the opportunity for a new store in the area in which you plan to enter business.

   Do not be over-enthusiastic in estimating your potential sales. A new business generally grows slowly, especially at the start. If you over-estimate your potential sales you are likely to invest too much capital in equipment and initial inventory, and commit yourself to heavier operating expenses than the actual sales volume attained will justify.

4. The amount which should be allowed for owner's salary will depend on the extent to which you draw on the business income for personal expenses. Some proprietors draw a regular monthly salary and the remainder of net profits irregularly or at the end of the year. Others reinvest a part of net profits in the business. The method of withdrawal of net profits, if the business is unincorporated, does not affect your income tax since salary, withdrawals, or profits retained in the business are all taxable and at the same rates.

   The owner's salary as a percent of net sales will generally decline with increases in sales volume. However, all other salaries and wages, as a percent of net sales, will generally increase. The two items together generally constitute a somewhat constant percentage of sales volume.

5. Occupancy, as used here, applies to the expenses of renting business property or to ownership expenses. For rented quarters the ratio covers rent and repairs for which the tenant is responsible. For owned premises the ratio covers such ownership expenses as property taxes, mortgage interest, insurance, depreciation and maintenance costs.

   If real estate is acquired for the business, enter under nonrecurring initial capital requirements on page 2 the total price if purchased outright. If the purchase is to be partially financed by a mortgage, enter the total cash payment. If business property is to be constructed, enter the total cost of construction. In each case full provision must be made for all of the initial costs incident to the purchase or construction. This requirement should be discussed thoroughly with the real estate agent, contractor, financing agency, or others whose services are employed in this connection.

6. Allowance should be made for depreciation of all fixtures and equipment in the determination of profits. The monthly depreciation rate should be entered in column 3 in the estimate of monthly operating expenses and profits. However, no provision for depreciation need be included in column 4 in the estimate of initial capital requirements.

7. Types of insurance for which provision may be made include fire, lightning, windstorm, use and occupancy, public liability, compensation, and robbery and burglary. Consult a reputable insurance company for full details of cost and coverage.

8. To estimate average inventory by using the operating ratios shown at the top of page 2 take 66 percent of your anticipated sales volume. This figure will represent "cost of goods sold," or the annual sales at cost value. Divide this amount by the number of stock turns per year (3) and the resulting amount will be the estimated inventory value at cost. For estimated sales of $60,000:

   $60,000 x .66 equals $39,600 divided by 3 = $13,200. When average inventory is computed on the basis of operating ratios it applies to the store already in operation, which maintains a somewhat larger stock than is essential for a new shop. Your initial inventory may be reduced by stocking a reasonable supply of major lines and filling in varieties and specialties as demand develops.

you reach predetermined sales volumes, the rent increases by a series of fixed percentages based on sales. This means that you do not reap the fullest benefit of improved sales. Sometimes, increased sales are made by decreased markups, but your lease does not take short markups into account. A graduated rental keeps pushing up your breakeven point and this makes it harder for you to reach your overhead figures and begin to make profit.

Choose Site in Center Carefully

Your site in a shopping center must be as carefully chosen as the center itself. Your location in relation to the anchor store or stores, as well as to the main public areas if there are any, is of utmost importance. In a two-level shopping center, the location near the escalators is a prime site. Also, a shop in a related area, for example, a specialty bakery next to a supermarket, can be profitable, while a shop in a nonrelated area, for example, a men's specialty shop between a series of ladies' stores, would have very little chance of success.

Buying a Going Business versus Establishing a New One

If you are going to relocate, should you buy an established business or start from scratch? Each alternative has its good and bad points. A going business comes with its equipment, merchandise, personnel, customer following, vendors, and, if you need it, a store name with a reputation. In some cases, you have very little extra to spend over and above the purchase price. Also, if you buy the shop on Monday, you can count on having a regular business day on Tuesday.

But should you buy a well-managed shop or a poorly run store? If you buy a money-making concern, the owner will usually ask a high price for everything he wants to sell, and then add "goodwill" to the purchase price. Yet, the personality of the owner may be so important that you will be unable to capitalize on the goodwill he has sold you.

Sometimes, buying a poorly run store is very worthwhile. It is usually sold at a bargain price and without such intangibles as goodwill. But you might still pay too much for it because of its poor merchandise assortments, improper fixtures, and an air of unattractiveness that repels both customers and vendors. Nevertheless, if the site is good and if you possess sound retail imagination, you may be able to transform a losing proposition into a very profitable business in a short time.

If you decide to start a store from scratch, you have the opportunity of creating it exactly as you want it to be. There are no old fixtures, equipment, or merchandise to consider. The shop can be planned as a complete unit even though limitations of capital may force you to undertake its completion in stages. Nevertheless, beginning mistakes can be very costly, building customer loyalty is usually a slow, painful process, and your assets may be expended before the store can become established and profitable.

How Soon Can You Make Money?

When a chain or a department store opens a new branch, it can afford to take the long view and lose money until the outlet begins to pay. But before *you* move, you must try to figure how long it will be until you can do a *profitable* business. Very few of your old customers may come to your new location and even under the best conditions it takes time for customers in the area to hear about you and decide to change their shopping habits. This is why you should increase your initial promotion expense to attract your old customers quickly as well as to inform consumers in the area of your store. Make sure that you can exist until your store is established and paying off.

If you are satisfied with the opportunities offered by the new site and feel that the move is worthwhile, engage a lawyer who has considerable experience in commercial rentals to examine your lease before you sign it. His advice and counsel can save you a lot of money and future aggravation. Remember that when you sign a lease you are bound to its terms as long as it lasts, and landlords are specialists in demanding conditions that benefit them, not you.

Moving Is a Serious Business

Do not be discouraged by the challenges you may face in moving, for it may offer you a greater opportunity for growth than you have at your present location. Retail giants like Macy's and Lord & Taylor in New York and Eaton's in Toronto moved from their original locations to new sites in order to grow and become successful enterprises. This chapter is merely trying to persuade you to think more than once before moving and make sure that if you decide to relocate the new site will be worthwhile.

WHAT THIS CHAPTER TOLD YOU

1. Today's customers are on the move and this affects the value of many retail locations.

2. Survey your present area and see whether your community and site have changed.

3. If your site is suitable but if your customers have changed, adjust your merchandising pattern to fit the new situation.

4. If the site is no longer profitable or you do not want to change your merchandising habits, think about relocating.

5. Determine if it is better to relocate in a downtown area or in a shopping center.

6. Make certain that the community and the site in which you wish to relocate have a future and that your move will be profitable.

7. Check the new area's retail services.

8. Fill a merchandise vacuum.

9. Decide whether to buy a going business or start a new one.

10. Determine how soon you can begin to make money.

11. Consult a lawyer before you sign the lease.

17

Make Every Inch of Your Store Pay

WHAT THIS CHAPTER IS ABOUT

One way to obtain the maximum return on your investment is to think of your store the way that a manufacturer thinks of his factory and an engineer thinks of machinery. Stores are places where sales are manufactured and fixtures are machines that help produce sales profitably. This chapter tells you how to make every inch of your store pay and how to keep it paying.

Old Methods of Thinking about a Store

Just because retailers deal with human beings is no reason why they should run their stores in an unpredictable and inefficient manner. Old-time merchants were called storekeepers because they believed that their stores were simply places to store merchandise until it could be sold. Consequently, they dumped goods wherever there happened to be an open space. Clothing, hardware, and grocery items were not separated but lay about in such a haphazard way that only the merchant himself knew where anything was, and sometimes even he forgot. Some stores today still use this method of handling merchandise.

New Methods Are Begun

Marshall Field, John Wanamaker, Timothy Eaton, and other retail pioneers found that it paid to make their stores neater and more orderly.

Finally, they grouped all the merchandise they thought belonged together in one area and called this area a *department*. Their stores became known as *department stores* because they contained a series of merchandise groupings which everyone (salespeople, customers, and executives) could easily identify. Later, this arrangement greatly facilitated stockkeeping, selling, buying, and supervision in the store.

As department stores expanded, space became an ever-increasing problem and executives were forced to make difficult decisions about the location and size of every department, both selling and nonselling. In order to make the best possible use of each inch of space, they experimented with different arrangements for locating fixtures, reserve and storage space, aisles, and customer and employee conveniences.

Stores Become Factories—With a Difference

About this time factories were discovering the value of efficiency and industrialists began to consult experts on machine layout, work flow, and the minimum employee effort necessary for maximum output. The large stores studied these factory methods and adopted those they could apply to situations in their own particular stores. They soon became aware of major differences between the approach of manufacturers and of retailers to this problem. For example, while a manufacturer sought to establish his factory site close to sources of transportation, material, power, and labor, a retailer's basic location requirement was customer convenience; and while a factory could use enormous and ugly pieces of machinery as well as esthetically unattractive work-flow arrangements, store fixtures and customer flow patterns must always be pleasing to the eye.

The essential difference between manufacturers and retailers, then, is that a manufacturer thinks of his factory in terms of machines while the retailer must constantly remember that his customers are of paramount importance. However, both the retailer and the manufacturer attempt to obtain the maximum amount of profit for every foot of space. Retailers do this by bringing customers and merchandise together for maximum sales and by making the best possible use of every cent they are forced to spend in operating their stores.

Delicate Decisions Required

The retailer must be constantly aware of the gross margin that every square foot of his store can produce so that he can make very delicate decisions in order to give just the right location and space to each department. He must also arrange his selling, nonselling, and service areas to obtain the maximum merchandise presentation and customer flow. He must remember that these decisions do not last forever. To obtain maximum profit in today's dynamic retailing, merchants must keep changing the size and location of their departments, even though this creates a certain degree of personnel resentment.

A Store's Selling Personality Begins with Its Front

Unlike a factory, where outside appearance has little value, a store's selling personality begins at its front, for most customers judge a store in the first place by its outward appearance. As a retailer, you go through this experience when you inspect stores in a strange city. You expect the merchandising procedures of shops whose fronts are brightly painted with bargain slogans to be different from those of shops that have dignified exteriors and quiet window displays.

If you can create a well-defined, easy to comprehend exterior, you will attract potential customers to your store and, at the same time, discourage those who are not interested in your merchandise from even entering the store. As a result, you will be able to give all your attention to potential buyers and not waste time, space, and energy on shoppers who have no desire to purchase your goods (Fig. 17.1). A front that does not have a positive store image loses potential customers who shy away from it and go to stores they understand, and it also brings in a certain number of people

FIGURE 17.1 This is an extremely attractive exterior of a specialty shop that caters to a young, fashion-alert clientele. Notice how the design immediately communicates to its potential customers its name and the kind of merchandise it carries.

Courtesy Judy's, Inc., Van Nuys, Calif.

who think it might be their kind of store and who are disappointed and angry when they discover that they misjudged it. A nondescript front, then, not only loses sales, it also increases expenses and creates customer ill will.

How to Plan Your Exterior Store Personality

Whether your store is located on a main street or in a shopping center, the first opportunity you have to make shoppers stop, look, and decide whether it is their kind of store is when they are walking, not driving, toward it. To attract the right kind of pedestrian, the store's exterior must stand out from all the others that surround it. You should be very conscious of the effect that various building materials have on people passing by. For example, fronts containing large areas of stone or metal create a very different impression from those that use wood. This difference is increased by the number, size, and depth of windows and the manner of dressing them, the height of the bulkhead, the brilliance or subtlety of the exterior lighting, and the way your store signature is designed. All these features must be planned to give the onlooker a strong and easily understood first impression of your store's personality.

If your store does not have traditional windows, the way its interior, particularly its front section, is presented should stop those passing by and permit them to quickly judge its personality and decide whether to investigate it further or walk past it.

Importance of Entrances

If your exterior appeals to potential customers and if your windows or interior interest them, then your entrance should gently, almost unnoticeably, lead them into the store. Entrances are an important part of your exterior design and they should be well-lighted and large enough for customer comfort. Wherever possible, steps, which are a customer hazard, should be eliminated and converted into a slight incline made of nonskid materials. Doors should be easy to open and wide enough for people with parcels to enter and leave freely. If a door is complicated in any way, people who fail to open it easily the first time become embarrassed and walk away. Some stores have eliminated doors during business hours by sliding them out of the way or by using an air curtain. An air curtain blows air at the entrance with sufficient force to separate the outside and inside atmospheres (Fig. 17.2).

How to Allocate Floor Space

As you proceed to create a strong internal store personality, you run into a number of problems because the floor space has to be divided into selling and nonselling areas that must be properly allocated to obtain

FLAT

Most economical. Merchandise can be brought out to the leased line or street line for maximum exposure. Can be completely visual or fitted with background panels. Minimum glass surface. Maximum reflection glare hazard. Poor viewing angle for sidewalk traffic.

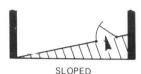

SLOPED

Effective traffic lead to door. More effective viewing angle for sidewalk traffic. Provides one feature window with background. Limited protected shopping area. Adds variety, but wastes selling space and the control of floor and ceiling materials can be very expensive.

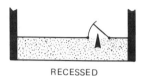

RECESSED

Protected shopping area. Some protection from reflection glare. Economical. Reduces interior sales area. Poor viewing angle from sidewalk approaches. Adds variety, but wastes selling space and the control of floor above and ceiling materials can be very expensive.

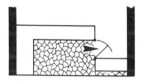

RIGHT ANGLED DOOR

Generous glass surface. Three good feature display areas. Protected shopping area. Novel entrance layout. Good sidewall display backgrounds. Fair viewing angles for sidewalk traffic. One or both windows can be visual. Applicable to exclusive stores. Requires professional display staff or service. Very expensive construction.

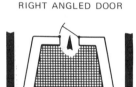

SPLAYED CLOSED

Good viewing angles for sidewalk traffic. Rear access aisles to service windows. Protected shopping area. Generous glass surface. Good protection from reflection glare. Requires width approximately 25' 0'' between walls.

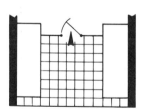

LOBBY

Provides complete visual front with generous side wall backgrounds. Protected shopping area. Carries effect of shop interior into windows and onto the street. Fair viewing angle for sidewalk traffic. Good protection from reflection glare.

FIGURE 17.2 Examples of entrances and their advantages and disadvantages.

Courtesy CML Design, Toronto, Ont.

maximum efficiency. Figure 17.3 gives you an indication of the main floor rent percentages used by some small and medium-sized stores. The only area that requires explanation is the right front third. This is charged with 20 percent of the total because most people turn to the right when they enter a shop. Since the entire front third of the store carries 47 percent of

5%	6%	5%
10%	12%	15%
12%	15%	20%
Window		Window

FIGURE 17.3 This is only one of the many variations used by store planners for the distribution of floor area rent. An extra amount should be charged to the departments that use the windows.

the total rent, great care must be taken to make sure that this section contains merchandise that serves your store best. It has been found that only one-quarter of your customers will go more than halfway into your store, and it has also been established that customers get a lasting impression about the merchandise you carry from what they first see when they enter. Consequently, using the front third as a merchandise catchall or locating stairs, elevators, or reserve or fitting rooms in these areas would be foolish indeed.

Locations for Nonselling Areas

It is obvious from Fig. 17.3 that the back or the left middle section of the store should contain as much of your nonselling and service areas as possible. Nonselling areas (receiving and marking rooms, storage space, and customer and employee conveniences such as rest rooms) should be adjacent to the back entrance or in the basement if it is sufficiently dry and if the ceiling is high enough for comfort. Stairs and elevators, too, should be placed as far back as possible. Fitting rooms and *forward* stock reserves should be conveniently close to the departments they serve. Usually, this involves area compromises with decisions being based on what arrangement is most profitable for the store as a whole.

With a little creative thought you can make the store's *vertical space* pay part of the rent. By making it a storage area, you increase the amount of the store's productive floor space. It can also be effectively used for displays because these can easily be seen by shoppers and their isolation from floor-level competition focuses attention on them.

Space for the office and the cash–wrap desk creates another set of problems. The best location for the office is on a mezzanine that overlooks the store. If this is impossible, place it in a back area, although when credit is important and the owner is his own manager, it may be desirable to locate it somewhere along the left side.

The position of the cash–wrap desk depends on a great many factors. In long, narrow stores that are not self-service the middle left wall seems desirable; in self-service stores the check-out counter should always be near the exit. In a square-shaped store the cash–wrap desk should be located in the front center. This is an expensive area, but it is very convenient to all departments, saves the convenience goods sales personnel much time and energy, and permits the merchant, who usually works in this area, a certain amount of overall store supervision.

Layout of Selling Departments

Decisions on the floor areas and locations of every one of your selling departments should be based on the comparative ability of each merchandise classification section and department to produce sales or profits.

Compare departmental sales and profits

Comparing inside and outside department sales per square foot became a very valuable tool when the operator of a hardware store decided to refixture his store which consisted of four departments: hardware, small electrical appliances, sporting goods, and automotive supplies. Both the sporting goods and the automotive supplies managers strongly urged that their departments be expanded, and both "guaranteed" more than enough sales and profits to pay for any additional space they obtained.

The owner was inclined to go along with the automotive supplies manager because the department was started when an aggressive automotive supplies chain unit opened across the street, and his pride tended to build up the "success" of that department in competition with the chain. He was damned if he wasn't as good a merchant as a chain any day.

Fortunately, however, the fixture company, a specialist in store operations, questioned the merchant's decision. It seemed to the fixture company that the sporting goods department looked very active and that the automotive supplies area appeared almost dead. In order to convince itself of the true situation, it compared the sales volume per square foot of each department in the store with national averages. The comparison showed that the sporting goods department was doing approximately 430 percent of the national average while the automotive supplies department was badly limping along with only 31 percent of the national average. It did not take the owner long to decide that he was paying too high a price to maintain his pride. He closed out the automotive supplies and used the space to extend his sporting goods department.

This is an example of the kind of emotional blind spot which a retailer can develop and which can become very expensive. To guard against this danger, you should be very careful to base your layout decisions on unemotional figures rather than on instinctive hunches or personal pride.

The departments that make the most profit need not be given prime positions. Distinctions must be made between shopping, convenience, and impulse goods. Merchandise that must be tried on, carefully examined, or thought about requires a quiet store area, placed as far back and off center as possible. Most convenience merchandise, however, should be easily accessible to customers while impulse items should be in the most heavily trafficked areas. However, some merchants stock this merchandise toward the rear in order to make customers walk the length of the store or when the cost of carrying these goods in front areas does not cover rent charges. These retailers feel that unless this kind of goods generates sufficient traffic, it should be moved to cheaper rental locations in the store.

Convenience, impulse, and shopping areas

Most customers can be led wherever you want them to go by the proper use of aisle tables, counters, lights, displays, and signs. For example, carefully arranged groupings of tables or counters influence shoppers to move to the right or left. Strategically placed fixtures that contain bargain merchandise attract customers to dead areas. Thus, by clever interior planning, you can expose customers to most of the merchandise in your store.

Guide your customers

A good store layout will help you to increase sales. When related departments (skirts and blouses; handbags and gloves; men's shirts and ties; garden supplies and outdoor furniture) are adjacent to each other, each department creates impulse or suggested sales for the other. A store that includes a bride's boutique and stocks undergarments and accessories for this merchandise will not only provide a thoughtful service for customers who patronize the department but should also sell more apparel to the bride and her wedding party.

Good layout increases sales

Some stores go even further by locating departments to suit customer thinking. They group gift china, linens, and silver and glassware items in a "gift suggestion" section. This layout gives shoppers as much related merchandise exposure as possible and therefore is one of the best ways of increasing sales.

There are many varieties of layout and many decisions to make before your store can attain maximum efficiency. But your plan should consider more than maximizing sales. A good layout should save the time and energy of your personnel. For example, if you place quick-selling impulse and convenience goods at the front of your store and locate the cash desk at the back, you will not obtain maximum sales and square foot efficiency. Doing this forces your salespeople to walk many unnecessary miles a day and loses many hours that should be used for stockkeeping and conserving their energy for selling purposes. For example, placing coats instead of dresses near fitting rooms creates considerable sales personnel and customer inconvenience and loses sales. A little thoughtfulness on your part when you plan your store layout can produce great rewards.

Good layout increases personnel efficiency

Employee and customer theft is a very serious problem in most stores, but few merchants realize how much it costs to replace a piece of stolen merchandise. For example, if an item that costs $10 and retails for $15 is stolen, two items must be sold just to recover its wholesale price. It takes another sale to recover the $5 markup of the stolen article and by then the overhead involved in selling three items may require a fourth sale. Theft, then, is a very large drain on your profit and every attempt should be made to reduce it.

A well-planned layout helps to discourage employees and customers from stealing. Employee theft is usually greater than customer theft because store personnel are constantly exposed to the merchandise and may enter and leave the store many times a day without arousing suspicion. One of the best ways to reduce employee theft is to lay out your nonselling areas according to the methods discussed in Chapter 6.

Customer theft can be discouraged by arranging your fixtures and merchandise displays to permit everyone, store personnel and shoppers, to see all selling areas of your store. If this cannot be accomplished, security equipment at strategic locations should be installed.

The position of your cash–wrap desk is also important because employees tend to gather around it when they have time on their hands. Therefore, whenever possible, it should be placed where it can command a good view of the selling area. Fitting rooms should be placed where employees can easily check customer traffic into and away from them. Expensive merchandise and impulse items should be located where shopper traffic is easiest to watch. In particular, they should be kept away from the store's entrance.

Laying out your store to prevent theft will only discourage, not stop, stealing. But everything you do to reduce theft will help you keep the profit you make on sales rather than have it contribute to the costs and markups of stolen goods.

If you want to obtain maximum benefit from your floor area, the first step is to plan the arrangement of your departments and fixtures on paper. You can take a sheet of blank paper, divide it into quarter-inch squares, and locate on it scale cutouts of your fixtures. You can make the cutouts yourself or you can purchase layout kits similar to the planning kit illustrated in Fig. 17.4. Whether you use a planning kit or a scale plan and cutouts of your own making, you will find it easy to rearrange your store according to the principles outlined in the preceding paragraphs.

When you relocate a department, make certain that it does not disrupt the efficiency of any of the other departments. Planning the store in this way highlights your problem departments and areas and helps you to reach reasonable solutions which, in most instances, will be a series of compromises. Before you make any final decisions, check your solutions by visiting stores that already have your ideas in operation. If the stores you visit are out of town or if they are not in direct competition with you, their owners will usually be most cooperative and helpful.

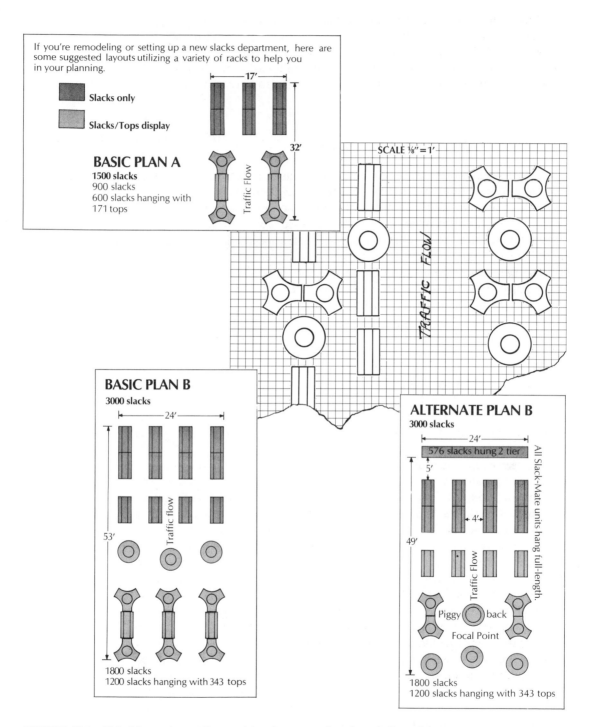

If you're remodeling or setting up a new slacks department, here are some suggested layouts utilizing a variety of racks to help you in your planning.

■ Slacks only

■ Slacks/Tops display

BASIC PLAN A
1500 slacks
900 slacks
600 slacks hanging with
171 tops

←——17'——→

32'

Traffic Flow

SCALE ⅛" = 1'

TRAFFIC FLOW

BASIC PLAN B
3000 slacks

←——24'——→

53'

Traffic flow

1800 slacks
1200 slacks hanging with 343 tops

ALTERNATE PLAN B
3000 slacks

←——24'——→
576 slacks hung 2 tier

5'

4'

49'

All Slack-Mate units hang full-length.

Traffic Flow

Piggy ◯ back
Focal Point

1800 slacks
1200 slacks hanging with 343 tops

FIGURE 17.4 This kit can be easily used to plan your store layout. It contains a simple grid sheet and cutout symbols to help you get the most efficient arrangement.

Courtesy Haggar Co., Dallas, Texas.

Lastly, mark the plan right on the floor of your store. This will further emphasize the relationship between selling, nonselling, customer, and service areas. Locating mechanical and electrical equipment is equally important. It is much cheaper and easier to erase and redraw chalk marks on a floor than to correct errors after the actual fixtures are in place.

How to Choose and Use Fixtures

If you plan to remodel or purchase new fixtures, make certain that they are made for the merchandise you intend to use in them. A good fixture organizes the merchandise in a logical manner and exposes a maximum of active stock within easy reach of both the customer and the salesperson. Since most fixtures need selling signs, the fixtures should have some means of holding the signs. A wrong fixture makes the merchandise unattractive to see and awkward to handle, but the right fixture in the wrong place is just a waste of good floor space. An example of the poor use of fixtures is to display bulky items on narrow shelves.

Ideal selling fixtures

A good functional fixture system sells merchandise and also stores and protects it. Yet, it is so unobtrusive that it does not detract from the merchandise itself. This asks a lot from fixtures and the trend today is for them to be adjustable, mobile, and functional. They come in standardized parts that are extremely flexible and can be joined together in many ways. Some have shelves and drawers that can be inserted and removed when desired; others can be used for hanging garments or displaying such long items as garden tools (see Figs. 17.5 and 17.6).

Functional fixtures

By the proper use of versatile and functional fixtures, the season's major items can always be displayed in the right area in the store. For example, a group of fixtures with shelves could display handbags, gloves, and scarves in the early Spring; then, by removing the shelves and adding hanging bars, they could be changed to a tops and pants section. As Summer approaches, swim suits and play clothes could be displayed until July when the same fixtures could be used for hanging clearance merchandise. In August and early September the area could be transformed into a back-to-school section that features sweaters on shelves over hanging pants. The next major change would be for Christmas when, by substituting shelves for the hanging bars, handkerchiefs, gloves, and scarves could be shown. In January the shelves could be removed and only the counter section used as bargain tables for clearances. As Spring approaches, the cycle could be completed by adding shelves for handbags, gloves, and scarves. This way, the same section of the store could be continuously used to its best advantage without moving its fixtures, and customers would always see the merchandise they were in the mood to buy.

Unless you have a very exclusive shop, it would be wise to look at fixtures with cool detachment and recall that a store is a place where people

Buy inexpensive fixtures

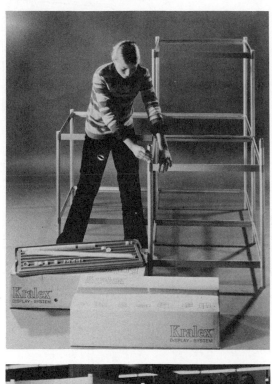

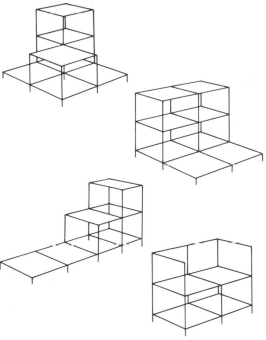

FIGURE 17.5 This versatile fixture system ensures effective presentation of specific ranges of merchandise. It is easy to assemble and dismantle and is light in weight yet sturdy.

Courtesy Alusuisse Metals, Fort Lee, N. J.

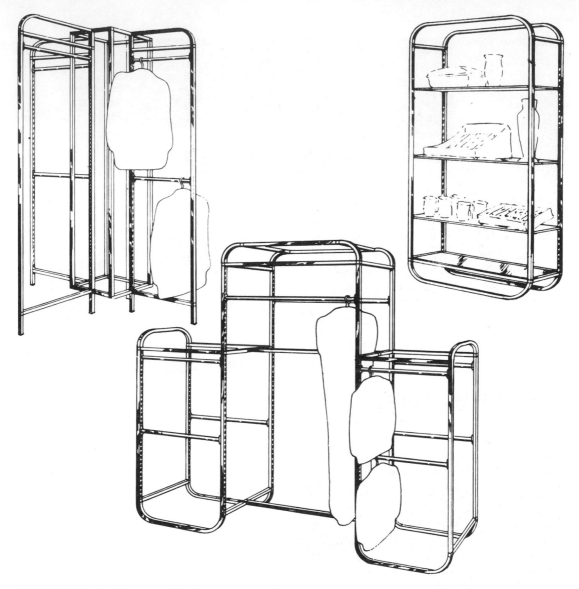

FIGURE 17.6 Another versatile fixture system that has considerable adjustability to handle a variety of display and customer selling needs.

Courtesy Structural Concepts Corp., Spring Lake, Mich.

come to buy merchandise, not to look at fixtures. Eye-catching fixtures defeat the main purpose of a fixture, which is to enhance the merchandise it displays, not to detract from it. You want people to talk about the wonderful merchandise you carry, not about your fixtures. Any money above the minimum requirements that you must put into fixtures can be better used to buy merchandise that yields a profit every time it turns over. Moreover, fixtures, like everything else in retailing, change rapidly and you should be prepared to accept new trends as they develop. If you buy expensive fixtures, you will naturally be very reluctant to change and your store will become increasingly outdated.

Salon Fixtures. Fixtures for different kinds of selling Fixture styles must be carefully chosen to fit your store image and help in the various forms of selling now used. Of these, salon selling is the oldest and the one still used in exclusive shops and departments where sales personnel handle all the merchandise. Salon fixtures should be distinctive and rich-looking but in an understated way. In this instance, expensive fixtures can be good business because they are part of the store atmosphere that these customers want. Fortunately, since styles in salon fixtures change slowly, the initial investment lasts a long time.

Sample Selling Fixtures. Fixtures for departments carrying such items as dinnerware or glassware should be chosen with good display in mind. They should help customers select the merchandise they want from floor samples before the customers go to a salesperson for the exact quantity, color, price, etc. They should also be adjacent to areas where the stock is stored and should be easily accessible to sales personnel.

Preselection Fixtures. In preselection areas customers are able to choose their wants because they see the store's entire range of merchandise. Sales personnel, however, are still important because they are required to instruct, demonstrate, and give a certain amount of guidance to customers. Fixtures in preselection departments must have a great capacity for merchandise display, storage, and customer accessibility, as well as a method for displaying sizes, prices, and product information. Most stores today use preselection fixtures for small appliances and silverware.

Self-service Fixtures. The best examples of self-service fixtures are in mass merchandising stores where customers can easily move about the store to select merchandise without sales personnel. Then they take their purchases to a cashier who completes the sale. The store's personnel are mainly engaged to keep stock, take cash, and wrap. Fixtures for these departments should stress flexibility and feature devices against pilferage. For example, it has been found that a narrow glass strip set at an angle on the front edge of a fixture reduces theft considerably.

Most stores use a variety of selling techniques and should plan their Use a variety of fixtures fixtures accordingly. For example, a men's store may use salon selling in its coat and suit departments, sample selling for its shoes, preselection for sports jackets and slacks, and self-service for shirts and ties. The store thus presents a varied and interesting atmosphere and at the same time it is making every inch of its space profitable.

If you revise your selling fixtures and policies, make certain that you The need to train yourself change too; otherwise, you will defeat the purpose behind the alterations. For example, the owner of a small grocery store can attempt to meet competition, make shopping easier, and reduce his own workload by altering his store from salon selling to self-service. However, if he is unwilling to revise his own selling habits, he will only create customer dissatisfaction and much more work for himself. When a customer shops in his new set-up, a retailer like this will still insist on "waiting" on her. He follows her around the store, grabs each prepackaged item she selects, and runs to the wrapping counter for a bag. Although he now has a cash register that adds and totals purchases, he still marks down the price of each item on the outside of a bag with the stub of a pencil and adds it to the previous total before returning the bag to the customer. If the customer selects 15 items, the grocer performs this procedure 15 times. By then, because he refuses to use a basket, he requires the customer's help to move the pile of merchandise that has accumulated.

In the meantime, other people have come into the store who select the items they need and walk over to the check-out desk, where they are forced to wait until the grocer has completed "serving" his first customer. No one is happy. The first customer does not require the help of the owner; indeed, she is embarrassed by his presence because he forces her to make instant decisions instead of allowing her the pleasure of handling merchandise, reading their labels, and selecting those articles that interest her. Again, because of the owner's salon selling techniques, she is not permitted to look around and buy on impulse. The other customers are annoyed and impatient because they believe that a self-service store should speed up, not slow down, shopping. The grocer, too, is unhappy. Not only has he used up a great deal of physical energy running back and forth, he also feels vaguely ill at ease about his handling of the first customer and very bad about keeping the other customers waiting. At the end of the day this grocer is extremely tired, both mentally and physically, and yet he hasn't done any of his stockkeeping, shelf arranging, or any of the other things he knows he should do to keep his store attractive and his merchandise up to date.

This unfortunate situation could have been avoided if the owner had remained near his check-out counter and had unpacked, checked, marked, and filled shelves while waiting for customers to complete their shopping. This example emphasizes the fact that fixtures alone cannot perform their function adequately. They must be correctly used by the store personnel.

The need to train personnel

If you alter your method of selling, you must not only change your own selling techniques, you also make certain that your staff understands and practices the new procedures. By doing this, you create an excellent opportunity to adopt and adapt many of the strengths inherent in large department and chain stores and still retain all the strengths that are yours because you are small. If the grocer in the above example joined a group of independents, he could buy merchandise and operate like a chain and still retain the quiet, friendly, and personal atmosphere that only a small store can develop. Customers could be greeted by name and with small talk and then be permitted to shop as they please while the grocer attends to his own affairs. However, he should help out shoppers who appear uncertain or confused.

When customers come to the check-out counter, he could apply his product knowledge to the needs of the individual shopper by suggesting an economy package, a multiple item, or a new product. In this way the grocer could increase sales and still make his customers *glad* to shop in his store.

Store planning, like every other retail operation, must be carefully and wisely thought through. Therefore, merchants should seek advice from experts in the field before deciding on definite department locations and fixture requirements. Most fixture manufacturers and many wholesalers employ consultants for this purpose, or you can engage a private firm of store designers. Some retail associations provide their members with a store-planning service. Some cooperative buying groups maintain staff designers who are eager to help member stores adopt the latest in fixture planning. But these experts can only suggest what should be done. The final decision, as in every aspect of your business, is yours alone.

Seek expert advice

Your cash register, wrapping desk, office equipment, receiving, marking, and other nonselling fixtures and equipment should be reviewed periodically to see what is new and whether you now require another kind of machine or fixture. It is important to remember that a fixture or a piece of equipment can only pay its way if the store has sufficient volume to use it to capacity. Expensive machines that lie idle for long intervals are very costly. It is equally expensive to hang on to old equipment instead of investing in machines that your business now requires. Some merchants group together to buy machines and thus reduce their individual expenses and make better use of the equipment; others rent machines, and still others hire specialists to perform the work.

Miscellaneous nonselling fixtures

In planning nonselling fixtures and floor areas, great care should be taken to reduce accident and fire hazards. This will not only bring down your insurance costs, it will also make your store a better place in which to work and shop.

Discreet background music either piped in from a company that offers this service or provided by your own system (not by radio which you cannot control) helps to make shopping a pleasant experience. Sometimes, however, music can be a nuisance because it may annoy your sales personnel or create customer ill will. Therefore, before you sign a contract for piped-in music, insist on a free trial period.

If you feel that your store requires major fixture changes but you cannot make them all at the same time, develop a master plan. In this way, as you make changes, you can maintain the store image you want to create. Then carry out your plan in stages that will best fit into the slower periods of your business. You should revise your plans as new ideas and trends develop, but this will be all to the good. You must move with the times and the times are always moving. But if you have a master plan, you can proceed with each stage and not jeopardize the store image you wish to create.

Planning major fixtures changes

1. A successful merchant thinks of his store as a sales factory, his equipment and fixtures as machines, and his personnel as machine tenders.

2. There are major differences between a factory and a store, for example, location and work flow, but the greatest difference is that a store must be planned to please customers but a factory need not be esthetically pleasing to anybody.

3. The objectives behind store planning are (a) to bring customers and merchandise together for maximum selling and (b) to make the best possible use of necessary expenditures.

4. Planning begins with your exterior. The exterior sets the tone of the store. The interior must confirm the image that the exterior creates.

5. Divide the interior into selling and nonselling service areas. Use rent per square foot as a guide.

6. Plan to use vertical as well as horizontal space.

7. Good interior layout increases sales, saves the energies of your personnel, and creates customer goodwill.

8. Fixtures should be flexible, enhance your store personality, suit the merchandise, and fulfill the selling techniques required of them.

9. If you alter your selling policies and fixtures, make certain that you and your personnel change too.

10. Seek expert advice on all areas of your store planning.

11. Break down your major fixture change plan into a series of interrelated stages; then, if necessary, modify them as you go along. This method insures a unified store personality that always follows the latest trends.

18

Organize Yourself and Your Employees for Continuous Expansion

WHAT THIS CHAPTER IS ABOUT

Planning the store area for maximum efficiency is only one side of the profit coin. You must also be able to organize the store's personnel so that each member contributes his best efforts toward making the operation successful. This chapter tells you what a retail organization means and how to go about coordinating every aspect of your business for continuous expansion and maximum profit.

Why Do Stores Progress or Fail?

Every retailer has seen stores rise rapidly and just as quickly level off or fade away. It is not unusual to see the town's largest department store prosper while the owner is active, but lose business rapidly when he dies and a member of the family or a trust company takes over the management. Then, just as it is about to expire, it may be sold to a new owner who brings it to life again. In other cases, it is the founder who fails to make progress and the member of the family or the new manager who saves the store and raises it to greater heights.

Perhaps your operation has reached a stagnant stage and you are conditioning yourself to be content with holding your own instead of fighting to expand because you feel that you are unable to cope with the next level of problems that a further increase in business will entail.

When you analyze any store's progress, you begin to realize that a successful merchant must have more ability than just that of being a good retailer. A good merchandiser can only go so far; then something else must be added or else the store's progress ceases. The "something else" is the owner's ability to organize both himself and his staff as he expands his operations. Most retailers can acquire an organizational competence if they want to do so because essentially this is the technique of coordinating all of the store's functions in an efficient and harmonious manner. It is like learning how to solve a constantly changing jigsaw puzzle by continually fitting the various activities of your store together so that you always obtain a satisfactory picture.

The Law of Human Limitations

A merchant who runs a store by himself must look after the buying, selling, financing, display, and store maintenance. No matter how hard he works, he soon discovers that it is impossible to do everything because he has only two hands and two eyes, there are only 24 hours in each day, and he cannot be in two places at once. Therefore, in spite of all his efforts and careful planning, he finds that he is subject to the law of human limitations that restricts the amount of mental and physical work that one person can do in any given time.

If his wife comes into the store, he discovers that this law determines every organizational function; for now he can divide his work and let his wife look after the selling and display areas while he spends all his time and energy on the other activities of his store. As business improves, he can afford to hire a part-time employee who is told to ticket the goods, keep the merchandise neat and clean, look after a certain amount of maintenance, and help the retailer's wife when she dresses the windows or works on interior displays. During busy times the part-time employee is also expected to sell.

Now the merchant can spend even more time attending to the store's major functions. When a full-time employee is engaged, the retailer gives him or her a certain number of routine jobs, and so it goes. As employees are added, the merchant assigns duties to them that he once had to perform all by himself. By the time he has hired three full-time salespeople and "retires" his wife, the work in the store might be organized as shown in Fig. 18.1.

Group Your Activities

You will see in Fig. 18.1 how the owner tried to group the store's activities and then divide them among the salespeople and himself. Every-

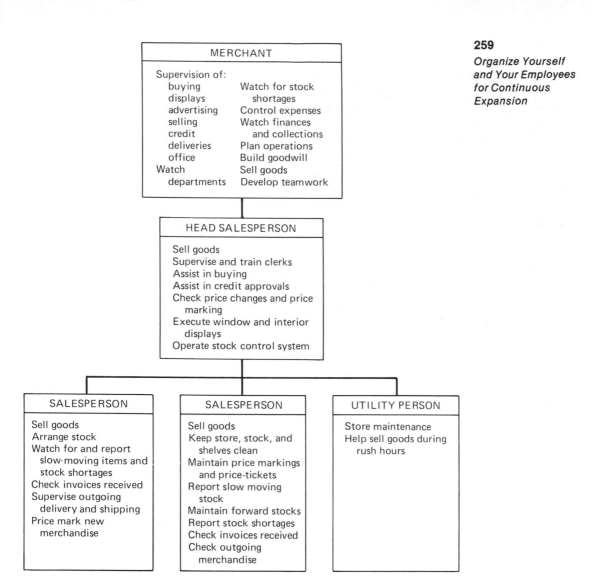

FIGURE 18.1   Organization chart for a small retail store.

one then understood his duties and how he fitted into the puzzle that made up the store's organization.

Tell Employees Where They Are on Your Chart

No matter how you organize your store, all employees must know where they fit into the organization and what their relationships are to the other employees in the store. This enables them to know how to operate in it. An organizational chart, then, is something like a map, but because there is nothing static about retailing, this chart must be changed from time to time to meet new conditions, either inside or outside the store.

Once you have grouped your store's functions and decided on the proper organizational structure, your next job is to assign specific duties to the employees so that they will know exactly what they are supposed to do.

Merchants make a big mistake when they hire employees and only tell them to "sell and keep the stock clean." The new employee asks, "What kind of selling am I supposed to do—pressure or nonpressure? Do I take turns or fight my way forward? Whom do I go to with customer complaints, and what happens if I have a personal complaint myself? Again, what does cleaning the stock mean? Does it require only dusting or does it mean I should report shortages as well? Are there other tasks I should know about?"

Some retailers deliberately avoid outlining employees' duties because they feel that definite job descriptions result in a minimum effort. Actually, the opposite is true. If employees are given specific tasks, they know that they will be checked on their ability to do the job satisfactorily. This creates a good atmosphere for discipline because there can be no buck passing and no pleas of ignorance.

Give Employees Authority and Make Them Accountable

Whenever a retailer assigns jobs, he must give employees the authority to perform them properly; otherwise, employees cannot be held accountable for results. For example, if the department managers are expected to buy, they must be permitted to sign all normal purchase orders without referring to those above them. If this is done, they can be held accountable for all the merchandise in their departments. However, if they are required to obtain OKs from their superiors before they make purchases, the superiors, not the managers, are responsible for the merchandise in their departments. Nevertheless, if buyers exceed their open-to-buys or are heavily loaded with slow-moving merchandise, their decisions should be closely checked by their superiors until the situation is corrected.

Develop Confidence in Your Staff

A major reason retailers fail to expand their business is their inability to develop confidence in their staff; in order to enlarge their operations, they must overcome the law of human limitations by assigning an increasing number of jobs to employees and delegating more and more of their authority. Yet, very few small and medium-sized retailers seem to be able to develop the necessary confidence in their staff that an expanding organization requires. Because most merchants feel that only they can do a good job, they keep interfering and breaking down their employees' authority and their accountability. Moreover, they are usually very liberal with criticism but very miserly with praise, and in many cases, they blame their employees for their own failures but take all the credit for the staff's successes. Actually, these merchants are responsible for both.

Final Responsibility Is Always Yours

You can assign tasks and give employees authority to do their jobs and so hold them accountable, but you can *never* give away responsibility. Thus, in the final analysis, the success or failure of the entire business is your responsibility. Creditors are not interested in alibis. They want their money—or else. Therefore, it is important that you realize that while you can assign jobs and delegate authority, you cannot give away responsibility.

Employees, then, should be selected with care and trained to do their jobs as you want them done. One reason for the importance of definite store policies and job descriptions is that they help to train employees to accept your beliefs, adopt your methods, and obey instructions. Otherwise, they, not you, are running the store. Besides, it is much better for all concerned to follow definite rules so that customers, salesmen, and other people may know what they can expect from your organization.

Proper Supervision Is Constant Supervision

There is little value in training personnel to do jobs as you want them done unless you constantly supervise their efforts. Employees are human and they tend to take shortcuts, invent their own way of doing a task which may be harmful to your overall plan, or forget what they were taught. You must keep after them and develop methods of overseeing and correcting their efforts without antagonizing them. This may require retraining, moving, or removing employees who are not performing properly. By alert supervision you can discover which of your policies are working and which should be strengthened. For example, you may have too narrow a price range for your buyers to buy properly, or you may not be lenient enough about customer returns. Proper supervision will reveal these faults early enough for you to correct them.

Make Changes Slowly

Habits are so ingrained in most people that when you decide to make a change, you must be careful to activate it in a series of small stages. Your employees will then accept each change and cooperate. If you move too quickly, they will resist your efforts and create an organization that is not what you want it to be at all. Also, by planning your new policies in small stages and supervising each one carefully, you can discover errors before they become serious and develop ways of overcoming them.

With the above general guides in mind, you can proceed to organize your store properly. First, decide what your objectives should be and then plan how to reach these objectives. Naturally, every merchant wants to make money, but each goes about satisfying this wish in different ways. Every retailer should establish the guides or policies that he hopes will lead him to his desired ambition. For example, one of your objectives might be a unified store personality. This requires a number of policy decisions that relate to your external and internal store characteristics. Once you have decided on your objectives and policies, you can plan the physical store as a whole, while retaining as much as possible of your present equipment.

1. Plan

Long-Term, Short-term, and Immediate Plans. Even if it were desirable to carry out the entire plan at once, lack of funds will most likely make it impossible to do so. Therefore, you break it down into a series of short-term plans and begin with what you consider to be most necessary and financially possible. Use the same procedure with other objectives. Your inventory may be in poor shape and you plan to correct this situation. You draw up a list of objectives such as the number of stock turns you desire, your ideal maintained markup, markdown percentages, etc. To achieve these goals, you develop a set of policies. For example, you might decide that your buyers must reduce their current number of vendors, stock must be aged and reduced according to a set schedule, department heads must be more careful in keeping up staple stock assortments, etc. In this instance, to announce all your policies at once would create a negative response. You must plan your approach so that you will attack the problem by a series of short-term plans that will educate your buyers and gain their cooperation with your new policies. In this way, your chances of reaching your objectives are much greater.

As you go about initiating, revising, and putting into practice your long- and short-term plans, you also plan next week's sales, next month's windows, and what to do with the lingerie department's lunch period today because it is short-staffed.

Plan Your Own Activities. Planning your *own* activities should become a habit, for a good organizer always plans his day, month, year, and even years. He also inspires his employees to plan their time. To plan is fairly simple; to carry out your plans is sometimes very difficult because most of them require a great deal of self-discipline and constant vigilance. However, these traits can be learned and in time they will become a habit.

Once you have a clear picture of your objectives and have drawn up a set of policies, you are ready to go about putting your plans into action. Divide the jobs to be done into easy to handle loads, check to see that they avoid duplication of tasks and dual subordination, and then see who of your employees is best suited for each task. Job planning in a small store is

2. Organize

much more flexible than in a large organization because the small store owner can usually rearrange chores to fit his personnel. The large organization, however, must find the employee to fit the job, for any tampering with its specifications can lead to a series of very complicated situations. Once you have matched your personnel to their tasks, check back to see that everything fits and that the organizational structure produces the teamwork necessary to benefit the store as a whole.

Be Very Careful When You Promote Employees. Be very careful when you promote employees from one organizational level to another or even when you move them from one job to another on the same level. Just because an employee is an excellent section head is not a reason to believe that he or she will make an excellent buyer. The same holds true for moving a top men's furnishing salesman to the clothing department. Frequently, the personality and skills that make an employee successful in one job may be the very reason why the employee becomes a miserable failure in another job.

Make Your Lines of Communication Short. Remember that the shorter you make the lines of communication that lead from you to the person doing the job, the better. Orders and ideas have a tendency to be misinterpreted when they are transferred from one person to another, and frequently they are not what the originator intended when they emerge at the end of the line. Another thing to remember in job planning is the law of human limitations. Because everyone is limited by his or her physical and mental abilities, to delegate too much work to an employee will produce poor results, but to assign the employee too small a task will weaken the incentive to do his or her best.

After the jobs have been allocated, plan how to explain their duties to the employees. This can be accomplished by private discussions, written orders, group meetings, or a combination of these. The method used should gain the employees' cooperation, make certain that they understand the tasks assigned them, and give them sufficient authority to carry them out. Then they can be held accountable.

3. Lead

Planning and organization are valueless until they are made to work. A leader must guide employees to a standard of maximum efficiency, and in small and medium-sized establishments the owner must provide this leadership. He alone can make or break his store operations.

Leadership Qualities. To be a leader, you must provide the initiative to get your plans going and have sufficient vitality and endurance to enthuse your employees with a desire to work and to remain at it when business is slow and inspire them to make an extra effort when business is brisk and the profit is there for the taking.

A good leader stops, listens, and thinks before he makes a decision, particularly when it will not be welcome to some of his employees, although it will, in his own view, benefit the store as a whole. Because a large percentage of decisions are necessarily unpleasant to one employee or another, the retailer must be able to persuade employees not only to accept his judgments, but also to put their hearts and souls into carrying them out. This is one of the most difficult arts a leader has to practise.

A retailer who is a leader does not shrink from responsibility. He accepts the difficulties entailed in running a store and realizes that everyone, including himself, makes mistakes. Thus, he blames himself for his own errors, but he quickly praises employees who work well. A good leader, then, is human as well as humane, and he has a great deal of understanding for those he leads. If you are a good leader, your employees will develop loyalty and morale. They will not only want to work for you, they will also be openly proud of your store and make customers and others conscious that it is a good store to deal with.

Even with good leadership, plans and organizational structures that look marvelous on paper sometimes become chaotic when put into practice. If this happens, *check for lack of coordination.* Perhaps you did a poor job of grouping related activities or did not define your organization and procedures clearly enough for your employees to understand what you wanted from them, how they fitted into the store, or how they were to act in certain situations.

4. Coordinate

Check communications system. If the communication system is operating poorly and if the flow of information down and up is stopped, diverted, or misinterpreted, you will find that employees are working at cross purposes. If you observe how news travels in your store, you will see that most of it moves along a natural system of friendship, coffee breaks, or social relations among the staff. A wise coordinator will adopt this natural flow and adapt his system to it, as far as is practicable.

Seek voluntary coordination. Because information has to be interpreted and accepted by those who receive it, the more voluntary coordination you can obtain from your employees, the better working organization you will have. This can be done by making your employees understand your major objectives and how you want to build your store around these objectives.

Another method is to create store traditions and morale by establishing a number of definite customs such as birthday cards for every employee, an annual dance, 10 year and 25 year clubs, etc. If in addition to these fairly usual customs you can develop a few unique ways to show that you appreciate the efforts of your employees, you will go a long way toward obtaining a strong store morale. Encourage your staff to give you suggestions about better ways to run the store. If you take each idea seriously and explain why it is impractical or unworkable, you will obtain a few that can have an enormously profitable effect on your store. These ideas should be rewarded. In any event, whatever you do to encourage active employee participation encourages better morale and better store coordination.

How to introduce new policies.　A wise merchant recognizes that while a store is full of rumors, it has no secrets, and he uses this fact to put out feelers on his proposed ideas and then interprets their reaction. He can then decide whether to formalize his ideas as policy and spend time in educating his staff or to introduce his plan in a series of small stages.

How to issue instructions.　Before giving an order to your staff, make sure that the order is reasonable, understandable, and complete in every detail. Otherwise, it will not be obeyed in the way you desire. If you issue an instruction that is unreasonable, say, for example, one that insists that your employees work extra hours on certain days, the instruction will not be obeyed by some and it will be poorly carried out by others. If you issue an order full of professional language, it will be misinterpreted or simply ignored, even though these terms appear to you to be the best way to explain the order.

Finally, if the instructions are not thought through to their logical conclusion, they leave the staff in confusion. For example, you might issue a new policy about customer returns by the following notice: "Henceforth, when a customer brings back merchandise (1) be very pleasant and polite and (2) tell the customer you will look after it." If you end your instruction at this point, your staff will be confused—how should they look after it? Give the customer a refund immediately? Give the customer a receipt and then send the merchandise back to the vendor for credit?

Because it is so easy for orders to be misunderstood or given an improper emphasis by employees, it is always wise to explain why you issued the instructions and where they fit into the store's functions. This can be done informally through individual discussions or formally through a staff meeting.

No matter what procedure you use to issue instructions, a number of your employees will tend to disregard new orders. They do this because they dislike change, disagree with you, or do not understand what your instructions mean and are too timid to ask for clarification. Therefore, you should plan to follow up any order, see that it is properly obeyed, and see that it does lead to better coordination then before it was issued. Otherwise, why make the change?

Simplified controls.　Because you are restricted by the law of human limitations, you must devise methods of extending yourself so that you can peer into every facet of your operation and watch how it is working. In some areas a quick look is sufficient, but in other areas a slower, longer look is needed. To do this, create a series of controls that will inform you where you are going and where your strengths and weaknesses lie.

Some of these controls will be internal, for example, the status of the bank balance, but others, such as the turnover, expense ratios, and net profit figures, will be both internal and comparative. You should also develop a series of individual controls that will tell you each salesperson's

**5. Establish
controls**

daily sales, each manager's gross margin, etc. These should be tied to standards so that every employee knows what is expected of him or her.

An ideal system contains a minimum of controls, all of which are simple to understand and inexpensive to keep and which are to be used to their fullest extent. Too many guides and standards are expensive to maintain, and complicated controls are useless because they will be ignored. If you pick strategic points in your store organization and control them, you will know how everything behind each point is functioning. Then it will only be necessary to investigate where the controls point to the development of a dangerous situation.

Correct faults early. Proper controls can highlight weaknesses. These should be corrected as soon as possible, for the longer a fault is permitted to lie unchecked, the harder it becomes to handle. For example, your controls may show how a portion of your floor area could be put to better use, but you know that to correct the situation will be unpleasant. Nevertheless, the longer you postpone the move, the more entrenched the present department becomes and the more difficult the final decision. Frequently, an adjustment could be forced on you, not by internal factors, but by external ones. For example, at one time the notions department might have been a source of large customer traffic and impulse buying, but today it is no more than a convenience for a rapidly dwindling proportion of your clientele. The fault does not lie with your store or the department manager but with changing customer habits. The sooner the space is filled with a current customer need that produces profits, the better.

Review constantly. Because retailing is so dynamic, you must periodically review every object, policy, and function in your store. Perhaps customer services are becoming too costly. If they are, how should these policies be changed and what kind of customer and employee education is necessary to make the new policies work? A review of your organization structure may reveal that the merchandise control office is wielding too much power over the merchandise function. Once you see that there is something wrong, correct the situation as quickly and efficiently as possible.

Are you the store's boss or its slave? If you never have time to think about your store as a whole because you are so busy with routine tasks, decide to stop being its slave and become its master instead. You can if you organize your store along the scientific lines discussed above. Then develop a new approach not only to your own duties and responsibilities but also to those of your employees. Learn how to plan and to discipline yourself so that you can control and coordinate your personnel for maximum efficiency, profit, and growth.

1. A retailer can continue to expand only as long as he is able to coordinate every aspect of his business for maximum profit.

2. Organize your business by analyzing and grouping the work to be done. Then, with the law of human limitations always before you, allocate specific duties to yourself and your employees.

3. Develop job descriptions for your employees and make certain that they understand what they are supposed to do, where they fit into your organization, and what authority they have to perform their tasks. Then they will know how to operate in the store and can be held accountable for the work they are hired to perform.

4. Remember that you can assign work and delegate authority but you can never give up ultimate responsibility.

5. Making certain that your employees are cooperating for greater profit and that all the store's functions are coordinated requires constant supervision, employee retraining, and organizational revisions.

6. There are five steps that a retailer should take to organize his store properly: (1) *Plan* the store's personality as a whole by deciding on the objectives and the policies required to reach these desires. (2) *Organize* the store by allocating jobs to those best suited for each task. (3) *Lead.* Leadership requires initiative, vitality, endurance, an open mind, the ability to make fair decisions, and a willingness to assume responsibility. Above all, be human and humane, and develop an understanding toward your employees. (4) *Establish coordination.* To keep your store running at top efficiency requires constant revision, for circumstances both inside and outside the store keep changing and demand the adoption of new coordination procedures. (5) *Establish controls.* Because you must operate under the law of human limitations, you require a set of controls that will tell you how every facet of your organization is doing.

19

How to
Pick Good Employees

WHAT THIS CHAPTER IS ABOUT

Because of the law of human limitations, you must delegate a number of store functions to others. As far as customers, vendor salesmen, and other people doing business with the store are concerned, the employee they deal with *is* the store. This chapter tells you how to select good employees, how to train them, and how to encourage them to give their best efforts toward making your store a profitable operation.

Employee Turnover Is Very Expensive

Large stores maintain expensive training departments to teach new employees how to perform their jobs according to the store's policies. Usually, this is the smallest part of the training cost, for stores cannot even estimate the expense caused by trainees' insulting customers through inexperience, misrepresenting goods, and losing sales because they lack merchandise knowledge or selling techniques. Some large stores, aware of trainee costs and the harm that new employees can do to the store's good-will, try to keep employee turnover to a minimum by making personnel a major operations division that can concentrate on such situations.

In a small store, good employees are even more important because they represent you personally and customers are not as tolerant of poor personnel in small stores as they are in larger organizations. In addition, it costs a lot of money, time, and energy to train sales personnel to adopt your organization's way of doing business. If a salesperson leaves shortly after he becomes a source of income instead of an expense, your loss is his gain for you have trained him to become an immediate asset to another employer. Constant turnover of help also reduces the morale of the store and tends to increase employee unrest. If you realize that employees are really your most important asset or your greatest liability, you will be very careful in selecting, training, supervising, and keeping them.

Yet, there is a great difference between a poor and lenient employer and a strict, but fair, one. Both soon create reputations among prospective workers. The poor employer drives away good potential personnel, no matter how lenient he may be; the strict employer, providing he is fair and pays according to effort, attracts good employees.

Employment Sources

There are a number of ways to obtain employees. If your store has pleasant working conditions, your current help may suggest the names of friends and acquaintances as well as members of their families who may want to work for you. In many instances, customers will give you the names of people who might be available or even hint about working in the store themselves. High schools and higher educational institutions provide a good and fairly intelligent source of part-time employees who, in some cases, can work into permanent positions. You can also place advertisements in trade papers because they are read by people in the field, some of whom are anxious to change jobs. The want ad section in newspapers usually brings in many applicants, but many of the applicants are unsuitable. As a last resort, various state employment services or private employment agencies can be contacted.

A good source that is sometimes overlooked is past employees. Keep a file on every good employee who leaves and use it when you need part-time help. These people are immediately productive and are worth contacting whenever the opportunity arises.

Pirating

Before you hire an employee who is working at another store, make sure that he really wants to leave and is not using you as a lever for a salary increase. An unscrupulous employee can obtain a substantial wage increase in this way and still remain at his first job. Again, taking away an employee by a more attractive salary offer creates a very unpleasant series of retaliations. Other stores will feel free to raid your staff and employee pirating wars benefit only employees.

To prevent pirating, it is wise not to offer an applicant any more than his going salary but to promise him an increase after a short period providing he proves satisfactory. This procedure will test the applicant's desire for a change and also clear you of any charge of pirating.

In most small and medium-sized stores the owner does his own hiring. You will cut down costs and save energy if you standardize your hiring procedures as much as possible. For certain jobs, your department manager can do the preliminary screening and send on to you only the most promising applicants to be interviewed by you before they are hired. It is your store and you must assume the ultimate responsibility for all its activities.

It is good policy to refuse at once applicants who are obviously unsuited for the job. Otherwise, they may read some hope into the interviews and think that you are going to accept them. This eventually creates an unpleasant situation and builds ill will. Of course, they must be refused tactfully, leaving them, if possible, with a feeling of warmth toward the store.

The final interview should do two things. You should gain pertinent information on the applicants and make up your mind whether or not they will be suitable for the job. Applicants should be given information on the store and the job so that they too can decide whether or not this is the store and the job for them. Deceiving applicants creates dissatisfaction and may result in excessive employee turnover. Give the applicants the facts and, if necessary, paint them blacker than they really are. Good prospects like challenges and if they accept them, they will be pleasantly surprised at the actual conditions and tend to build up morale and loyalty all the faster.

It is a good practice to design and print your own application form because it creates a businesslike atmosphere. It is not necessary to have all applicants fill out the form. Use it only for those in whom you are interested. The form shown in Fig. 19.1 provides for all pertinent information. It should be used as a guide for the interview itself and if the applicant is hired, it becomes a permanent record. Watch for any omissions when the prospect fills in the form, because omissions sometimes indicate an unpleasant experience that you should know about. You yourself should carefully determine the reasons for these omissions during the interview. An area you should be very clear about is the number of job changes and the reasons for them. It is important to contact references, but remember that few applicants are foolish enough to give references that may be detrimental to themselves. Most references are lenient and uncritical in their observations on applicants. An entirely unbiased report on an applicant may of course be prepared by your credit bureau.

Some stores leave new employees to learn as they go along. This procedure can be very costly, for the employees are not only useless until they know what is expected of them, they can also do a great deal of harm before they learn their jobs. By training prospects you make them productive sooner and you save the time and effort of other employees who otherwise would be forced to do a half-hearted supervisory and training job on the new employees just to prevent them from becoming nuisances or to keep

WORTH'S

Application for Employment

DATE _____

MR.
MRS.
MISS.
Name in full — Print   Wife's or Husband's Name   Maiden Name

ADDRESS
No.   Street   City   State   TELEPHONE NO.

HOW LONG AT ABOVE ADDRESS   PREVIOUS ADDRESS

| | | | | | | Single ( ) | Separated ( ) | |
| DATE OF BIRTH: | Mo. | Day | Year | Height | Weight | Age | Married ( ) | Divorced ( ) Widowed ( ) |

NAME AND ADDRESS OF CLOSEST RELATIVE   RELATIONSHIP TO YOU

HAVE YOU ANY HISTORY OF: Rheumatism Yes ( ) No ( ) Back Condition Yes ( ) No ( ) Hernia Yes ( ) No ( ) Nephritis Yes ( ) No ( )

Diabetes Yes ( ) No ( ) Tuberculosis Yes ( ) No ( ) Allergy Yes ( ) No ( ) Mental Illness Yes ( ) No ( )

MAJOR OPERATIONS Yes ( ) No ( )   SERIOUS ACCIDENT OR ILLNESS Yes ( ) No ( )

DATE AND KIND?   DATE AND KIND?

HAVE YOU ANY DEFECTS IN SIGHT, HEARING, SPEECH OR BODY? Yes ( ) No ( )

HAVE YOU EVER SIGNED A WAIVER FOR PHYSICAL DISABILITY?   WHEN?   WHY?

HAVE YOU EVER RECEIVED WORKMEN'S COMPENSATION?   WHEN?   WHY?

How many in your immediate family? (Include yourself)	NAME (of each one working)	RELATIONSHIP	OCCUPATION	EMPLOYER

WERE YOU EVER IN OUR EMPLOY? Yes ( ) No. ( ) DEPT.   POSITION   FROM   TO

HAVE YOU ANY RELATIVES EMPLOYED BY WORTH'S   Yes ( ) No ( ). NAME OF RELATIVE   DEPT.

ARE YOU SEEKING: PERMANENT WORK ( ) OR SEASONAL WORK ( )   FULL TIME ( ) PART TIME ( )   AFTER SCHOOL AND SAT. ( ) SAT. ONLY ( )

FOR WHAT POSITION DO YOU APPLY?   SOCIAL SECURITY NUMBER

DO NOT WRITE BELOW THIS LINE — PLEASE CONTINUE ON OTHER SIDE

DATE EMPLOYED	DEPT.	POSITION	RATE	STORE NUMBER
TERMINATED: DATE	REASON			RATING
REHIRED— DATE	DEPT.	POSITION	RATE	STORE NUMBER

FIGURE 19.1   The information on this application form gives a complete record of the applicant's history and other necessary data.

Courtesy Worth's, Westbury, Conn.

EACH QUESTION MUST BE ANSWERED ACCURATELY AND FULLY. UNTRUTHFUL STATEMENTS WILL CAUSE REJECTION OF YOUR APPLICATION.

Record of Employment

			FROM		TO	
			MONTH	YEAR	MONTH	YEAR
PRESENT OR LAST EMPLOYER	POSITION YOU HELD					
NUMBER AND STREET OR AVE.	IF SALESPERSON, WHAT DID YOU SELL?					
CITY AND STATE	REASON FOR LEAVING					

			FROM		TO	
			MONTH	YEAR	MONTH	YEAR
NEXT PREVIOUS EMPLOYER	POSITION YOU HELD					
NUMBER AND STREET OR AVE.	IF SALESPERSON, WHAT DID YOU SELL?					
CITY AND STATE	REASON FOR LEAVING					

			FROM		TO	
			MONTH	YEAR	MONTH	YEAR
NEXT PREVIOUS EMPLOYER	POSITION YOU HELD					
NUMBER AND STREET OR AVE.	IF SALESPERSON, WHAT DID YOU SELL?					
CITY AND STATE	REASON FOR LEAVING					

Education

	NAME OF SCHOOL	ADDRESS	No. of Years	Course	Year of Graduation
GRAMMER					
HIGH					
COLLEGE				Degree	
OTHER					

Personal References

GIVE NAMES AND ADDRESSES OF TWO PERSONS (**NOT RELATIVES OR FORMER EMPLOYERS**) WHO HAVE KNOWN YOU FOR MORE THAN A YEAR AND CAN VOUCH FOR YOUR HONESTY, CHARACTER AND HABITS.

NAME	STREET and CITY	OCCUPATION

I certify that the statements made by me on BOTH SIDES of this application are true, complete, and correct to the best of my knowledge and belief and are made in good faith. I understand that if I knowingly made any misstatements of facts, I am subject to disqualification or dismissal and to such other penalties as may be prescribed by law or Personnel Department regulations.

_____
Signature

FIGURE 19.1 (continued)

them out of trouble. Training also reduces employee turnover and improves morale and store loyalty which go a long way toward making a successful store.

If you cannot spend the time training new employees yourself, the job must be delegated to someone else. In most stores there are people who like this kind of work and who do it very well. You must make it clear to these employees that you consider the time spent with the new people productive and that their time will be considered when you review their contribution to the store. The time spent in training should take place whenever there is very little activity in the store. You can work out a training schedule with your senior employees or let them submit one for your approval. But just because you delegate the training job to someone else does not absolve you from the results. If employees are poorly trained, they will harm you, not their teacher. Therefore, make it a point to check up on new employees and see that they learn the store's routines, procedures, and outlook properly.

Who does the training?

Plan your training program to accomplish two purposes: (1) It should make your new employees aware of what you are trying to do. This means instruction on the history of your store, its policies, and its objectives. Employees should be told why you adopted the methods under which you are now operating and they should also be informed about your future goals. (2) It should tell new employees *exactly* what their jobs are and then teach them how to do the jobs *your* way. This includes your approach to customers, your method of writing out sales slips, how you keep stock, etc. It may require a relearning process on the part of new employees, but if you explain *why* you do things as you do, they will understand and quickly acquire your methods of operating.

The purpose behind training

Training Is a Never-ending Process

To obtain maximum efficiency, employee training must be considered a never-ending process. Once employees have satisfactorily undergone their initial instruction, their training should be continued through a regular series of short meetings in which parts of their jobs are reviewed or updated. They should then be encouraged to discuss their work and suggest ways to improve it. If properly handled, these meetings will produce the added bonus of reducing tensions among employees and between them and their superiors. It should also help to build morale and encourage store pride and loyalty. If possible, the meetings should be held on store time but when it is necessary to hold one in the evening, simple refreshments should be served and compensation should be made for the extra time the employees spend on store work.

Some stores have adopted a policy of promoting only from within, and and they formally rate their employees every 3, 6, or 12 months. Thus,

Promotion policies

employees always know exactly how the store feels about them and what their chances are for advancement. This system has the advantage of making the more ambitious employees work their hardest to get ahead, but it can boomerang, too, and make workers who see no advance in prospect do less than their best. It also creates a certain degree of unhappiness and dissatisfaction, for in many instances the opinion the store holds about an employee differs greatly from his opinion of himself.

It is not necessary for a small or medium-sized store to rate its employees formally, but a periodic review of each worker should be undertaken, ending in an interview between the boss and the employee concerned. These interviews may be unpleasant or embarrassing, but they should be held, because everyone likes to know what the boss thinks of him or her, one way or the other. If you have any criticism or suggestions on how employees can improve their performance, this is the time to discuss them. If the employee is in danger of being fired, the employee should be made aware of it and that there will be a trial period during which he or she will be judged and told the results.

Stores that have a policy of promoting from within sometimes discover that no one on the staff can fill a certain job. They must then resort to a number of subterfuges that are soon discovered by the staff. Consequently, there will be a reduction in morale and confidence in the store policies. It is better to state that although you try to promote from within, it is not always possible to do so.

Transfer policy

In large stores employees who are dissatisfied with one job can be given another; in chain stores they may be moved to a different city or locality. A small store does not have this job flexibility. Nevertheless, since losing a trained employee is expensive, a great deal of thought should be given to seeing whether or not an employee can be retained for another job. Unhappy employees are poor workers and sometimes very little is required to make them content. Perhaps a shift to another department in which the employee would feel more at home or more productive or perhaps a move to another, more understanding, supervisor may be the solution. But trying to force unhappy employees to stay where they are because transferring them may appear to be weakness on your part is foolish indeed.

Dismissal

No one likes to dismiss an employee for inadequacy, because no matter how it is done, the person concerned can be hurt very deeply. The smaller the store, the more personal your relationships with your employees and the harder dismissal becomes. Therefore, before you take this step, make sure that there is no other way out and that your conscience is clear. Then plan the interview so that it will do least injury to the employee's pride and to the store's goodwill. By this time, you should know the employee's thinking processes fairly well, and if you can keep your emotions from becoming involved, the interview can be conducted with a certain amount of control. In this way you can ease the employee's pain and lessen the interview time and your own embarrassment.

There is more to working in a store than wages. Intangibles such as your attitude to employees and their feeling toward you and the store, and physical amenities such as pleasant employees' rest rooms, the distance an employee has to travel each day, hours of work, etc., are plus and minus factors that must be considered.

A salary, however, is tangible, and the money an employee has in his envelope is the most important tangible of all. In the old days employees were offered so much a week and they could either accept it or go elsewhere. Today, salaries have become more involved because some employers have discovered that their help produce more if they are offered the minimum wage and given opportunities and incentives to increase it by their own efforts.

Since there is no perfect wage plan, there will never be a wage plan that will satisfy everyone concerned. The best ones are compromises that are fair to employers, satisfactory to most employees, meet minimum wage laws and, when necessary, union requirements. Only a certain percentage of your sales volume can be allotted to salaries, and if this is too high, you are bound to lose money. Nevertheless, your method of paying wages should make most of your employees happy.

To do this, it should be understood by your staff and it should be flexible enough to change with today's dynamic conditions. Wage systems in some stores are so complicated that no one but management can understand them. This means that employees do not know how much they are going to earn and so cannot plan their own living expenses properly. Also, a good plan should provide an incentive for every employee to produce more for the store. For example, not all salespeople are alike in their ability to sell; therefore, there should be some system to reward the better ones. This makes for more satisfied personnel and better sales volume.

Wage Plans

Straight Salary. This is easily understood, but it is not very flexible. Also, it does little to differentiate the poor from the good salesperson. However, in certain sales areas where customer service is most important and time must be spent with each customer, straight salary can be best.

Straight Commission Plan. Here, salespeople get a percentage of what they sell and are permitted a drawing account based on their probable earnings. This is balanced at regular intervals and if employees owe the store money, they are sometimes allowed to carry it over into the next period. In this case, most stores reduce employees' drawings until they make up the shortage.

If the commission is too low for the potential sales volume and if the salesperson's deficit mounts, employee turnover is very large. Straight commission plans also overemphasize sales volume and thereby cut down on the time that should be spent building up customer goodwill. Such a plan also tends to create high-pressure selling and causes returns to be greater. If, however, salespeople are properly trained, they will learn that their commissions are based on net, not gross, sales and that dissatisfied customers making returns take up a lot of time that could be spent in productive selling.

Salary Plus Commission Plan. These plans attempt to combine the best features of straight salary and straight commission plans. Here, the employee is given a basic salary and then a commission on sales. Following are three variations of these plans:

1. A base salary is paid plus a single commission rate on all sales.
2. A quota is set for each salesperson and he or she gets a small commission on all sales up to the quota. The salesperson then receives a larger percent on all additional sales above the quota. The basic pay, of course, is constant.
3. A basic salary is paid plus commission only on sales that are over a quota.

The employee knows his minimum salary and can plan his expenses accordingly. He also has a direct incentive to increase his sales.

However, some of these plans are difficult to understand and are expensive to maintain. Percentages vary from month to month and from department to department. To have the greatest incentive, commissions should be paid as soon as possible after the period ends, and this may become an expensive bookkeeping procedure. Problems also arise when an employee moves from one department to another if the departments have different quota percentages. Finally, quotas must be set low enough for employees to benefit from the quota periods, but if the quotas are set too low, they create a high salary-to-sales ratio and this is bad from the employer's standpoint. If, however, quotas are set too high, the salespeople's incentives are lost.

Spiffs or P.M.'s (Premium Money). These are special cash bonuses that are given to employees who sell particular items of merchandise. They are usually placed on slow-selling items when the employer feels that it is cheaper to pay spiffs than to reduce the merchandise, although sometimes he may offer a spiff and also mark down the item. Spiffs must be carefully handled, particularly in the service store. No salesperson should sell something just for the spiff, for this kind of selling can build up customer ill will toward the store. Spiffs can become very expensive.

Salary Plus Bonus Plan. This plan is used mainly in large stores, chains, and branch stores. A straight weekly salary plus a six-month or yearly bonus is given to certain personnel. For example, it can be paid to either department managers or to all employees in a department of the store who exceed a set quota. This plan is difficult to understand because quotas are difficult to determine because they involve such store operations as sales volume, gross margins, and direct as well as a certain number of indirect

Salary plans for selling and nonselling employees

expenses. Nevertheless, if properly planned and explained, this plan creates a very productive team atmosphere and also develops an environment in which unproductive employees eliminate themselves. This technique also builds store morale.

Pension Plans. More and more stores are undertaking this kind of incentive. Usually, the plan is based on employees' salaries and their length of service. At retirement, employees receive set amounts that can be paid in a single sum or in a series of monthly payments. Such schemes include a life insurance policy that insures that when an employee dies his or her estate would receive the same amount of money as would have been paid had the employee lived to receive the pension.

Pension plans are proving valuable in keeping good employees. Employees should be eligible to join only after they have worked in the store long enough for the store and the employees to decide whether or not a career in the store will be profitable for both employer and employees.

Before getting involved in a pension plan, seek advice from a specialist in pension planning.

Miscellaneous Benefits

Most stores give employees a discount on the merchandise they carry. This discount can range all the way from a small percent off retail prices to cost price plus a small handling charge. It can also vary according to the employee's position, length of service, department, or season. For example, most new employees are not entitled to a discount until they have worked a certain length of time. They keep their sales slips, and after the trial period, they turn them in and receive a discount credit for their purchases to date. Many stores either give their employees a larger discount at Christmas and permit extra shopping privileges or they set aside a morning or an evening for this purpose.

Employee discounts

Some employees abuse discount privileges and buy for relatives and friends as well as themselves. To stop this practice, some stores record each employee's purchases and thus they are able to determine what each employee buys. Other stores set a limit on the amount that an employee may purchase at a discount and often eliminate discounts on certain sale goods. Employee discounts should be carefully controlled because they can be very costly to a store.

Some larger stores give permanent employees as many insurance benefits as possible, but for the small store most insurance plans are too costly. Nevertheless, if insurance plans can be instituted, perhaps with employee participation, they should be.

Life and hospital insurance

Many department and chain stores go to great lengths to make their employees feel happy, contented, and loyal to the store or chain. They

Employee services

have large recreation rooms and all kinds of competitions between employee groups and outside groups. They also have such extracurricular activities as acting, bowling, and hobbies that a group of employees may desire. Some large department stores and chains publish a store paper that contains articles of a general nature as well as new policy decisions, gossip, pep talks, etc. The small store owner cannot do these things, but if he thinks about his employee relations, he will be able to develop a number of group activities such as an annual dance, Christmas party, picnic, etc., that will keep his employees happy and contented and that will build up store morale.

However, the best service you can give your employees is to take a real interest in their problems and, when necessary, offer advice, counsel, and financial aid to help them overcome a difficult situation. Many large stores have personnel departments to perform these functions, but by their very nature, personnel departments are impersonal and therefore unsatisfactory. What most employees want and need is continuous personal contact with their employer. This relationship can only take place in small and medium-sized stores.

Because unions find it difficult and uneconomical to unionize small and medium-sized stores, you may never have to deal with them. But if they do try to organize your employees, be very careful in dealing with them. The National Labor Relations Act of 1935 prohibits employers from interfering with unions, discriminating against union members, and refusing to bargain with their representatives. You should realize that while a union knows how to turn every point of this and other laws to their advantage, you may have very little knowledge of whether or not any action you may take is legal. So no matter how frustrated or angry you feel, before you take any action, seek advice from the NRMA, your trade association, or a competent lawyer on how to handle negotiations.

Dealing with unions

WHAT THIS CHAPTER TOLD YOU

1. Employees are your most expensive item and a great deal of time and consideration should be given to selecting, training, and supervising them.

2. It is best to develop a routine system for interviewing, hiring, training, and dismissing employees.

3. It is most important to train every new employee in your way of operating and to keep him away from customers as much as possible until this is accomplished.

4. Promote employees as much as you can, but keep your policy flexible.

5. Although employees need more than wages to be contented, money is most important. Sales personnel can be paid a straight salary, straight commission, a combination of salary plus commission, a straight salary plus spiffs, or any combination of these plans.

6. To work well, any wage plan must be easy to understand and must be fair to both employer and employee.

7. In addition to wages, employees might receive discounts on purchases, vacations, and sick leave with pay. Whenever possible, life and hospital insurance plans should be provided. However, nothing equals your interest in their personal welfare.

8. Many stores have installed pension schemes that have proved useful in reducing employee turnover and building store morale.

9. Most stores try to create employee group activities outside of business, for example, bowling, picnics, etc.

10. Be very careful how you negotiate with unions.

20

How to Cope with Government Legislation and Consumer Movements

WHAT THIS CHAPTER IS ABOUT

If you think that because you are an independent retailer you can run your store as you please, forget it! Those days are over. More and more federal, state, and local laws, as well as consumers, both as individuals and in political pressure groups, are restricting the way you can do business. The first part of this chapter outlines some major laws and regulations that affect your operations and discusses how to cope with them; the second part deals with consumers who may or may not be your customers and suggests a number of techniques that will improve your status with them and in turn will build up your store's reputation and goodwill.

How to Cope with Government Legislation

As unrestricted free enterprise permitted the larger manufacturers, wholesalers, and retailers to eliminate effective competition, some of them were able to set unfair prices on their goods and to produce and market products that were hazardous to purchasers. Eventually, their smaller competitors became so incensed with these unfair and harmful practices, they forced various levels of government to try to stop or control the more unethical ways of doing business by passing a series of laws and regulations.

Why government legislation became necessary

Laws Against Price-fixing. A pioneer attempt to control price-fixing was the Sherman Anti-Trust Act of 1890 which attempted to make all forms of price-fixing and agreements to divide the market illegal where these

Laws that control prices

practices would lessen competition and lead to a monopoly condition. Major adjustments to this Act were the Clayton Act and the Federal Trade Commission Act (1914), the Robinson–Patman Amendment (1936), and the Celler Amendment (1950). The purpose of these Acts and Amendments was to strengthen the concepts that were contained in the Sherman statutes.

Although the Federal Trade Commission was created in 1915 to assist in enforcing federal anti-trust laws, most states felt that it was too difficult for the Commission to police federal price control laws at the local level. Therefore, they passed their own laws against conspiracies, combinations, and restraints of trade.

You must understand how these laws affect your method of doing business with your suppliers, for, in some instances, disobeying them can lead to very serious consequences. For example, under the Robinson-Patman Act, a retailer is equally guilty along with the vendor if he knowingly accepts an illegal concession offered by the vendor. Therefore, if you are not certain of the legality of a price arrangement, seek the advice of the NRMA, your trade association, or a competent lawyer before you agree to it.

Truth in Advertising. Because some manufacturers and retailers tend to use misleading and exaggerated techniques to promote their goods, the federal government and most states have legislated against this practice. The most important federal "truth in advertising" laws are the Wheeler-Lea Act and the Food, Drug and Cosmetic Act, both passed in 1938, and the Consumer Protection Bill (1969) which permitted the Justice Department and the Federal Trade Commission to take action on such harmful selling practices as bait and switch selling, withholding appropriate refunds on deposits, attempting to make customers buy unneeded goods and services, misrepresenting guarantees, and the brand and quality of certain merchandise, etc.

Laws to regulate promotions

Because of the confusion that resulted from the truth in advertising laws, the Federal Trade Commission issued a set of guidelines about its interpretation of deceptive statements in retail prices. For example, retailers cannot claim or imply that a price has been reduced unless the quoted former price was actually one that was on the merchandise for a sufficient length of time to make it a base price. Thus, you are forbidden to mark an item for a day or two at, say, $19.95 and then advertise it as a big reduction at $14.79. Again, if you claim that your prices are lower than manufacturer's list or that they are lower than those of your competitors, you must be able to prove that they are really below the manufacturer's and below those of your important competitors.

Truth in Labeling. When manufacturers and other distributors realized that under self-service arrangements a product's package or label was an important selling tool, some of them created labels and packages that falsified the true nature of their goods. In 1966 the federal government took action against this practice by passing the Fair Packaging and Labeling Act, usually called the "Truth-in-Packaging Act." Among other provisions, it authorized the Federal Trade Commission and the Food and Drug Administration to take action against distributors who use misleading pictorial matter on their packages or labels or who do not list the ingredients, net quantity, and size when they quote the number of servings. It also defined the use of such words as "jumbo," "giant," and "cents off."

Consumer groups helped to write this legislation and they have continued to be very active in supporting revisions to the Act as they find other techniques marketers have created to promote their products but which, in some way, harm or deceive those who purchase them. Although you have no legal responsibility for seeing that your distributors obey this law, you have an obligation to point out infractions to them. If they disregard your comments, you should report them to the proper authority. If more retailers assumed this watchdog responsibility, it would help to build more consumer confidence in the goods stores offered them.

Laws that regulate consumer credit

If you operate your own credit facilities, make sure that you know the laws and regulations that have been passed by the federal government and those of your state for they spell out in great detail how credit can be legally extended to your customers. See Chapter 15, page 216.

Laws that regulate labor

Before 1935 most attempts by workers to form unions were considered to be unlawful agreements in restraint of trade. That year, the National Labor Relations Act gave employees the legal right to organize and prevented employers from interfering with the process in any way or from discriminating against union members. In 1947 the Labor Management Relations Act, called the Taft–Hartley Act, not only strengthened the 1935 law but also sought to protect employees against union abuses. Since then a number of other federal acts have established very strict rules of employee-employer relations.

Since these statutes are periodically updated, you should be very careful in your relationship with unions, for although your knowledge of labor law may be very sketchy, theirs will not only be current but they will also have the capability of maximizing any infringement of these laws you might make through design or ignorance. Thus, before you take any action against a union you would be wise to discuss the situation with an experienced labor lawyer, the NRMA, or your trade association.

Until 1964 all retail organizations were exempted from the Fair Labor Standards Acts (1938), sometimes called the Wage and Hour Law, which established minimum wages, maximum hours, overtime pay rates, and other conditions of employment. Since then most stores and their employees have come under the Act and since it is revised from time to time, it is important that you keep current with the changes because they intimately affect your relationship with your employees.

Another law that may affect you is Title VII of the Civil Rights Act

(1964) which established equal employment opportunities as a civil right. Unless you familiarize yourself with this Act, you may get into hiring and firing difficulties and you may be sued by an employee for discriminating against him or her in matters of wages, job assignments, etc.

Because many states have passed their own labor laws, statutes, and regulations and because they keep revising them, you should know what they are and how they differ from those of the federal government. Because these laws at both levels are in a constant state of review and revision, it is imperative that you find a means of keeping abreast of all changes that affect your relations with your employees.

Taxation

Acting as tax collectors for federal, state, and local governments has become as much a function of retailing as buying and selling because all levels of government have discovered that stores are convenient depots for them to collect both direct and indirect taxes. A *direct tax* is one that is paid by the person on whom it is legally imposed, i.e., it is collected directly from the customer who makes a purchase in your store. Although these taxes do not increase retail prices, they are politically unpopular because they emphasize a tax burden that a legislature is imposing on consumers, most of whom are voters.

An *indirect tax* is imposed on one person but is paid in part or wholly by another, for example, manufacturers and importers pay the government for any tax levied on them, but retailers in effect return this tax when they pay their invoices to these resources. Retailers then consider indirect taxes as part of their initial cost and add their normal markup to them. In this way, customers pay both the tax and the retailer's markup as well. Politicians like indirect taxes because they are hidden from voters who direct their anger at merchants for raising their prices to cover these taxes rather than at the politicians who set them.

Although it may be difficult for you alone to demonstrate how indirect taxes affect your retail prices, you should clearly show customers that you make no profit on the direct tax. However, in view of the growing strength of consumerism, it is important that retailers support a campaign that would inform the public about the effect of indirect taxes on retail prices.

Unlike income, direct and indirect taxes, unemployment, social security, and business taxes as well as all license fees are considered current expenses and should be deducted from operating profit.

When you think of it, a lot of federal, state, and local tax money goes through your hands in a year. Because none of it belongs to you, make very certain that every penny you take in and pay out can be easily traced by any official who comes to audit your account. Since penalties for attempts to falsify tax accounts are usually severe, make sure that your accountant sets up a proper system to record the movement of tax monies.

Again, make it a point to find out how you should operate as a tax collector and to receive notices of all changes that affect your tax collection and payment functions.

It is very important to realize that the laws discussed above in no way cover all you should know about the federal, state, and local laws that affect your particular business. Moreover, you should be aware that a number of government commissions and private research agencies are constantly looking into various aspects of business practices that may be important enough to warrant legislation. It's up to you to be alert to the vast variety of government legislation at every level that restricts your freedom to act as a pure independent. Remember that ignorance of the law is no excuse for breaking it.

Keep current on all laws that affect your business

Therefore, you should develop a method of keeping current with every law that affects your business. A good way to do this is to catalogue the laws in a logical sequence and store them in loose-leaf binders. Then you can throw away those that are no longer current and insert new ones or revisions of old ones.

Remember that you are a merchant not a lawyer. Therefore, when problems concerning government regulations occur that require an experienced expert, consult one. Trying to solve a problem on a do-it-yourself basis may turn out to be a very time-consuming, humiliating, and expensive method of handling any difficult situation involving government regulations.

Legislation and Consumers

This section merely scratches the surface on how to cope with consumer legislation and consumer movements. Its purpose is to demonstrate that consumerism is not only here to stay but it is also a powerful political force that is recognized by presidents, officials, and politicians down to the local level. Moreover, consumers of every income and educational level are becoming more and more aware of their rights; therefore, you can expect your customers to react with increasing recognition of their ability to redress any action on your part that they perceive as harmful to themselves.

How to cope with consumer movements

Successful retailers have always understood the difference between customers and consumers (see Chapter 1). For example, Marshall Field unashamedly catered to women customers; he was one of the first merchants to hire female clerks for his lingerie section and he also created and vigorously enforced the store's motto, "Give the lady what she wants." This policy was strictly adhered to even when it was obvious that the occasional "lady" was taking advantage of that policy. On the other hand, he knew that his main consumer segment consisted of the higher-income Chicagoans and made certain he carried what they wanted. He might have called his dual policy "customerism" and "consumerism," for he realized that he must not only bring customers, who might be servants or their employers, to his store, but to keep them coming back and to expand his clientele, he must sell them goods that would be consumed with pleasure and satisfaction.

The difference between customers and consumers

Because consumer activists have not been able to develop a universally accepted definition of consumerism, some have interpreted consumerism as anything they believe is detrimental to them in some way, for example, polluted air or loud noises, while others consider it to be as narrow as a two-cent rise in the retail price of bread.

Consumerism

The shortest and, to retailers, the most important definition of consumerism was expressed in 1970 by Mrs. Virginia H. Knauer, who was then a Special Assistant to the President for Consumer Affairs. She revised the old marketing concept of "Let the *buyer* beware" to "Let the *seller* beware," and thus shifted the responsibility of the marketplace from consumers to all levels of marketers. However, since most consumers only deal with retailers, this marketing level has become the main focus for consumer irritation with whatever they perceive as a consumer evil that is being generated by the marketing process.

Consumers are the bosses of the marketplace

Most marketers agree that consumers are the bosses of the marketplace because the success of any consumer product is based on the amount of dollars consumers are willing to spend on it. However, consumerism claims that marketers have overlooked the fact that this concept can only operate fairly when buyers are able to make intelligent judgments on the use value to them of the products offered in the marketplace. Thus, in pioneer days "buyer beware" was a workable marketing principle because most consumers knew the composition of every product merchants carried. But as manufacturing became more complex, consumers lost this ability to make intelligent value judgments on an increasing number of items because they no longer knew the ingredients, composition, or manufacturing process of these goods.

Consumer laws against health hazards

Some manufacturers took advantage of this inequality between buyer and seller and flooded the market with an increasing number of harmful and dangerous goods and/or, with the cooperation of retailers, made exorbitant claims on their use value. Since the federal government was committed to the free-enterprise system, it took no active part in redressing this inequality until the excesses of manufacturers and retailers became so great that the public demanded that laws be passed to protect them from the more blatant marketing evils.

The first legislative step in consumer protection was the Food, Drug and Cosmetic Act (1906) which forbade the adulteration and misbranding of food sold in interstate commerce. This Act was strengthened in 1938 and 1962 and no doubt will continue to be amended as major changes occur in the manufacturing and marketing of these products.

In 1907 the government again reacted to consumer pressure by passing the Meat Inspection Act which empowered the Department of Agriculture to inspect slaughtering, packing, and canning plants that shipped meat in interstate commerce. Diseased meat is destroyed and pure meat is stamped U.S. Government Inspected. This Act was amended in 1967 to force the states to raise their inspection standards to those of the federal government.

The first of these was the Food, Drug and Cosmetic Act of 1906, which was later strengthened by the Wheeler–Lea Act of 1938, the Fair Packaging and Labeling Act (1966), and the Consumer Protection Bill (1969).

As the federal government became more involved in protecting consumers against harmful selling practices, the character of its legislation became more specific and detailed. For example, in 1939 it passed the Wool Products Labeling Act which forced producers to label the kind and percentage of "wool," "reprocessed wool," and "reused wool" on all products, except carpets, rugs, mats, and upholsteries that contained wool. Moreover, the names of the manufacturers or distributors must also appear on the label which must remain on the goods until it passes into the customer's hands.

Another example is the Fur Products Labeling Act (1951) which required manufacturers and distributors to name the animal that produced the fur, its country of origin, whether bleached or dyed, and whether made up of paws, tails, bellies, or waste furs. Retailers may substitute their own labels, but they must retain the information from the original label for three years.

While other laws like the Textile Fiber Identification Act (1958) and the Fair Packaging and Labeling Act (1966) sought to give consumers more merchandise knowledge, the Federal Cigarette Labeling and Advertising Act (1966) demonstrated a new concern of the federal government toward consumer protection. It requires that cigarettes sold in interstate commerce be packaged and labeled with the warning, "Warning: The Surgeon General has determined that cigarette smoking is dangerous to your health."

The Consumer Credit Protection Act (1968) was concerned with selling practices that could be laid directly to retailers who conducted harmful credit operations. A sequel of this Act was the Fair Credit Reporting Act (1970). These Acts gave consumers much more knowledge about the extent of their contractual obligations to a particular retailer and also afforded them some recourse against secret credit ratings.

Because warranties and guaranties are so difficult to define, federal laws to protect consumers against these selling practices are still in the advisory stage. Nevertheless, when the harmful effects of these selling practices produce sufficient consumer protest, some remedial form of legislation will be enacted.

These acts are concerned with protecting consumers against buying products that might cause them physical harm. For example, the Flammable Act of 1953 placed prohibitions on manufacturing, importing, and transporting clothing that is so highly inflammable that it is dangerous when worn by individuals. The Flammable Fabrics Act (1967) extended these prohibitions to interior furnishings, fabrics, and materials.

The Federal Hazardous Substances Labeling Act (1960) made manufacturers of such household products as cleaning agents, paint removers, and polishers print labels that warn consumers about the hazards that might result from their use. In 1966 the Child Protection Act prevented the marketing of potentially harmful children's toys and articles.

The same year (1966) saw the passage of the National Traffic and Motor Vehicle Safety Act which directed the Secretary of Transportation to issue safety standards for 1968 automobiles. Among the areas to be covered were impact-absorbing steering wheel and column, safety door latches and hinges, safety glass, dual braking system, and impact resisting gasoline tanks and connections. Tires had to meet load standards for fully loaded vehicles (including baggage), be labeled with the name of the manufacturer or retreader, and contain safety information, for example, the maximum permissible load for the tire.

Notice how most of these laws, and these are a very small sampling of those actually passed, have become increasingly specific and detailed in their desire to protect consumers. You can expect this kind of law to increase as consumers become more vocal and organized and thus better able to pressure the federal government to give them more product knowledge about the goods that appear in the marketplace and more protection against whatever harmful selling practices retailers and other marketers might be tempted to use.

Consumer protection acts become more specific

Until 1962 when the late President Kennedy formally acknowledged that the federal government had a direct responsibility to protect consumers against harmful marketing practices, it required a great deal of public pressure before Congress made any attempt to balance the seller–buyer equation. Although the overt reasons for consumer boycotts were the rapid rise of both unemployment and retail food prices, the laissez-faire attitude on the part of the government was a major underlying factor in the organization of the sporadic consumer protests that took place in the early 1900s and 1930s. However, these boycotts were shortlived, for whenever unemployment and food prices declined, consumers soon reverted to their old method of reacting to the marketing system on an individual basis; either they continued to patronize a certain store or they gave their business to a competitor.

Consumer legislation did not come easily

A number of supermarket boycotts were again organized by consumer activists in 1966 because food prices had increased dramatically and real purchasing power had as dramatically declined. This time, however, the organizers were irritated by more than the price of food; they also resented the fact that while the prices of most consumer products were increasing rapidly, their after-purchase satisfaction continued to decrease.

Marketers defended the system by insisting that consumers were not compelled to purchase any products offered to them and since they were better educated than their forefathers, they should be able to act more intelligently in the marketplace than their ancestors. What these defenders of the system studiously overlooked was the fact that the marketing process in the 1960s had become so complex that most consumers knew far less about the satisfaction value of the products retailers offered them than did their ignorant forebears.

What consumers wanted was to restore the balance of the seller–buyer equation by forcing sellers to give buyers sufficient product information to enable them to make value judgments on the goods they might want to purchase and to protect them from harmful products. Further, because consumers were better educated, they were much more aware of their power in the marketplace and were also able to articulate their desires so that they not only influenced other consumers but government as well.

John F. Kennedy was the first president to perceive that since consumerism had become so powerful a political force, it was expedient for him to assume a leadership role in its future evolution. Therefore, on March 15th, 1962, he sent a message to Congress in which he broadly defined consumer rights as (a) the right to safety, (b) the right to be heard, (c) the right to be informed, and (d) the right to choose.

Presidents assume leadership

Lyndon B. Johnson not only reaffirmed these rights, he was also more specific in his approach. He tried to control sales "rackets," automobile insurance, and product warranties. Richard M. Nixon in a message to Congress, February 24th, 1971, suggested the creation of a new Office of Consumer Affairs in the Executive Office of the President, which would be responsible for analyzing and coordinating all federal activities in the field of consumer protection.

There is little doubt that succeeding presidents will continue to demonstrate their interest in protecting the consumer in the marketplace and that their example will be emulated by government officials down to the local level.

A great deal of consumer literature is being printed by the federal government, consumer groups, and the public media. For example, the Department of Agriculture publishes pamphlets that seek to give consumers more knowledge about how to buy food. The Department of Commerce has issued pamphlets on tires, textiles, and adhesives. In 1970 the General Services Administration established a Consumer Product Coordination Information Center to give consumers information on products it has developed through its own research development and procurement activities.

Consumer education

Among the many functions of the Office of Consumer Affairs in the Executive Office of the President are those that provide policy guidance on how product information should be released, how consumer complaints should be handled, and how to encourage and coordinate consumer education programs. This office also distributes its own consumer education and protection booklets and twice a month it publishes a consumer news letter on federal government consumer programs which includes a supplement that summarizes *Federal Register* items that are deemed of particular interest to consumers.

The Department of Commerce has also established a National Business Council for Consumer Affairs that contains over a hundred members. The objectives of this council are to examine consumer–business problem areas that pertain to warranties, product safety, packaging, labeling, and credit and to try to solve these problems by voluntary action.

The best-known consumer magazines are *Consumer Bulletin* published by Consumers Research, and the more popular *Consumer Reports.* There are also a large number of consumer articles being printed by newspapers and magazines and by some of the consumer associations themselves. All this literature is augmented by radio and TV programs.

Some manufacturers and the larger retail organizations have joined the educators by including consumer "experts" as part of their staff. These employees write on consumer subjects, handle complaints, and, in general, perform a public relations function as they relate to consumers.

Courses on a vast variety of consumer subjects have been introduced at all levels of school and university curricula and more and more books on areas of consumer interest appear in bookstores. All signs indicate that consumer education will continue to grow and make itself an important part of the consumer movement.

Even this short discussion on the growth and power of the consumer movement should illustrate that now more than ever before you must seriously consider how consumers will react to every contact they make with you and your store. Today, customers are not only your boss because they have the mobility to patronize your store or move to a competitor's, but as consumers or as agents for consumers they are also able and willing to wield an increasing amount of legal clout. Therefore, you must take all the necessary steps to protect yourself by knowing the federal, state, and local laws that have been passed to protect consumers. In this way you can avoid carrying merchandise that is not properly labeled, running illegal promotions, or giving credit in a manner that can be contested in court. If you have any doubts about any consumer legislation, consult NRMA or your trade association before you take action.

What consumerism means to you

You should also create an information system that will keep you up-to-date with changing consumer interests. The best way of doing this is to subscribe to as much consumer literature, both government and private, as necessary. By simply skimming through these publications, you should be able to get the feel of consumer shifts from one important area to another. If any of these concern your operation, you can then plan how to cope with it so that it will increase, not decrease, your sales and so that it will build goodwill. For example, if consumers find favor in some of the merchandise you handle, you can incorporate their remarks into your promotions; if they do not find your merchandise favorable, investigate the reasons why they don't and, if necessary, cease carrying this merchandise until the manufacturer upgrades it to standards that are acceptable to consumers.

The technique described above is the *back office* way to cope with consumerism. The *front office* technique is to build a good rapport with your customers, particularly those you think are their leaders. Encourage these customers to analyze your merchandise, your services, etc. Remember that analysis is not only finding fault, it also includes pointing out the store's good points. You can increase your contacts with this group by forming a "Consumer's Council" and holding formal meetings with them where more intense discussion of your store's operations can take place. Some recompense could be made for their time.

Front office technique

Since you are also a consumer, you should become actively involved in consumerism. This will alert you to what consumer activists are thinking and will also help create goodwill for your store. Moreover, it will give you an opportunity to suggest how consumers and marketers can initiate a series of dialogues that should be beneficial to both sides of the seller–buyer equation.

Become involved in consumer activities

The best way to become a consumerist is to join an active consumer organization. Consumers Union is one of the most influential and important of these bodies. Its magazine *Consumer Reports* reports on the findings of tests performed on consumer products randomly purchased from retail stores. It is also very active in promoting consumer education and has published pamphlets on such topics as interest rates, guaranties and warranties, life insurance, product safety, and how to select a doctor. Again, it supports consumer research projects, the International Organization of Consumer Unions, and subsidizes experts at regulatory and legislative hearings.

The Consumer Federation of America is a national organization that includes state and local consumer groups, the National Consumers League, as well as labor unions and the National Council of Senior Citizens. It acts as an information clearing house for its member groups and also performs certain fact-finding and analyses of consumer interest activities.

Although these organizations might be useful to you at the state or national level, the best way to begin is to join the consumer activists in your area. If necessary, your newspaper, radio, or TV station should be able to give you the current status and background of local consumer activities. With this information, you can plan whatever action you feel that you should take to help the movement.

WHAT THIS CHAPTER TOLD YOU

1. Your freedom to operate as an independent merchant is being continuously reduced by various federal, state, and local laws, as well as by the activities of consumer activists.

2. You should develop a method of keeping current with every law that affects your business.

3. Because many of these laws are difficult to understand, when necessary and before taking any action, seek the advice of a lawyer, accountant, tax consultant, NRMA, or your trade association.

4. Since consumerism is here to stay, learn how to cope with the movement and with individual consumerists.

5. The best way to do this is to accept the movement and plan how to use it to increase your sales and customer goodwill.

6. Keep current on all federal, state, and local laws that protect consumers and, when necessary, consult a lawyer, NRMA, or your trade association before taking any action.

7. Develop an information system that will keep you up-to-date with changing consumer interests and whenever these are appropriate, use them to increase your store's sales and goodwill.

8. Try to build a good rapport with your customers, particularly with their leaders.

9. Join and become active in consumer movements.

291
*How to Cope
with Government
Legislation and
Consumer
Movements*

21

How to
Use Money Profitably

WHAT THIS CHAPTER IS ABOUT

Most small merchants think of money as something that goes from the cash register into the bank. It is then used to pay invoices, operating expenses, and business taxes. Whatever is left is divided between the retailer and government income taxes, with the government receiving the lion's share. But this kind of money, called *cash,* is actually a very small part of the financial resources, or capital, with which a successful merchant works. Much more important is his ability to borrow money and obtain credit.

Capital, then, can be as tangible as a five-cent piece or a five-dollar bill or as intangible as a bank loan or "30 days net" terms of payment. No matter what its form, it is a retail tool like an advertisement or a window display, and if properly used will make more money for your business. Merchants who do not know how to manage money always suffer from lack of it. Yet, they probably have, or could obtain, sufficient capital for their needs if they knew what to do or where to go for it. This chapter tells you how to manage your capital so that you obtain the most out of every cent you handle.

Kinds of Capital

There are two main kinds of capital, *equity* and *borrowed. Equity* capital is what you own. You pay no interest on it and it does not have to be paid back. *Borrowed* capital is money that belongs to someone else who expects to get it back with interest.

Following are the three main ways in which a business uses capital:

1. *Fixed capital* is money spent on such things as fixtures, equipment, buildings, etc., which cannot be turned back into cash quickly but which you must have in order to do business.

2. *Working capital* is money used to buy stock, pay wages, utilities, rent, etc. It is money spent to make money.

3. *Liquid capital* consists of cash or disposable securities like certificates of deposit, stocks, or bonds. Every merchant should have a reserve of liquid capital to take care of any emergency that may crop up in the course of doing business.

There are no standard proportions for the distribution of capital. They are set by the particular time and situation in which the store happens to be. But spending too much for fixed assets means that you will have too little for working and liquid capital, and vice versa. Review your proportions from time to time and see whether or not they should be changed. Let your accountant, banker, and records of similar stores guide you. Remember, however, that your situation may be unique and so may require a different proportion of capital breakdown from normal.

How to Get Capital

Your own capital

Your first source of capital is that of keeping your personal living costs down and investing these savings plus whatever profit the business produces into increasing the store's ability to make more money. Never starve your store in order to keep up with the Joneses. Personal financial sacrifices for your business at crucial times will eventually put you ahead of your friends and neighbors.

Review your expenses

This is a constant source of extra money. Compare your expenses against last year's and against those of other businesses (Fig. 21.1). If your total is going up or is out of line with the average store, break it down into as many different categories as you can, for example, management salaries, office salaries, selling salaries, etc. Then check back to see *why* some of them are so high.

Instead of being a creature of habit or tradition, look around for new ways to cut costs even a little. Remember that a penny saved here and there soon mounts up to dollars that can be used to produce more dollars and more net profit.

Yet, sometimes it pays to spend money. It is good business to purchase or rent a machine or install a new system if it will save you money in the long run. The only true guides to spending are constant vigilance and flexibility.

Take all cash discounts

One of the best ways to make money is to ask for and take every cash discount you can get. 2/10 can equal 36.7 percent interest per annum, and even 1/10 pays 18.35 percent. Again, if you have the finances and the

INCOME STATEMENT DATA	Sales Under $100,000	$100,000 to $200,000	$200,000 to $500,000	Sales Over $500,000
NUMBER OF STORES	130	268	340	104
NET SALES VOLUME....................	$70,669	$161,470	$319,236	$819,005
Current Year's Sales vs. Previous Year	+9.69%	+10.10%	+14.68%	+14.37%
Gross Sales	102.70%	102.49%	103.18%	102.63%
Less: Total Deductions.............	2.70	2.49	3.18	2.63
Net Sales........................	100.00	100.00	100.00	100.00
Cost of Goods Sold.................	71.72	65.38	66.22	68.75
Margin............................	28.28	34.62	33.78	31.25

PAYROLL AND OTHER EMPLOYEE EXPENSES

	Sales Under $100,000	$100,000 to $200,000	$200,000 to $500,000	Sales Over $500,000
Sararies—Owners, Officers, Managers .	9.27	7.81	6.22	3.84
Salaries—Sales Personnel............	4.02	7.71	7.09	7.36
Salaries—Office Help................	.59	1.33	1.69	1.65
Salaries—Other Employees............	2.04	1.08	2.42	2.76
Federal and State Payroll Taxes........	.71	.84	.93	.84
Group Insurance	.23	.18	.22	.23
Benefit Plans	.04	.19	.28	.62
TOTAL PAYROLL AND OTHER EMPLOYEE EXPENSES...........	16.90	19.14	18.85	17.30

OCCUPANCY EXPENSE

	Sales Under $100,000	$100,000 to $200,000	$200,000 to $500,000	Sales Over $500,000
Heat, Light, Power, Water............	1.22	.90	.74	.59
Repairs to Building..................	.32	.31	.23	.26
Rent or Ownership in Real Estate*.....	3.22	3.28	3.01	2.53
TOTAL OCCUPANCY EXPENSE...........	4.76	4.49	3.98	3.38

OTHER COSTS OF DOING BUSINESS

	Sales Under $100,000	$100,000 to $200,000	$200,000 to $500,000	Sales Over $500,000
Office Supplies and Postage	.36	.40	.43	.38
Advertising........................	1.52	1.58	1.64	1.51
Donations.........................	.08	.07	.06	.05
Telephone and Telegraph.............	.51	.33	.29	.33
Bad Debts.........................	.20	.25	.25	.50
Delivery (Other than Wages)...........	.74	.49	.43	.41
Insurance (Other than Real Estate and Group)...............	1.18	.84	.77	.61
Taxes (Other than Real Estate and Payroll)..............	.80	.61	.53	.42
Interest on Borrowed Money (Other than Mortgages)	.85	.44	.51	.52
Depreciation (Other than Real Estate) ..	1.09	.64	.66	.59
Store and Shop Supplies..............	.48	.46	.35	.38
Legal and Accounting.................	.42	.35	.36	.28
Dues and Subscriptions..............	.13	.11	.08	.06
Travel, Buying, Entertainment.........	.15	.16	.22	.27
Unclassified.......................	.72	.50	.73	.69
TOTAL OTHER COSTS OF DOING BUSINESS .	9.23	7.23	7.31	7.00

	Sales Under $100,000	$100,000 to $200,000	$200,000 to $500,000	Sales Over $500,000
TOTAL OPERATING EXPENSE............	30.89	30.86	30.14	27.68
NET OPERATING PROFIT.................	(2.61)	3.76	3.64	3.57
Cash Discounts and Other Income.....	1.51	1.20	1.30	1.35
NET PROFIT (Before Federal Income Tax) ...	(1.10)	4.96	4.94	4.92

*Ownership in Real Estate includes Taxes, Insurance, Depreciation on Land and Buildings and interest on Mortgages.

FIGURE 21.1 These profit and loss statements are based on a range of profits, sales, and expenses. This permits hardware retailers to judge their performances and to make practical decisions on how to improve their operations. NRMA or your trade association should have similar data.

Courtesy National Retail Hardware Association, Indianapolis, Ind.

resource is willing to accept anticipation, you have another way of making more profit on your inventory dollars. If a vendor refuses to give you a cash discount or anticipation and if it will not damage your credit rating, try for longer dating. However, never pay any bill until its due date. You should be able to use the money as profitably as any of your creditors. Thus, if an invoice is dated August 13th, 2/10, n/30, you can accept it (after taking off the discount) on August 14th if you like, but date the payment August 23rd, that is, take your full ten days.

Providing that you can maintain a proper markup, the quicker your stock moves, the more gross margin you make. For example, if you carry an average retail stock of $50,000 and make $15,000 every time it moves in and out of the store, and it does this twice a year, your gross margin will be $30,000. If you can turn your stock just one more time, your margin will become $45,000. Your expenses would increase with the extra volume but not significantly, for your major overhead expenses have already been taken care of in the first two turns.

The longer old equipment and merchandise stay in the store, the less they are worth. Unlike real antiques, these items do not appreciate in value, but some retailers get stubborn or sentimental about an old fixture or piece of equipment. They hate to see it go because it reminds them of the good old days. Other retailers set a minimum price for old equipment. If they cannot get their price, they prefer to keep the article—and they do. They want to sell a cash register that cost $1,000 back in the 1960s for $1,000. What these retailers refuse to understand is that it is better to take $100 or even $50 for the register and use the money for new equipment that will produce sales and profits *now*.

The same illogical ideas are held about old merchandise. A merchant may have paid $60 for a suit five years ago, but it certainly is not worth that today. If he can get $30 for it, he should take it, buy something he can sell for $45, and make $15 profit. The truth is that if he keeps the suit long enough, it will simply fall apart on the hanger and not be worth anything at all. By selling equipment and merchandise at sacrifice prices before they get too old, the retailer can obtain more capital to work with and also have more room for new items in his store.

Another way to manage capital is to have efficient methods for collecting receivables. Some stores maintain an easy credit policy, but most successful merchants insist that their customers pay on time. It not only gives them more money to work with but a paid-up charge customer is also free to make other purchases. The sooner delinquent accounts are dealt with, the better chance the retailer has of collecting them and the easier it becomes to maintain customers (see Chapter 15 for a discussion on consumer credit).

There are institutions that will buy your accounts receivable for a fixed rate on the dollar. Selling accounts receivable this way is usually done either on the basis of nonrecourse or on the basis of recourse. *Nonrecourse* means that when the finance company accepts a charge account, you are no longer responsible for payments. Selling accounts on *recourse* gives you a higher percentage on the dollar, but the finance company charges you for all customer defaults. Some finance companies permit you to collect payments and operate your credit department as though your customers were still dealing exclusively with you; others send out notices to your customers and ask that payments be made directly to them.

Sell accounts receivable

Before you sell your accounts receivables, shop around, compare the *real* discount rates and other costs, and estimate potential customer ill will. Then see if it is worthwhile or if it is better to obtain the necessary capital in some other way.

Most credit card companies have a sliding scale of charges that is usually based on sales volume; some convert credit purchases into cash more quickly than others do. Therefore, if you want to accept credit cards, bargain for each company's lowest rates and try to get your customers to use the cards of those companies that charge the least or give you the quickest conversion into cash. Since most customers who use more than one credit card have little loyalty to a particular credit card, if you suggest that they use the one you profit from the most, they will likely go along with your wishes.

Accept credit cards intelligently

Vendors who supply you with merchandise are an excellent source of working capital because normally they give you 30 days, 60 days, or even a longer time to pay for the goods they sell you. But they will only give you these terms instead of insisting on COD (cash on delivery) if you have a good credit reputation. The best way to build a sound credit status is to pay all your bills promptly and ask for and take all the cash discounts you can get. If you are unknown to a supplier, he will probably look up your credit in a book put out by a firm like Dun & Bradstreet that specializes in investigating and estimating the credit standing of most businesses in the United States and Canada. You should know what these firms think about your credit and if you disagree with their conclusions, make it a point to ask them how to improve your rating. Usually, it pays to take their suggestions and establish a better credit status (Figs. 21.2 and 21.3).

Use suppliers as a source of working capital

Sometimes it is possible to ask suppliers for longer dating so that you will have more time to dispose of their merchandise before you pay for it. Remember that when you ask for discounts you improve your credit, but when you ask for longer terms, you may hurt your standing or cause rumors to spread that you cannot meet your bills. Therefore, consider unusual credit extensions carefully.

Sometimes manufacturers, wholesalers, and franchisers will give

Key to Ratings

	ESTIMATED FINANCIAL STRENGTH		COMPOSITE CREDIT APPRAISAL			
			HIGH	GOOD	FAIR	LIMITED
5A	Over	$50,000,000	1	2	3	4
4A	$10,000,000 to	50,000,000	1	2	3	4
3A	1,000,000 to	10,000,000	1	2	3	4
2A	750,000 to	1,000,000	1	2	3	4
1A	500,000 to	750,000	1	2	3	4
BA	300,000 to	500,000	1	2	3	4
BB	200,000 to	300,000	1	2	3	4
CB	125,000 to	200,000	1	2	3	4
CC	75,000 to	125,000	1	2	3	4
DC	50,000 to	75,000	1	2	3	4
DD	35,000 to	50,000	1	2	3	4
EE	20,000 to	35,000	1	2	3	4
FF	10,000 to	20,000	1	2	3	4
GG	5,000 to	10,000	1	2	3	4
HH	Up to	5,000	1	2	3	4

CLASSIFICATION FOR BOTH
ESTIMATED FINANCIAL STRENGTH AND CREDIT APPRAISAL

FINANCIAL STRENGTH BRACKET

1 $125,000 and Over

2 20,000 to 125,000

EXPLANATION

When only the numeral (1 or 2) appears, it is an indication that the estimated financial strength, while not definitely classified, is presumed to be within the range of the ($) figures in the corresponding bracket and that a condition is believed to exist which warrants credit in keeping with that assumption.

ABSENCE OF RATING DESIGNATION FOLLOWING NAMES LISTED IN THE REFERENCE BOOK
The absence of a rating, expressed by the two hyphens (--), is not to be construed as unfavorable but signifies circumstances difficult to classify within condensed rating symbols. It suggests the advisability of obtaining a report for additional information.

EMPLOYEE RANGE DESIGNATIONS IN REPORTS OR NAMES NOT LISTED IN THE REFERENCE BOOK

Certain businesses do not lend themselves to a Dun & Bradstreet rating and are not listed in the Reference Book. Information on these names, however, continues to be stored and updated in the D&B Business Data Bank. Reports are available on such businesses and instead of a rating they carry an Employee Range Designation (ER) which is indicative of size in terms of number of employees. No other significance should be attached.

KEY TO EMPLOYEE RANGE DESIGNATIONS

ER 1	Over 1000 Employees
ER 2	500 - 999 Employees
ER 3	100 - 499 Employees
ER 4	50 - 99 Employees
ER 5	20 - 49 Employees
ER 6	10 - 19 Employees
ER 7	5 - 9 Employees
ER 8	1 - 4 Employees
ER N	Not Available

© *Dun & Bradstreet, Inc.* 1974
99 Church Street, New York, N.Y. 10007 18B-7 (730801)

FIGURE 21.2 If you want to see *your* rating, ask your bank manager to look it up in Dun & Bradstreet. If you feel that it is not a fair rating, present your case to Dun & Bradstreet, Inc., New York.

Courtesy Dun & Bradstreet, Inc., New York.

retailers who have reputations as good merchants extended dating and even financial support on very easy terms. These resources are not philanthropists. They need outlets for their goods and services and the more "loyal" stores they have buying their merchandise and their services, the safer their operations become, the better they can plan, and the cheaper they can produce sales. But having a resource act as your financier has great disadvantages and dangers. You are forced to deal with him and that may not be

BUSINESS INFORMATION REPORT

BASE REPORT

SIC	D-U-N-S	© DUN & BRADSTREET, INC.		STARTED	RATING
56 11	04-426-3168	CD 26 MAR 15 197-		1946	DD1
	FRANK'S MEN'S SHOP	MENS CLOTHING			
	SANDERS, FRANK, OWNER				

10 SOUTH BROAD AVE
NEWARK OHIO   43055
TEL 614 206-4555

SUMMARY

PAYMENTS	DISC PPT
SALES	$104,684
WORTH	$40,032 F
EMPLOYS	4
RECORD	CLEAR
CONDITION	STRONG
TREND	UP

PAYMENTS

HC	OWE	P DUE	TERMS	FEB 19 197-	SOLD
3000	1850		2 10 30	Disc	Over 3 yrs
500	200		2 30 60	Disc	Over 3 yrs
3000			1 10 30	Disc Ppt	
7412	1400		30	Ppt	Over 3 yrs

FINANCE

	Dec 31 196-	Dec 31 197-	Dec 31 197-
Curr Assets	$ 42,213	$ 43,312	$ 46,364
Curr Liabs	7,732	8,031	7,383
Working Cap	34,481	35,281	38,981
Worth	34,895	36,902	40,032
Sales	96,890	102,559	104,684

Statement Dec 31 197-

Cash	$ 8,243	Accts Pay	$ 7,101
Accts Rec	7,492	Taxes & Accruals	282
Mdse	30,629		

Current	46,364	Current	7,383
Fixts & Equip	1		
Prepaid Exp	1,050	NET WORTH	40,032
	-----------		-----------
Total Assets	47,415	Total	47,415

Sales 197-, $104,684; gross profit $36,485; drawings by owner $9,463; net profit $3,130. Annual rent $4,200. Fire insurance on mdse $30,000, fixts $5,000. Fixts & Equip less depreciation of $6,475.

Prepared from statement signed FRANK'S MEN'S SHOP by Frank Sanders, owner, Feb 18 197-. Prepared by E. A. Fames, Jr., independent accountant.

-----0-----

Mar 15 197-, Sanders said that sales were up 4% so far this year. Profits are expected also to increase as expenses have remained constant. He estimated merchandise at $32,000 and owes about $8,000 in accounts payable, all of which is current.

BANKING

At a local bank balances average medium to high four figures on a routine non-borrowing basis. Account satisfactory.

HISTORY

Trade name registered July 10, 1946.

SANDERS, born 1917, married. 1935 graduated high school. 1935-43 employed by Newark Department Store as assistant sales manager, men's wear department. 1943-46 U. S. Navy. 1946 started this business.

OPERATION

Retails medium priced line of men's suits, slacks, shirts, hosiery and accessories. Features nationally advertised brands, including
(CONTINUED)

FIGURE 21.3 A sample Dun & Bradstreet report on a men's wear store. Note that the rating given in this case is DD1. This means that this retailer has a high rating of $35,000 to $50,000.

Courtesy Dun & Bradstreet, Inc., New York.

best for your business. In both the short and long run, the freedom to choose suppliers will make your business more successful.

A supplier will sometimes offer you goods on a consignment basis, i.e., he owns the merchandise and you only pay for what you sell. Goods on consignment increase the merchandise selection in your store at no cost to you, but there are very obvious dangers. They can compete with the goods you already own and you have no right to reduce consigned merchandise. Never take goods on consignment just because they are offered to you. First think of how the merchandise will look in your store and whether it will have a harmful or beneficial effect on your total operation.

Consignment merchandise

Usually, fixtures and other equipment can be purchased on extended terms or with a conditional sales agreement that permits you to pay for them in installments. In some instances, you may be able to arrange a lease and purchase agreement. However, examine these plans very carefully because all of them are more expensive than an outright purchase or one with a cash discount. But they may be worthwhile if you can use your money more profitably elsewhere.

Money, like merchandise, must be kept moving. Excess money lying in your current account only earns a profit for the bank—you get nothing for it. If your current account contains more money than your business requires but you want to keep your capital liquid, shop banks for the best interest rates on a savings account. You will be surprised how these institutions compete with each other for deposit accounts. You can also buy Treasury bills, notes, bonds and short-term certificates, or, if you feel more adventurous, see your banker or a reputable investment broker about easily marketable securities.

Put excess money to work

When you require outside money, don't be afraid to borrow it. It can be good business to obtain outside loans providing that you can pay them back as agreed and that the interest you pay is considerably less than the profit you make.

Use other people's money

Before you make an appointment with a lending institution, decide how much money you need, what you intend doing with it, the possible results of the investment, and how you expect to repay the loan. Then discuss the proposal with your accountant and, if necessary, revise the plan to make it stronger. The accountant should then prepare it and go over it with you until you understand what every figure means and are able to answer intelligently any questions the loan officer might ask (Fig. 21.4). Sometimes it is better to have the accountant accompany you on the interview. His fee for this service should be minimal when you consider his advice on the practicality of the loan and how it should be handled, his ability to write it out so that it makes sense to the lender's interviewer, and the time he spends coaching you or accompanying you to make the presentation successful.

How to prepare a proposal for a loan

```
                    SMALL SIZE SHOPPE

                   YOUR MATERNITY SHOP

                 For year ending July 31st.

                    Explanatory Notes


SALES                                                        $83,931.33

COST OF SALES
        Inventory July 1                      21,627.13
        Purchases                             57,497.07
                                              79,124.20
        Less: Inventory July 31               23,874.00          55,250.20

                GROSS TRADING PROFIT                             28,681.13

EXPENSES
        Store and office salary                8,563.51
        Rentals                                7,500.00
        Advertising                            1,458.66
        General, Office and Accounting           947.20
        Store expenses                           854.30
        Insurance and Taxes                      828.82
        Light, Heat and Water                    701.10
        Telephone                                479.66
        Interest and Bank Charges                364.24
        Packing and Shipping                     920.37
        Unemployment Insurance & Workmen's Compensation  116.85
        Car Expenses (75%)                       579.36          23,314.07

            Net Profit before Depreciation                       5,367.06

Less: Allowance for Depreciation on - Fixtures    930.00
                                     - Car (75%)  555.00          1,485.00

                                          NET PROFIT            $3,882.06
```

FIGURE 21.4 Profit and loss statement to supplement bank's evaluation of a small business.

One of the best places to borrow money is a bank. This is why it is poor policy to change banks unless you think that there is an advantage in doing so; for the longer you deal with one bank, the better record you build up and the more of its services you should be able to obtain. **Where to borrow money**

However, since it is the bank manager who recommends your loan, make sure that he is your kind of banker. He should be willing to assume risks and take the blame if he guesses wrong. He should also be a small businessman's banker and so be more interested in lending money to small businesses than in negotiating with large corporations. He must have faith in small businessmen and want to help them grow because he feels that his own business will increase as his clients become more prosperous. Finally, it is most important that the bank manager you deal with have a number of retail accounts similar to yours.

When you find this kind of bank manager, trust him and cultivate him as a valuable friend and counselor. His attitude and outlook are important for your business and he can advise you with a great deal of insight because he knows how other stores like yours are functioning. But remember that he is no merchant and so may not fully understand what appears to you to be a simple business proposition. Nevertheless, when he disagrees with your proposal, think it over carefully; then if you still like it, go ahead in spite of his advice.

Face Loans.   There are various ways you can borrow money from a bank and each one lends itself to a specific situation. If you require a small loan for a very short period, the banker may suggest a *face loan.* This is a loan without any security and is given because the banker trusts you and wants to help you over a temporary financial difficulty.

Overdraft.   For bigger loans and longer periods, the manager may suggest an overdraft credit. This permits you to overdraw your current account up to a prearranged limit. It is based on your needs, the banker's experience with you, and the securities you can offer. The advantage of this loan is that you pay interest only on the money you actually borrow. For example, you may establish an overdraft credit of $10,000, but if you overdraw $5,000 for five days, you pay interest only on the $5,000 for the five days. If this is at 6 percent per annum, the charge will amount to $4.11.

Term Loans. Another kind of loan is called a *term loan.* Here the banker offers you a definite amount of money which you promise to repay within a certain time, usually in monthly installments. For example, a $2,400 term loan might be paid back in two years by monthly payments of $100 plus interest. Term loans are helpful when you require fixed capital because it will take some time for the money to earn its way.

Of course, you can work with all three loans or a combination of them. This is where a competent banker can be of help. His business is to lend money, but he is not in business to lend you all the money he estimates you can be secured for. If he is a conscientious banker, he will suggest whatever amount and kind of loan he thinks is best for the particular circumstances and then let you have it at a reasonable cost.

Bankers require collateral for all loans except face loans. *Collateral* means assets that are easy to liquidate, for example, stocks, bonds, or life insurance policies. You sign over to the bank as much of these as is necessary until your loan is repaid. If you are unable to meet your obligations, the bank sells the collateral, deducts its loan, and returns any balance to you. Banks will sometimes take a lien on property or fixtures, although they prefer not to. They will also give you a certain amount of credit on assigned accounts receivable.

Although a banker lives by lending money, he prefers not to give you any if he feels that you will not be able to pay it back. Banks are not equipped to sell their client's assets, and they do not want to do so. Therefore, when a banker gives you his reasons for refusing a loan, take them seriously. However, since his judgment is that of a banker, not a merchant, review the idea and if you still like it, look around for other sources of capital.

Endorsed loans

Sometimes a bank requires that a loan be endorsed. This means that the bank wants someone who is a good credit risk to sign his name to the loan. Then, if you cannot make your payments, the bank collects from the endorser who, in turn, does what he can to get his money from you.

Small Business Administration

A good source for loans is the Small Business Administration which, in 1958, through the Federal Small Business Investment Act, was licensed to establish investment and development companies at the local level to lend money to small businessmen who need money but have been turned down by private sources. To find out where the Small Business Administration offices are located in your area, write the U.S. Small Business Administration, Washington, D.C. 20416.

Lending institutions

In addition to banks and the Small Business Administration, there are institutions that will lend you money. Some finance corporations and private persons will discuss a loan with you, and there are occasions when you might use them. But before you accept a loan, shop around and figure out the *real,* not the *apparent,* costs involved. For example, a $2,400 loan for two years at 6 percent per annum on a *reducing balance* repayable at $100 a month would cost you $150.05. The same amount for the same time with a *repayment schedule* of $126 per month would cost you $624.

Distinguish between the real and the apparent cost

The difference between the two loans lies in the way they are handled by the lending institution. When you get a loan with a *reducing balance,* you pay interest only on the money you actually borrow. If, for example, on January 1st, you obtain a loan of $2,400 at 6 percent, with a reducing balance, your interest payment on February 1st would be approximately

$$\$2,400 \times \frac{6}{100} \times \frac{1}{12} = \$12$$

If, on February 1st you pay back $100 of your loan, you are then borrowing only $2,300 during February, so on March 1st your interest payment would be approximately

$$\$2,300 \times \frac{6}{100} \times \frac{1}{12} = \$11.50$$

If you keep paying back your principal as agreed, by January of the second year you will be using only $1,200 of the lender's money for that month. Therefore, on February 1st of the second year, your interest payments would be

$$\$1,200 \times \frac{6}{100} \times \frac{1}{12} = \$6, \text{ etc.}$$

If you cannot obtain a loan on a reducing balance, be very careful to find out how much the one you are being offered will really cost. Lending institutions today are legally obliged to tell you what a loan will cost, but some of them add on hidden costs which, of course, is a roundabout way of increasing their interest rate. For example, you might be offered $2,400 for two years at 13 percent per annum on the principal. The interest would be $624. However, the lending institution might add the $624 to the $2,400 and make you sign a note and become responsible *at once* for $3,024, not $2,400. Such a loan works out to a *real* interest rate of 24.96 percent per annum.

Look for hidden costs

When you are offered this kind of loan, always ask about interest rebates. You might find that if you accepted the loan outlined above on January 1st and wished to pay back the $2,400 on February 1st, you would only receive a rebate of 92 percent of the $624, or $574.08. The interest, then, for the month, would be $49.92. If you wanted to clean it up at the end of February of the second year, you might only receive back 20 percent of $624, or $124.80, etc.

Institutions and individuals who loan money at high *real* interest rates defend this practice by saying that they are willing to accept greater risks than those who use only the reducing balance method. Usually, they do not demand the same high liquidity of collateral and they are not as interested in the reasons for the loan as are those who offer money on a reducing balance. They are in business to risk their money and so are prepared to sell whatever collateral is necessary to make their loans good.

The best source, but not the only source, for a business loan with a reducing balance is your bank. As a rule, banks do not want to seize and sell property and so they take great care to make certain that a business loan will be profitable and can be repaid. Figure 21.5 shows the kind of detailed evaluation of a business that a bank may make before granting a substantial loan. (See pp. 304–5.)

One of the best ways to keep your credit (borrowing capability) high is to arrange to pay your commitments as promised. To do this, you should develop a system that will tell you days, even months, ahead whether or not you are going to have sufficient money to meet your commitments as they fall due. Then you will never be short of funds and be forced to make partial payments on some of your commitments while you scurry around looking for distress money which you will have to borrow at exorbitant interest rates. This planning technique is called *cash flow* and it prepares you for financial crises and gives you enough time to negotiate a proper loan or to make arrangements with your creditors that will not endanger your credit standing.

Plan to meet your commitments

A simple but effective cash flow system is to take a wide sheet of ruled paper and at the top mark the bank days for as many weeks ahead as you think necessary. Then, as you accept invoices, enter the amounts under their

How to develop a cash flow system

NAMES AND OFFICES OF OFFICIALS OR PARTNERS	M. or S.	AGE	
John Smith - Sole Owner		47	NAME Small Size Shoppe
			NATURE OF BUSINESS Retail Womens' Wear P.O. Bankton
			(if not in your district explain on reverse why account is on your books)
			STATEMENT AS AT 31st December 19___

Item No.	ASSETS	Customer's Valuation omit cents	Manager's Valuation omit cents	LIABILITIES	omit cents
	LIQUID ASSETS			**FLOATING LIABILITIES**	
	Cash	343	343	Hometown Bank 3rd & Main	4,819
	Accounts Receivable $ 2,193.			Outstanding checks	2,518
	Bills Receivable $ _____			Wholesalers	16,493
	Total $ 2,193.			Sundry Parties	
	Less Reserve ____ $ ____ (Extend net total)	2,193	1,974	Sales Tax	
	Merchandise Held for Sale	23,874	21,487	Wages Due and Accrued	
	(Total Sales for Year $ 83,931)			Taxes _____ (Arrears $ _____)	
				Payments on Mtgs. and Agts. for Sale, Past Due ____ Prin.	
	Prepaid expenses	632	–	Interest	
				Payments on Mtgs. and Agts. for Sale _____ Prin.	
				Due within 12 months	
				Interest	
	(Insurance on Liquid Assets $ 22,000.) TOTAL LIQUID	27,042	23,804	TOTAL FLOATING	23,830
	FIXED ASSETS (Household Effects not to be included) Furn. & Fixt. 9,572.			**DEFERRED LIABILITIES** (Payments Deferred 12 mos. or longer)	
	Deprec. 5,850.	3,722	2,791		
	Automobile 3,242				
	Deprec. 1,513	1,729	1,297		
				Mortgages and Agreements for Sale ____	
				(Last Verified _____ 19___)	
	Real Estate Unencumbered Goodwill	2,573			
	(Insurance on Buildings _____)				
	(Insurance on Equipment and Fixtures $6,000.)				
	*(Property Searched _____ 19___)			SURPLUS	11,236
	*Report on reverse any discrepancies, joint tenancies or other special features revealed.			(Manager's Estimate of Surplus $ 4,062.)	
				(Liability as Endorser or Guarantor $ _____)	
				(Give particulars on reverse)	
	Life Insurance $ 5,747. c.s.v. $ 1,281			Is Statement Audited? Yes	
	Name of Beneficiary Ruth Smith - Wife	35,066	27,892	If so, by whom? Wm. Jones & Co. C.P.A.	35,066

FIGURE 21.5 One bank's evaluation of a business. The overdraft amount will be set by the bank's main office and will be based on this report and the manager's recommendation.

due dates on the sheet. Also plan for recurring withdrawals like rent, salaries, petty cash, your own "salary," etc. When you have the system working properly, it will tell you how much cash you require in the bank to meet every day's expenses as far ahead as you wish to plan.

To find out whether or not you will have enough money to meet these withdrawals, put down on paper your *real* balance (not the balance your bank book shows, but the one in your check book, which should always be kept up to date). Now look up last year's sales figures and, if you have a customer credit operation, its receipts and then estimate how much money you will be depositing for the period for which you are planning.

By adding your estimated cash to your actual current balance and subtracting your estimated withdrawals, you should know approximately whether or not you will be able to meet your commitments. If you see that you are going to have difficulty a month or even longer from today, decide how much money you will require and how long it will take you to pay it back. Then meet with your bank manager or other lending sources and begin to negotiate a loan and/or write your main creditors to suggest an

	LOANS	TRADE BILLS		POSITION OF ACCOUNT			FACE VALUE	MANAGER'S VALUATION

Highest Past 12 Months __Sep.__ 19___ $ _7,036._ 19___ $ _____   As at __June 4__ 19_____   SECURITY:

Lowest Past 12 Months __June__ 19___ $ _2,602_ 19___ $ _____   Loans $ _2,654._ _____   A/A $5,747. Life Ins. c.s.v.

Date on which Loans including Overdrafts last liquidated in full: Trade Bills $ _____ M/V $ _____   81/31(1954) John Smith - $5,000.

(If not liquidated within 12 months give reason in paragraph (E) below and state what is being done to have account cleaned up.) __December__ 19____   Indirect $ _____   Fire Insurance - $28,000. Loss to Bank.

NOTE:—Aim to explain the Manager's opinion of the customer's responsibility and the basis of the Manager's valuations. If space inadequate for remarks attach sheet of explanatory notes.

(A) Receivables. State total rated "good", "fair", "weak" and also total carried longer than 12 months.

(B) Basis of inventory valuation, etc. State Manager's estimate of total amount of slow-moving goods.

(C) Efficiency of bookkeeping methods. Submit copy of profit and loss statement if available.

(D) List individual properties of real estate separately showing relative encumbrance and amount of fire insurance.

(E) Liabilities.

(F) Comment on points of special significance bearing on customer's position or claims to credit.

(G) If new account state how acquired and reason for leaving former bankers. Are recent reports from former bankers and outside enquiries satisfactory?

The firm operates at 10 Richmond Street in this city - specializing chiefly in maternity wear. The store handles a diversified line of well known, branded women's clothing lines with emphasis on small size. Sales are made chiefly to transient off street clients although the firm has a good number of long standing, regular customers. Credit is extended (and carried on the books) to reliable customers who have dealt with the firm for many years. Classified as good - borne out by negligible bad debt experience. Other requests for credit are channelled through Standard Discount, without recourse. We deduct 10%. Merchandise consisted of items usual to this type of business - dresses, coats, suits, some sportswear and as mentioned maternity wear, with the valuation being made at lower of cost or market for statement purposes. All staple lines - we value at 90%. Operations and earnings during the period were satisfactory but we have cautioned Smith regarding allowing his drawings to exceed earnings. This feature will be watched in the future. The firm's working capital position is relatively thin, however, full utilization of trade credit is taken (minimum-60 days) which permits the bank overdraft to keep within its limits and show fair fluctuation. Smith is a hard working, conscientious individual who devotes his full time and energies to the business. In view therefore of our long and satisfactory association and bearing in mind the prime security held, we feel we can safely conduct the account on the basis outlined.

This section need not be completed in accounts operating under an authorized credit.

Maximum Credit Limits and Basis on which Account is to be Conducted

To Expire __June 5__ 19____   Rate of Interest __8__ %

Loans $ _3/5,000._   Approved Trade Bills $ _____

(1) Secured by

A/A $5,747. Life Ins. c.s.v.

Fire Ins. Fixt. $6,000.
Stock $22,000. L.T.B.

(2) Purpose of Loans: (if the account is being carried in liquidation this fact should be recorded.)

To carry existing advances and assist the firm finance their general operations.

(3) <u>Time</u> and <u>Source</u> of Repayment

Sale of merchandise and collection of accounts receivable - periodic liquidation through year during busy sales seasons.

(OLDEST YEAR FIRST)	19	19	19	19	19	19
Liquid Assets	28,632	30,806	26,282	23,800	27,042	
Floating Liabilities	24,402	25,700	22,430	19,344	23,830	
Liquid Surplus	4,230	5,106	3,852	4,456	3,212	
Fixed Assets	5,341	5,242	9,849	8,119	8,024	
Mortgage Debts						
Fixed Surplus	5,341	5,242	9,849	8,119	8,024	
Total Surplus	9,571	10,348	13,701	12,575	11,236	

John Doe   Manager

Date Submitted _____ 19____

FIGURE 21.5 (continued)

extension or a division of their accounts into a series of smaller payments. In this way you avoid panic financing which is not only very expensive but bad for your peace of mind.

How to shop for a loan

If you have a good reason to borrow money and if you have sufficient acceptable collateral to back it up, go to your banker first. If he refuses to grant the loan, think it over. If you are still convinced that the extra money can increase your profit, shop a few banks and consult the Small Business Administration. If all of them turn down the proposition and you still want to go ahead, shop other loan institutions and private lenders; then compare *real* costs. They might not only charge you high interest rates, but you might also find the occasional private lender who wants to take an active part in the business or who will ask for other terms. If you want to accept a loan from a private individual, consult your accountant and your lawyer. Since it is going to cost a lot anyway, a few extra dollars to protect your interests is a good investment.

Borrowing money is a business tool, but it should not be taken lightly.

It might pay you to obtain $2,400 at a real interest rate of 24.96 percent, but you should know the *real* rate and then estimate your chances of making the borrowed money pay more than the cost involved.

Sometimes you can make money, as well as obtain more capital, by reorganizing your business. There are advantages in being independent, such as the ease with which you can start a business and the freedom you have in running it. When you are on your own, if you do a poor job, there is no one to criticize you but yourself, but if you do a good job, you receive all the profits which you can use to live on or plow back into the business to make more money. In addition, tax departments ask less of individual proprietors. They demand a minimum of records and allow business losses to be deducted from personal income.

Money obtained by reorganization

But like everything else in the retail business, the individual proprietorship has its disadvantages. Because *you* are the business, what happens to it if you become sick or die? Again, no man has the ability, energy, or time to perform every retail function properly and so the business is bound to suffer. Further, a single proprietor is personally liable for all debts incurred in the operation of his business and all the profits are taxable as personal income whether they are withdrawn or not. In any event, as he continues to expand, the single proprietor usually will require more money than he can obtain personally. He should not wait until this happens to consider other ways of organizing his business to protect his investment and to get more capital on which to grow.

Under an ownership arrangement, you sell parts of your business to one or more people who then have an interest in your operation. This form of organization has advantages: two or more heads should be better than one, particularly if you choose your partners intelligently. Look for people with whom you can work without much argument and who have business talents that are different from yours. You should then have a smooth-running and well-rounded business management team. The fact that most or all of the partners contribute capital should increase the worth of the business and permit it to expand. Again, unless specially provided for, each partner has unlimited personal liability and this should increase the amount of credit on which the business can draw. If the business loses money, each partner can deduct his portion of the loss from his personal income.

Partnerships

Gloomy Side of Partnerships. Unless there is a special arrangement, not only is each partner personally liable for all business debts, but he is also responsible for the business actions of all the other partners. If one of them decides to be a "big shot" and orders expensive fixtures, signs a long-term lease at an exorbitant rent, or performs any other ridiculous act in the name of the partnership, all the partners are held personally liable. Another disadvantage is that partnerships automatically dissolve on the death or voluntary withdrawal of any of the partners. Although special arrangements can be made to take care of these contingencies beforehand, the procedure is cumbersome and the loss of a partner might mean the virtual liquidation of the business. Again, instead of all the profits belonging to you, they must be shared and disposed of according to the partnership agreement. This can lead to a great deal of argument. Some partners might want to reinvest their earnings to help build the business still further, but others might feel that they require every cent for their personal use.

Engage an Expert Lawyer. If you decide to form a partnership, engage a lawyer who is an expert in drawing up partnership agreements. Nothing is so frustrating as to own a business, take in partners, and then discover that you can no longer act freely and you cannot dissolve the partnership without forfeiting a great deal of your equity in the business.

Because neither a single proprietorship nor a partnership answered certain basic business requirements, the corporate form evolved. This eliminated personal liabilities and the risk of a business dissolving because certain individuals left it for one reason or another. A corporation is a legal entity that limits one's liability to the funds that one invests in it, and it continues to exist even after any or all of the original owners decide to leave. That is one reason why corporations can increase their capital by selling shares in the business to anyone who wants to buy them or by borrowing from the public by issuing bonds. Theoretically, these stocks and bonds can be bought and sold again and again without affecting the management of the business, although in practice ownership may change or be influenced by outsiders who buy up a sufficient amount of stocks and/or bonds.

The corporate form also permits a business to function differently from a proprietorship or a partnership. For example, in a single proprietorship or a partnership, the income tax department does not recognize a wife's salary as a business expense, but a corporation can pay a wife a salary if she actually puts in time because she is considered an employee of the company. Again, a corporation is permitted to establish a pension plan for its employees, with the business paying most or all of the premiums. If you and your family are the principal employees in such a company, you share most of the benefits.

Disadvantages of Corporations. The corporate form has many disadvantages, but for a small business, most of them can be minor. The corporation charter must set forth what the business is supposed to do. It cannot change or enlarge on these activities unless it sets up a new organization and obtains a new charter. Corporations are required to obey many extra regulations, make more reports, and keep better books than are other business organizations, because by law a corporation is not a personal business but a public one. This usually requires more paper work and office staff and thus can be more expensive than the other business forms. But forcing a retailer to keep proper books may be a good thing and can save him money in the long run.

While you are small, the corporate form will not help your company's credit rating. In fact, you will have to pledge more of your personal assets

WHAT FORM OF BUSINESS ORGANIZATION?

Individual Proprietorship

One person as sole owner.
No legal organization requirements.
Unlimited personal liability for business debts.
Termination upon death of owner.
Relative freedom from Government control.
No income tax levy on business (but on owner only).

Partnership

Two or more persons as co-owners.
Definition of partner's rights and duties by partnership agreement and State partnership law.
Possible requirement for filing certificate under State law.
Unlimited liability of each partner for all debts of firm.
Capacity of one partner to bind others when acting within scope of business.
Termination upon death or withdrawal of a partner.
Relative freedom from government control.
No income tax levy on partnership itself.

Corporation

Creation as a legal entity pursuant to State law.
Stockholders as owners who are separate and distinct from corporation.
Requirement for obtaining charter from State.
Required payment of filing fees and capital stock taxes.
Continuity unaffected by death or transfer of stock shares by any or all owners.
Limited financial liability for stockholders.
Subjection to more Government control than a proprietorship or partnership.
Income tax levy upon corporate profits and, in addition, upon dividends after they are paid to stockholders.

FIGURE 21.6 Advantages and disadvantages of the various ways to organize your business.

Source: Department of Commerce, Washington, D.C.

than you would under the other two forms because your creditors cannot go against your personal worth. They can only seize the money that has been invested in the corporation. Since this is usually a small sum, they will probably demand your personal endorsement on all the corporation's debts.

To figure out which form of business is the best for you at any time, consult both your lawyer and your accountant. They will discuss the advantages and disadvantages of partnership and corporate arrangements and suggest which form would be better for you in the long run. There is usually no rush to jump from a single proprietorship to either a partnership or a corporation. Each form should evolve as your business grows. It then becomes one of the reasons why you are able to run a business successfully. **Consult your lawyer and accountant**

No matter how advantageous a partnership or a corporate arrangement may look, before you say "Yes" think very carefully about your happiness under either of these business situations (Fig. 21.6). Remember that the moment either one becomes a fact, you lose your independent status. From then on you must answer to other people, but if they displease you, they cannot be summarily fired. They must leave voluntarily and this usually means that a financial settlement has to be arranged that may be difficult for you to meet, and/or you will have to deal with new partners, shareholders, or bondholders who will continue to curtail your freedom of action. Therefore, if you want to be 100 percent independent, be satisfied to move ahead slowly but with your freedom intact. **Do you want to be 100 percent independent?**

WHAT THIS CHAPTER TOLD YOU

1. Money is a commodity like inventory, and a retailer's ability to merchandise it can help him make a profit or end up with a loss.

2. Money, i.e., capital, consists of cash plus your ability to get credit and loans.

3. You use capital in three ways: (a) to buy fixed assets like fixtures, (b) to make it work for you by purchasing goods and selling them at a profit, and (c) to keep a liquid reserve for unforeseen emergencies.

4. The way you spend your money should vary with circumstances, but if you spend too much on fixtures you will have less to spend on merchandise, etc.

5. You can build up capital by investing and reinvesting your own money, by cutting down on your personal and the store's expenses, taking all cash discounts, getting faster merchandise turnover, selling old equipment and merchandise, collecting or selling accounts receivables efficiently, accepting credit cards, using suppliers as a source of working capital, and putting excess money to work.

6. The main sources of outside money are (a) the banks, (b) the Small Business Administration, (c) lending institutions and private sources, (d) suppliers, (e) selling accounts receivable, (f) credit cards.

7. Use a cash flow system to plan and control your obligations.

8. Capital can be obtained through three main organizational forms: (a) single proprietorship, (b) partnership, (c) corporations.

9. Each form has advantages and disadvantages which should be carefully studied with the help of experts before a decision is made to move from one form to another.

10. Entering into a partnership or corporate structure entails a loss of personal independence.

22

Make Your
Investment Dollar
Pay Good Dividends

WHAT THIS CHAPTER IS ABOUT

One of the laws for which retailers can be thankful is the one that forces every businessman to keep a set of books. Yet, many small retailers regard this requirement as a real nuisance and they attempt to reduce their income tax by juggling the figures so that their records are meaningless. This chapter tells you how to keep correct records so that you can understand and control all your operations, and then it tells you why small retailers who "save" a few hundred dollars in taxes may lose thousands in the process.

The Value of Correct Bookkeeping

A correct set of books is a true record of the activity of your day-by-day and year-by-year business. It permits you to compare your current figures against those of other years, and it gives you a sound basis for decisions about what is going to happen tomorrow, in the next six months, or in the coming year. A good bookkeeping system enables you to see weaknesses in time to correct them and to recognize the areas where you are strong so that you can build them up to be even stronger. You can also plan ahead with a great deal of accuracy and confidence and then control your plans. Doing these things will bring in many more dollars than the "savings" you might make through inaccurate records.

The two kinds of records that you should keep are operational records and merchandising records. The first group tells you how your business is operating and is a concern of management. The second group informs you about the movement of goods and is used by merchandising people like buyers and department managers to control inventories. Chapters 7 and 8 dealt with merchandising records. This chapter discusses how to interpret operational recording systems.

Bookkeeping Records

To find out whether you made a profit or a loss in any period (usually a month or a year), you simply subtract what the business spent from what it received. To do this accurately, you must have a method of entering everything that the business takes in and everything that it pays out. If you do an entirely cash business, you can write down each day's sales on the left side of a sheet of paper and enter what you pay out on the right. Then by subtracting one total from the other, you know how big a profit or loss you have.

However, since few businesses today are sufficiently simple to be operated in this way, more complicated systems have been developed to record cash sales, credit sales, vendor purchases, checks written, etc. This information is gathered together in a general ledger from which informative statements can be obtained. Since mistakes can easily occur in such systems, a method of checking the accuracy of the entries has been devised. This is called the *double entry bookkeeping system* and is used by most businesses today.

Advantages of an Accountant

If you have no training in bookkeeping, it is best to employ an experienced retail accountant to set up the initial system and teach you how to use it. This money is well spent because inaccurate records are not only useless but also dangerous. If, however, you do not want to keep the books yourself and if you find an accountant expensive, hire a part-time bookkeeper. Then you will have more hours per day to devote to jobs that will make you money.

Hiring a part-time bookkeeper may be good time and money management, but before you reject the accountant idea, consider seriously what he can do for you in addition to keeping your books. He usually delegates an apprentice to do the detail work and because this person's wages are nominal, your charges are accordingly relatively small. When you hire a retail accountant, you are able to draw on his experience and knowledge whenever you have a retail or financial problem because he has a number of clients who run businesses similar to yours and his advice will be based on more than his ability to read figures.

An experienced retail accountant can sometimes save you much more on income and other taxes than his fee. He still will be responsible for the accuracy of the books and will give you advice on how to answer any questions the tax people may ask. But you should always remember that he is an accountant, *not* a retailer, and certainly does not have your retailing ability or personality. Therefore, while his advice should always be encouraged, you are not obliged to accept it. You are the only one who can make final decisions on all matters that pertain to your business.

Operational Records

Books of records are of little use until they are gathered together in a form that permits you to compare your current operations with your past figures and with those published by the government and trade associations. This should be done every month, as well as once a year. Two forms, the balance sheet and the profit and loss statement, have been developed for this purpose. It is not important for a retailer to know how to draw up these statements, but it is very important that he knows how to use them.

How to Compare Operational Statements

The operational statements of large stores usually contain many more detailed breakdowns than you need and also may report figures on such operations as leased areas with which you are not concerned. For comparison purposes, however, you should know how to group external published figures so that they resemble your statements as much as possible. Again, some accountants differ in their headings, for example, they may use "gross profit" for "gross margin." Others handle some items in a way that differs from yours, for example, they might show cash discounts as a deduction from gross cost of merchandise sold, whereas you might consider it as "other income." But it is easy to move these figures to where you want them so that you can easily compare the statements.

Balance Sheet Headings

The balance sheet (Table 22.1) is compiled to give Mr. Smith a picture of his store at a certain date. It is a frozen or still view of how he did from one period to another. The statement contains two sides, assets and liabilities, with the assets showing what the business is worth and the liabilities showing what it owes, including Mr. Smith's equity, i.e., the capital he has invested in it.

There are two kinds of assets: current assets and fixed assets. *Current assets* (shown in Table 22.1 as $50,350) are those Smith expects to turn into

Assets

TABLE 22.1 Smith's Gift Shop, Balance Sheet

Current Assets				Current Liabilities		
Cash on hand and in bank			$ 1,600	Bank loan	$15,000	
Accounts receivable	$13,100			Bills payable	1,500	
Notes receivable	11,050			Accounts payable	3,800	
	24,150			Accrued liabilities	1,200	
Less provision for bad debts	1,150		23,000	Total current liabilities		$21,500
Inventory			20,250			
Accrued assets			40			
Prepaid expenses			460			
Investments at current value			5,000			
Total current assets			$50,350			
Fixed Assets				**Proprietorship**		
Equipment at cost		6,600		Capital investment		32,450
Less depreciation		3,000	3,600			
Total assets			$53,950			$53,950

cash to pay his current liabilities. *Fixed assets* ($3,600) are those he uses to operate the business and are not expected to be converted into money. Current assets are necessary for the continuing operation of the business, such as buying, promotions, operating expenses, etc., but fixed assets are also necessary in order to have the fixtures and equipment with which buying and selling can be done.

Current liabilities ($21,500 in Table 22.1) are those debts Smith expects to pay off within a short time. *Long-term liabilities* could be a mortgage loan on his business premises. The *proprietorship* heading ($32,450) tells him how much he has invested in the business in cash or by leaving part of each year's profit in the business.

Profit and Loss Statement

The profit and loss statement (Table 22.2) takes a different view of Smith's operation. This is a picture of the buying and selling activities of his business during a set period to show whether it made a profit or a loss. The statement does this by looking at three main facets of Smith's merchandising operations:

1. How much merchandise he really sold during the period.
2. How much money he made by selling these goods.
3. Whether the expenses he thought necessary to make the sales resulted in a profit or a loss.

The gross sales figure, show in Table 22.2 as $104,500, is the sum of all the sales the business made during the period. But since some of these purchases came back, returns and allowances must be deducted from gross sales ($104,500 minus $4,500) in order to obtain the net sales figure of $100,000.

Again, according to Table 22.2, Smith began the period with $16,600 worth of stock at cost. During the period he received merchandise costing him $65,000, returned $900 of it, and received allowances of $250. Therefore he really spent $63,850 on merchandise. He also paid $750 to have the merchandise moved from the vendors' places of business to his store, thus increasing the cost of goods to $64,600. During the period, therefore, he handled $81,200 worth of goods at cost.

At the end of the period he took inventory and found that he had $20,000 worth of merchandise in the store. (This figure does not necessarily represent what he paid for the goods but rather the lower of cost or market value.) To this he added $250 for transportation charges and made the total cost of goods in the store $20,250. Therefore, he must have moved $60,950 worth of goods at cost out of his store. Most of this was paid for by his customers, some was stolen by shoplifters and/or his employees, sales might

TABLE 22.2
Smith's Gift Shop, Profit and Loss Statement

Sales				
Gross merchandise sales			$104,500	
Less: sales returns	$ 4,000			
sales allowances	500	4,500		
Net sales				$100,000
Cost of Goods Sold				
Inventory 1st of period			$16,600	
Gross merchandise purchases		65,000		
Less: purchases returns	900			
purchases allowances	250	1,150		
Net purchases		63,850		
Plus: transportation		750	64,600	
Total merchandise handled			81,200	
Inventory end of period	20,000			
Plus: transportation	250		20,250	
Gross cost of merchandise sold			60,950	
Less cash discounts earned			1,300	
Net cost of merchandise sold			59,650	
Net loss on alterations			850	
Total cost of merchandise				60,500
Gross Margin				39,500
Total Operating Expenses				25,000
Net Income				14,500

have been rung up incorrectly, or other mistakes were made that would increase the amount of merchandise that moved out of the store. But because he took cash discounts totaling $1,300, the merchandise really cost him only $59,650. Since he lost $850 on alterations, this too must be added to his merchandise costs. If he had made a net profit on alterations or repairs, it would have decreased his merchandise costs.

He is now ready to calculate the total cost of merchandise sold, which is $60,500. By simply subtracting this figure from the net sales, he knows that he received $39,500 (gross margin) from selling goods that cost him $60,500.

This picture begins with the $39,500 Smith made by selling goods that cost him $60,500. Expenses of running the business must be paid from this amount and by preparing a very detailed record of these expenses, Smith knew that they totaled $25,000. (Note: Since Smith is a single proprietor, expenses do not include his "salary" or "drawings.") This leaves a net income of $14,500 and it is this amount that Smith must report when he makes up an income tax statement.

Profit and expense view

If Smith's gift shop is a partnership, the $14,500 would be divided among the partners, according to their agreement. Then each one's share would be considered his income regardless of what salaries or drawings were recorded during the year.

However, if the business is incorporated, Smith must be given a salary. If this amounted to $12,500, the total operating expenses would be $37,500 ($25,000 plus $12,500) and net operating income would be $2,000. The corporation would pay income tax on this amount and then the stock-holders would decide what to do with the balance.

How to Use These Statements

Knowing what goes into a balance sheet and profit and loss statement is the first step in learning their value and how to use them to judge the success of your operation. But one statement by itself is of very little use. For example, are liquid assets of $23,000 too much? Is $3,600 worth of fixed assets too little? And is the merchant in our example a good retailer because he made $14,500 net profit from sales of $100,000? To answer these questions and many others, the statement must be compared with the store's past performance and with outside figures.

Some Balance Sheet Ratios and Percentages

By comparing your balance sheets against published statistics, you can find out a great deal about the strengths and weaknesses of your business, as well as your current trends (Fig. 22.1).

This will tell you how strong your current position is. The equation is **Current ratio**

$$\frac{\text{current assets}}{\text{current liabilities}}$$

Using the amounts from Table 22.1, we see that this ratio is

$$\frac{50,350}{21,500} = 2.3:1$$

This means that current assets are more than twice current liabilities. A 2:1 current ratio is usually considered the necessary safeguard for most businesses, but yours may be peculiar and require a different ratio. The only way to tell is by knowing your own trend and by comparing this ratio with those of businesses similar to yours.

Cash and accounts receivable (quick assets) should be considered in relationship to current liabilities. You might have a good current ratio, but it might be the result of a slow inventory that is difficult to convert into cash. In the example the quick assets are (cash) $1,600 plus (receivables) $23,000 plus (investments) $5,000 = $29,600. The ratio, then, is **Quick assets to current liabilities**

$$\frac{\$29,600}{21,500} = 1.38:1$$

Line of Business (and number of concerns reporting)	Current assets to current debt	Net profits on net sales	Net profits on tangible net worth	Net profits on net working capital	Net sales to tangible net worth	Net sales to net working capital	Collection period	Net sales to inventory	Fixed assets to tangible net worth	Current debt to tangible net worth	Total debt to tangible net worth	Inventory to net working capital	Current debt to inventory	Funded debts to net working capital
	Times	Per cent	Per cent	Per cent	Times	Times	Days	Times	Per cent	Per cent	Per cent	Per cent	Per cent	Per cent
5641 Children's & Infants' Wear Stores (44)	5.37	4.06	16.50	16.90	6.25	6.45	**	5.9	5.0	24.6	69.4	73.0	31.3	20.1
	2.81	2.49	10.00	10.83	3.85	4.29	**	4.5	17.6	47.8	107.5	102.5	60.9	31.0
	1.72	0.71	3.45	4.26	2.75	3.21	**	3.6	42.0	97.5	198.0	159.6	84.0	62.2
5611 Clothing & Furnishings, Men's & Boy's (190)	4.56	4.62	13.71	17.01	4.54	5.35	**	6.1	5.3	24.3	57.7	63.4	36.6	12.1
	2.98	2.79	8.16	10.39	3.22	3.80	**	4.3	12.1	46.0	98.2	89.3	61.7	25.1
	1.97	1.07	3.57	4.17	2.23	2.70	**	3.1	24.2	85.0	174.2	127.9	95.1	46.8
5311 Department Stores (179)	4.44	3.31	10.19	13.08	4.69	5.72	**	7.0	13.1	24.7	55.1	59.0	42.9	19.0
	2.90	2.07	6.76	8.81	3.26	4.26	**	5.5	32.5	43.7	90.7	77.5	69.2	40.2
	2.09	0.96	2.90	4.04	2.65	3.32	**	4.4	62.4	70.0	131.1	108.7	103.0	70.0
Discount Stores (187)	2.65	3.11	16.06	22.17	8.18	11.22	**	6.9	14.6	48.2	86.0	108.4	52.3	20.4
	2.09	1.61	11.36	12.50	5.72	6.88	**	4.9	32.3	77.5	129.7	139.8	67.2	39.2
	1.55	0.75	5.14	6.40	4.17	4.68	**	4.0	56.5	124.4	204.3	195.2	97.7	76.7
5651 Family Clothing Stores (94)	4.84	4.29	12.74	14.85	4.95	5.59	**	7.0	5.5	20.3	58.2	50.7	37.1	22.5
	2.93	2.28	7.27	9.03	3.21	3.67	**	4.8	12.1	43.6	103.8	87.1	58.4	35.4
	2.13	1.01	4.13	4.60	2.19	2.74	**	3.6	26.5	76.5	158.7	123.7	89.3	54.9
5252 Farm Equipment Dealers (89)	2.88	3.85	14.37	21.66	7.26	10.28	24	5.9	9.5	43.0	100.5	80.1	60.2	11.0
	1.60	1.80	7.98	10.23	5.00	5.68	37	4.0	17.5	146.4	198.5	145.9	86.5	26.8
	1.35	0.99	4.54	6.23	3.02	3.34	59	2.6	39.7	213.7	257.4	239.1	113.9	48.0
5969 Farm & Garden Supply Stores (73)	3.30	6.13	23.26	41.67	5.23	9.23	**	14.6	18.6	25.0	61.8	40.0	72.6	24.1
	1.97	2.99	12.71	20.01	3.13	5.94	**	8.8	39.7	46.1	78.6	79.5	115.4	57.7
	1.41	1.85	6.32	12.50	2.33	4.07	**	5.7	65.7	89.0	128.0	138.9	212.7	118.7
5712 Furniture Stores (177)	5.61	4.78	13.70	13.98	4.78	6.28	37	6.9	4.9	21.3	45.9	32.2	55.7	9.1
	2.76	2.75	8.16	8.18	2.78	2.95	97	4.8	11.9	55.7	96.9	66.4	91.2	21.7
	1.74	1.07	3.69	3.78	1.61	1.64	191	3.5	26.3	117.2	192.9	118.5	139.5	40.2
5411 Grocery Stores (134)	2.50	1.63	15.39	32.59	14.24	31.36	**	23.1	49.1	37.8	64.7	79.2	67.9	26.6
	1.81	0.91	9.41	18.20	10.30	21.10	**	16.1	72.1	60.8	100.4	130.7	91.8	64.6
	1.38	0.53	5.06	9.67	6.60	12.55	**	11.9	99.9	93.6	169.1	204.4	129.3	148.5

**Not computed. Necessary information as to the division between cash sales was available in too few cases to obtain an average collection period usable as a broad guide.

Line of Business (and number of concerns reporting)	Current assets to current debt	Net profits on net sales	Net profits on tangible net worth	Net profits on net working capital	Net sales to tangible net worth	Net sales to net working capital	Collection period	Net sales to inventory	Fixed assets to tangible net worth	Current debt to tangible net worth	Total debt to tangible net worth	Inventory to net working capital	Current debt to inventory	Funded debts to net working capital
	Times	Per cent	Per cent	Per cent	Times	Times	Days	Times	Per cent	Per cent	Per cent	Per cent	Per cent	Per cent
5251 Hardware Stores (90)	6.00	4.81	14.20	20.34	4.52	5.49	**	5.7	4.9	17.4	41.0	64.1	24.9	8.1
	3.23	2.81	8.75	10.14	3.20	3.68	**	4.0	14.5	36.9	100.0	86.5	49.0	28.8
	2.09	0.99	2.72	4.04	1.96	2.38	**	3.2	26.1	79.7	174.2	122.0	82.1	54.2
5722 Household Appliance Stores (82)	2.70	3.85	17.70	25.58	8.61	9.14	16	7.9	9.1	45.1	95.4	60.5	74.8	8.4
	1.82	2.04	9.30	11.28	4.83	6.11	34	5.4	17.4	101.3	203.8	118.6	102.4	27.8
	1.38	0.88	5.79	7.13	2.81	3.81	79	4.2	39.5	194.1	313.4	198.3	170.1	50.9
5971 Jewelry Stores (76)	4.83	6.75	13.49	14.60	2.98	3.22	**	3.9	3.6	25.1	48.7	61.9	39.5	9.4
	3.17	3.61	8.44	9.12	2.02	2.37	**	2.7	9.6	44.2	89.4	84.5	63.2	19.7
	2.10	1.92	4.14	4.22	1.64	1.83	**	2.4	21.6	83.3	139.8	120.0	94.8	38.2
5211 Lumber & Other Bldg. Mtls. Dealers (170)	4.57	3.60	13.72	17.54	5.25	6.93	33	8.7	11.2	20.9	56.8	51.4	46.5	11.2
	2.62	2.37	9.05	10.89	3.43	4.57	53	6.0	22.1	45.6	90.1	74.2	78.0	37.2
	1.85	1.53	4.59	6.22	2.42	3.06	71	4.2	43.4	81.2	141.5	102.4	132.4	60.9
5399 Miscellaneous General Mdse. Stores (74)	5.82	3.80	13.79	15.99	5.80	6.07	**	6.6	7.6	19.0	57.9	59.5	26.0	13.8
	3.62	2.15	8.21	8.94	3.34	3.80	**	4.3	16.9	37.1	121.8	36.6	52.9	43.9
	1.89	1.03	2.58	3.08	1.94	2.31	**	3.1	34.7	81.4	177.3	142.6	80.0	80.7
5661 Shoe Stores (86)	5.09	3.09	10.54	13.42	4.74	5.70	**	4.9	6.2	21.4	54.6	79.3	34.8	4.8
	2.76	1.68	6.32	6.97	3.65	4.55	**	3.8	12.5	45.4	92.9	106.0	50.0	19.0
	2.07	0.59	2.17	2.30	2.81	3.09	**	3.1	25.6	86.8	153.1	154.0	66.5	49.6
5531 Tire, Battery & Accessory Stores (55)	4.36	5.00	15.22	20.45	5.21	7.54	**	8.2	6.6	23.5	56.0	59.1	31.8	19.7
	2.21	2.03	9.62	12.32	3.50	4.80	**	5.3	16.3	52.3	76.3	90.2	91.4	30.1
	1.71	0.99	3.85	5.13	2.62	3.38	**	3.9	35.4	116.8	181.8	129.7	149.4	63.7
5331 Variety Stores (64)	4.75	3.87	15.27	19.15	5.48	7.22	**	5.1	14.1	19.6	50.5	90.9	31.1	15.2
	3.00	2.11	8.81	11.39	3.55	4.61	**	4.1	24.4	39.3	73.5	124.3	42.9	43.0
	2.06	1.07	3.72	4.62	2.59	3.37	**	3.0	51.4	66.9	105.4	156.4	69.2	66.1
5621 Women's Ready-to-Wear Stores (167)	4.32	4.52	15.78	21.30	5.95	7.45	**	10.0	7.0	27.3	69.2	46.0	53.8	15.0
	2.81	2.30	8.53	10.96	3.96	4.92	**	6.7	18.2	49.2	100.1	72.3	87.2	33.2
	1.82	0.98	4.26	5.14	2.67	3.27	**	5.0	37.8	92.4	163.1	114.8	129.7	56.0

**Not computed. Necessary information as to the division between cash sales was available in too few cases to obtain an average collection period usable as a broad guide.

FIGURE 22.1 Notice that each ratio has three figures. The center one in bold type is called the *median* because it is obtained by arranging all the figures used in order of size with the best one at the top and the poorest at the bottom. The one figure that falls in the middle of the series becomes the median. The figure halfway between the median and the top of the entire series is called the *upper quartile*. The figure halfway between the median and the bottom of the series is called the *lower quartile*. This reporting system is infinitely more useful than straight averages because you have a much better idea of the level of your figures against those of the reporting stores.

Courtesy Dun & Bradstreet, Inc., New York.

A ratio of 1 is considered conservative for most businesses, but it might be unhealthy for your business. Comparisons with standard figures and your own history must be used to evaluate this figure properly.

This ratio indicates whether or not you have enough cash on hand to meet your current obligations and take advantage of discounts or special cash buys that come up. The equation is

Cash to current liabilities

$$\frac{\text{cash}}{\text{current liabilities}} = \frac{\$1,600}{21,500} = .08$$

This is usually figured as a percentage of net worth or, in this case, Mr. Smith's capital investment:

Liabilities to net worth

$$\frac{\$21,500}{32,450} \times 100 = 66.2\%$$

This percentage tells you whether you own a large share of the assets of the business or whether you are buying them with your creditors' money.

$$\frac{\$20,250}{50,350} \times 100 = 40.2\%$$

Inventory as a percentage of current assets

This percentage figure helps you to discover whether you are putting too much or too little money into your inventory. It should be checked with your sales and inventory ratio, i.e., your turnover ratio, in order to draw a better conclusion.

Profit and Loss Statement Ratios and Percentages

This is the cost of goods sold over the average inventory. To find the average inventory, add the opening and closing inventories together and divide by two. In the example this is

Turnover Ratio

$$\frac{\$16,600 + 20,250}{2} = 18,425$$

Using these amounts, we see that this ratio becomes

$$\frac{\$59,650}{18,425} = 3.2$$

This means that during the year goods averaging $18,425 in value have moved in and out of your store 3.2 times. Providing that you marked them properly, every time this happened a profit should have been created. This is one of the most important ratios for you to watch.

$$\frac{\$100,000}{23,000} = 4.4$$

This is an extremely valuable ratio to merchants who do a big credit business. In the example, 4.4 means that the annual rate of sales is 4.4 times the amount of receivables outstanding. Again, whether this is good or bad has to be judged against other figures, both internal and external.

$$\frac{\$39,500}{100,000} \times 100 = 39.5\%$$

This percentage tells you what you made on the merchandise that moved out of the store during the period. It is the key percentage in the operating statement, and its trend should be carefully watched.

$$\frac{\$25,000}{100,000} \times 100 = 25\%$$

This percentage means that you spent 25¢ on expenses for every dollar you took in in sales. Like the gross margin percent, it is a very important figure, and in order to be accurate you must include in the expenses an estimate of your own salary, a proper rent if you own the property on which the store stands, and any other expenses that non-owned stores charge against their profit and loss statements. Try to be very realistic about these estimates because this percentage figure can tell you whether or not you are operating a good business. If you are showing too high an expense to sales ratio, find out why and do something about it.

Any expense that you want to watch can be segregated by your bookkeeping system and calculated as a percentage of net sales. These percentage figures can be plotted from period to period and compared with outside sources. Expenses can be broken down in many ways. The simplest, and the one used by most small stores, is called *natural division of expenses.* This method puts into one account all your payroll expenses, into another your advertising expenses, etc. If you want to use percentage comparisons correctly, you must be careful to include in each account only those items that other stores include (Fig. 22.2).

$$\frac{\$4,500}{104,500} \times 100 = 4.3\%$$

This tells you the percentage of returns and allowances you made during the period. Unless you have a good reason for a high percentage, this figure should be kept as low as possible. Notice that the base in this equation is the *gross* sales, not the *net* sales.

	Usual Costs (Table 4, Column 1)	Usual Costs Applied to $38,889 Sales	Actual Costs in $38,889 Store	Difference	Diagnosis
Salaries:					
Proprietor	8%	$ 3,111	$8,400	$5,289	Proprietor's withdrawals high. May be losing sales through insufficient help.
Employees	6%	2,333	437	−1,896	
Rent	2%	$ 778	$ 900	$ 122	Satisfactory since heat is included.
Other expenses:					
Heat	0.3%	$ 117	Included in rent	—	See above.
Light and power	0.8%	311	$ 263	$ −47	Well controlled.
Taxes and licenses	0.5%	194	204	10	Satisfactory.
Insurance	0.4%	156	164	8	Satisfactory.
Interest paid	0.3%	117	None	117	No big debts.
Repairs	0.2%	78	57	−21	Good results.
Delivery	0.3% = 6.3%	117	4	−113	Customers may want this service.
Advertising	0.7%	272	694	422	Are extra payments productive?
Depreciation	0.8%	311	80	−230	May need more new fixtures.
Bad debts charged off	0.1%	39	Included in miscellaneous	—	Better to show amount separately.
Telephone	0.3%	117	Included in miscellaneous	—	Better to show amount separately.
Miscellaneous	1.6%	622	270	−352	Well controlled.
Cost of merchandise sold	69%	$26,833	$27,745	$ 912	Better buying control needed.
Turnover of merchandise stock (times a year)	3.5	—	3.1	—	
Average merchandise investment	$8,000	—	$ 9,033	$1,033	Opportunity revealed to cut merchandise stock investment

FIGURE 22.2 How following a natural expense classification system can aid in analyzing store operations.

Courtesy Eli Lilly & Co., Indianapolis, Ind.

322

For a small retailer, the cost of trying to reduce his income tax comes very high. There are many easy ways that he can do it, such as charging a percentage of his personal expenses to the business or taking merchandise from the store without recording it. Retailers who practice these techniques do not realize how much they tempt employees to steal (both merchandise and cash). Because they have no proper accounting system, they cannot tell whether some of the employees are dishonest until they are caught. Even the most high-principled employees must waver at the thought that they can increase their incomes by simply copying their boss and taking merchandise out of the store without making sales slips or by not recording cash sales and pocketing the money. For who is to know?

Another way some retailers attempt to avoid paying income tax is to lower sales figures, thus making the gross margin smaller. A very common method is to undervalue inventory, that is, reporting a figure that will give a gross margin percent which the retailer thinks the tax departments will accept without further investigation. The merchant who undervalues his closing inventory should realize that this figure becomes the opening inventory of his next period and that if he keeps on falsely lowering inventories for a number of years *he must buy, but not sell, more and more goods.* He therefore gets into a position where he must pay cold cash for merchandise that has to lie in out-of-the-way places in his store until it rots. The example in Fig. 22.3 shows how a merchant could eventually lose thousands of dollars a year by fixing closing inventories to "acceptable" gross margins. Actually, the only people who make money by this system are those who sell merchandise to such retailers.

An honestly valued inventory could result in more taxes, but it could also mean that more money would be left to make profit for your business or to spend on yourself. Or you may carry insurance for the real value of your inventory, but all that the insurance companies will give you on a total merchandise loss is the amount shown on your books. If you claim "over-insurance" they might refund your premiums, but that is all.

Some small merchants try to keep two sets of books, one for themselves and the other for the tax departments. This seldom succeeds, for few retailers are competent bookkeepers, and most of them become careless about making entries in the second set of books. In any event, the time and energy they spend in doing this is enormous. If they spent it in buying, selling, and managing their stores, they would be way ahead in real money, even after giving the tax departments their share.

Importance of Honest Bookkeeping

You can now see how important it is to keep a correct set of books. For example, most ratios and percentage figures are worthless unless you report

COMPARISON BETWEEN "ACCEPTABLE" AND TRUE GROSS MARGINS

"Acceptable" Gross Margin (28%)	True Gross Margin

First Year

	"Acceptable"		True
Sales	$100,000	Sales	$100,000
Opening inventory...$10,000		Opening inventory...$10,000	
Plus purchases 70,000		Plus purchases 70,000	
Total mdse. handled.. 80,000		Total mdse. handled.. 80,000	
Closing inventory.... 8,000		Closing inventory.... 10,000	
Cost of goods sold.........	72,000	Cost of goods sold.........	70,000
Gross margin.............	28,000	Gross margin.............	30,000

NOTE: You now have $2,000 worth of merchandise you have bought and paid for in cash, but which you cannot sell because of your "acceptable" gross margin.

Second Year

	"Acceptable"		True
Sales	$100,000	Sales	$100,000
Opening inventory...$ 8,000		Opening inventory...$10,000	
Plus purchases 70,000		Plus purchases 70,000	
Total mdse. handled.. 78,000		Total mdse. handled.. 80,000	
Closing inventory.... 6,000		Closing inventory.... 10,000	
Cost of goods sold.........	72,000	Cost of goods sold.........	70,000
Gross margin.............	28,000	Gross margin.............	30,000

NOTE: You now have $4,000 worth of merchandise which you cannot report. Of this, approximately $2,000 is already one year old, and $2,000 worth of new merchandise cannot be reported.

Third Year

	"Acceptable"		True
Sales	$100,000	Sales	$100,000
Opening inventory...$ 6,000		Opening inventory...$10,000	
Plus purchases 70,000		Plus purchases 70,000	
Total mdse. handled.. 76,000		Total mdse. handled.. 80,000	
Closing inventory.... 4,000		Closing inventory.... 10,000	
Cost of goods sold.........	72,000	Cost of goods sold.........	70,000
Gross margin.............	28,000	Gross margin.............	30,000

NOTE: You now have $6,000 worth of merchandise which you cannot report. Of this, approximately $2,000 is more than two years old, $2,000 is more than one year old, and $2,000 of new merchandise cannot be reported.

Fourth Year

	"Acceptable"		True
Sales	$100,000	Sales	$100,000
Opening inventory...$ 4,000		Opening inventory...$10,000	
Plus purchases 70,000		Plus purchases 70,000	
Total mdse. handled.. 74,000		Total mdse. handled.. 80,000	
Closing inventory.... 2,000		Closing inventory.... 10,000	
Cost of goods sold.........	72,000	Cost of goods sold.........	70,000
Gross margin.............	28,000	Gross margin.............	30,000

NOTE: You now have $8,000 worth of merchandise which you cannot report. Of this, approximately $2,000 is three years old, $2,000 is two years old, $2,000 is one year old and $2,000 is new merchandise that cannot be reported.

FIGURE 22.3   Comparison between "acceptable" and true gross margins.

Profit Planning Sheet
For Business Control

Devised by

THE NATIONAL RETAIL HARDWARE ASSOCIATION

Firm _____

Address _____

FIRST STEP: Plan expense for this year.

Enter actual expense for last year in each classification. If classifications do not agree with yours, change to agree with your records. In no case include shop labor and freight with expense. Then enter planned expense for this year.

(Use nearest dollar figures)   (Use nearest dollar figures)

Expense Item	Actual Last Year	Planned This Year	Expense Item	Actual Last Year	Planned This Year
A Salaries, Owner			M Depreciation, Delivery Equip'm't		
B Salaries, Clerks			N Depreciation, Furniture and Fixtures		
C Salaries, Office			O Depreciation, Building		
D Office Supplies and Postage			P Rent		
E Advertising			Q Repairs		
F Donations			R Heat, Light and Water		
G Store Supplies			S Insurance		
H Telephone and Telegraph			T Taxes		
I Losses, Notes & Accounts			U Interest on Borrowed Money		
K Salaries, Delivery			V Association and Other Dues		
L Other Delivery Expense			X Unclassified		
			Y Total Actual Expense Last Year and Planned This Year		

SECOND STEP: Plan margin for this year.

Determine percentage of margin for the past five years by filling in columns below.

(Use nearest dollar figures)

	19 ___	19 ___	19 ___	19 ___	19 ___
1. Enter year for which figures are given.					
2. Enter under each year the amount of merchandise inventory at beginning of that year.					
3. Enter total amount of merchandise purchased each year. Include shop labor and freight.					
4. Add amounts on lines 2 and 3.					
5. Enter amount of merchandise inventory at end of each year.					
6. Subtract amounts on line 5 from those on line 4 giving cost of goods sold during year.					
7. Enter total net sales for each year. Merchandise returned by customers should be deducted first.					
8. Enter cost of goods sold from line 6, same column.					
9. Subtract amounts on line 8 from those on line 7. The result is the margin.					
10. Divide amounts on line 9 by those on line 7. The result is percentage of margin on sales.	%	%	%	%	%

11. Planned margin that can reasonably be expected, based on experience as shown on line 10 .... _____%

THIRD STEP: Find sales required to pay expenses and leave 5% for profit.

12. Deduct 5% for profit from planned margin (line 11_____% which leaves percentage available for expense of _____%

13. Expense_____% (line 12) equals planned expense of $_____ (Line Y, planned column)

14. 1% equals $_____100% will then be the amount of sales necessary .... $_____

Example: If expense is 20% of the planned sales and amounts to $10,000, 1% will be 1/20 of $10,000 or $500. 100% will equal 100 times $500 or $50,000, amount of sales.

FIGURE 22.4 Profit planning sheet. Although these steps for profit planning are suggested for hardware stores, they can be easily adapted to any kind of retailing.

Courtesy National Retail Hardware Association, Indianapolis, Ind.

FOURTH STEP: Plan monthly sales.

In the first three columns below enter net sales by months for the past three years.

In Column A, add the sales for each month for the three years. Thus line 15, Column A will be the total of January sales for three years. Line 27, Column A, will be the sum of the total sales for three years.

In Column B, enter the percentage of total sales usually obtained in each month. To find, divide total sales for each month, Column A, by the sum of the total sales for three years, line 27,

Column A. Thus, if total sales for three years are $150,000 and total sales for three Januaries, $7,500, the probable sales for January will be 7,500 ÷ 150,000 or 5%.

In Column C, enter the planned sales for each month. First, enter in Column C, line 27, the planned sales for the year from line 14 in Third Step. Then multiply the planned sales for the year by the percentages in Column B. Enter result in Column C. Thus, if planned sales are $50,000 and it is found in Column B that 5% of the yearly sales result in January the planned sales for January will be $50,000 multiplied by .05 or $2,500.

(Use nearest dollar figures.)

	19 __	19 __	19 __	Column A Total of Months	Column B Mthly. Pctgs.	Column C Planned Sales	
15. January					%		January
16. February					%		February
17. March					%		March
18. April					%		April
19. May					%		May
20. June					%		June
21. July					%		July
22. August					%		August
23. September					%		September
24. October					%		October
25. November					%		November
26. December					%		December
27. Total					100 0 %		Total

FIFTH STEP: Determine the amount of purchases required to leave a desired investment in merchandise inventory at end of the year. Follow instructions below.

(Use nearest dollar)

28. Enter planned sales for this year (line 14, Third Step)	
29. Enter planned margin (planned sales as above, multiplied by per cent. of margin, line 11, Second Step)	
30. Deduct amount on line 29 from that on line 28. The result is the approximate cost of goods sold	
31. Enter amount of merchandise inventory desired at end of this year	
32. Add amounts on line 30 and 31	
33. Enter actual inventory at beginning of this year	
34. Deduct amount on line 33 from that on line 32. The result is planned purchases for this year	

SIXTH STEP: Plan monthly purchases. (Follow similar procedure as in Fourth Step.)

In the first three columns below enter net purchases by months for the past three years. The amounts should include freight paid, also shop labor. Merchandise returned to wholesalers or manufacturers and credited by them during a given month should be deducted from purchases for the month.

In Column D, add the purchases for each month for the three years.

In Column E, enter the percentage of total purchases usually

obtained in each month. To find, divide total purchases for each month, Column D, by the sum of the total purchases for three years, line 47, Column D.

In Column F, enter the planned purchases for each month. First, enter in Column F, line 47, the planned purchases for the year from line 34, Fifth Step. Then multiply the planned purchases for the year by the percentages in Column E. Enter result in Column F.

(Use nearest dollar figures)

	19 __	19 __	19 __	Column D Total of Months	Column E Mthly. Pctgs.	Column F Pl. Purchases	
35. January					%		January
36. February					%		February
37. March					%		March
38. April					%		April
39. May					%		May
40. June					%		June
41. July					%		July
42. August					%		August
43. September					%		September
44. October					%		October
45. November					%		November
46. December					%		December
47. Total					100 0 %		Total

FIGURE 22–4 (continued)

all your sales. If your inventory is a fixed one instead of a true one, the money you spend on bookkeepers and accountants is largely thrown away.

You Can Control Your Store

With accurate ratios and percentage figures you can control all your store's operations. Without them, or with made-up figures, the store runs you. Accurate figures will tell you not only that your inventory is heavy, but also how much heavier it is than it was at the same time last year or than it is in the average store. They will also permit you to scrutinize and judge every expense and decide how to keep your capital in proper balance and watch your gross margin and net profit. Moreover, you can do something about the weaknesses that appear in these comparisons before they prove fatal, and you can see where you are strong and build up these areas. Finally, accurate figures permit you to foresee trends and develop methods of capitalizing on them as they become strong or to drop them when they pass their peak.

You Can Plan

Accurate figures enable you to plan how you want your store operated and then build up a set of controls that will tell you how close your actual day-to-day, week-to-week, month-to-month, and year-to-year operations are to your plans (Fig. 22.4). If they vary too much from reality you can see your actual situation soon enough to do something about it. For ways to plan and control merchandise, markups, markdowns, turnover, etc., see the discussion of the six-month plan in Chapter 7.

WHAT THIS CHAPTER IS ABOUT

1. The key to business success and expansion is the planning and control of all your operations.

2. To do this, you must have a correct set of books and a good system of internal control.

3. You must be able to read and understand your figures and do what they tell you.

4. An accountant who has retail clients and is interested in their welfare will be able to interpret your statements and help you to judge their meaning. But remember that he is an accountant, *not* a retailer. You, not he, should make the decisions.

5. You can best plan and control your store by constantly comparing its current operations with your past figures and with outside figures.

6. You should make a practice of using ratios in planning and controlling the operations of your store. When used in this way, balance sheets and profit and loss statements are of inestimable value.

7. Retailers should realize that working out fictitious book figures to save a few hundred dollars in income taxes means losing thousands of real dollars that could be used to further their business or to enjoy life.

How to
Keep Records

WHAT THIS CHAPTER IS ABOUT

Chapter 22 told you *why* bookkeeping should be as accurate as possible. This is easy when the number of daily transactions in your store is so small that either you or a part-time bookkeeper can accumulate the data and enter them in a short time. But as your business expands, so do the number of transactions and eventually this forces you to develop more sophisticated systems to keep on top of the data you require to control the store's merchandising operational activities. This chapter discusses the major merchandising and operating record-keeping systems retailers use to give them the information they want when they want it.

Record-keeping Equipment

The record-keeping equipment you require should be based on the amount of information you need to gather to produce the data necessary for planning and controlling your merchandising and operating systems. The objective is to begin with a manual system and then as your needs grow to introduce advanced equipment and systems *before* the old ones become so slow and cumbersome that you are unable to obtain the information you need quickly enough to control all the functions of your store.

Manual Records

When you first opened your store most likely it was small enough to require only a part-time bookkeeper who *manually* wrote out whatever

records, statements, and controls you required. However, as business
picked up, the number of merchandise and operational entries increased until you required a full-time bookkeeper to keep your information up to date.

With increased business it became obvious that your bookkeeper could not cope with the entries that had to be made to stay on top of the job. At this point you entered the second stage, which was to install a number of mechanical aids that would help increase the data gathering procedures. These would have been a more sophisticated cash register, an adding machine, a desk calculator, a bookkeeping machine, and manual equipment to reduce the number of repetitive operations required to handle payrolls and accounts receivable.

Introducing these innovations was expensive and perhaps disturbing to your head bookkeeper who had to learn how to use them and teach them to the staff. But the alternatives were to hire more part-time and full-time employees or have the present ones fall so far behind in their work that what they produced was ancient history and therefore useless for planning or making day-to-day decisions.

Automatic Equipment

The third stage begins when business expansion forces you to think about introducing *automatic* equipment into the office. By this time you should have discovered that the bookkeeping market is very competitive and so varied in the choice of equipment and systems that selecting the automatic equipment you think you require will be very difficult. Therefore, you should decide to start your research for this stage of your office operation well in advance of the time you expect to install it.

You should begin by writing out the broad criteria of your research. The criteria should contain such factors as (a) the only equipment that you will consider will be relatively easy for your bookkeeper (who by this time should be your office manager or controller) to understand, operate, and supervise with a minimum of instruction and (b) that the equipment will contain sufficient potential to be integrated with whatever advanced equipment you may want to introduce as your office and control needs become more sophisticated. Other important criteria are that the equipment should give you the information you require quickly and accurately enough for active use and that its cost and maintenance should be reasonable in relation to its serviceability.

Where Should Research Begin?

A good place to begin your research is to ask your accountant for the names of noncompeting stores that are using machines and systems he believes would satisfy the requirements of your third stage. Visit these stores and inspect their operations. Then ask what they would do to improve their present equipment and systems. From these investigations you should be

able to decide which manufacturers you want to contact. Make it a point to
look at equipment and systems that are less sophisticated as well as those that are more advanced than you think you will require. In this way, you will be in a better position to judge the kind of equipment and systems you really need.

It is also very important to keep your accountant and office manager informed about all your findings and to involve them in the final decision making. After all, since they are the ones who will be responsible for keeping the equipment operating and turning out the information you and your executives will require, their cooperation is essential.

In your research you will soon discover that stores that use automatic equipment operate either a tabulating or an electronic data processing (EDP) system to perform their office and control functions.

Tabulating Systems

A tabulating system uses punch cards or tapes which are fed into machines that sort, tabulate, and print the information asked for. It is much faster and more accurate than manual systems, it is also considerably less expensive and easier to install than EDP, and it is less expensive to maintain. However, compared to EDP, it is very slow and cumbersome and extremely limited in the number of processes it can perform. Moreover, tabulating operators must be carefully trained because the machines must be fed by a number of different routine requirements.

EDP Systems

Because EDP systems are able to store or "remember" whatever facts you want to give them and can operate with almost incredible speed, in seconds they are able to receive data and reassemble them in any form you or your executives may desire. For example, they are so versatile that they can be programmed to give you the movement of your merchandise by department, classification, and stockkeeping unit (SKU) as they happen or at the end of certain time periods. Moreover, the SKUs can be broken down by price, size, color, material, or any other factor you or your buyers require for decision making. They are also able to alert fashion buyers to their slow- and fast-selling items, and staples can be reordered automatically. They will produce open-to-buy reports and other information controls your buyers require to keep on top of their merchandise areas (Figs. 23.1, 23.2, 23.3, 23.4, 23.5, 23.6).

EDP is invaluable in playing such merchandising games as how many items must you sell at $X to make $Y profit. Now, if you lower the price to $R, how many more must you sell to reach the $Y? If you raise the price to $Z, what quantity must you dispose of to obtain your target profit? It can also project the results of various turnover patterns, develop alternative

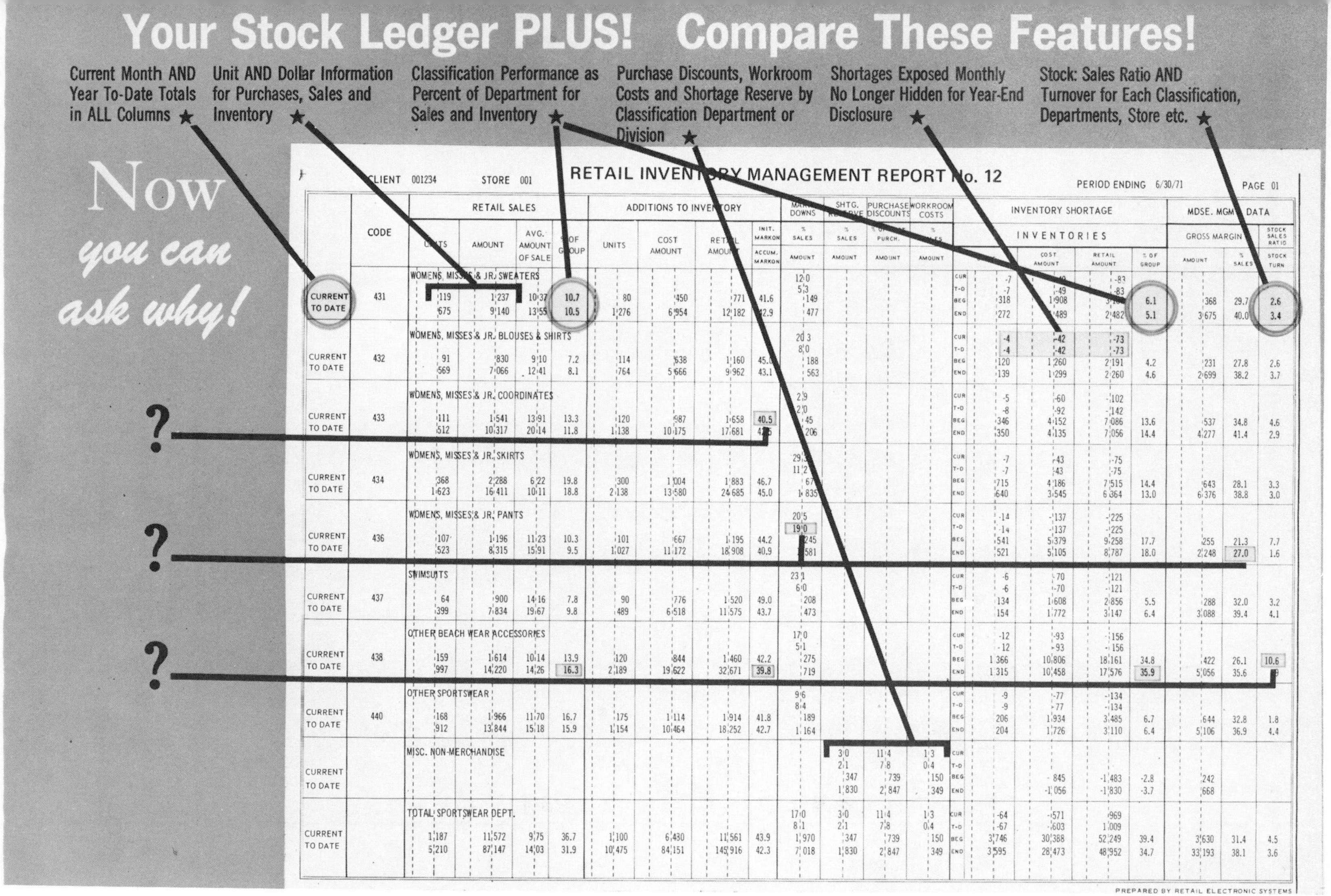

CLIENT 001234 STORE 001

RETAIL INVENTORY MANAGEMENT REPORT No. 12

PERIOD ENDING 6/30/71 PAGE 01

	CODE	Retail Sales: Units	Amount	Avg. Amount of Sale	% of Group	Additions to Inventory: Units	Cost Amount	Retail Amount	Init. Markon / Accum. Markon	Mark Downs: % Sales / Amount	Shtg. Reserve: % Sales / Amount	Purchase Discounts: % of Purch. / Amount	Workroom Costs: % / Amount		Inventory Shortage / Inventories	Cost Amount	Retail Amount	% of Group	Mdse. Mgmt Data: Gross Margin Amount	% Sales	Stock Sales Ratio / Stock Turn
WOMENS, MISSES & JR. SWEATERS																					
CURRENT TO DATE	431	119 675	1,237 9,140	10.37 13.55	10.7 10.5	80 1,276	450 6,954	771 12,182	41.6 42.9	12.0 5.3 149 477				CUR T-D BEG END	-7 -7 318 272	[illegible] -49 1,908 1,489	-83 -83 [illegible] 2,482	6.1 5.1	368 3,675	29.7 40.0	2.6 3.4
WOMENS, MISSES & JR. BLOUSES & SHIRTS																					
CURRENT TO DATE	432	91 569	830 7,066	9.10 12.41	7.2 8.1	114 764	538 5,666	1,160 9,962	45.[illegible] 43.1	20.3 8.0 188 563				CUR T-D BEG END	-4 -4 120 139	-42 -42 1,260 1,299	-73 -73 2,191 2,260	4.2 4.6	231 2,699	27.8 38.2	2.6 3.7
WOMENS, MISSES & JR. COORDINATES																					
CURRENT TO DATE	433	111 512	1,541 10,317	13.91 20.14	13.3 11.8	120 1,138	987 10,175	1,658 17,681	40.5 4[illegible]	2.9 2.0 45 206				CUR T-D BEG END	-5 -8 346 350	-60 -92 4,152 4,135	-102 -142 7,086 7,056	13.6 14.4	537 4,277	34.8 41.4	4.6 2.9
WOMENS, MISSES & JR. SKIRTS																					
CURRENT TO DATE	434	368 1,623	2,288 16,411	6.22 10.11	19.8 18.8	300 2,138	1,004 13,580	1,883 24,685	46.7 45.0	29.[illegible] 11.2 67[illegible] 1,835				CUR T-D BEG END	-7 -7 715 640	-43 -43 4,186 3,545	-75 -75 7,515 6,364	14.4 13.0	643 6,376	28.1 38.8	3.3 3.0
WOMENS, MISSES & JR. PANTS																					
CURRENT TO DATE	436	107 523	1,196 8,315	11.23 15.91	10.3 9.5	101 1,027	667 11,172	1,195 18,908	44.2 40.9	20.5 19.0 245 581				CUR T-D BEG END	-14 -14 541 521	-137 -137 5,379 5,105	-225 -225 9,258 8,787	17.7 18.0	255 2,248	21.3 27.0	7.7 1.6
SWIMSUITS																					
CURRENT TO DATE	437	64 399	900 7,834	14.16 19.67	7.8 9.8	90 489	776 6,518	1,520 11,575	49.0 43.7	23.1 6.0 208 473				CUR T-D BEG END	-6 -6 134 154	-70 -70 1,608 1,772	-121 -121 2,856 3,147	5.5 6.4	288 3,088	32.0 39.4	3.2 4.1
OTHER BEACH WEAR ACCESSORIES																					
CURRENT TO DATE	438	159 997	1,614 14,220	10.14 14.26	13.9 16.3	120 2,189	844 19,622	1,460 32,671	42.2 39.8	17.0 5.1 275 719				CUR T-D BEG END	-12 -12 1,366 1,315	-93 -93 10,806 10,458	-156 -156 18,161 17,576	34.8 35.9	422 5,056	26.1 35.6	10.6 [illegible]
OTHER SPORTSWEAR																					
CURRENT TO DATE	440	168 912	1,966 13,844	11.70 15.18	16.7 15.9	175 1,154	1,114 10,464	1,914 18,252	41.8 42.7	9.6 8.4 189 1,164				CUR T-D BEG END	-9 -9 206 204	-77 -77 1,934 1,726	-134 -134 3,485 3,110	6.7 6.4	644 5,106	32.8 36.9	1.8 4.4
MISC. NON-MERCHANDISE																					
CURRENT TO DATE											3.0 2.1 347 1,830	11.4 7.8 739 2,847	1.3 0.4 150 349	CUR T-D BEG END		-845 -1,056	-1,483 -1,830	-2.8 -3.7	242 668		
TOTAL SPORTSWEAR DEPT.																					
CURRENT TO DATE		1,187 5,210	11,572 87,147	9.75 14.03	36.7 31.9	1,100 10,475	6,430 84,151	11,561 145,916	43.9 42.3	17.0 8.1 1,970 7,018	3.0 2.1 347 1,830	11.4 7.8 739 2,847	1.3 0.4 150 349	CUR T-D BEG END	-64 -67 3,746 3,595	-571 -603 30,388 28,473	969 1,009 52,249 48,952	39.4 34.7	3,630 33,193	31.4 38.1	4.5 3.6

PREPARED BY RETAIL ELECTRONIC SYSTEMS

FIGURE 23.1 Notice the amount of merchandise data contained in this report and how it highlights the status of the important control areas of each merchandise category. For example, why is the current gross margin of the women's, misses, and junior pants so low when compared to its to-date percentage?
Courtesy Retail Electronic Systems, Staten Island, New York.

SEASON MERCHANDISING PLAN REPORT

CLIENT 2345   STORE 01   CLASS/GROUP 603 MENS SLACKS   PERIOD ENDING OCTOBER 31, 19

HISTORICAL INFORMATION

MONTH	B.O.M. STOCK	SALES MONTH	SALES STOCK SALES RATIO	SALES SEASON	MARKDOWNS MONTH	MARKDOWNS %	MARKDOWNS SEASON	MARKDOWNS %	RECEIPTS	E.O.M. STOCK
FEB	8000	1000	80	1000	25	25	25	215	1925	8900
MAR	8900	1250	72	2250	75	6.0	100	44	1825	9400
APR	9400	1050	89	3300	375	114	475	144	2225	10200
MAY	10200	1375	87	4675	310	227	785	167	1385	9900
JUN	9900	2800	35	7475	415	70	1200	161	1715	8400
JUL	8400	2100	40	9575	210	216	1410	148	1810	7900

POSITION / PLAN

E.O.M. STOCK	MONTH	B.O.M. STOCK	SALES MONTH	SALES STOCK SALES RATIO	MARKDOWNS MONTH	MARKDOWNS %	PLAN ON ORDER	PLAN ADJUSTMENTS	PLAN OPEN TO BUY	PLAN E.O.M. STOCK
8900	FEB	7200	1200	8.3	100	8.3				
9400	MAR	8100	1450	8.6	135	8.6				
10200	APR	8800	1300	6.2	210	16.2				
9900	MAY	9100	1525	5.4	85	5.4				
8400	JUN	9000	3300	5.8	190	5.8				
7900	JUL	7500	2175	10.6	220	106				
	TOT.		11600	8.5	940	8.5				

PREPARED BY: RETAIL ELECTRONIC SYSTEMS, INC.

FIGURE 23.2 Notice that this plan was made four months before it became operative and that the merchandiser used the historical information to guide him in working it out. At first glance, it seems very optimistic because the BOM stocks are consistently lower than the historical trend while the monthly sales projections are considerably higher.

Courtesy Retail Electronic Systems, Staten Island, New York.

SEASON MERCHANDISING PLAN REPORT

CLIENT 2345 STORE 01 CLASS/GROUP 603 MENS SLACKS PERIOD ENDING FEBRUARY 28, 19

HISTORICAL INFORMATION

MONTH	B.O.M. STOCK	SALES MONTH	SALES STOCK SALES RATIO	SALES SEASON	MARKDOWNS MONTH	%	MARKDOWNS SEASON	%	RE-CEIPTS	E.O.M. STOCK
FEB PLN	7200	1200	60	1200	100	83	100	83	2200	8100
FEB ACT	7600	1050	72	1050	25	24	25	24	2200	8725
FEB VAR	-400	-150		-150	-75		-75			-625

POSITION / PLAN

MONTH	B.O.M. STOCK	SALES MONTH	SALES STOCK SALES RATIO	MARKDOWNS MONTH	%	ON ORDER	ADJUST-MENTS	OPEN TO BUY	E.O.M. STOCK
MAR	8100	1450	55	125	87	300	625	1350	8800
APR	8800	1300	67	210	162	100		1710	9100
MAY	9100	1575	57	85	54	200		1360	9000
JUN	9000	3300	27	190	58	250		1740	7500
JUL	7500	2175	35	230	106	210		1695	7000

PREPARED BY: RETAIL ELECTRONIC SYSTEMS, INC.

FIGURE 23.3 and **23.4** These figures illustrate what happens when an original plan proves too optimistic. Notice that the merchandiser has only revised his original planned figures to June. Obviously, he wants to wait until he obtains his actual April figures before revising his original July plan and he may wait until the actual May information reaches him be- fore deciding what to do about August. Nevertheless, when the May data arrive, he should be able to plan his opening inventory (BOM stock) for September and so make up his initial fall and winter season plan.

Courtesy Retail Electronic Systems, Staten Island, New York.

SEASON MERCHANDISING PLAN REPORT

HISTORICAL INFORMATION

MONTH	B.O.M. STOCK	SALES MONTH	SALES STOCK SALES RATIO	SALES SEASON	MARKDOWNS MONTH	%	MARKDOWNS SEASON	%	RE-CEIPTS	E.O.M. STOCK
MAR PLN	8100	1450	61	2650	125	116	225	84	2275	8800
MAR ACT	8725	1375	64	2475	60	43	85	34	1635	8925
MAR VAR	-625	-75		-225	-65		-140		-640	125

POSITION / PLAN

MONTH	B.O.M. STOCK	SALES MONTH	SALES STOCK SALES RATIO	MARKDOWNS MONTH	%	ON ORDER	ADJUST-MENTS	OPEN TO BUY	E.O.M. STOCK
APR	8800	1200 / 1300	67	210	162	210	125	1475	9100
MAY	8900 / 9100	1450 / 1575	57	135 / 85	54	300		1260	9000
JUN	8735 / 9000	3035 / 3300	27	190	58	300		1690	7500
JUL	7500	2175	35	230	106	250		1655	7000
AUG	7000	2000	35	100	50			3100	8000

PREPARED BY: RETAIL ELECTRONIC SYSTEMS, INC.

FIGURE 23.4

SALES ANALYSIS REPORT #1A

CLIENT NO. 001234   STORE NO. 001   PERIOD ENDING 07/31/   PAGE 01

	CODE	DESCRIPTION	GROSS SALES AMOUNT	**** SALES RETURNS **** AMOUNT	% OF GROSS SALES	************* NET SALES ************* UNITS	AMOUNT	AVERAGE AMOUNT OF SALE	% TO GROUP
CURRENT	341	SHIRT L/S WHITE	585.20	35.20	6.0	110	550.00	5.00	33.8
TO-DATE			2,587.20	137.20	5.3	500	2,450.00	4.90	38.2
CURRENT	345	SHIRT L/S FANCY-COLOR	1,001.70	101.70	10.2	180	900.00	5.00	55.3
TO-DATE			3,339.00	189.00	5.7	630	3,150.00	5.00	49.1
CURRENT	349	SHIRT S/S WHITE	122.36	7.36	6.0	19	115.00	6.05	7.1
TO-DATE			608.93	33.93	5.6	95	575.00	6.05	9.0
CURRENT	351	SHIRT S/S FANCY-COLOR	67.33	7.33	10.9	10	60.30	6.00	3.7
TO-DATE			253.92	13.92	5.5	40	240.30	6.00	3.7
CURRENT		TOTAL DRESS SHIRTS	1,776.59	151.59	8.5	319	1,625.30	5.09	74.0
TO-DATE			6,789.05	374.05	5.5	1,265	6,415.00	5.07	77.9
CURRENT	361	SPT SHRT L/S KNIT	151.20	11.20	7.4	20	140.00	7.00	24.6
TO-DATE			746.90	46.90	6.3	100	700.00	7.00	38.6
CURRENT	363	SPT SHRT S/S KNIT	37.17	2.17	5.8	5	35.00	7.00	6.1
TO-DATE			148.54	8.54	5.7	20	140.00	7.00	7.7
CURRENT	365	SPT SHRT YR L/S WOVEN	127.56	7.56	5.9	20	120.00	6.00	21.1
TO-DATE			318.00	18.00	5.7	50	300.00	6.00	16.5
CURRENT	367	SPT SHRT WW L/S WOVEN	159.90	9.90	6.2	25	150.00	6.00	26.3
TO-DATE			594.72	34.72	5.8	94	560.00	5.96	30.9
CURRENT	369	SPT SHRT YR S/S WOVEN	106.10	6.10	5.7	20	100.00	5.00	17.5
TO-DATE			106.10	6.10	5.7	20	100.00	5.00	5.5
CURRENT	371	SPT SHRT SW S/S WOVEN	26.63	1.63	6.1	5	25.00	5.00	4.4
TO-DATE			15.93	.93	5.8	3	15.00	5.00	.8
CURRENT		TOTAL SPORT SHIRTS	608.56	38.56	6.3	95	570.00	6.00	26.0
TO-DATE			1,930.19	115.19	6.0	287	1,815.00	6.32	22.1
CURRENT		TOTAL SHIRT DEPARTMENT	2,385.15	190.15	8.0	414	2,195.00	5.30	100.0
TO-DATE			8,719.24	489.24	5.6	1,552	8,230.00	5.30	100.0

FIGURE 23.5 Notice how the sales analysis report (the top portion of this figure) highlights the importance of Code 345 L–S fancy-col. shirts and the comparative weakness of the sport shirts category. The report also alerts the buyer that the summer season is over because the L–S dress shirts are really beginning to move. Since the season is just begin-ning, one of the problems the merchandiser should immediately try to solve is the large percentage of returns of colored dress shirts. If he finds the answer early enough, it will mean better sales, turnover, etc., and more important, fewer dissatisfied customers.
Courtesy Retail Electronic Systems, Staten Island, New York.

SALESCLERK ANALYSIS REPORT #1A

CLIENT NO. 001234   STORE NO. 001   PERIOD ENDING 07/31/   PAGE 02

	CODE	DESCRIPTION	RATE	GROSS SALES AMOUNT	****SALES RETURNS**** AMOUNT	% OF GROSS SALES	****NET SALES**** UNITS	AMOUNT	NET COMMISSION
CURRENT	13	L. SIMPSON	1.5	760.00	60.00	7.9	60	700.00	10.50
TO-DATE				3,187.70	175.70	5.5	210	3,012.00	37.16
CURRENT	17	R. BUTLER	2.0	1,144.80	84.80	7.4	80	1,060.00	21.20
TO-DATE				4,377.50	247.50	5.7	316	4,130.00	70.40
CURRENT	20	H. STONE	1.0	480.35	45.35	9.4	30	435.10	4.35
TO-DATE				1,154.04	66.04	5.7	105	1,088.00	10.88
CURRENT		TOTAL CLERKS		2,385.15	190.15	8.0	170	2,195.00	36.05
TO-DATE				8,719.24	489.24	5.6	631	8,230.00	118.44

FIGURE 23.6 This figure warns the personnel department to investigate H. Stone. If he were on vacation during part of July, his poor sales figure could be understood, but why are his returns so high for the month? Moreover, the to-date figures show that he is by far the poorest of the three salesmen. Perhaps he should be replaced.
Courtesy Retail Electronic Systems, Staten Island, New York.

six-month plans, and give merchandisers whatever other data they require before they decide on a policy plan or objective. This kind of game planning was almost impossible before EDP because most merchandisers were too impatient to wait for answers that had to be produced by slow, cumbersome, and often inaccurate manual or calculating machine processes. With EDP, the answers are almost instantaneous.

Although merchandisers have become most appreciative of the help they can receive from EDP, retailers first used it as an office tool because it could be easily programmed to maintain the general ledger and handle all payroll and accounts payable routines. It could also turn out profit and loss, balance sheet, and other informative statements at whatever management levels and intervals executives desired, as well as to produce such important control procedures as budget planning, sales forecasting, etc.

Moreover, EDP is invaluable in stores that have a large credit volume because with its memory capabilities and speed, it can authorize charge transactions almost instantly. It is also able to give the credit manager an age report on every credit customer and also run off lists of delinquent, slow pay, and inactive accounts.

The ability of EDP to segregate credit customers became a very valuable promotional tool, for now promotions could be geared to special segments of credit customers as well as to a general list. Merchandisers then used EDP to obtain information on what credit customers were buying and not buying in the store. In this way they could discover their merchandise strengths and weaknesses. Because EDP was also able to develop customer profiles, i.e., the age, sex, marital status, income, etc., of the store's credit users, they could make decisions on these customers' probable response to a new item, merchandise category, price range, etc.

Two of the main advantages of installing most EDP systems are their *modularity* (increased capacity and services can be added with comparative ease) and *compatibility* (advance systems can be substituted with a minimum of disruption). Both these advantages give EDP a very long life.

EDP Can Be a Disaster

Although EDP is a system for all functions, its adoption in your store could be a disaster. Its complexity and the sophistication of its performance can easily confuse you and result in your making a succession of errors. For example, for maximum efficiency, the capabilities of each piece of equipment should be able to integrate its functions with the operations of the other units. Yet, it is very easy for you to decide on a cash register that is much too advanced for the data you have to give it. This is also true of the number, the time intervals, and the kind of reports you require from the system.

There is also the danger that you might underestimate your requirements and so be unable to receive the service you expect from the system or overestimate them and receive a lot of useless but very expensive information. Or your choice of a service bureau might result in a series of unnecessary problems.

What about the human factor? Will your office staff be comfortable working with the system and will your executives use it to increase their decision-making capabilities? In some instances, office employees will try to sabotage your systems because they are unable to understand their relationship to them or they believe that they will supplant them. Buyers may have no faith in EDP reports and thus disregard them or may discourage their use because they think that EDP can perform so many of their buying functions that it will cause them to lose their jobs.

There is also the possibility that you have an inflated understanding of EDPs capabilities. For example, you may believe that it is a panacea for every problem, so when a difficult situation arises, all that you have to do is to ask it for the best solution. Yet, EDP can never replace human judgment or decison-making processes; it can only use the data it receives from human beings (input) and use it according to instructions given to it by a human being (programmer). If the input is inadequate or if it is poorly programmed, or both, it will produce erroneous and perhaps dangerous information.

Another disadvantage of installing an EDP system is the difficulty you will have in making it operate properly. Even though most EDP manufacturers and EDP service firms have developed systems packages, the ones they select to suit your particular needs will still have to undergo a certain amount of alteration and testing. Then its faults (bugs) must be worked out (debugged). Both operations take time and add to office staff, pressure and cost. To these inconveniences you must add the burdens of employee training and executive education.

Finally, even though most or all of the equipment can be rented and charged against current expenses, the systems' initial and maintenance costs will likely be higher than that of a tabulating system.

Because the decision on whether the advantages of EDP outweigh its disadvantages is up to you, a good way of arriving at a conclusion is to write out in consultation with your accountant and your staff *exactly* what you and they want from a computer system. These needs should be placed under such headings as the following: (a) What controls and reports do we require? (b) Why do we need them? (c) How fast must they be received? (d) How often are they needed? (e) What decisions can be made from them? These headings should then be broken down into their component parts. For example, "what reports do we require?" may contain balance sheets, profit and loss statements, six-month plans, expense budgets, open-to-buy, the movement of SKUs, etc. "Why do we need them?" may question the necessity of a hardware buyer's knowing the rate of sale of green garden hose by size, length, and price.

Then, against each subhead, rate the capabilities of a tabulating and an EDP system. In this way, your decision whether to include a tabulating system becomes almost automatic. If it remains, its probable useful life should be considered, and if this is long enough to be acceptable, the cost of both systems should then be studied. Finally, you and your accountant should discuss the organizational changes required under the system you wish to adopt.

As a result of your deliberations, if you decide to install a tabulating system, remember that business growth will eventually force you to adopt EDP. Therefore, you should maintain your contacts and research in the EDP market. This will not only reduce the time and energy required when you decide that an EDP system must be installed, but your continued association with the dynamics of the market will also make the judgment of your needs much more reliable.

WHAT THIS CHAPTER TOLD YOU

1. The number of transactions the business does and the speed at which you require control and decision-making information dictates the record-keeping equipment you require.

2. You should move into more advanced techniques and/or equipment *before* the old systems become too slow to help you control all the aspects of your business.

3. The usual evolution is from manual systems to mechanical systems to automatic systems.

4. Automatic systems can be built around either tabulating or electronic data processing equipment.

5. The advantages and disadvantages of automatic and EDP systems should be carefully studied before you decide which one would be best for your store.

6. Since this research takes a great deal of time, you should begin shopping the bookkeeping systems market well in advance of the time you expect to install the new systems.

7. Because each new bookkeeping system installation is very expensive and requires a great deal of retraining of your staff, you should make very certain that the method and equipment you adopt will have a long enough life to make the capital outlay and staff re-education pay off.

8. Keep in constant contact with your accountant. Although his advice should be carefully considered, remember that only you can make the decision on which system the store should install.

24

How to
Control Your Merchandise
and Operating Expenses

WHAT THIS CHAPTER IS ABOUT

Newspapers are full of stories of large-scale disasters, but they rarely report the kind of small-scale tragedy that a business failure can create. That is why we never learn about the numbers of retailers who get into trouble because they have had no merchandise controls or the retailers who are forced into bankruptcy because they could not control their expenses. No one knows how much more income tax retailers pay than they are required to by law because they do not keep good records. This chapter discusses some of the necessary steps that every merchant should take to control the money he invests in inventory as well as the amount he spends to dispose of these goods.

Retail Inventory Method

A merchant who has expanded his business to the point where he can no longer supervise the movement of his merchandise personally must think about running it by other means than instinctive decisions. To continue to grow, the retailer must be able to plan, control, and expand his merchandising operations in an organized manner. To do this, he needs a system that will inform him how his inventory is doing at any given moment. For the majority of progressive merchants, the retail inventory method provides the base from which stems much of their merchandise planning and control.

Merchandise control begins with the retail inventory method

Although taking the physical inventory of every item in the store at the lower of cost or market value is the most reliable way to value stock, in practice, it has many faults. It is very time-consuming, clumsy to operate, and, because it is entirely subjective, tends to create a great number of errors. Moreover, as retailing became more dynamic and competitive, merchants wanted to know their stock position at the end of each day, and the cost method proved very inadequate for this purpose.

At the same time, because merchandise is turned back into cash only when it is sold, not when it is purchased, these retailers began to understand the importance of thinking about an item at its selling price, not at its cost. They also realized that a customer is not concerned that an item cost the retailer $100. If $89.50 is what the customer wants to pay for it, that is all the retailer can sell it for and therefore that is all it is worth at retail.

The need for fast but controlled merchandise decisions and the development of a more sophisticated way of thinking about inventory eventually led to the creation of the retail inventory method, by which a merchant can tell *at any time* the *approximate* value of the goods in his store at retail and the lower of its cost or market value. This system requires that the merchant keep a running total of the merchandise in his store at both cost and retail. At any time, then, by simply subtracting the cost of the goods from their current retail (which might differ from the original price because of price changes), he can find his dollar markup and his markup percent on retail.

If, for example, the average markup of an inventory is 40 percent of retail, then the current cost or market value of this merchandise is 100 percent minus 40 percent, or 60 percent. If the current retail of the merchandise is $30,000, then the lower of its cost or market value is $30,000 × .60, or $18,000. This cost or market value, of course, may differ from the original cost of the goods because they may have depreciated or appreciated in value since they were bought. Following are the figures in statement form:

	Cost	Retail	Markup ($)	Markup (%)
Beginning inventory	$15,000	$ 23,000		
Purchases	60,000	102,000		
Total merchandise handled	75,000	125,000	$50,000	40
Complement of markup percentage				60
Retail inventory at end of period		30,000		100
Cost of inventory at end of period ($30,000 × .60)	18,000			

The retail method is the quickest system yet devised to give a merchant up-to-the-minute inventory values that also automatically include transpor-

| DATE | BEGINNING INVENTORY AND ADDITIONS | | | | | | | | | NET SALES | MARK DOWNS | |
| | PURCHASES | | | FREIGHT AND EXPRESS | ADDITIONAL MARK UP | ACCUMULATED | | | | | | |
	COST	RETAIL	%			COST	RETAIL	%			AMOUNT	%
Opening	13,568	21,814	37.8			13,568	21,814	37.8				
Feb.	4,589	7,646	40.0	36	29	4,625	7,675	39.7	3,938		554	14.1
To date	18,157	29,460	38.4	36	29	18,193	29,489	38.3	3,938		554	14.1
Mar.	3,993	6,649	39.9	50	11	4,043	6,660	39.3	5,685		84	1.5
To date	22,150	36,109	38.7	86	40	22,236	36,149	38.5	9,623		638	6.6
Apr.	7,562	12,659	40.3	41	149	7,603	12,808	40.6	4,964		895	18.0
To date	29,712	48,768	39.1	127	189	29,839	48,957	39.1	14,587		1,533	10.5
May	4,596	7,714	40.4	55	26	4,651	7,740	39.9	6,531		66	7.6
To date	34,308	56,482	39.3	182	215	34,490	56,697	39.2	21,118		1,599	2.4

FIGURE 24.1 Departmental inventory ledger. The departmental inventory ledger is one of the most important controls that the retail method develops. It is to merchandise control what the dashboard is to your car. By watching these figures month by month and comparing them to planned operations, a retailer should be able to correct weaknesses before they become serious, and he should be able to make strong areas even stronger.

tation charges and it is the only system that continuously values goods at cost or market, whichever is lower. Using the information that the retail method gives him, a merchant can draw up monthly balance sheets and profit and loss statements for both the store and its departments and so plan and control not only merchandise but all store operations as well (Fig. 24.1).

Physical inventory must still be taken at least once a year, but the retail inventory method makes this a very simple procedure. Since there is no need to estimate the cost or market value of each item, all that has to be listed are the retail prices on the tickets. At that time, if a significant difference occurs between the book and the physical inventories, the implication is that a

| DEDUCTIONS | | | | INVENTORIES | | | | COST OF SALES | | GROSS PROFIT | | TURN-OVER |
| EMP. DISC., ETC. | | SHRINKAGE | TOTAL | COST | RETAIL | BY | AVERAGE STOCK AT RETAIL | COST OF MERCHANDISE SOLD | WORK-ROOM COSTS-NET | AMOUNT | % TO SALES | |
AMOUNT	%											
				13,568	21,814	1						
55	1.4	39	4,586									
55	1.4	39	4,586	15,365	24,903	2	23,358	2,828		1,110	28.2	0.17
99	1.7	57	5,925							2,044	35.9	
154	1.6	96	10,511	15,767	25,638	3	24,118	6,469		3,154	32.8	0.40
113	2.3	50	6,022							1,340	27.0	
267	1.8	146	16,533	19,746	32,424	4	26,195	10,093		4,494	30.8	0.56
140	2.1	65	6,802							2,418	37.0	
407	1.9	211	23,335	20,284	33,362	5	27,628	14,206		6,912	32.7	0.76

stock shortage has occurred, and immediate steps should be taken to discover how it happened.

The retail method also enables the retailer to reduce his merchandise insurance because he need pay only on the goods he has in the store at the beginning of every month. In case of fire or any other accident, the retail method establishes the amount of the loss without delay. Thus, the time involved in receiving a settlement is shortened.

Disadvantages of the retail inventory method

The retail inventory method requires more bookkeeping and more work for buyers and clerical staff. Initial retail prices must be marked on each invoice and thereafter all price changes (up, down, or canceled) must be accurately recorded (Fig. 24.2). Therefore, if it is not constantly supervised, it will give out wrong and possibly dangerous inventory value. Also, the store must be very carefully departmentalized and this too entails more work for everybody.

Moreover, this method can be dishonestly manipulated. Fictitious retail pricing will overvalue inventory cost, fictitious markdowns will undervalue

CHANGE IN RETAIL PRICE   09801

REASONS FOR MARK DOWN			
1	Competition	5	Net Wholesale
2	Clear Outs	6	Damaged Mdse.
3	Advertised Sale	7	Price Line Change
4	Prestige Merchandise	8	Special Purchase

IMPORTANT
← A REASON MUST BE GIVEN FOR EVERY MARK-DOWN

MARK DOWN		MARK UP	
MARK DOWN CANCELLATION		MARK-UP CANCELLATION	

Store_____ Dept _____

Date_____ 19___

MERCHANDISE	CLASS	UNITS	OLD PRICE	NEW PRICE	PRICE CHANGE	AMOUNT OF CHANGE	
							TOTAL

Buyer_____ Countersigned_____ MARKING ROOM

FIGURE 24.2 Notice that this price change report is serially numbered and the reason for any price change must be noted by the person making it.

Courtesy Worth's, Waterbury, Conn.

it, and deferred or too heavy markdowns at strategic times will either over-value or undervalue the goods.

Further, it cannot be used in certain retail businesses, such as made-to-measure clothes or custom-made drapes, where labor is a large part of the cost of the goods. Again, when the retail inventory method is introduced, the taxable profit can be high. In this instance, however, tax departments are normally very cooperative and a reasonable settlement can usually be negotiated.

Conclusion

The retail method is best for stores that carry staple and fashion merchandise, for stores whose stock undergoes quick obsolescence, or for stores in which stock shortages are a problem. If your operation permits its use and you are ambitious to grow, the retail inventory method should be installed as soon as possible. Although you can plan and control merchandise by reducing monthly sales and inventories to their estimated *cost,* this method is not recommended because both estimates can be so far out of line that they are dangerous.

The retail inventory method will cost you money to install and its upkeep is more expensive than the cost system. But once it is understood and used properly, it will pay large dividends, not only in money but also in the assurance that comes when you have an exact knowledge of how the merchandise in your store is moving. Such information permits you to plan and control all your operations with a confidence that usually results in big profits.

Shoplifting and Employee Dishonesty

Theft by customers and employees can become a major and very expensive problem for most stores. Although it can never be eliminated, it can be reduced if the techniques outlined in Chapters 6 and 19 are carefully followed. In addition to these methods, you can install a burglar alarm system, employ security guards, or hire an agency that specializes in detecting customer and employee dishonesty. Although these precautions may be expensive, if you are in a district where pilferage is commonplace, they will be far cheaper than what you will lose in merchandise or cash.

One of the best ways to discourage customer and employee stealing is to adopt a strict policy of prosecuting everyone who is apprehended. This policy should be advertised by having signs placed in strategic places, for example, in fitting rooms and washrooms throughout the store. Court action takes time, money, and a certain amount of unpleasantness, but once your reputation as a retailer who prosecutes dishonest people becomes known, it will discourage stealing and the number of incidents can drop dramatically.

You can further reduce customer shoplifting by covering the selling areas of your store with sufficient staff at all times. Since most stores hire too few floor personnel, when shopper traffic is high these employees are too busy waiting on customers or completing sales to watch shoppers who are just as busy stealing merchandise.

A good practice is to hire help whose only responsibility at busy times is to watch shoppers. These employees should be trained to politely answer questions put to them by shoppers and to resist being persuaded to wait on one customer so that his or her partner can steal merchandise. They should also be instructed how to recognize potential shoplifters (Fig. 24.3) and the various methods they employ to pilfer goods. Finally, they should be carefully instructed on when and how to apprehend a shoplifter, for unless this is performed correctly and legally, you can be subject to an expensive damage suit. *All* your staff, not just the security personnel, should be instructed in customer shoplifting practices and detection, as well as how to apprehend shoplifters, but it should be strongly stressed that it is better for the staff to alert the security personnel to take action rather than to perform it themselves.

Although a great deal of publicity is given to customer stealing, most surveys indicate that the largest percentage of pilferage is performed by

LOSS PREVENTION CHECK LIST

I. Customer Prevention check list

Identify the shoplifter:
> A shoplifter can be young, old, rich, poor, male, female, black, or white and wearing anything. General characteristics that identify shoplifters:

1. Shoplifters use their hands to steal. If you are suspicious of someone, watch his/her hands.
2. Shoplifters are constantly looking to see who is watching them so they have a tendency to look quickly from side to side. Watch their heads for quick movements.
3. In attempting to conceal merchandise on their person, shoplifters often exhibit quick, jerky movements of arms and body.
4. Some shoplifters use diversionary tactics like fainting while their accomplice grabs the merchandise.
5. The clumsy shoppers who drop items repeatedy on the floor may not be just clumsy; they may want you to arrest them so that they can sue you.
6. Shoplifters may make numerous trips to the same counter or area until they have an opportunity to steal.
7. A shoplifter who appears to be a hard-to-fit customer may be walking around with store clothes under his or her own clothing.

Specific actions of shoplifters:

1. They may use various activities to distract the clerk's attention.
2. A bulky look or unnatural walk.
3. Asking to see more articles than a salesperson can control.
4. Sending a clerk away for more merchandise.
5. Two or more people shuffling merchandise at the same display.
6. Carrying unpurchased merchandise around the store.
7. Placing bags on the floor next to clothing racks.
8. Large groups of teenagers roaming through the store.
9. Wearing out-of-season apparel.
10. Removing merchandise from the counter and then turning their back to the salesperson.
11. Prolonged lingering around counters without wanting assistance.
12. Asking for extra bags or boxes.
13. Women with large purses.
14. The "early bird" or last minute shopper who attempts to take advantage of laxness in security.

Ways to prevent customer shoplifting:

1. Exchange information among stores on security ideas and on shoplifters.
2. Use specially designed mirrors for employees to observe blocked or screened-in areas.
3. Keep expensive, high-loss items in a locked showcase.
4. Do not display expensive or high-loss items near entrances or exits.
5. Use dummy displays or dummy packages on counters.
6. Arrange small items so they must be unhooked from a stand to be removed.
7. Station employees in strategic locations to observe customers.
8. Establish these company rules on shoplifting and enforce them:
   a. Wait on all customers promptly. Shoplifters do not need or want the attention of clerks.
   b. Avoid turning your back on a customer.
   c. Never leave your section unattended.
   d. Be especially alert when groups of juveniles enter the store.
   e. Prevent children from loitering and handling merchandise.
   f. Closely observe people with baby carriages.
   g. Watch people with large handbags, shopping bags, umbrellas, and folded newspapers.
   h. Observe people wearing loose coats or dresses.
   i. Be alert to people who carry merchandise from one location to another.
   j. Don't allow merchandise to lie around on counters if it belongs somewhere else.
   k. Watch people wearing heavy coats in warm weather.

FIGURE 24.3 Some important loss prevention ideas adapted from the "Loss Prevention Check List" prepared by the Operations Division of the NRMA.

Reprinted by permission of the NRMA, New York.

General rules for all floor personnel:

DO'S
1. Be alert—keep your eyes open.
2. Watch customers—anticipate their actions.
3. Be attentive—be helpful—be courteous.
4. Watch for shoplifter characteristics.
5. Be a good merchandise housekeeper.
6. Call your manager if in doubt.

DON'TS
1. Do not accuse a person of being a thief.
2. Do not be diverted from your job.
3. Do not permit children to loiter unattended.
4. Do not discuss customers except in confidence.
5. Do not lose your head—keep calm.
6. Do not touch, accuse, threaten, or attempt to detain a shoplifter—call your manager.

Remember: alert and wide-awake salespeople, aware of what is going on around them, are the most effective possible deterrent to shoplifting. Prompt and attentive service not only discourages shoplifters but pleases regular customers and builds business for the store.

II. Employee Prevention check list

1. Are *all* employees' packages checked in and out?
2. Do *all* store people enter and leave from one entrance?
3. Are *all* sales to employees made by someone other than themselves?
4. Do *all* employees have lockers and are these inspected at invervals?
5. Are outside shoppers used to check *all* high shortage departments?
6. Are night watchmen and cleaning staff required to check in and out of the store?
7. Are *all* cases with valuable merchandise such as furs and jewelry provided with locks and inspected at intervals after store closing to make certain locks are used?
8. Are *all* fitting rooms inspected at intervals for items and/or unused hangers?
9. Are *all* perimeter and other stockrooms provided with locks and regularly checked?
10. Is the marking room provided with locks and any entry prohibited unless marking room manager is present?
11. Are *all* delivery bins inspected at intervals with check-ups on whether routed packages have been recorded?
12. Are *all* cash register users each provided with own money bag and contents regularly checked?
13. Are *all* customers receiving cash refunds written to verify their receipt of the money?
14. Is "Will Call" or "Layaway" handled in separate area and *all* files and packages regularly checked for accuracy and possible return to stock?
15. Are frequent checks made of *all* waste paper disposal areas to make sure containers are empty?
16. Are *all* cash register readings made daily and kept separate from employees turning in cash?
17. Are *all* cashiers' "overs and shorts" watched to discover any constant discrepancies?
18. Is there a proper routine for control in issuing *all* salesbooks, refund books, and the turning in of used books?
19. Are regular test checks made to discover unmarked merchandise in various departments?
20. Is *all* unticketed and unmarked merchandise required to be re-ticketed to insure selling at the proper price?
21. Are inventories, before and after selling, required on *all* merchandise that is sold at off-price for limited periods, so proper markdowns will be taken?
22. Is *all* merchandise to be displayed on counter tops or tables counted each morning and evening to check possible pilferage?
23. Are *all* top-of-the-counter quantities of concealable items kept small so some "eyeball" control can be kept of such items as jewelry, cosmetics, hosiery, handkerchiefs, and the like?
24. Are *all* sales personnel, departments heads, and assistants trained and constantly counselled on the need for nonstop watchfulness of exposed merchandise to curtail shoplifting?
25. Is there a clearly written, taught, and understood manual for *all* these policies and procedures?

employees. One way to reduce this percentage is to carefully check on every applicant's honesty record. However, this does not mean that you should categorically reject anyone who has a record of dishonesty. The age and circumstances that led the applicant to steal should be considered and if these now seem unimportant, they should be disregarded. Hiring someone with a record of dishonesty often leads to a very grateful and loyal employee who will repay you many times over for your decision to trust his ability to remain honest.

Expenses

How to plan expenses and profits

Most small retailers neglect to plan and control expenses. This results in whim-spending, i.e., giving advertising too much money or starving the office. If you plan your expenses by using inside and outside percentage figures based on net sales as well as gross margin percent as guides, you should do a much better job of controlling expenses. Remember that expenses must be paid for out of gross margin; if you have anything left, it becomes the profit you made on your operations. For example, if you make a gross margin of $30,000 and you pay out $25,000 in expenses, your operating profit is $5,000. Therefore, by planning and controlling your gross margin and expenses, you automatically plan and control your operating profit.

However, it might be easier for you to plan your operating profit and gross margin. In this case, the difference will be total operating expense, i.e., planned gross margin $30,000, planned profit $5,000; therefore, planned expenses are $25,000.

Still another way is to plan your expenses and profits and then add these two figures together to arrive at your planned gross margin, i.e., planned expenses of $25,000 plus planned profits of $5,000 equals planned gross margin of $30,000. To make any of these plans work, you must be realistic about every element in the plan. For example, if you plan $100,000 as net sales, with a planned gross margin of 30 percent and expenses of $25,000, and make your sales figure, a profit of $5,000 will be realized. But if you make only $50,000 net sales with a 30 percent margin and expenses of $25,000, you will end up with a $10,000 *loss*.

How to control expenses

Once your target expense figures are set for the coming year, break them down into two six-month periods as you did with the merchandise control plan (see Chapter 7). You are then able to control every expense week by week or month by month, by departments, and for the store as a whole. However, expenses have certain peculiarities that must be recognized before they can be planned and controlled properly.

Ways of looking at expenses

Certain expenses are *fixed,* for example, rent, taxes, etc., which are almost the same whether you make one or a thousand sales. Others, like salaries, wrapping, etc., are *variable,* that is, they increase or decrease according to the number of sales you make.

Another way of looking at expenses is to classify them as *uncontrollable,* like rent, or *controllable,* like salaries. It must be remembered, however, that even uncontrollable expenses should be examined and planned for because they can sometimes be reduced. For example, if rent is too high in one department, it can be reduced by making the department's area smaller. For department purposes, planned expenses can be divided into *direct,* e.g., salaries and advertising, and *indirect,* e.g., management salaries, office expenses, etc. Expenses can also be grouped into *natural divisions* like advertising, payroll, etc. (Fig. 24.4) or according to expense centers, that is, all expenses incurred in keeping the store clean or in selling goods, etc.

The best way for you to group expenses is the way they are grouped by the majority of stores in your trade. For example, if you are in the hardware business, you will want to compare your operation to the general hardware field, and so you should break down expenses according to the form shown in Fig. 24.5. Notice that all store expenses must be included in your profit and loss statements. If you are a single proprietor, you must "give" yourself a realistic salary, and if you own the property, a realistic rent. Again, if your wife and other members of the family act as employees, they should be given salaries that are equivalent to those you would pay for outside help doing the same work. In a partnership, the owners should "receive" salaries commensurate with their functions. All personal expenses like nonbusiness travel or repairs to your house should be eliminated from the profit and loss statement.

**Best way to
group expenses**

By developing a realistic profit and loss statement, you will be able to judge how profitable your business is. It will enable you to make more reliable comparisons between your operation and outside ones, and it will also highlight your strengths and weaknesses. You will then be able to know which areas to concentrate on to give you more profit and which require a new approach in order to build up their strength.

By making net sales equal 100 percent and then translating all dollar expenses into a percentage of sales, you can compare your store's operations with those of stores doing ten times as much or one-tenth as much as you do, and you can do so for several years back and thus develop trends. But remember that if your net sales or expense figures are fictitious, comparisons are worthless.

**Every expense
is a percentage
of net sales**

Divide the year into two six-month periods and enter last year's actual expenses in dollars and as a percentage of sales. By looking at past, present, and comparative dollar figures and percentages, estimate your planned future dollar expenses month by month. Total these and if they seem realistic, work them out as a percentage of planned sales. Now see whether or not the total planned dollar expenses closely approximate the difference between the planned gross margin and your planned profit. Do the same for

**How to set up
an expense
control budget**

```
┌─────────────────────────────────────────────────────────────────────┐
│                    NATURAL DIVISION OF EXPENSES                      │
│                                                                     │
│   01. Payroll                      13. Depreciation                 │
│   02. Allocated Fringe Benefits    14. Professional Services        │
│   03. Advertising Media Costs      16. Bad Debts                    │
│   04. Taxes                        17. Equipment Rentals            │
│   05. Supplies                     18. Outside Maintenance and      │
│   07. Services Purchased               Equipment Service Contracts  │
│   08. Unclassified                 20. Real Property Rentals        │
│   09. Travel                       90. Expense Transfers In         │
│   10. Communications               91. Expense Transfers Out        │
│   11. Pensions                     92. Outside Revenue as Other     │
│   12. Insurance                        Credits                      │
└─────────────────────────────────────────────────────────────────────┘
```

FIGURE 24.4   From the 1976 edition of the *Retail Accounting Manual,* published by the Financial Executive Division of the NRMA, New York.

While this breakdown is used by some independent retailers for internal controls as well as for internal and external comparisons, other independents accumulate natural expenses by a technique known as expense centers. This method permits them to determine and control certain expenses for a specific area of their store's operations. But in order to compare any expense or expense center properly, make sure it includes only what it *should* include. For example:

Payroll should include salaries, wages, commissions, bonuses, spiffs, prizes for sales contests, vacation pay, sick leave pay and all other such items. It should *not* include labor costs in alteration departments or service departments which belong in the cost of merchandise.

Services Purchased consists solely of charges made by outsiders, such as cleaning services, repair and maintenance done by other organizations, purchase of delivery service from an outside agency, etc.

Traveling includes transportation, hotel bills, taxi fares, meals, tips and incidentals spent by employees of the business when traveling for business purposes, providing they are reimbursed for them. It does not include local carfares or automobile hire, which should be charged to "Unclassified."

Insurance should be charged with the cost of all insurance, whether actually paid for or provided for through reserves. The cost of term insurance should be distributed evenly over the term for which protection is furnished.

Property Rentals includes only the cost of renting land, buildings, offices, warehouses, outside storage, garages, and display windows which are actually used in the operation of the business. Rental of living quarters definitely does not belong here, nor do taxes, maintenance, or insurance paid directly by the store on rented property.

INCOME STATEMENT DATA	All Hardware Stores	Low Profit Stores	High Profit Stores	Your Figures
NUMBER OF STORES	842	279	268	
NET SALES VOLUME	$288,638	$261,462	$260,542	$ . . . .
Current Year's Sales vs. Previous Year	+13.65%	+11.39%	+13.42%	. . . . %
Gross Sales	102.92%	102.59%	103.48%	. . . . %
Less: Total Deductions	2.92	2.59	3.48	. . . .
Net Sales	100.00	100.00	100.00	100.00
Cost of Goods Sold	67.16	69.72	64.67	. . . .
Margin	32.84	30.28	35.33	. . . .
PAYROLL AND OTHER EMPLOYEE EXPENSE				
Sararies—Owners, Officers, Managers	5.96	6.32	5.73	. . . .
Salaries—Sales Personnel	7.00	7.19	6.67	. . . .
Salaries—Office Help	1.52	1.67	1.29	. . . .
Salaries—Other Employees	2.36	2.74	2.00	. . . .
Federal and State Payroll Taxes	.86	1.06	.69	. . . .
Group Insurance	.20	.25	.14	. . . .
Benefit Plans	.36	.36	.23	. . . .
TOTAL PAYROLL AND OTHER EMPLOYEE EXPENSE	18.26	19.59	16.75	. . . .
OCCUPANCY EXPENSE				
Heat, Light, Power, Water	.75	.80	.73	. . . .
Repairs to Building	.26	.27	.24	. . . .
Rent or Ownership in Real Estate*	2.80	3.20	2.69	. . . .
TOTAL OCCUPANCY EXPENSE	3.82	4.27	3.66	. . . .
OTHER COSTS OF DOING BUSINESS				
Office Supplies and Postage	.53	.41	.36	. . . .
Advertising	1.58	1.69	1.49	. . . .
Donations	.06	.05	.06	. . . .
Telephone and Telegraph	.31	.34	.27	. . . .
Bad Debts	.30	.43	.19	. . . .
Delivery (Other than Wages)	.45	.55	.36	. . . .
Insurance (Other than Real Estate and Group)	.78	.84	.66	. . . .
Taxes (Other than Real Estate and Payroll)	.56	.54	.47	. . . .
Interest on Borrowed Money (Other than Mortgages)	.55	.80	.43	. . . .
Depreciation (Other than Real Estate)	.66	.61	.59	. . . .
Store and Shop Supplies	.35	.43	.31	. . . .
Legal and Accounting	.34	.40	.24	. . . .
Dues and Subscriptions	.09	.08	.08	. . . .
Travel, Buying, Entertainment	.19	.22	.17	. . . .
Unclassified	.62	.67	.58	. . . .
TOTAL OTHER COSTS OF DOING BUSINESS	7.37	8.06	6.16	. . . .
TOTAL OPERATING EXPENSE	29.45	31.92	26.57	. . . .
NET OPERATING PROFIT	3.39	(1.64)	8.76	. . . .
Cash Discounts and Other Income	1.31	1.10	1.48	. . . .
NET PROFIT (Before Federal Income Tax)	4.70	(.54)	10.24	. . . .

*Ownership in Real Estate includes Taxes, Insurance Depreciation on Land and Buildings and Interest on Mortgages.

FIGURE 24.5 By filling in the "your figures" column, a hardware merchant can tell how well or how poorly he has been operating compared to other retailers in the hardware business. Then, by using this information as a guide, he can plan his own profit and loss statements by years, six-month periods, months, weeks, and even days. Retailers in other kinds of business can use the same planning technique by asking their trade association for figures that relate to their trade.

Courtesy National Retail Hardware Association, Indianapolis, Ind.

whatever departments you wish to control by this method and see whether or not their sum agrees with the total store figures.

Next, review each expense (fixed and variable, controllable and uncontrollable) and see where it can be reduced. If necessary, break each one down further. For example, supplies can be examined by looking at the amount of paper, boxes, twine, office stationery, etc., you have bought. Then see whether or not cutting out certain sizes of bags or boxes will permit you to buy larger quantities of the ones you want to keep so that you will qualify for additional discounts or find out whether or not group buying will reduce these costs. Again, is it necessary to use all those office forms and is there an easier or in the long run a cheaper way to keep records?

Every expense should be judged by its productivity for the store. If in one month a department has 3,000 sales transactions and its selling salaries are $1,500, then each transaction costs 50¢ in selling salaries alone. If you divide your entire payroll by all the transactions the store has made, i.e., cash and credit sales, returns and allowances, you can discover what each transaction really costs in salaries. If any of these unit costs are too high, examine them even more closely to see where they can be reduced. For example, customer returns and allowances may be way out of line. This could be a result of poor selling because your salespeople are untrained or too lazy to make certain that every piece of merchandise leaving the store is in first-class condition or that the purchase is really what the customer wants.

How to judge expense productivity

Also, ask yourself if each expense is really necessary and if you should spend so much on it. Some expenses can be cut if you plan for their peaks and valleys. This is particularly useful in reducing costs required to handle the store at its busiest and slowest times. If you can plot the hours, days, weeks, and months when you do the largest and the smallest volume and then plan how much sales staff, office personnel, wrappers, etc., are required to give customers sufficient service, you can hold your personnel costs to a minimum. Any savings that you can make without harming sales or your store personality will either permit you to give customers better prices or reward you with a higher operating profit.

Once the season begins, watch your open-to-spend control as carefully as you do your merchandise open-to-buy. If you are forced to make a large unplanned expenditure, see if you can postpone or sacrifice enough planned ones to cover the contingency. If this is impossible, you must revise your budget and your profit accordingly. However, if you increase either your sales volume or your gross margin, you can afford to increase your expenses and end up with the same planned profit.

How to control expenses

Your accountant's advice should be sought and carefully considered, particularly if he takes the long view and suggests changing the form of your organization. There may be many tax advantages to be gained by going

Best form of organization

from an individual proprietorship to a partnership or a corporation and he should be able to show you what these are. Of course, there are disadvantages in every organizational form and the tax savings may not be worth the extra clerical work or the personal aggravations that a change might entail (see Chapter 21).

If your accountant has sufficient retail experience, he should be most helpful in advising you when to end your fiscal year, which does not have to coincide with the calendar year. Most retailers end their year on January 31st, but it may be better for you to end yours on July 31st or May 31st. Because it is not good practice to change the year end too often, be sure that the advantages of any change outweigh the disadvantages for some time to come.

Fiscal year

Government officials look differently at agreements which you make with your family (short arm's length) and those you make with strangers (arm's length). They scrutinize family arrangements very carefully, but they are less suspicious of contracts entered into with persons who are not related to you by blood, marriage, or adoption. You should therefore be very careful to find out the probable governmental attitudes toward business arrangements that involve your immediate family. For example, how will the government regard the terms of a lease between your wife and yourself, or what will their opinion be on the loan agreement between your wife and your business?

Family and nonfamily arrangements

If your wife and any of your children work in the store as legitimate employees and you report their salaries to the income tax people, their wages should be charged as a business expense. The revenue people will then decide on their validity. However, if their salaries are lower or higher than the going wage for the kind of work they do, more realistic figures should be incorporated into the profit and loss statements you use for comparative purposes.

Employment of wife and children

Make sure that you charge every possible business expense against your gross margin figure. For example, if you can establish that you use your car for both personal and business reasons, get a ruling on the percentage of this expense that will be allowed for business purposes. Then keep all your gas, repair, parking, and washing bills, etc. To these, add the allowable depreciation and then take the agreed upon percentage of this figure as a business expense.

Personal and business expenses

Traveling, entertainment, and other expenses can be treated in the same way. The income tax people will accept most reasonable claims, and every cent that you can legitimately charge against the business reduces your net profit and consequently your income tax.

Because it is possible to make considerable savings by knowing how to build up reserves, not only for fixtures but also for inventory and bad debts, discuss your inventory procedures and how to treat your outstanding

Make sure of your reserves

accounts receivable and accounts payable with your accountant. If the tax people agree to your methods, they expect you to keep using them from year to year. Therefore, if you want to make changes, you must convince them that the reason for adopting a new procedure is to give you a better system of controls rather than to reduce your income tax.

Sometimes it pays to sell a piece of furniture or equipment for cash and then buy a new one, but at other times a trade-in or a lease agreement may be best. Here, again, your accountant's advice may save you money. He can also advise you on the best way to depreciate these assets, for there are several methods that can be used for this purpose. Your accountant should know which are permissible for each asset and which is best for your business.

Furniture, fixtures, and equipment

Sometimes an expense can be considered as belonging to the current or to the following year. Your accountant can be most helpful in calculating the results of both situations. But remember that your annual profit and loss statement and balance sheet are to be used for more than reporting your income tax and as an internal control technique. They will be carefully examined by your banker and by such credit sources as Dun & Bradstreet. Although you should try to avoid showing too large a profit, you should make the business look as healthy and progressive as possible.

Good years versus bad years

If you do not know about allowable expenses and permissible deductions, you can overstate your income and pay larger taxes than necessary. Federal, state, and local tax laws are constantly changing and usually you have neither the time to study them nor the experience to judge how the changes will affect your business. That is the job of your accountant; if he is competent and knows your business and its financial problems, he is worth retaining. Always remember, however, that he can only give advice. You must make the final decision yourself.

It is easy to overstate income

Insurance

All the work, effort, and money that you put into the store can be wiped out by a fire, lawsuit, flood, or theft. Yet, most small merchants never carry sufficient insurance to take care of these hazards. They are like soldiers in the firing line—they believe that the bullets are always meant for the other fellow, not for them. The only time merchants think about being sufficiently insured is after something does happen, and then it is too late. Most small merchants protect their families with life insurance, but they do not realize that a business is just as likely to have a fatal accident as its owner. In many cases, business insurance can be worth much more to a retailer's family than his life insurance, for without a business, the family's main source of income dies. So protect your business investment by remembering that it *can* happen to you, and when it does, you can be wiped out.

How to protect your store and your investments

Since it is very costly to buy coverage for every contingency, some gamble must be taken, but before deciding what this gamble should be, investigate various kinds of insurance and figure out their costs. Then see how much you can spend for insurance and still keep within your budget.

What insurance to get

You should always be fully insured against fire, water, and employee and general public liability. You should also carry insurance on such equipment as elevators, boilers, sprinklers, and automobiles, as well as some form of business interruption insurance. Then if your budget permits, take out life insurance with the business as beneficiary or set up an approved pension plan. In this way, you can protect your business and increase the value of your estate. If money is still available, cover the business against such contingencies as theft, burglary, loss of accounts receivable and, perhaps a blanket policy on goods in transit should be considered.

It is best to give all your insurance to one agent because in this way you become a good account and he will put himself out to give you service. Because there are a variety of ways to buy insurance and an experienced agent can help you decide which are best for your business at a particular time, before you decide on an agent, make sure that he is reliable and has a fairly large retail clientele. As you grow, it may be more beneficial to move from one form of insurance to another, so review your insurance set-up periodically. It is a good practice to occasionally permit a competing insurance agent to examine your policies and make suggestions that might save money. You buy insurance as you do merchandise and your business should be given to the agent who produces the most valuable policies for your needs.

How to insure

Get your agent to explain what each kind of insurance covers and, what is more important, what it *does not* cover. Ask for as many comprehensive policies as possible, for these cover a great many risks in one policy. Thus, you can obtain better protection with less cost because the insurance company's handling expenses are reduced when one policy takes the place of, say, five. Also pay particular attention to whether the insurance covers present replacement costs or original costs less depreciation. Take as many multiple-year policies as you can because they are issued at substantial discounts.

What to look for

When the broker has gone, spend a little time reading each policy yourself to see if what he said is correct. If you have any questions, telephone him and if his explanation does not satisfy you, consult your accountant or lawyer. It is your money and your risk. It will be too late *after* the accident to discover that you are not covered for a particular situation.

When an accident occurs, immediately notify your agent or the insurance company involved. They will tell you whether or not you have a claim and if you do what to do about it. They will also begin to move the claims machinery so that the time lapse between accident and payment is reduced to a minimum. However, be careful about signing statements. Read

What to do when you have a claim

and understand every document before you sign. If you are in doubt about what it says, take it to your lawyer. Once you sign your name to a document you are committed to whatever it says. If the document is in order, your lawyer's assurance that it is all right is well worth his fee. If it is not completely satisfactory, he will see the dangers you only dimly feel and will tell you what to do about them.

Ask your agent how to reduce insurance costs. He should not only give you as many comprehensive policies and multiple-year terms as possible, but he should also suggest that installing fire extinguishers, fire doors, or sprinkler systems or that better illumination in the store will lower premiums substantially and thus allow you to buy more insurance. The idea is not to spend less money on insurance. The idea is to buy more protection. For example, if you use the retail inventory method, you can report your inventory situation to your agent monthly and thus pay only for the merchandise you actually have in the store.

How to save on insurance premiums

You should also consider co-insurance because it gives more coverage than ordinary insurance for the same money. But co-insurance requires a high coverage, usually 80 percent; otherwise, in case of a loss you can suffer heavily. Have your agent explain the advantages and dangers of co-insurance until you clearly understand all its implications. Then decide if it or straight insurance is better for you. If you give your business to one agent and you want to take advantage of multiple-year premiums, comprehensive policies, and blanket insurance, ask him to stagger the policies so that the premiums do not fall due at one time or ask him how you can arrange to pay him in monthly installments and thus ease your cash outlay. In this way, you are able to plan and control your insurance, as you should every other aspect of your business.

Protect Your Estate

An important factor in making any major decision on the way your business should be operated should be its effect on your estate. For example, will a partnership or a corporate arrangement protect your estate better than operating as a single proprietor? Again, after consultation with your accountant and lawyer, you should periodically review and revise your will. The amount of your estate keeps changing and so do your responsibilities. Moreover, estate laws are constantly being rewritten and some of these revisions may take more of your hard earned wealth than necessary. They can also affect the disposition of your estate. While drafting your first will may take time and can be expensive, making further changes should be routine and therefore be minimal in cost and time.

1. For most stores, the retail inventory method provides the best basis for planning and controlling all store operations. It should be used by every merchant who can use it and who wants to continue to grow and be successful.

2. It will pay you to engage the services of an experienced retail accountant to advise you on the best way to organize your business for income tax purposes.

3. All your work in building up a business can be nullified if you are not properly insured.

4. Since most small merchants cannot carry insurance for every contingency, they must make choices.

5. Giving all your insurance to one agent should result in getting the most insurance for your dollar, but keep checking up on him to make sure that he is doing his best for you.

6. Protect your estate by consulting both your lawyer and accountant.

25

What It Takes To Be a Successful Retailer

WHAT THIS CHAPTER IS ABOUT

One of the saddest facts about retailing is the number of people in it who should be doing something else. Only when it is too late do these people realize that merchants must have more than capital to be successful. This chapter discusses some of the essential qualities retailers should possess, and it discusses how to overcome most of the deficiencies that prevent retailers from being more successful than they are at present.

False Ideas about Retailing

Because successful merchants advertise their success constantly and publicly, most people imagine that all retailers make money. For example, they believe that merchants make 50 percent on most of the merchandise they sell, and a 100 percent profit on items like furniture and jewelery is thought to be standard. Moreover, the general public thinks that retailing requires little experience, education, knowledge, or intelligence. Many people think that all a man needs to open a store is some money. If he is fortunate, he will make a good living; if he is less fortunate he will, at least, live comfortably. In the popular mind, then, retailing is purely a matter of luck and nothing else.

Therefore, parents buy stores for their problem children and hope for the best; people with money stake poorer relations to a business and think that it will solve their problems; and many people without a trade open a small grocery store believing that they will make a living or at least that they will always have food in the house. If one is lazy or does not like the work he is now doing, the obvious answer is to become a retailer. To all these people there seems no easier or more delightful way to earn a good living than to be your own boss, come and go as you please, and "work" by standing around talking to customers.

The Truth about Retailing

When this country was in its early stages of development, anyone with a little capital and some merchandise resources could make a living by running a shop, but this is no longer true. To be a successful retailer, even a small one, under present conditions takes more than money, resources, and a store. Today's successful merchant must have very well-defined qualifications, and the more successful he is to become, the more pronounced these qualifications must be.

A Liking for People

Retailing is a people business. Thus, human beings, not goods, are a merchant's real stock in trade, for no other business or profession deals with so constant a flow of people. The first qualification of a successful merchant, then, is a genuine liking for people. That is why successful merchants enjoy talking to everyone who comes into their stores. The proprietor who walks around his shop as though the people in it were non-existent not only has a staff that is dissatisfied but customers who will avoid his store as much as they can. Warm and enthusiastic salespeople attract shoppers to a store and reflect the owner who is sincerely interested in people.

If people bother you, sell your store and get into a business in which the human element is an unimportant factor.

A Liking for Your Customer Group

It is not enough to like people in general, you must have a particular fondness and empathy for the customer segment you seek to serve. This may be the working man, the white-collar class, an ethnic group, the very fat or thin, the very tall or short. Whichever it is, you must thoroughly understand the customer segment and its problems. You need not desire to associate yourself socially with your customers, but you must feel that by selling them merchandise bought especially for them you are helping to make their lives happier and pleasanter.

Your choice of customer segment and your desire to work with it can come in a number of different ways. For example, when F. W. Woolworth was ten years old, he went into the best store in his town to buy a birthday present for his mother. Though he had five pennies clutched in his hand, he was rudely chased out because he didn't belong socially and he was so obviously poor. This experience resulted in Woolworth's deep urge to provide low-income families with a store where they could buy "fancy" goods and be treated with respect. Eventually, he developed such advanced merchandising methods that he could carry luxury items like ribbons and lace at prices even the lowest wage earners could afford. More recently, another poor boy, Sol Polk of Chicago, remembered how hard his mother worked because she could not afford the mechanical aids that wealthier housewives used. He opened a small discount house in Chicago for low-income families and by aggressive promotions saw it grow into one of the largest discount houses in the United States.

J. C. Penney, the founder of one of the largest retail chains in the United States, had a great deal of customer empathy. When he was still in his first store in Kemmerer, Wyoming, he ordered a lot of dresses that were four to six inches longer in front than in the back. The style was unorthodox but practical, because he had noticed that the stomachs of a great number of the wives of miners and sheepherders, who were his chief customers, remained enlarged after pregnancy. The dresses proved very popular and continued to sell until foundation garments became a part of every woman's wardrobe.

Retail Imagination, Vision, and Initiative

These examples illustrate more than customer empathy. They demonstrate the rich imagination of true merchants who can accurately picture customer wants and who have the vision to improvise methods of merchandising them. But imagination and vision are futile unless retailers have the initiative to make their ideas work. This sometimes requires a great amount of optimism and persistence. F. W. Woolworth failed three times before he discovered that he must broaden his merchandise to include ten-cent items as well as five-cent items in his stock and that his stores must be located only in heavy traffic areas.

Merchandise Knowledge

Consumer protection

It seems hardly necessary to mention that retailers should know what the merchandise they handle consists of, what it is supposed to do, and how it actually performs. Yet, few merchants have sufficient merchandise knowledge. They believe the extravagant claims of their suppliers and only after the merchandise creates customer dissatisfaction do they become aware of its faults. A long list could be made of stores that sold apparel and curtains that burst into flames when exposed to the heat of a match, garments that would not hold a crease or wrinkled too easily, and furniture that fell apart under normal use. If retailers knew their merchandise, they would reject harmful and faulty items like these at once. In this way, they would build goodwill for their stores by fulfilling one of the main functions of a good merchant: to protect customers from shoddy merchandise. It would also add to their reputations as merchants who understand and agree with the basic concepts of consumer protection.

Merchandise knowledge leads to better products and/or lower prices. The merchant who knows his products and wants to keep his customers satisfied is constantly suggesting ideas to manufacturers that will make their goods more salable. A more efficient slide fastener, a sturdier seam, a more durable finish are some suggestions merchants have made which manufacturers have been happy to accept and implement. This necessary characteristic of a successful merchant reinforces his desire to cooperate with consumers and creates goodwill for him and his store.

Better products

Finally, merchandise knowledge is a must for customer selling. For example, a customer might think he needs toggle bolts, but if the retailer has merchandise knowledge he will tactfully ask what they are to be used for and then, if they are to be used in a situation in which resistance to vibration and stress is most important, he will suggest that the customer buy lock nuts instead.

Better customer selling

In addition to his knowledge of staple merchandise, a retailer must study new products as they come on the market. Consumers cannot possibly keep up with this kind of merchandise and so they expect the retailer to advise them on what is best for their particular needs. New man-made materials, for example, require careful study on the part of the merchant so that he can give his customers the best after-purchase satisfaction. This is particularly true in stores where salespeople have a duty to explain to every customer how certain items should be used and taken care of for longer use or wear. Salespeople should take for granted that customers will not read the merchandise information labels and therefore it is their duty to explain to every purchaser the information that the label contains. This customer service can be rendered only when the merchant himself knows about the merchandise he carries and then makes certain that his employees also have this knowledge.

The results of more thorough merchandise knowledge are reductions in returns, more satisfied customers, and more people coming into the store because they value the authoritative advice they are given. It also places the merchant in the forefront as a consumer-oriented retailer.

Overall Retail Experience

The longer you have been in business, the more experience you should have acquired to help you to recognize opportunities and avoid pitfalls. The greatest number of retail businesses fail during the first three years, and approximately 90 percent of these failures are caused by their owners' lack of experience in one retail function or another. For example, a very successful department store buyer decided to go into business for himself. He failed in 18 months, because his shop was poorly located for his customer segment and he attempted to use department store merchandising techniques without realizing that these had to be scaled down to small store standards.

This man might have become a successful independent if he had had the ability to learn plus sufficient capital to pay for his mistakes. But few people have this extra money. Therefore, it would have been wiser if he had worked in a small store long enough to gain an overall experience of how this kind of shop should be operated. With this knowledge combined with what he had learned as a department store buyer, his chances of success in running his own business would have considerably increased.

However, if you are already in the retail business or see a real opportunity to enter it, you can try to absorb more knowledge of retailing by initiating discussions with successful retailers in your field, studying books on retailing or asking the Small Business Administration, NRMA, or your trade association or trade publications for solutions to your problems.

Physical, Emotional, and Mental Stamina

Merchants in small businesses should not only be strong enough to move merchandise and fixtures in their stores, they should also have sufficient good health and stamina to stand on their feet for many hours at a time and still think about store problems instead of aching backs, painful arches, or high blood pressure.

Because they work under great mental and emotional pressure, retailers must be able to stand up under these pressures. Otherwise, they will be overcome by the enormous amount of detail and the number of decisions they must make day after day. The hardware merchant who denies that he carries a hose bracket which a customer bought from him only an hour earlier, or the proprietor who argues that all his fabrics are colorfast when an obviously faded dress is returned cannot operate a successful business for any length of time. Some retailers are so indecisive that they keep changing their minds and create a lack of confidence in their staff, suppliers, and customers; other retailers antagonize and embarrass their employees by scolding them publicly. These are only a few of the hundred and one manifestations that betray a retailer's mental and emotional imbalance and could destroy his business.

Most of these retailers could adjust very well to other jobs. They should sell out and seek employment in fields where they are not subjected to the long, hard, constant pressure that retailing entails.

Common Sense

Few leading merchants became famous because of their high intelligence, but all were credited with having an uncommon amount of common sense. The distinction is important because intellectual capacity alone is not enough in retailing. Intelligence must be coupled with common sense or the ability to grasp and organize facts quickly and then to make a series of sound and practical decisions. Common sense also includes the rarer characteristic of admitting mistakes early enough to use imagination and vision and so capitalize on them.

Whenever Marshall Field felt that the country was headed for a depression, he liquidated his stock for ready cash. This technique temporarily created a heavy operating loss, but it enabled him to use the money he obtained in this way to buy distress and bankrupt merchandise and sell it at bargain prices that pleased his customers and still gave him a very handsome profit. As a result, he made, not lost, money during economic crises.

Management and Executive Ability

A retail business is only as big as its owner. A merchant who does well and begins to expand eventually faces a number of situations that demand new management concepts. As his store develops he may be able to merchandise more profitably, but he can still lose money and stop growing if he continues to think and act as he did when he first started business. Such a retailer finds it difficult to hand over the increasing load of routine duties to subordinates, and the jobs he does assign are so poorly defined that employees are confused about what is expected of them. Moreover, because he hates to give up any function, he denies employees the necessary authority to perform their work properly.

This man only criticizes, never praises, and seldom explains, consults, or takes suggestions from others. He runs a one-man show and never lets anyone forget it. As a result, he works so long and so hard on unnecessary tasks that he has no time for planning, initiating, leading, supervising, and controlling his store. He ceases to grow and then begins to lose his competitive position. Because so many retailers lack administrative and executive skills, Chapter 18 has been devoted to this subject.

Courage

Courage in customer relationships

To list courage as a necessary qualification for a retailer to have may seem peculiar, yet sometimes merchants require a great deal of courage to be successful. John Wanamaker had courage when he put price tickets on his merchandise and permitted no bargaining, and even more courage when he announced that he would give cash refunds to customers who claimed that they were not satisfied with the goods they bought in his store. Wanamaker needed courage not only to face the monetary risks of these innovations but also to ignore the jeers of his competitors who eagerly looked forward to his downfall.

Courage in new merchandising ideas

Introducing new merchandising ideas takes courage. It required courage for R. H. Macy to expand his small specialty shop into a department store and for F. W. Woolworth to build his first, tiny shop into a chain. Both these merchants had to take great risks when they developed new and untried methods of retailing. Courage was needed by merchants who pioneered in mail order selling, supermarkets, discount houses, catalogue stores, and warehouse stores. These retailers were not only forced to invent the technology of their kind of merchandising, but in every case they also had to overcome the strong opposition of established retailers. Moreover, every step they took was full of danger because in most instances their financial resources would not permit them to absorb a severe loss.

Fortunately, retailing continues to attract adventurers who have the courage to experiment with new and sometimes revolutionary merchandising ideas. The vast majority begin their careers as independent merchants who open small shops and then start to develop their own version of retailing. Most of these independents fail and leave to take other jobs, some learn from their failures and try again, and others become discouraged and if they reopen their stores, they conduct business along traditional lines.

Consumers owe a great debt of gratitude to these courageous merchants, for they are the ones who succeeded in permitting very large segments of consumers to upgrade their life-styles by being able to satisfy wants that up to then were beyond the consumers' ability to own or even to rent.

Courage in personnel relations

Some retailers show courage in their relations with their personnel. For example, J. C. Penney, founder of one of the largest department chain stores in the world, never permitted anyone to climb up the executive ladder until that person had selected and trained someone else to take over his or her job; and as the person moved up in the company he or she participated more and more in its responsibilities and its earnings. Even today Penney's belief in the dignity of the human being is strikingly illustrated by the company's refusal to bond employees even though over a billion dollars pass through their hands every year.

Another noteworthy example of courage in personnel relations is Sears' policy of hiring handicapped persons to perform certain functions in their organization and its pioneer program of employing, training, and promoting, without bias, women and all minority groups.

Organizational courage

Sometimes a retailer needs organizational courage. He must make decisions that he feels will benefit the store in the long run, even though he knows that the decisions will be disliked by his employees and others actively concerned in the business. Such a man was James O. McKinsey who, as chairman of Marshall Field & Co., in 1935 courageously closed out the company's wholesale division because it had lost $12,000,000 in 5 years. Because this action entailed letting go approximately 800 employees and a loss of face for the company, it took many years before Marshall Field executives would admit that McKinsey had made the right decision.

More than Hard Work

Successful retailers work all the time. During the day they are busy supervising staff, seeing that customers are served, and making countless major and minor decisions, most of which must be right. At night and on vacations they shop windows, read advertisements, and think up promotions to better their operations. But hard work and long hours do not automatically lead to success. Many corner groceries stay open from 7 A.M. to 12 P.M. seven days a week, but their owners barely make a living.

What counts is the *way* a retailer works. Successful merchants can distinguish between what is most important and what is less urgent and they can organize their days so that they handle the most essential matters first. Also, they try to avoid details that can be handled by someone else. In this way, they have more time to supervise the whole store. A retailer who spends his entire day receiving, checking, marking, and getting goods on the floor is certainly working hard, but he accomplishes very little. Any of his clerks could perform these duties. What he has done, however, is to neglect those tasks that only he can do. These could be supervision of displays, advertisements, and promotions, as well as the buying and selling operations of his staff. Working hard, then, calls for job selection, careful planning, and, most difficult of all, self-discipline. With practice, any merchant can acquire good work habits, and the more he practices them, the more satisfactory will be the results.

Willingness to Take a Chance

All business is risky, but retailing is the most risky of all. No matter how much customer empathy a merchant may have, no matter how much research he does before trying something new, he deals with people and this makes results largely unpredictable. Only after the attempt has been made can reasons be discovered why it succeeded or failed. Yet to stay in business, risks must be taken and the risks that are to be successful must be greater than those that fail. In the fashion field every season is a gamble. Even in the more staple goods styling changes are becoming more frequent. Although the adoption of scientific methods and sound retail techniques minimize a merchant's mistakes and permit him to take greater advantage of his more fortunate buys in order to succeed, he must still take chances and experiment with new merchandise and new merchandising ideas.

Figure-mindedness

Because retailers constantly think in such terms as cost, markup, markdowns, and percentages, retailers must be figure-minded. It is not enough for them to know how to add, subtract, multiply, and divide. They must also realize the importance of accuracy because decisions based on mathematical errors can be fatal. But most important, they must have the ability to understand what figures mean in a retail sense. For example, when a merchant is offered a clearance of 15 gross of an item at $14.40 a gross, net, FOB store, he must realize that the lot will cost him $216 and that it contains 2,160 units. Then he must know whether or not he can afford the outlay, if

there are enough units for a promotion, and whether or not he can store and
display the item properly. In order to arrive at a retail price, he must figure out what profit he wants from the purchase and his chances of making it through selling the item at such prices as 15¢, 2 for 25¢, or 3 for 39¢. At any point, a mathematical mistake can result in a wrong conclusion, and instead of working with a hot promotion, he can have more than 2,000 lemons on his hands. Using hand calculators and markup charts or playing the "if" game with EDP will speed your ability to work out the necessary mathematics, but they cannot tell you what to do with the answer. This remains your responsibility.

Flexibility

Because the small retailer must perform and oversee so many different functions, he must have a great amount of job flexibility. During a single morning he may be consulted on pricing, advertising, window display, office procedure, and credit arrangements. He may also be called upon to soothe an irate customer, make a major policy decision, discuss and refuse to sign an order for merchandise, and ask another buyer why he or she has not ordered certain items.

Under today's retail dynamics, merchants must acquire another kind of flexibility—the ability to change with the times. Habit, conservatism, and laziness are a retailer's main weaknesses; progressiveness and a sense of pioneer adventure are his main strengths. Flexible merchants were the first to recognize the value of pleasing customers by initiating a one-price policy, free delivery, and other customer services. Today's flexible retailers are experimenting with reducing customer services in return for lower retail prices, specializing in merchandise that will attract a small subsection of consumers, concentrating on those consumers who prefer to do their shopping by out-of-store techniques, etc. Tomorrow will bring many more revolutionary ideas and merchants who seek change will capitalize on these trends and become more successful, but merchants who remain traditionalists will first ignore and then fight the new ideas and finally lose out to their more flexible competitors.

Liking the Retail Business and Your Store

Most retail giants showed an early liking for retailing. When F. W. Woolworth was 16, he took a bookkeeping course because he thought that it would help him get a job in a retail store. Because there were no jobs available, he spent the next 4 years on his father's farm during the day and clerking at night in a store whose owner paid him nothing for his services. Marshall Field's father, too, was a farmer, but Field wanted to be a retailer so much that he got his first clerking job when he was 15. He lasted only 2 weeks and was sent home to his father with the message that Marshall was not suited to the business world, but the experience certainly didn't kill his enthusiasm for retailing. When he died, he was one of the best known and richest merchants in the world.

Having most of the qualifications discussed above will not make you a successful retailer. You must also be happy in your work and proud to be a merchant. When a stranger asks you what you do, are you proud to say, "I am a retailer"? Or do you hedge and feel ashamed to reply? Do you encourage your children to enter your business or do you try to persuade them to enter another field that, in your view, is more honorable and carries more prestige? Do you wake up with the desire to get down to the store as soon as possible and meet the day's tasks with relish and enthusiasm? Do the hours go by quickly because every minute contains so much excitement and interest that closing time comes all too soon? Do you look for things to do that will keep you there just a little longer? Are you glad to keep open Saturdays, Sundays, and the odd evening because there is no place you would rather be than in your store?

How you answer these, and similar questions, will reveal your feelings about retailing and your store. If you believe that the main reason you are in retailing is to make money and that another career would not only give you a livelihood but make you happy as well, you should seriously investigate the possibilities of selling your store and pursuing another occupation.

Liking Your Kind of Retailing

Aside from liking retailing in general, you must enjoy your associations with your particular customer segment and kind of business. Does the merchandise you handle give you a sense of pride and pleasure? Do you like the smell of your store with its strong aroma of leather or wood? Obviously, if you dislike the merchandise you handle, you can hardly expect your customers to respect it or consider it worth buying.

Are you sincerely interested in the people who come in during the day and are you eager to talk to them? Do you find real satisfaction in discovering and providing for their merchandise needs? Do you enjoy making a sale, not only because of the profit involved but also because you feel that the merchandise you sold will make the customer happier? If, on the contrary, you feel that your customers are beneath you and that serving them is a demeaning experience, you may be certain that they will sense your attitude and reject your sales efforts.

Sometimes a merchant likes retailing but dislikes his customer segment. He would be wise to decide what consumer group will give him the most satisfaction and then develop his store to appeal to these people.

Not all Qualifications Are Necessary

To be a retailer, then, is not as simple as it looks, and the fact that so many unqualified and inefficient merchants still manage to stay in business only shows how quickly a good merchant can get ahead. Moreover, to be successful it is not necessary to have all the retail qualifications discussed above. If you like people and are proud and happy to work with your consumer segment, you should evaluate your abilities and then, as the opportunity arises, handle only those retail functions you do best. You can hire specialists to perform the tasks in which you are weak. For example, if you are a good buyer but a poor controller, employ someone to set up, operate, and interpret merchandise budgets. If you are a poor buyer but are good with figures, you should employ someone who has strong merchandise sense and let yourself be guided by him or her on style, but not on quantities. Spending time on jobs that you do poorly is wasteful and expensive not only because the jobs are never done properly, but also because they prevent you from performing the activities that you do well. In the long run, the successful merchant is one who learns to accept his own limitations and to understand and control the increasingly involved managerial techniques that every sound business has to employ to expand.

WHAT THIS CHAPTER TOLD YOU

1. To be a successful retailer, you should have (a) a genuine liking for people, (b) a special empathy for those in the customer segment you seek to serve, (c) retail imagination, vision, and initiative, (d) merchandise knowledge, (e) overall retail experience, (f) physical, emotional, and mental stamina, (g) common sense, (h) managerial and executive ability, and (i) courage.

2. You must also be (a) willing to work hard, (b) willing to take risks, (c) figure-minded, and (d) flexible.

3. Further, you must also (a) like the retail business and your store and (b) like being a merchant in the particular consumer category you are serving.

4. Successful retailers need not have all these qualifications, but they must at least have 1(a), 1(b), and 3(a), and 3(b) above.

5. As you grow, you should perform only those retail functions that are most important and come easiest to you. Specialists may be hired for the other functions, but in the long run, a business can only be as big as its owner's ability to organize and control every aspect of his business.

26

Retailing Comes of Age

WHAT THIS CHAPTER IS ABOUT

Within the last century retailing has developed from a relatively minor to a very major part of the distributive system. The change took place so rapidly that most merchants are unaware of the important role they now play in the country's economy. This chapter tells you how it occurred and how retailers should look at themselves in their new role.

What Retailers Used to Do

Long before World War 1, most of the goods bought by consumers were staples. Stores could carry little else because manufacturing was primitive, importing expensive, and transportation slow and cumbersome. Retailers bought goods in bulk, broke them down into smaller quantities, and then stocked them until they were required by their customers. Under these conditions, neither the retailer nor his customers had much to say about the merchandise they bought and consumed. They merely took what they could get.

For example, a typical general store stocked commodities such as salt, sugar, tea, and other staple groceries, and nails and hardware that were shipped in by freight to the nearest railroad station. It took considerable maneuvering by able-bodied men to handle and place these items in the store, and once set, they were seldom moved. However, the merchant personally selected most dry goods and fancy groceries on trips to the city and brought them back in a wagon drawn by a good team of horses.

Before and after World War I manufacturing improved so rapidly that by the end of World War II, America was able to make almost everything it needed and in most cases produce more than it could consume. At the same time it made such tremendous improvements in its methods of communication and transportation that goods could be ordered more quickly and transported across the country with increasing speed.

Status of Retailers Begins to Change

As manufacturing, communication, and transportation improved, alert retailers discovered that it was profitable to order more frequently and cut down the size of each order. This technique was made easier by the intense competition that developed among the retailers' suppliers who no longer waited for orders to come to them, but began to seek out merchants to try to please them with a constant flow of new products. Once retailers became aware of their changed status, they began to look for and demand merchandise that they thought their customers would like. Then, they ceased to be *stockers* of consumer goods and became *shoppers* of goods for their customers.

Customers Become more Sophisticated

Over the years consumers changed too. As their incomes and buying power increased, they became dissatisfied with staple merchandise and began to look for items that were different and exciting. Those retailers who could select from the manufacturers' offerings what their customers wanted, increased their clientele, and became successful; those who carried on as though a merchandising revolution was not taking place soon dropped behind and were lost.

Retailers Grow in Importance

As manufacturers increased their skill and productive capacity, those who produced consumer goods began to see that *distribution,* not production, was their chief worry, and they saw that the best channel to dispose of their products was through retail outlets. They also discovered that the more successful retailers had trained themselves to judge merchandise offerings in terms of their ability to please their customers, not themselves.

If these retailers became enthusiastic over a new item, its manufacturer could feel confident that he had a product that would sell at the consumer level; but if retailers as a whole rejected the item, he knew that it had little chance of reaching the ultimate consumer. Those manufacturers who recognized the growing importance and power of the retailer began to invite a few influential merchants to "preview" and criticize new items before putting them into production.

The next step was for manufacturers to discuss new product ideas with retailers while they were still in the planning stage. Today, some retailers have considerable influence at the manufacturer's level, and all retailers, simply by accepting or rejecting merchandise offerings, shoulder a major responsibility for the standard of goods that come onto the consumer market.

Retailers Begin to Dictate

As certain retail organizations grew in size and buying power, they could afford to develop their own special brands of merchandise and plan promotions well in advance of the season. Thus, they began to work early with manufacturers, who learned to use this advance retail information to build up their own lines. A great many of today's conveniences and the continued rise in our living standards can be traced in great measure to the forward thinking, planning, and initiative of these retailers.

When retailers become lazy and forget their function as interpreters of future customer demand, the economy suffers. Had automobile dealers in the early 1960s been alert retailers, they would have been aware of the increasing consumer desire for smaller and less expensive cars and that the largest percentage of this need was being filled by imports. It was not only their resonsibility to forward this information but also to insist that manufacturers begin to develop American made cars that would satisfy this new consumer trend. When dealers neglected to do so strongly enough, there was a significant decline in the sales of American built cars that only was overcome when manufacturers began to produce the kind of compact cars their customers wanted.

Economic Importance of Retailers

During the 1950s most economists and other specialists who plan ways to keep the economy healthy began to realize the important role that retailing was playing in the country's economy, for by then America had evolved from a society whose prime concern was manufacturing to one whose main interest was consumption. Under this new economic structure, retailing, whose function was to move goods from producer to consumer, was acknowledged to be such an important control element that economic planners would recommend that retailing be encouraged or discouraged according to whether they thought the economy should be expanded or contracted.

The Retailer Becomes a Supershopper

Today, the variety of items that manufacturers put on the market is almost endless and any retailer who buys and stocks merchandise like the general store merchant of pioneer days will have a short business life. The successful retailer today must perform the difficult task of selecting an increasing small number of items from a growing quantity of similar products and carry just enough of them to last until something new comes along. This has forced him to be very alert and to discover almost minute differences in manufacturers' offerings; for if he is not expert enough to judge the best of these products, he will lose customers. The retailer, then, has become a supershopper who not only prejudges his customers' wants and attempts to make manufacturers produce them, but he also constantly shops the manufacturers' markets, both at home and abroad, in order to buy what he considers to be the best all-round values for his customers. As the world grows smaller, the retailer's supershopping function and his responsibility for increasing the living standard of his customers has been intensified.

The Retailer's Job Is to Protect His Customers

Because the retailer has so much real control over the merchandise he buys and because he is essentially supershopping for his customers, consumers believe that he should be held responsible for the quality and price of the merchandise in his store. They want him to protect them and to do his best to give them quality goods at the lowest possible price. In response to these demands, some of the larger stores have developed their own research and testing laboratories to make certain that the merchandise will perform as promised. They are also very careful to state in their advertising only what they *know* the item will do, for example, "machine washable and machine dryable," etc. In many cases, they refuse merchandise because it does not come up to their standards, although to all outward appearances it is satisfactory.

Retailers Must Build Public Confidence

This practice has built up tremendous public confidence in these stores. If other merchants would use private testing services, they too would be fulfilling their duty to their customers and would increase their own reputations as responsible retailers. By performing these functions, retailers would not only help to keep the distributive channels flowing at a healthy speed, they would also raise the country's standard of living. Indeed, a great many labor-saving devices that the consumer uses today, the trend toward health products and clothing that is easier to care for, as well as better quality products at comparatively lower prices, are, in a large measure, the result of retailers insisting that manufacturers think about what will satisfy the ultimate consumer.

The Primary Retail Function Remains

Yet, in spite of these new duties and responsibilities, retailing has not changed in its essential purpose, which is to buy and sell goods at a profit.

Since prehistoric times retailers have always performed this useful function. It could have begun when one caveman who made too many arrows and another caveman who made too many bows "sold" them to a third caveman who made his living by stocking and trading them with others as they were required. As transportation developed, merchants and traders sought out both their suppliers and their customers, and we have exciting stories of caravans with their rich and exotic cargoes crossing the desert, of ships plying the seas in search of new trade routes and new countries, and of wars being fought to hold and develop trading territories. All these events increased the wealth and importance of the merchant princes who worked under the protection of the dominant powers. The history of the Hudson's Bay Company, the oldest retail organization in the world, is full of stories about its struggles with its competitors over trade with the Indians.

Thus, throughout history merchants have performed the same basic function; they bought in bulk whatever they thought their customers would want, broke it down into whatever small units consumers required, and then attempted to sell it at a profit.

What Is a Retailer's Profit?

What is the definition of retailer's profit? Retailers make two kinds of profit: *gross profit,* which is sometimes called *gross margin,* and *net profit.* For example, if an article costs a retailer $1 and he sells it for $1.50, he makes 50¢. This is his *gross profit,* and most people feel that it is too high. Indeed, it would be if it meant that retailers could pocket 50¢ on every $1.50 item they sold.

What the public fails to realize is that the retailer must use his gross profit to pay all his expenses, give himself a salary equivalent to one that he would get if he worked for someone else, pay interest on the money he has invested in his store, and permit him to set aside enough money to improve his business. What is left, and this is usually a very small percentage of his sales, is his *real profit.*

The Retailer's Services

Any profit a merchant makes is rightfully his because he has performed a number of important services for his customers. Almost everything people buy, from their first to their last breath, either quickly like food or more slowly like furniture and cars, must be purchased from one kind of retailer or another. Moreover, the enormous amount of goods that today's consumers demand for their existence, comfort, and prestige and at prices that range from one cent to thousands of dollars are housed in locations that must be carefully selected for their operational convenience. To accomplish this, retailers must perform the very risky task of anticipating their customers' needs and having these items in their stores when their clientele decides to purchase them.

Think how unhappy a young girl who has been invited to her first formal would be without our current retail system. Where would she buy a dress that would impress her escort and be the sensation of the evening? She might learn the names of manufacturers who make formals, but this would not help her very much. She would not know which firms were best for her, what styles they manufactured, the materials they carried, how they were sized, whether or not they were reliable, what their prices were, etc. Also, she might not have enough cash to pay for the dress and even if she borrowed the money, she would not know what would happen if the dress did not fit and she had to return it. All her accessories would have to be purchased in the same way.

Consumers with Retailers

Under today's retail conditions, this young girl can shop in any number of stores and enjoy the excitement of searching for the kind of dress she wants to wear. In these stores she can actually see, try on, and compare a great variety of dresses from a number of different manufacturers. Moreover, she knows the price of each dress and whether she can buy it for cash or on credit terms. She need not compare the competence of the various manufacturers, and she does not have to be an expert on materials or workmanship. She leaves that to the retailer whom she trusts as a specialist in these matters. Moreover, in some stores she can expect the professional advice from salespeople who have been trained to suggest the style, material, and color that are best for her. In most instances, stores will make whatever alterations are necessary. She shops for her accessories in the same way.

Satisfying her wants is a pleasurable experience for this young girl only because some retailers prejudged her needs, shopped the manufacturers for her, and brought a wide choice of dresses and accessories to their stores *before she knew she wanted them.*

Manufacturer's Price versus Retail Price

Because moving merchandise from producer to consumer via the retailer is a complicated procedure, the following question arises: What prices would manufacturers have to charge if they decided to sell goods *direct* from their factories to the consumer? At first sight, it would seem that these prices should be lower than those ordinarily charged by retail stores, although somewhat higher than wholesale. They would have to cover the cost of additional personnel to take care of the greater volume of individual sales, returns, correspondence, etc., that unit selling creates.

However, whenever manufacturers do decide to go retail and open up a series of shops, their costs and consequently their selling prices increase enormously. Now they must meet all expenses like taxes, salaries, advertising, etc., that running any store involves. Eventually, they must make as large a gross margin as competing retailers and thus their prices would have to be comparable.

The difference between the manufacturer's price and the retail price, then, must still cover the costs of buying merchandise in bulk, transporting it to a store, and assembling and packaging it in quantities that customers can handle, plus the cost of storage and rent, and the losses caused by obsolescence, markdowns, and merchandise shortages. These standard costs are increased by those services that customers expect to receive when they shop in a certain kind of store. Retail prices, therefore, vary according to these special services. For example, an article in a self-service clothing store should be cheaper than the identical item in a shop that has a variety of customer services.

Although retailing is an expensive service, even the Communists, who thought retailers were the worst kind of capitalists and liquidated them when they came into power, soon learned the error of their thinking. Merchandise distribution became so chaotic in the U.S.S.R. that the government was forced to open a series of stores which performed most of the classic functions of retailing in the free enterprise world, including that of pricing goods for net profit.

Be Proud of Your Net Profit

Everyone expects to be paid for his labor. This is as true for manual laborers and machine workers as it is for doctors, lawyers, and scientists. In the long run, people's wages, salaries, and fees vary according to their ability to produce. In this respect, the retailer is no different from any other worker, for his net profit varies according to his ability to merchandise properly. Thus, a retailer should be proud if he ends his year with a net profit, because it proves that he has done a good job for his fellow citizens. It can never be too high because monopoly practices in retailing cannot exist for any length of time. It is so easy to go into the retail business that whenever a merchant develops a new idea that results in unusually high profit, he soon has a great number of imitators who eat into his market and reduce his profit, thus bringing it into line. Supermarkets, discount houses, and warehouse stores are good illustrations of this fact.

Retailing Is Largely a Risk Business

Aside from such ordinary business risks as depressions, recessions, wars, strikes, and shortages, the retailer must be compensated for a number of special risks. Manufacturers work mainly with machines and with people who are merely machine tenders. They can, therefore, accurately estimate what a particular operation will cost and how many units they can produce from the material they use. The retailer is not so fortunate, for he deals with free-willed human beings, and this fact, in spite of all modern retail techniques, makes his business unpredictable. No one, not even psychologists or motivational researchers, can judge with mechanical accuracy how any group of people will react to any merchandise situation.

In addition to the unpredictable idiosyncrasies of his customers, most retailers are plagued with the vagaries of the weather. This is most important in fashion and sporting goods because a late spring, a cool summer, a hot fall, or a mild winter can ruin a merchant. Indeed, not only must the weather be "correct" for each season, but it must also be "right" on those particular days and hours of the day when most customers want to shop these kinds of stores. Retailers, then, must take these risks into consideration when they set retail prices.

The Retailer Is Community Minded

When the retailer carried his store on his back or in a wagon, he did not hesitate to misrepresent his merchandise and charge as much as he could for it. But when he settled down and became part of a village, town, or city, he realized that his future depended on the faith that the community placed in him. Moreover, he began to understand that a healthy and prosperous community meant good business for him, and therefore he gave his time, energy, and money to build up the area in which he was situated. In many villages the general store became the community meeting place and today many merchants are mayors or other high civic officials; and as community services developed, merchants became increasingly active in working with these agencies.

Consumerism Affects Retailing

Before the consumer movement of the 1960s, customers who disliked the way a store treated them went somewhere else, and if they felt strongly enough about their experience, they denounced the store whenever an opportunity arose. Thus, the only harm they did the store was on an individual basis. But today, if a complaint is sufficiently serious, the customer can report it to a number of government agencies and consumer organizations. When this happens, the merchant is forced to deal with much more than an individual consumer and this knowledge has forced many stores to revise their customer policies so that they are more in line with the way consumers believe retailing should be practiced.

The Need for Scientific Retailing by Independent Merchants

Recent government statistics show that approximately 87 percent of all stores in the country are independently owned. Moreover, these stores

account for more than 60 percent of the total retail sales in the country. A
little less than 95 percent of these stores employ fewer than 20 persons.

If the independent is to continue to hold or increase his share of the market, he must stop doing business in a haphazard way. Inefficient retailing only increases consumer costs and harms the economy. Independent retailers should realize that they have just come out of the cracker barrel stage and that scientific retailing is here to stay and is developing at an increasing speed. Merchants who take advantage of new scientific retailing techniques learn to make their stores produce more and more per square foot, and they also learn how to adopt and adapt new merchandising ideas as they appear. Retailers who do not learn new methods fall by the wayside. According to Dun & Bradstreet, 90 percent of business failures were a result of inefficient management.

Retailing Has Become Professional

As successful retail organizations grew, they had to discard their old hit-and-miss methods. Department stores, and later the chains, developed a series of principles and techniques that any store today can adopt and tailor to its needs. Because merchandising geniuses like John Wanamaker and J. C. Penney are still rare, large retail organizations are run by men who think of themselves not as instinctive merchants but as professional retailers. They operate their business according to accepted principles, although each store practices these according to its own retail philosophy. For example, a basic retail principle is to make a net profit, but whether a store makes it on a high markup and a low turnover or on low prices and a high turnover is a matter of practice. It is a principle that retailers must sell to customers, but the kind of customer a retailer tries to attract is a matter of practice.

There is, however, more to being a professional retailer than establishing a set of principles and practicing them. Retailers must formulate a code of ethics so that every merchant who wants to deserve the name "professional" will try to do more than just run a store to make money. He will know that he must constantly and conscientiously perform a highly ethical and skilled professional service that his customers will understand and appreciate.

The need for more professionalism in retailing has been recognized by educators who have developed a variety of vocational and academic courses on the subject that are offered to full-time and part-time students at every educational level. Some of these courses are of a general nature, but others are highly specialized and deal, for example, only with retail buying or retail administration practices. It would certainly pay you to take advantage of these courses as a way of refreshing or updating your retail knowledge.

If courses are not offered in your area, you can enroll in correspondence courses that are recommended by your trade association or the NRMA. They will also suggest books on retailing as well as trade magazines that should help you keep current on retail developments in your area. Also, the "If You Want More Information" section in this book, beginning on page 390, is very useful because it contains the names and addresses of major publishers of retail books, retail associations, trade journals, and trade services. By consulting these lists you should be able to communicate with resources that can help to solve many of your retail problems.

WHAT THIS CHAPTER TOLD YOU

1. Since prehistoric times retailing has consisted of buying merchandise in bulk, breaking it down into smaller quantities, and storing it until consumers want to buy it. Until recently most of these goods were staples and both the retailer and the consumer accepted what was produced without question.

2. Improvements and competition at the manufacturing level and the increasing ease of communication and transportation permitted the retailer first to suggest and then to dictate the kind of merchandise he wanted to purchase for his customers.

3. As incomes increased, consumers became more and more difficult to satisfy. Merchants began to anticipate customer wants and to shop for them.

4. The increasing variety of goods and the shrinking world caused the retailer to become a supershopper who scoured the world markets and sought to buy the best merchandise for his customers at the lowest prices. In this way, he immeasurably increased the living standards of most consumers.

5. Retailing is an expensive service and the retailer must mark up his goods to cover all expenses and gain a small return for his labor. Considering the risks involved, if the retailer ends his year with a net profit, he should feel that he has done a good job for the community and himself.

6. Over the years a set of retail principles has been developed that merchants should study as an aid to becoming better retailers.

7. Because retailing has become so important to the economy, merchants should begin to think of themselves as professionals and should develop a code of ethics that will help to build up consumer confidence in stores of all sizes. They should also take advantage of retail courses that are given at every educational level.

27

There'll Always Be
an Independent Retailer

WHAT THIS CHAPTER IS ABOUT

When department stores were developing, pessimistic students of retailing predicted the end of the small, independent merchant. The same gloomy prophecy was made when chain stores became prominent in the retail system. Yet, the independent is still with us, and judging by current trends, he is here to stay. This chapter tells you why the prophets were wrong and how the independent retailer can increase his business by not only developing his own strengths but also adding to them the strengths of large retail operations.

The Small Retailer Is a Chronic Worrier

When he has a good day, the small retailer shrugs and says, "What about tomorrow?" When he has a good week, he cries unhappily, "What about next week?" Even when his year ends with a handsome profit, he complains, "How will I meet my day-to-day figures next year?" He also worries about his competition. When he hears that a competitor is going to open a small store on his street or in a neighboring shopping center, his heart misses a beat; if it is a big store, his heart stops entirely, for he immediately pictures himself out of business.

Why He Worries

If a small store owner feels this constant fear and insecurity, he has no faith in his ability as a retailer, He probably runs his business by instinct and thus has nothing to fall back on but his own experience. Moreover, if he uses any control figures, most likely they are only internal comparative sales figures. No wonder he feels that he is isolated, that he is living dangerously, and that every move by a competitor is a direct threat to his existence.

He Need Not Worry

In reality, any retailer who is alert to his customers' wants, who knows how to satisfy them, and how to operate his business properly need not worry. In fact, he should welcome competition because it will bring more customers to his area and permit him to increase his volume.

The Independent Is Here to Stay

Whenever a new method of retailing, for example, department, chain or discount stores, and/or catalogue houses, grew large enough to attract the attention of the prophets of gloom (which include many independents), they began to shout that the end of the small retailer was at hand. Sometimes their prognostications so frightened the federal and state governments that they passed laws to weaken the large retail organizations and to encourage the ability of the small merchant to survive. History shows that these laws were ineffective, for large and small retailers continued to thrive as though the laws did not exist.

What happened, and still happens, is that large retail organizations must fight each other rather than the smaller stores in order to hold or increase their segment of the mass market. Their very existence and growth depends on volume and that is why they dominate the variety, discount, and food store field. Independents, however, can make a good living on a comparatively small sales volume and so can successfully operate stores that give consumers convenience of location or carry the kind of merchandise or offer services that the large organizations cannot supply.

Statistics show that since the turn of the century over 85 percent of retail establishments in the United States have been one-store operations and that these have accounted for approximately 60 percent of all retail sales. Another way the figures show the predominance of the independent is that well over 75 percent of all retail establishments since 1900 were operated by no more than five paid employees.

Figures Check with Facts

These figures seem fantastic because most people do not realize that small independents cannot dramatize their existence with a steady barrage of advertisements and gimmicks that form such an integral part of chain and department store promotional programs. Thus, small stores make comparatively little impact on public consciousness. Also, department and chain stores are physically large and are situated in downtown city cores and large shopping centers where they can be seen and remembered by great numbers of shoppers, whereas independent stores are usually small and are often located where they make little impression on people passing by.

The Yellow Pages of any telephone book show that while large metropolitan areas contain a small number of department stores and even more chain units, thousands of small independent shops are open for business. Moreover, while department and chain store units are few and far between in small towns and villages, these areas are served by great numbers of independent retailers.

These statistics show that the independent has little to fear from either chains or department stores in the foreseeable future.

What About Me?

You may, however, find this general picture of little comfort, and you may say, "These overall figures are no doubt interesting, but I know that in my town, on my street, or in my shopping center, and certainly in my shop, business is not only bad—it is getting worse. Yet, people are buying merchandise, so they must be dealing with chain, department, or discount stores, mail order houses, catalogue stores, or some other kind of retailers. They certainly are not coming to me."

If this is true and if you really are losing more customers than you think you should, does the fault lie with your competitors or with yourself?

It is easy to blame the other fellow. You can always complain, "How can a small merchant like me compete against large retail operators? Just look at their prices! They can sometimes sell cheaper at retail than I can buy wholesale." Or, "How can a small man advertise or promote like a large store?" And so on.

What History Tells Us

Is it impossible to compete with department and chain stores or are you using this as an excuse? History is full of little fellows who successfully overcame their powerful enemies.

The fight between David and Goliath is a good example. David defeated Goliath because he recognized his opponent's weaknesses and his own strengths. Because he realized that physical contact with the giant would be fatal, he deliberately planned to keep out of his opponent's reach. He also knew that he had no chance of conquering Goliath with any of the weapons ordinarily used at that time. So he selected one that Goliath would not expect and in which he was especially skilled. This was the slingshot. The outcome of this confrontation was that "David smote Goliath from afar."

Big Retailers' Weaknesses versus Small Stores' Strengths

Like David, the small independent merchant need not be frightened by retail giants; instead, he should examine the big retailers' weaknesses and strengths and see how he can turn these to his advantage. For example, a major weakness of department and chain stores is their lack of good human relations; yet in no business is this quality more necessary than in retailing. It is almost axiomatic that the larger the retail operation, the more difficult it becomes for executives to have their orders carried out correctly by their employees or for important information, gathered at the lowest level, to travel correctly up to the top. Large retail organizations use a great many methods to overcome these deficiencies, but they can never achieve the face-to-face relationship of the small independent who tells his salespeople what he wants done and then sees that it *is* done or of salespeople who can easily let the boss know what their customers are thinking.

Lack of good human relations

The inability to obtain good human relations is particularly striking in chain store operations. Personnel at headquarters are so preoccupied with running the chain by figures that they find little opportunity for personal contact with either store employees or the chain's clientele. Store managers, too, have little time for customers or employees and in spite of advanced electronic data processing techniques, they still spend most of their working days and a great deal of their energy filling in reports and dealing with other routine matters.

Human relationships in chain stores are particularly poor

Also, salespeople in chain stores are unable to develop enthusiasm toward their customers. The larger and more extended the store units, the more the salespeople tend to think of themselves as very small cogs in a very large machine. Most salespeople in chain stores feel that customers are a nuisance because they take up time that could be better spent in counting, sorting, and rearranging stock. This is particularly true in self-service stores.

Some chains have become conscious of the bad state of their customer-employee relations and are spending huge sums of money to inform the public how friendly, smiling, and warm their personalities really are. But unless they operate under totally different principles from those they are now using, these chains will continue to fail at the store level where human relations count most.

Chains attempt to improve customer-employee relations

How different the shop of an independent can be if the owner cares enough to make it so! He can personally impress on his staff the important part they play in the success of his store and the value of good customer relations. In fact, the more the owner stays on the floor himself, greeting customers by name and making small talk before turning them over to the sales clerk, the better the customers will like his shop. The more he watches and even participates in each sale, the more people will enjoy shopping in his store. Everyone likes to be called by his name and questioned about his

The small independent's great strength is in human relations own and his family's health, for these are very warm and human gestures in an all too cold world. Like all major retail pioneers, Marshall Field spent the greater part of his day greeting customers, seeing that they were properly served, and adjusting complaints. In fact, it was while he was settling one of these complaints that he used the famous phrase, "Give the lady what she wants."

Alterations of policies, even in small routines, become increasingly more complicated and expensive as retail organizations expand their operations. For this reason, most department and chain stores tend to suffer from inertia and inflexibility. This means that they meet consumer or economic changes only after a harmful time lag. For example, it required several years of steadily declining sales for department and variety chain stores to accept and challenge the merchandising techniques of promotional and warehouse stores.

If the independent is anything, he is *flexible.* He can come into his store at any time, including Sunday, rearrange his windows, move his stock, mark it up or down, and introduce a new policy at a moment's notice. The tragedy of most independents is that they seldom use this business flexibility. Instead, they wait until the big fellows move, and by then all the advantage they could have had is lost.

The large retailers' inherent inertia and inflexibility are partly responsible for the fact that under adverse conditions they appear less able to control their overhead than the smaller store. Consequently, they are more vulnerable to reverses in customer trends and economic cycles than are the independents. For example, department stores fought self-service and self-selection for years while they complained about the increasing difficulty they encountered in holding their expenses down to profitable levels. The alert independent is always able to cut costs, even though this may entail his missing a trip to Florida, keeping his car another year, or even smoking 50-cent instead of $1 cigars.

Neither department nor chain stores can maintain their volume unless they have excellent customer locations. Department stores developed because they were in the center of town and convenient to most customers. When these customers moved to the suburbs and when downtown areas became congested and shopping unpleasant, department stores lost volume. Some attempted to bolster sales by low-cost parking, store renovation, and branch stores; others simply closed their doors and ceased operations. Chain stores, too, realized that they must have 100 percent locations, but they developed a different technique to achieve this purpose. They sought to rent, not own, their stores and so were able to move with their customers much more easily.

The independent need not require high volume to exist. He can, therefore, do well in areas that could not profitably support a department or chain store. This is a great strength for the small store, because he can often operate without department or chain store competition. Small villages, towns, suburbs, growing and declining areas, and side streets adjacent to main traffic areas are all natural locations for the small independent. Here he performs a necessary service and, if he has the ability, he can develop and grow. The small independent can also do well in the same areas as larger stores because he does a different kind of business and attracts a different class of customer; he receives the benefit of large customer traffic flow and, if he operates properly, his business can be very successful indeed.

Special Weaknesses of Department Stores

Ideas are slowly accepted

Essentially, a full-line department store consists of a number of small specialty shops, called *departments,* under one roof and one management. These departments are run by executives who have certain restrictions on the manner in which they can operate. They must try to maintain target markups, give or refuse certain customer services, use window display and advertisements according to plan, and so on. From top management's point of view, it is essential that their executives obey store policies and act in cooperation with every other executive because this is the only way a common front can be presented to every customer who shops in the store.

This system means that executives who have more than average ability and initiative must restrain themselves for the good of the store as a whole. Even when an executive has a worthwhile idea he or she may have difficulty selling it to top management because the executives are seldom close enough to the actual operations to envisage the idea's possibilities. In addition, an idea may not be accepted because what may be good for some departments would be harmful for others. As chain stores experience the same organizational difficulties, both kinds of retailing make improvements very slowly and cautiously.

Not highly specialized

Although department stores consist of a series of specialty shops, in practice, these shops sometimes lose their specialty store appeal. Buyers must produce a large volume of sales in order to absorb their overhead figures and make a profit. This means that they must enlarge their customer segment; yet they cannot carry merchandise in too great a breadth because they need depth for sales volume. Therefore, they tend to standardize the merchandise in their departments and play it safe, for if buyers take a chance and lose, they are severely penalized because unsold merchandise reduces their open-to-buy until it can be disposed of. The quickest way this can be accomplished is to clear it at reduced prices. This lowers their markup and they must then work hard to obtain goods they can sell at higher than average markups in order to bring the department back to normal. After a few such experiences, even the most adventurous buyers become cautious.

Because a small store does not require a comparatively large sales volume to make a profit, the owner can afford to specialize in as narrow a customer segment as he pleases. Moreover, if he likes a merchandise idea, he can try it out. If it fails, he can shrug it off and attempt another technique. Only when an innovation proves sufficiently successful do larger retailers adopt and adapt it to their own purposes. Thus, the ability of the small independent to carry on experiments is extremely important to the whole retail structure. For example, Clarence Saunders developed the idea of self-service in his small grocery store in Memphis, Tennessee. He tried to sell his idea to the A & P, but when the A & P refused it, he patented the technique, called it *Piggly-Wiggly,* and leased it out to other independents. It became so successful that grocery stores of all sizes adopted and adapted it to fit their particular operations.

Special Weaknesses of Chain Stores

While most of the merchandise in department stores tends to be standard, mass merchandisers can only handle goods that are highly standardized, mass-produced, and sold in great quantities. Thus, while prices in both organizations may be lower than specialty stores, the merchandise they contain for the most part lacks interest and excitement.

Merchandise standardization

What a weakness for a small store to exploit! It leaves the independent with many opportunities in which his main competition is from other independents who cater to the same consumer segment.

In order to keep their prices as low as possible, chains cannot afford many customer services. They usually sell for cash, discourage returns, have hardly any distinctive atmosphere, and the service of their sales personnel leaves much to be desired. Again, most chain store managers are too busy to do more than take orders from the head office and handle the daily merchandise intake and outgo. Thus, customers are disregarded until they approach a clerk or check-out counter with the selected item, cash, or credit card.

Lack of customer services

The independent usually runs his store with more leisure and less pressure and without the enormous amount of detailed reports that chains need to operate properly. Therefore, he can see what is happening in his shop, give customers his personal attention, and, when necessary, make exceptions to his usual customer policies. All this creates goodwill and better business for the store.

Large Retailers' Strengths

Large retailers operate with a number of strengths that small store merchants can turn to their advantage once they know how to practice the principle of adopt and adapt. This means that they know how to *adopt* some of the large department and chain store operating techniques and *adapt* them to suit their own businesses. If they do this properly, they add to their own strengths as small independents and thus have the best of all possible retail operations.

Principles of adopt and adapt

Large retailers have an advantage over most small merchants because they have learned to plan and control every facet of their organizations. Early in their history these organizations realized the dangers of operating by instinct and guesswork and they began to develop procedures that would tell their executives as quickly and precisely as possible what was taking place in every corner of their business. Today, by using past, present, and comparative records and gauging future trends, executives of big retailing concerns plan all their operations with care and precision.

Planning and control

For example, when buyers of large stores go to market, they have very definite ideas of what to buy, how much to buy, and from whom to buy. Moreover, once the goods arrive on the floor, they receive a constant flow of information about the way customers treat each item. Thus, they know which of the goods they have purchased are "runners," which are "lemons," which price lines are selling, and so on. Using this knowledge, they can readjust their plans and make whatever changes they deem necessary. They also use similar planning and reporting techniques to control expenses. But since plans without discipline are useless, these organizations insist that their personnel exercise sufficient self-control to make their plans work.

Every independent should adopt the big retailers' control techniques because once he knows what is happening in his store, he can plan his business properly. But he must also learn to discipline himself or his plans will not work out. The small retailer should no longer say, "I think I'll try a dozen or two" or ask, "Miss Jones, how are we doing with that $29.95 dress?" His open-to-buy should tell him whether he can order one dozen, two dozen, or none at all. His records should show him whether or not the $29.95 dresses are selling. How a small merchant adapts these techniques to his particular business is a very individual matter; but it should result in a shop that is run not on emotion, as most small stores are today, but on knowledge.

Is the small merchant afraid of large retailers because they are bigger or because they operate more efficiently than he does? As long as all the stores in a community operate inefficiently, every retailer makes a living at his customers' expense, but as soon as an efficient organization moves into the area, the established merchants begin to lose their clientele and the most inefficient of them go out of business.

Big store efficiency versus small store inefficiency

So to be successful, small stores need to be efficient. For example, one independent who has consciously combined the advantages of a small store with the strengths of a large operation did over a million-dollar business in a store approximately 80 feet deep with a 20-foot frontage. One reason for his success is that ever since he opened the store, he kept records of the style, color, size, price, vendor, and movement of every article in his shop which, in the course of a year, added up to over a million items. Using this information, he was able to buy and plan promotions 6, 12, or 18 months ahead. It would have taken a very unusual set of circumstances to upset this retailer's calculations. Changes in business conditions and customer demands never surprised him because he was always sufficiently aware of them to plan for and take advantage of every consumer and economic trend.

Large stores are aware that population is constantly shifting and that sites that are good today will most likely be only fair a few years from now and very poor 20 years hence. Chains are constantly closing down stores that customers no longer patronize in sufficient numbers and are opening new ones in locations where they feel that a greater number of people want to shop.

Large stores are conscious of customer flow

The small store owner, too, should be conscious of his customer flow and be flexible enough either to move with his customers or to change his merchandise policies to suit his new clientele. Many a small merchant has gone out of business because he has become stubborn and said, "My customers can come to me, or else." The "or else" in this case means bankruptcy.

Large retail organizations have learned the futility of trying to please everyone, and thus they specialize, both in the kind of goods they carry and in the kind of people they want to attract. Each organization tries to create a unique personality so that everyone knows the merchandise it carries. For example, most customers who want to see wide assortments of refrigerators or raincoats would go to Sears' rather than to Woolco.

Large stores develop a unique personality

What about *your* store? What are you doing to make its personality so unique that everyone in your area knows exactly what merchandise you carry, your price range, your services, and everything else your name stands for? Moreover, by adopting the large stores' principle of building a better personality and adapting it to your business, you will become a better merchant because the more you learn about your specialty, the more consumers in your area will recognize you as an authority on the goods you carry.

One obvious strength of department and chain stores is that their enormous resources permit them to operate on a scale that is impossible for the independent. They can employ high-salaried people to specialize in a single function like buying, selling, advertising, display, or control, but the small retailer must perform all these functions himself, and many more besides.

Large stores' enormous resources

For example, large stores can buy at quantity prices, create styles, develop special labels, and control the quality of merchandise in their stores. If a small store tried to do this, it could run into all kinds of difficulties and frustrations. Sometimes a small merchant spots a runner early in the season and quickly reorders what he thinks he can use. Then he sits around and chews his nails because the best part of the season is over before the merchandise comes in. This happens because the manufacturer must wait until he has accumulated enough orders from other small merchants to make production profitable. Large stores do not have this problem; they can order a large enough quantity for a manufacturer to go into production at once.

Special chain
store advantages

Although chain store buyers work from a central office, they constantly receive reports on how every item they bought is moving from each unit in the chain. The more area these units cover, the quicker buyers know their runners and their lemons, and thus the sooner they can reorder running items and get rid of slow movers. The only time the small retailer finds out what is selling outside his store is when he reads the trade papers or talks to vendor salesmen. Thus, he frequently decides on his runners much later than do the chain buyers and then he runs out of wanted items before the height of the season.

In addition, chain store buyers are always in the market; buying is all they do, all day long, every day of the week. Moreover, since they specialize in specific merchandise areas, they become expert enough to develop new items which can be confined to them; or they redesign certain manufacturers' goods and sell them at lower retail prices. Since most people who shop in chains are more interested in price than in brand names and know that most chains stand behind their goods, branded or unbranded, they buy with confidence. It is not surprising then that chains sometimes carry merchandise that the small independent has never seen and never even knew existed.

Independents
collectively can
compete with
large stores

Independents can adopt the huge resources and strengths of large retailers by grouping together. Then, collectively, they can possess as much resource potential as any large organization. Some resident buying offices have successfully adopted group buying and operating techniques for their retail accounts, while independents who belong to "chains" like Rexall drug stores, Red and White grocery stores, and True Value hardware stores have also succeeded beyond all expectations. These retailers are able to merchandise and operate like their largest competitors, yet they are able to retain all their inherent advantages because basically they remain independent merchants.

Advantages and
disadvantages
in being an
independent
retailer

If the small retailer uses his inherent strengths and adopts and adapts the strengths of his large competitors to his own business, he should not worry about chains and department stores, or even his smaller competitors. If he practices or improves on the principles discussed in this book, he can make a good to an excellent living and still retain his independence. Moreover, only his own ambition will dictate whether he remains at his present size or continues to expand. Because he is his own boss, he can set his own work and leisure time and if he wishes to participate in community or any other activities, he need not ask anyone's permission to take time out of his working day. Because his success is due entirely to his own ability, he can be proud of his accomplishments and when the time for retirement approaches, he can plan the way he wants to dispose of his business.

Of course, there are disadvantages in being an independent retailer. For example, lack of capital may slow business growth, the responsibility for making every decision can be very exhausting and sometimes frightening, and there is always the danger that the business will run the merchant rather than the merchant run the business.

But for those people who want to live their lives as independent retailers, the advantages of running their own stores greatly outweigh the disadvantages. So when all is said and done, this book will have been worthwhile if it helps the thousands of small and medium-sized merchants who want to enjoy the fruitful life of an independent retailer in a free-enterprise system.

WHAT THIS CHAPTER TOLD YOU

1. Statistics show that the independent retailer is here to stay.

2. This is so because department and chain stores have a number of inherent weaknesses that the independent can exploit.

3. The basic weaknesses of chain and department stores are (a) lack of good human relationships, (b) inflexibility and inertia, and (c) they require 100 percent locations and large customer areas. These weaknesses can become the strongest part of the independent stores' operations.

4. Special department store weaknesses are (a) new ideas are accepted with great reluctance and (b) merchandise tends to be dull and unexciting. These department store weaknesses can be developed into small store strengths.

5. Special chain store weaknesses are (a) they can handle only standardized, mass-produced, large-volume merchandise and (b) they lack consumer services. These weaknesses, too, can be made into small store strengths.

6. Both department and chain stores are strong in the following: (a) they have developed an ability to plan and control every facet of their organization, (b) they constantly strive for efficiency, (c) they are very conscious of the need for locations that are convenient to their customers, (d) they use highly developed merchandising techniques (e) they have enormous resources, and (f) they can afford to hire highly trained specialists.

7. Independents can meet the large stores' strengths by (a) applying the principle of adopt and adapt to their own operations and (b) joining a group of independent retailers.

8. Although there are disadvantages in being an independent, the disadvantages are outweighed by the advantages of your earning a worthwhile living and still being your own boss.

9. Practicing the principles discussed in this book should help independents to enjoy a worthwhile life while making a satisfying living.

If You Want
More Information

HOW TO USE THESE LISTS

The lists below are not meant to be complete but are sufficient to get you started if you want more information on retailing in general, or on any specific retail problem.

This book has emphasized the advantages of cooperative action and here is an excellent opportunity to put it into practice. Get some of the merchants in your community to contribute to a fund to buy retailing books. The group of retailers as a whole should select the titles so that they will cover the widest possible variety of subject matter. When they arrive, the books should be studied and discussed by the group and then donated to the local library so that everyone in the area can use them. In this way, you and other retailers will build up goodwill for retailing as well as acquiring a reference library that will help improve your retail techniques.

Some Publishers of Books on Retailing

Since there is a continuous stream of retailing books and pamphlets being published, no list can remain up-to-date for very long. The publishers listed below are the best known in the retail field and you should begin by writing each of them for their latest list on retail subjects. Then you can select those that most interest you and your group and go on from there.

Clarke-Irwin & Co., Ltd., Toronto, Ont.
The Dryden Press, Hinsdale, Ill.
Fairchild Publications Inc., New York, N.Y.
Harcourt Brace Jovanovich, Inc., New York, N.Y.
Houghton Mifflin Co., Boston
John Wiley & Sons, Inc., New York, N.Y.
John Wiley & Sons Canada, Ltd., Rexdale, Ont.
McGraw-Hill Book Co., New York, N.Y.
McGraw-Hill-Ryerson Ltd., Scarborough, Ont.
The Macmillan Co., New York, N.Y.
Prentice-Hall, Inc., Englewood Cliffs, N.J.
Prentice-Hall of Canada Ltd., Scarborough, Ont.
Dow Jones-Irwin, Inc., Homewood, Ill.
The Ronald Press Co., New York, N.Y.
South-Western Publishing Co., Cincinnati, Ohio

Some Retail Trade Journals*

Appliances

Dealerscope
115 Second Ave., Waltham, Mass.
Mart Magazine
Berkshire Common, Pittsfield, Mass.
Merchandising Week
1 Astor Plaza, New York, N.Y.

Automotive

Auto Merchandising News
234 Greenfield St., Fairfield, Conn.
Canadian Automotive Trade
481 University Ave., Toronto, Ont.
Revue Moteur
(*See* Can. Automotive Trade)

Books

Publishers Weekly
1180 Avenue of the Americas, New York, N.Y.

Children's

Earnshaw's Infants, Girls & Boyswear Review
393 Seventh Ave., New York, N.Y.
Juvenile Merchandising
370 Lexington Ave., New York, N.Y.

*Publishers' complete addresses only appear the *first* time mentioned.

China392

China, Glass & Tableware, Ebel-Doctorow Pub. Inc.
1115 Clifton Ave., Clifton, N.J.

Curtains

Curtain, Drapery & Bedspread Magazine
(See China, Glass & Tableware)

Druggists

Drug Topics
550 Kinderkamack Rd., Oradell, N.J.
Drug Merchandising
(See Canadian Automotive Trade)

Fabrics

American Fabrics and Fashions
24 E. 38th St., New York, N.Y.
Sew Business
1271 Avenue of the Americas, New York, N.Y.

Fashions

California Apparel News
1016 S. Broadway Pl., Los Angeles, Cal.
Clothes
380 Madison Ave., New York, N.Y.
Women's Wear Daily, Fairchild Publications
7 E. 12th St., New York, N.Y.
Style
(See Canadian Automotive Trade)

Floor Covering

Floor Covering Weekly
919 Third Ave., New York, N.Y.

Florists

Florist
20900 Northwestern Highway, Southfield, Mich.

Footwear

Footwear-News
(See Women's Wear Daily)
Shoe & Leather Journal
1450 Don Mills Rd., Don Mills, Ont.

Furniture

Furniture News
P.O. Box 1569, Charlotte, N.C.

Home Furnishings Daily
(See Women's Wear Daily)

Home Goods Retailing
(See Canadian Automotive Trade)

Furniture & Furnishings
(See Shoe & Leather Journal)

General Merchandise

Chain Store Age, Gen. Mdse. Edition
2 Park Ave., New York, N.Y.

The Discount Merchandiser
641 Lexington Ave., New York, N.Y.

Volume Retail Merchandising
109 Railside Rd., Suite 102, Don Mills, Ont.

Gifts

Gifts & Decorative Accessories, Geyer-McAllister Pub. Inc.
51 Madison Ave., New York, N.Y.

Groceries

Progressive Grocer
708 Third Ave., New York, N.Y.

Supermarket News
(See Women's Wear Daily)

Canadian Grocer
(See Canadian Automotive Trade)

Epicier
(See Canadian Automotive Trade)

Hardware

Hardware Age, Chilton Co., Inc.
Chilton Way, Radnor, Pa.

Hardware Merchandiser
7300 N. Cicero Ave., Chicago, Ill.

Home & Auto, Harcourt Brace Jovanovich, Inc.
757 Third Ave., New York, N.Y.

Hardware Merchandising
(See Canadian Automotive Trade)

Hosiery

Hosiery and Underwear
(See Home and Auto)

Intimate Apparel

Body Fashions/Intimate Apparel
(See Home and Auto)

Jewelry

Jewelers Circular/Keystone
(See Hardware Age)
Modern Jeweler
15 W. 10th St., Kansas City, Mo.
Canadian Jeweler
(See Canadian Automotive Trade)

Luggage

Luggage and Leather Goods
80 Lincoln Ave., Stamford, Conn.

Management

Stores
100 W. 31st St., New York, N.Y.

Men's

Daily News Record
(See Women's Wear Daily)
Men's Wear
(See Women's Wear Daily)
Men's Wear of Canada
(See Canadian Automotive Trade)

Office Supplies

Office Product News
645 Stewart Ave., Garden City, N.Y.

Sporting Goods

Sporting Goods Business
1515 Broadway, New York, N.Y.
Sports Merchandiser
1760 Peachtree Rd., N.W., Atlanta, Ga.

Toys

Playthings
(See Gifts and Decorative Accessories)
Toys
(See Home and Auto)
Toys and Playthings
146 Bates Rd., Montreal, Que.

The Journal of Retailing, New York University
202 Tisch Hall, Washington Sq., New York, N.Y.

Retail Advertising Week
101 Fifth Ave., New York, N.Y.

Visual Merchandising
407 Gilbert Ave., Cincinnati, Ohio

Some Retailers' Associations

This list, like the book publishers, and trade journals, is not complete because retailers' associations keep appearing and disappearing. This is particularly true of the smaller associations. Again, a number of associations have area offices which are not listed below. If you want to know whether a specific retail trade has an association or an area office, write the National Retail Merchants Association in the United States or the Retail Council of Canada in Canada.

National Appliance & Radio-TV Dealer's Association
318 W. Randolph St., Chicago, Ill.

Automotive Parts & Accessories Assn.
1730 K St., N.W. Washington, D.C.

Motor Accessories Marketers Assn. of Canada
95 Thorncliffe Park Dr., Toronto, Ont.

American Booksellers Assn., 800 Second Ave., New York

Canadian Booksellers Assn., 2 Bloor St. E., Toronto, Ont.

National Association of Retail Druggists
1 E. Wacker Dr., Chicago, Ill.

National Association of Retail Grocers of the United States
2000 Spring Rd., Oakbrook, Ill.

Canadian Federation of Retail Grocers
29 Old Oak Rd., Toronto, Ont.

National Retail Hardware Assn.
964 N. Pennsylvania St., Indianapolis, Ind.

Canadian Retail Hardware Assn.
290 Merton St., Toronto, Ont.

National Home Furnishings Assn.
1150 Merchandise Mart Plaza, Chicago, Ill.

Retail Jewelers of America
1025 Vermont Ave., N.W., Washington, D.C.

Canadian Jewelers Assn.
663 Yonge St., Toronto, Ont.

National Lumber & Building Materials Assn.
1990 M St., N.W., Washington, D.C.

Mass Retailing Institute
570 Seventh Ave., New York, N.Y.

Menswear Retailers of America
390 National Press Bldg., Washington, D.C.

American Retail Federation
1616 H St., N.W., Washington, D.C.

National Retail Merchants Assn.
100 W. 31st St., New York, N.Y.

Retail Council of Canada
74 Victoria St., Toronto, Ont.

Retail Merchants Assn. of Canada
1780 Birchmount Rd., Scarborough, Ont.

National Shoe Retailers Assn.
200 Madison Ave., New York, N.Y.

Canadian Retail Shoe Assn.
2510 Yonge St., Toronto, Ont.

National Sporting Goods Assn.
717 N. Michigan Ave., Chicago, Ill.

National Association of Variety Stores
7646 W. Devon Ave., Chicago, Ill.

Index